Language in the Trump Era

Early in his campaign, Donald Trump boasted that "I know words. I have the best words," yet despite these assurances his speech style has sown conflict even as it has powered his meteoric rise. If the Trump era feels like a political crisis to many, it is also a linguistic one. Trump has repeatedly alarmed people around the world while exciting his fan base with his unprecedented rhetorical style, shock-tweeting, and weaponized words. Using many detailed examples, this fascinating and highly topical book reveals how Trump's rallying cries, boasts, accusations, and mockery enlist many of his supporters into his alternate reality. From Trump's relationship to the truth, to his use of gesture, to the anti-immigrant tenor of his language, it illuminates the less obvious mechanisms by which language in the Trump era has widened divisions along lines of class, gender, race, international relations, and even the sense of truth itself.

JANET MCINTOSH is Professor of Anthropology at Brandeis University. Her work focuses on linguistic and sociocultural anthropology in the United States and sub-Saharan Africa. Her second book, *Unsettled: Denial and Belonging among White Kenyans* (2016), received Honorable Mention in the American Ethnological Society's Senior Book Prize, and in the Victor Turner Prize for Ethnographic Writing. She is on the Editorial Boards of Oxford Studies in the Anthropology of Language (Oxford University Press) and the journal *Cultural Anthropology*.

NORMA MENDOZA-DENTON is Professor of Anthropology at University of California, Los Angeles. She is past President of the Society for Linguistic Anthropology of the American Anthropological Association. Best known for her book *Homegirls: Language and Cultural Practice among Latina Youth Gangs* (2008), she publishes on language and politics, youth, migration, and visual cultures.

T0371247

Language in the Trump Era

Scandals and Emergencies

Edited by

Janet McIntosh
Brandeis University

Norma Mendoza-Denton
University of California, Los Angeles

CAMBRIDGE
UNIVERSITY PRESS

University Printing House, Cambridge CB2 8BS, United Kingdom

One Liberty Plaza, 20th Floor, New York, NY 10006, USA

477 Williamstown Road, Port Melbourne, VIC 3207, Australia

314–321, 3rd Floor, Plot 3, Splendor Forum, Jasola District Centre,
New Delhi – 110025, India

79 Anson Road, #06–04/06, Singapore 079906

Cambridge University Press is part of the University of Cambridge.

It furthers the University's mission by disseminating knowledge in the pursuit of
education, learning, and research at the highest international levels of excellence.

www.cambridge.org
Information on this title: www.cambridge.org/9781108841146
DOI: 10.1017/9781108887410

© Cambridge University Press 2020

First published 2020

A catalogue record for this publication is available from the British Library.

Library of Congress Cataloging-in-Publication Data
Names: McIntosh, Janet, 1969– editor. | Mendoza-Denton, Norma, editor.
Title: Language in the Trump era : scandals and emergencies / edited by Janet
McIntosh, Norma Mendoza-Denton.
Description: Cambridge, United Kingdom ; New York, NY : Cambridge
University Press, 2020. | Includes bibliographical references and index.
Identifiers: LCCN 2020013351 (print) | LCCN 2020013352 (ebook) | ISBN
9781108841146 (hardback) | ISBN 9781108887410 (ebook)
Subjects: LCSH: Trump, Donald, 1946 – Language. | Rhetoric – Political aspects –
United States – History – 21st century. | Communication in politics – United States –
History – 21st century.
Classification: LCC E913.3 .L36 2020 (print) | LCC E913.3 (ebook) |
DDC 973.933–dc23
LC record available at https://lccn.loc.gov/2020013351
LC ebook record available at https://lccn.loc.gov/2020013352

ISBN 978-1-108-84114-6 Hardback
ISBN 978-1-108-74503-1 Paperback

For Jennifer Jackson (1975–2015)

Contents

Figures

Tables

Contributors

H. SAMY ALIM is the David O. Sears Presidential Endowed Chair in the Social Sciences and Professor of Anthropology at University of California, Los Angeles, and the Founding Director of the Center for Race, Ethnicity, and Language (2010). His recent books include *Articulate While Black: Barack Obama, Language, and Race in the US* (Oxford, 2012, with Geneva Smitherman), *Raciolinguistics: How Language Shapes Our Ideas about Race* (Oxford, 2016, with John Rickford and Arnetha Ball), and the *Oxford Handbook of Language and Race* (Oxford, 2020, with Angela Reyes and Paul Kroskrity).

AOMAR BOUM is an associate professor in the Department of Anthropology at University of California, Los Angeles. He is the author of *Memories of Absence: How Muslims Remember Jews in Morocco* (Stanford University Press, 2013), and coauthor of the *Historical Dictionary of Morocco* (Rowman and Littlefield, 2016), *The Holocaust and North Africa* (Stanford University Press, 2019), and the *Historical Dictionary of the Arab Uprisings* (Rowman and Littlefield, 2020).

DEBORAH CAMERON is Professor at the Faculty of Linguistics, University of Oxford. Her recent books include *Feminism* (Profile Books, 2018) and *Gender, Power and Political Speech* (with Sylvia Shaw, Springer, 2016).

KIMBERLY CERÓN graduated from University of California, Los Angeles in the class of 2019.

CAROL COHN is Director of the Consortium on Gender, Security and Human Rights at University of Massachusetts Boston. She is the author of *Women and Wars* (Polity Press, 2013).

OSCAR GAYTÁN graduated from University of California, Los Angeles in the class of 2018.

DONNA M. GOLDSTEIN is Professor of Anthropology at University of Colorado Boulder. She is the author of *Laughter Out of Place: Race, Class, Violence, and Sexuality in a Rio Shantytown* (University of

California Press, new edition 2013), and two special issues in the journal *Culture, Theory and Critique.*

CELESTE GÓMEZ graduated from University of California, Los Angeles in the class of 2020.

KIRA HALL is Professor of Linguistics in the Departments of Linguistics and Anthropology at University of Colorado Boulder. Her latest books include *The Oxford Handbook of Language and Sexuality* (forthcoming, coedited with Rusty Barrett) and *Parsing the Body* (under review, coedited with Mary Bucholtz).

JOHN HERNÁNDEZ graduated from University of California, Los Angeles in the class of 2020.

ADAM HODGES is an adjunct assistant professor of linguistics at University of Colorado Boulder. His books include *When Words Trump Politics: Resisting a Hostile Regime of Language* (Stanford University Press, 2019) and *The "War on Terror" Narrative: Discourse and Intertextuality in the Construction and Contestation of Sociopolitical Reality* (Oxford University Press, 2011).

MATTHEW BRUCE INGRAM is Assistant Professor of Communication Studies at Dakota State University. His recent publication, "YouTube Commentaries on Trans Time-Lapse Videos: Transforming Misgendering Stances into Pedagogical Moments," is part of a special issue in the journal *Somatechnics* concerning Trans Narratives.

MARCO JACQUEMET is Professor of Communication and Culture at University of San Francisco. His publications include *Ethereal Shadows: Communication and Power in Contemporary Italy* (coauthored with Franco Berardi; Autonomedia 2009) and *Credibility in Court: Communicative Practices in the Camorra's Criminal Trials* (Cambridge University Press, 1996).

MARCO ANTONIO JUÁREZ graduated from University of California, Los Angeles in the class of 2019.

BRUCE MANNHEIM is Professor of Anthropology at University of Michigan. His books include *Authority, Hierarchy, and the Indigenous Languages of Latin America: Historical and Ethnographic Perspectives* (edited with Alan Durston, University of Notre Dame Press, 2018), and *The Dialogic Emergence of Culture* (edited with Dennis Tedlock, University of Illinois Press, 1995).

JANET MCINTOSH is Professor of Anthropology at Brandeis University. She is the author of *The Edge of Islam: Power, Personhood, and Ethnoreligious Boundaries on the Kenya Coast* (Duke University Press, 2009); *Unsettled: Denial and Belonging among White Kenyans* (University of California

Press, 2016); and numerous journal articles in linguistic and sociocultural anthropology.

NORMA MENDOZA-DENTON is Professor of Anthropology at University of California, Los Angeles. She is the author of *Homegirls: Language and Cultural Practice in Latina Youth Gangs* (Wiley-Blackwell, 2008), and over fifty chapters and journal articles in the fields of linguistics, anthropology, communication, and education.

MAGALY RESÉNDEZ will graduate from University of California, Los Angeles in the class of 2021.

OTTO SANTA ANA is Professor of Chicana, Chicano, and Central American Studies at University of California, Los Angeles. He has published four books and fifty academic pieces, chiefly on how language is used to validate unjust social inequity. He has served as an expert on major civil rights legal cases regarding the public discourse of elected officials. His formal declaration in defense of DACA was submitted as part of an amicus brief to the US Supreme Court.

NATASHA SHRIKANT is Assistant Professor in the Department of Communication at University of Colorado Boulder. Her work analyzing tensions between structure and agency during the communicative negotiation of racial, ethnic, and cultural identities appears in journals such as *Discourse and Society, Discourse and Communication, Pragmatics, Gender & Language, Journal of International and Intercultural Communication*, and *Ethnic and Racial Studies.*

JACK SIDNELL is Professor of Anthropology at University of Toronto. He is the author of *The Concept of Action* (with N. J. Enfield, Cambridge University Press, 2017), editor of *Conversation Analysis: Comparative Perspectives* (Cambridge, 2009), and co-editor of *Conversational Repair and Human Understanding* (Cambridge, 2013), *The Handbook of Conversation Analysis* (Wiley-Blackwell, 2012), and *The Cambridge Handbook of Linguistic Anthropology* (Cambridge, 2014).

SYLVIA SIERRA is Assistant Professor at the College of Visual & Performing Arts, Department of Communication & Rhetorical Studies, Syracuse University. Her book *Millennials Talking Media* is under contract with Oxford University Press.

JAMES SLOTTA is Assistant Professor of Anthropology at University of Texas at Austin. He has published recent articles in *Language in Society, Language and Communication, American Ethnologist*, and many other venues.

GENEVA SMITHERMAN is University Distinguished Professor Emerita in the Department of English at Michigan State University. She is the author of *Articulate While Black: Barack Obama, Language, and Race in the US* (Oxford, 2012, with H. Samy Alim), *Word from the Mother: Language and African Americans* (Taylor & Francis 2006), and *Talkin' that Talk: Language, Culture, and Education in Africa America* (Routledge 2000).

ROBERTO SOLÍS graduated from University of California, Los Angeles in the class of 2019.

BRION VAN OVER is Assistant Professor of Liberal and Creative Arts at Manchester Community College. He is the author of articles in journals such as *Journal of Applied Communication Research* and *Cultural Studies*.

QUENTIN WILLIAMS is Associate Professor in the Linguistics Department at University of the Western Cape. He is the author of *Remix Multilingualism* (Bloomsbury Press, 2017), and coauthor of *Making Sense of People and Place in Linguistic Landscapes* (Bloomsbury Press, 2018) and of *Neva Again: Hip Hop Art, Activism and Education in Post-Apartheid South Africa* (HSRC Press, 2019).

Acknowledgments

I'm grateful to Brandeis University for the Norman Award research funds that assisted in the production of this book, and for Brandeis' funding of my participation in the 2017 American Anthropological Association meetings where we first staged a panel on this subject. Thanks to the AAA attendees who encouraged us to expand the panel into a teachable book, and to the contributors for bearing with us through a complex process so that their wonderful work could be part of this volume. I am exceedingly grateful to Sasha Martin for being the *deus ex machina* who descended to take care of a thousand fiddly editorial details, making astute suggestions and supportive notes to each author along the way. Particular thanks to Isabel Collins of Cambridge University Press for her responses to so many questions, to Andrew Winnard, and to the external reader who offered such supportive comments. To my older son Tobias, many thanks for the cover design concept!

To the veterans and service members who have helped shed light on the politics of military language (see my "Crybabies and Snowflakes" chapter within): Thank you for being willing to speak with this anthropologist. Ben Schrader offered insights from a most valued perspective. Heartfelt gratitude to the brilliant members of the Cambridge Writer's Circle who offered feedback in the context of long-standing friendship: Manduhai Buyandelger, Elizabeth Ferry, Smita Lahiri, Ann Marie Leshkowich, Heather Paxson, and Chris Walley. Jen Roth-Gordon, you are the most prompt and thorough reader I can imagine, making tough but immensely helpful suggestions; thank you so much for your help. And special gratitude to my parents, Ken and Peggy McIntosh, for their everlasting solidarity, and to Tom, Tobias, and Theo for supporting me with love while I worked on this project during an already impossibly busy time. We dedicate this book to the memory of Jennifer Jackson, who would have been anguished by the Trump era but would have tucked right into analyzing it with the compassion, humor, and insight of someone who understood disparate corners of America. She was my good friend and remains an example to me, in head and heart.

Janet McIntosh

I would like to pay homage to the linguistics/anthropology scholars who have passed away and who inspired us to write this book. They include Jennifer Jackson (1975–2015), Jane Hill (1939–2018), Chuck Goodwin (1944–2018), Barney Bate (1961–2016), Joshua Fishman (1926–2015), and Ivan Sag (1949–2013). All of them have written insightful political-linguistic-anthropological pieces and are constantly in mind as "shadow subjects," as interlocutors in interiority, and as we write and think about these issues. Our field and our world are lesser in their absence.

Audiences at the American Anthropological Association, UCLA's Discourse Lab and Co-operative Action Lab, Berkeley Linguistics Department, the Linguistic Society of America's Linguistics Institute in Kentucky, and Duke University have given feedback on various portions of this work. Nomi Stoltzenberg with the Center for Law, History, and Culture at University of Southern California invited me to their West Coast Literature and Law conference "Trump Reads! Literature and Law in the Age of the Donald." The interaction in this venue with writers and legal scholars was extremely important in the development of my ideas.

Thanks to Andrew Winnard at Cambridge University Press and to Isabel Collins, whose editorial flair and support have been invaluable. Extra gratitude to Sasha Martin, who good-humoredly helped with so many details for this book to come together.

Other friends and colleagues who have been sounding boards for various aspects of this work include Aomar Boum, Rodolfo Mendoza-Denton, Ozlem Ayduk, Galey Modan, Rudi Gaudio, Jeff Maskovsky, Erin Debenport, Bambi Schieffelin, Samy Alim, Candy Goodwin, Sandro Duranti, Ellie Ochs, Julio Serrano, Kit Woolard, Sherry Ortner, Tim Taylor, Perry Gilmore, Sonya Pritzker, Can Aciksoz, Zeynep Korkman, Sarah Abrevaya Stein, Frederick Zimmerman, Keith Walters, Penny Eckert, John Rickford, Susan Slyomovics, Nadjib Berber, Miriam Meyerhoff, David Myers, Daria Roithmyer, Amy Wilentz, Susan Gal, Greg Thompson, Benjamin Smith, Dennis and Carol Preston, Jemima Pierre, Peter Hudson, Jack Sidnell, Otto Santa Ana, Luis Manuel Olguín, Brackette Williams, Jonathan Rosa, Hannah Appel, Jessica Cattelino, Noah Zatz, and Susan Ettner.

Tyanna Slobe deserves special thanks as an indispensable research assistant. Molly Bloom, Courtney Ryan, Ashley Stinnett, Tania Rhodes, Colleen Cotter, Tad and Claire Park, Stefanie Jannedy and Bettina, Justus, Jacob, and Karsten von Eitzen, Abdeslam Ait Tastift, Nezha Garimi, and all the Boums from Marrakech to Foum Zguid have kept me sane with talk and friendship.

And ultimately, this book is inspired by and dedicated to the thinkers of the future, the thunderbolts of inspiration and whirlwinds of action who are Teo and Kai Mendoza-Ayduk, Ryan Ait Tastift, and most especially Maggie Boum-Mendoza, who loves great ideas!

Norma Mendoza-Denton

Note on Transcription Conventions

Unless otherwise specified by an author, we use a variation on the transcription system developed by Gail Jefferson for the analysis of conversation (Harvey Sacks, Emanuel A. Schegloff, and Gail Jefferson. 1974. "A Simplest Systematics for the Organization of Turn-Taking for Conversation." *Language* 50: 696–735, at 731–33). Transcription conventions used throughout include the use of CAPITALS to indicate talk spoken with special emphasis. Colons after a vowel indicate an elongated vowel sound. A left bracket ([) marks the onset, and a right bracket (]) marks the offset of overlapping talk. Numbers in parentheses – for example, (1.2) – note the length of silences in seconds, while a single period in parentheses (.) indicates a micropause of less than 0.1 seconds. A dash (-) marks the cut-off of the current sound. An equals sign (=) indicates "latching," where talk starts up in especially close temporal proximity to the end of the previous talk. Transcribers' comments and non-verbal action descriptors are italicized in double parentheses ((*like this*)); single parentheses, (like this), around talk indicate a problematic hearing. Punctuation symbols are used to mark intonation changes rather than as grammatical symbols: a period indicates a falling contour; a question mark, a rising contour; and a comma, a falling-rising contour, as might be found in the midst of a list. Each line of text (without a hard return) indicates talk spoken within a single breath group.

Occasionally some of the authors in this volume have transcribed the same conversation differently, paying attention to different details of interaction, tone, or gesture. We have retained the authors' intended transcriptions insofar as possible, since these are not inconsistencies but theoretically motivated by different "noticings."

When the transcribed talk is a monologue, authors have transcribed for content, using standard punctuation rather than the above transcription conventions, occasionally adding their own emphasis (which they have marked as such).

Grammatical solecisms, spelling and punctuation errors, and other infelicities in Trump's tweets have been left unedited.

Note on Ethnonyms and Phenotypic Descriptors

We have opted to capitalize both "Black" and "White" (while recognizing there is no uniform identity within these groups), when, taken in context, the terms indicate a racialized identity. In the context of Trump's politics, racial identity has been foregrounded for many, and White identity is increasingly self-conscious, particularly in hostile juxtaposition to its racial others. In a few instances, we use lower case when these terms foreground phenotype over identity (as in, "black and brown women").

Introduction: The Trump Era as a Linguistic Emergency

Janet McIntosh

> This is the creation story of Donald Trump becoming president of the United
> States. His whole brand is: *I will say things that the other guys won't.*
> Ben Rhodes, former speechwriter for President Obama[1]

Early in his campaign, Donald Trump boasted: "I know words. I have the best
words" (Trump 2015). And yet, one of the enduring paradoxes of Trump's
presidency has been the upsetting and contradictory nature of his language. Our
popular understanding of language leads us to expect words to pin down
meaning, but language in the current political moment equivocates, collapses,
gives us false starts and electric shocks. From the Trump administration's
earliest pronouncements of the "largest ever" inaugural crowd size, to his
tweeted insistence in March 2020 that the White House's chaotic response to
the COVID-19 outbreak was "perfectly coordinated" (Trump 2020a), language
in the era of Donald Trump seems less about describing reality than about thick-
fingered manipulation: *We have said it, and thus have made it so.*[2] Precedent
and previous use matter less than the reality-generating properties and the
bluster of words.

The Trump era feels like a political emergency to many, but it also feels like
a linguistic one. Language has been repeatedly enlisted to produce and fortify
Trump's reality, and it has scandalized liberal Americans as it inaugurated the
tone of Trump's presidency – from "Make America Great Again," which critics
felt suggested a racist, nativist atavism, to the T-shirts at conservative rallies
reading "Trump 2016: Fuck Your Feelings." The controlled, subtle oratory of
Obama; the reassuring paternalism of Reagan; the elegant inspiration of JFK –
such verbal artistry would be behind us. In his crude terms, Trump would tap
into and exacerbate global currents of right-wing populism, complete with
White victimhood, xenophobic fear mongering, and resurging patriarchy (van
Dijk 2005; Wodak 2015). He would bring demagoguery to the surface of
American politics, with all its appeal to popular prejudices (Hodges 2019a,
Steudeman 2018, Young 2018), while he and his appointees would attack "the
experts" in just about every domain while fomenting paranoid conspiracy
theories (Warzel 2019). Critics would charge that his followers, some of

them evangelicals convinced Trump's presidency was ordained by God, were in cult-like thrall. And with Trump, the nation would enter not only a new political era, but also a new linguistic one, in which language would be weaponized in vindictive fashion, forging a new kind of presidential power.

As a result of their political and linguistic differences, left and right are now so polarized it's as if we are living in different realities. By late 2019, Trump's critics saw a president deserving of impeachment on multiple grounds, while his supporters saw a leader saving the country, not destroying it. To capture these extremes, some on the far right (sometimes known as the alt-right) have used an image from the classic sci-fi film *The Matrix*, in which the heroic Neo is offered a choice between a "red pill," which represents brutal truths, or a "blue pill" that would let him bask in illusion. Alt-righters say that, like Neo, they opt for the "red pill," confronting an underlying reality leftists are in denial about: namely, that America is being smothered by big government; that men are oppressed and imperiled by feminism; that White people are victims of reverse racism; and that immigrants, Muslims, LGBTQ+ individuals, and other minorities are destroying the fabric of the nation (cf. Kakutani 2018: 86).

There's a link between this red pill/blue pill logic and language, for one of the most striking things about this era is that the very same speech events and verbal stylings that buoy Trump's supporters leave his detractors aghast. Different readings of reality have been linked to different readings of the same utterances and the same linguistic style. But, far from understanding Trump as a guy who "tells it like it is" or as a dementia victim whose spelling errors alone should disqualify him from presidency (the extreme poles of these oppositional readings of language), we have to understand these very framings as ideological products, backlashes, and accretions of not only racially inflected political priorities but also class-based sentiment.

What Can a Language Studies Approach Contribute?

At the heart of this book is an encouragement to think about how language both "means" things and "makes" society. Obviously, language communicates content through word meaning and the way we combine words into sentences. But as Jennifer Jackson (2013) has explained, linguistic anthropology encourages us to explore fleeting or seemingly minute verbal moments and their interpretation in context to understand the tricks behind the magic. Donald Trump is somehow using language – from word choice to less obvious interactional oscillations – to enlist members of the public in his distortions, breeding new social dynamics and a species of presidential authority many Americans have hardly recognized. How is he pulling this off? How, to paraphrase Jackson, can we examine language and its contexts to understand how the rabbit got put in the hat in the first place?

Linguistic anthropologists, sociolinguists, and other language scholars have developed a suite of concepts that will aid us in understanding language in Trump's time. Some of this work draws on tools from "rhetoric" as it was traditionally understood; namely, the verbal arts of "persuasion" (for more on Trump's rhetorical persuasion, see Hodges 2019a, Lockhart 2018, Skinnell 2018b). But in recent decades some have construed rhetoric more broadly, merging it with other approaches in language studies and nesting the study of utterances within broad social dynamics. Speech can provide ways of identifying in-groups and out-groups, ways of signifying personalities and feelings, and ways of signaling competence, authenticity, or allegiance. We see that language often *does* something beyond just referring or describing; it sets up storylines that aim to constitute reality, breathes life into identities constructed on the fly through interaction, establishes hierarchies, and enlists people into patterned rituals of social life. In the current political moment, it has also made large portions of the population feel decidedly outraged and unsafe.

To understand how Trump's language works and why it terrifies, to grasp as fully as possible the capacious significance of any given speech event, requires an expansive sense of context. It requires understanding the backdrop of ideas about power, and it sometimes requires understanding how any given speech act reaches backward and forward in time to articulate with other, related speech acts – treating language, in other words, not as a matter of narrowly construed "persuasion," but as a matter of anthropology. Anthropologists understand the meanings of events and utterances by looking to broader contexts. In some cases, this means exploring how meaning is made interactively, attending, for instance, to the way speakers unwittingly collude to construct a jointly shared linguistic activity and to crystallize the relationship between them as they go. In others, it means broadening farther outward to examine the significance of a speech event in ideological, historical, national, even international context. And it can include exploring objections and resistance to any given linguistic construction of reality.

As we address these dynamics in the Trump era, we bring tools from linguistic anthropology and language studies to a wider audience, defining them carefully for the public and using them to address questions such as these:

- Why have the communicative dynamics of Trump's campaign and presidency felt so different from any other, and how did his gestures, words, and tweets help put him in power while fracturing the nation so deeply?
- Why do both Trump's supporters and detractors feel assailed by language dynamics, caught in a kind of "mutual minorityhood" when it comes to their preferred forms of speech?
- How does Trump get away with his prevarications (or at least try to)?

- How does Trump manage to get people to align with him in speech events ranging from roundtables to rallies, setting up a particular type of presidential authority?
- How does Trump use language to prop up his narrow construals of reality, including masculinist and White supremacist claims to power?
- How does Trump's language directly and indirectly signal a storyline about imperiled whiteness and dangerous "others," both domestic and foreign? And how have some of these "others" responded to Trump?

In this Introduction, I review select, recurrent linguistic dynamics of Trump's presidency ("select," because the later chapters address many additional vital topics; "recurrent," to set the stage). If Trump's rise has felt to some like a linguistic emergency, this can only be understood by exploring competing American "language ideologies"; that is, collective beliefs linking ideas about language to ideas about the way the social world is or should be. I start by historicizing some changes in American ideologies of (and expectations for) presidential communication, changes that have happened in tandem with mass mediation. I then engage with the widespread language-ideological disagreements about "political correctness" (or PC), disagreements that have fed a situation of verbal "mutual minorityhood" I explain below. This leads me into the disagreements about how to locate meaning in Trump's linguistic style – that is, the form, rather than the semantic content, of what he says. While the right's embrace of Trump's supposedly "authentic" style often overlooks the dismaying inhumanity of his policies, I suggest the left's fixation on Trump's verbal errors also brings a risk: namely, playing on class prejudices at the expense of analyzing more consequential world-shaping aspects of language and, indeed, policy in the Trump era. In the final sections, I discuss the prevarication, gaslighting, and word policing Trump and his administration have used to bend political and social reality, reasons for the rapid rise in profanity across the political spectrum, and the spread of hateful speech. These changes, felt by many as verbal scandals and crises, furnish the backdrop for the focused chapters that follow.

Presidential Language: A Brief Comparative History

Presidential appeal and credibility hinge on what political insiders call "message," or "the politician's publicly imaginable 'character'" (Lempert and Silverstein 2012: 1–2). Message isn't so much about what politicians literally state about the issues, but rather what they convey about their "identity and personal values" by way of "all manner of signs that creatively gesture toward this persona without explicitly describing it." Presidential language, then, helps to create the political figure's holistic message or brand.

Historically, American presidential candidates have worked within fairly predictable constraints of language ideology to convey their message, particularly the expectation that they show seriousness, erudition, and "statesmanlike" qualities through composed, polished language. Lincoln's Gettysburg address, for instance, achieved its fame partly through his "priestly, Eucharistic" style that connected the public with the sacred (Silverstein 2003: 57). For a long while, it was conventional for presidents to preserve formality by addressing the public as if reading from a written document or (starting in the 1950s) a teleprompter – with perhaps a bit of ad lib for humor or immediacy – when giving a planned speech. The American public has also tended to value direct displays of conviction and intention in presidential speech.

In recent decades, expectations for presidential language have shifted along with mass media technology. Franklin D. Roosevelt took advantage of the radio age with his weekly "Fireside Chats" – the first time in history that a large segment of the public could listen simultaneously to their president in their homes. Although Roosevelt deliberately chose common words to create more intimacy than the elite formalisms he used elsewhere, the addresses were still painstakingly drafted, and sounded more like oratory than informal "chatting" (cf. Lim 2003). Still, the era merged at least the promise of an accessible touch with high presidential formality.

With the television era, visual polish became crucial to success. The first televised presidential debate in 1960 broadcast a tanned, unflappable JFK next to a pallid, sweating Richard Nixon (a contrast visible even on a black-and-white TV screen). Kennedy's chiseled confidence enhanced his delivery throughout his presidency, as did his inspirational oratory, with poetic style that connected him to a transcendent sense of purpose. His inauguration speech marked him as the charismatic steward of a new America: "Let the word go forth from this time and place ... that the torch has been passed to a new generation of Americans." Ronald Reagan, a seasoned Hollywood actor, brilliantly exploited the medium of television by coordinating with camera operators to visually "illustrate" his words. In his inaugural speech, for instance, the cameras panned over the great monuments in Washington, DC, as Reagan gained reflected glory from the monuments' "visual majesty" (Jamieson 1998). He was also a master storyteller, invoking deeds from heroic Americans, dipping into choice quotations from poetry and scripture, and managing to make Americans feel as if they all were bettered by the reflected glory of great men (and I do mean men). Though Reagan's critics gleefully compiled examples of his grammatical solecisms (Green and MacColl 1983), some of which may have been early signs of the Alzheimer's that would take his life, his addresses to the public were often models of craftsmanship.

After Reagan, the Bush dynasty that came before and after Bill Clinton marked something of a verbal come-down. George H. W. Bush's Vice

President, Dan Quayle, was ridiculed for years for a 1992 incident in which, at an elementary school in Trenton, New Jersey, he amended a student's (already correct) spelling of "potato" by adding an "e" to the end of the word. The event presaged the post-Clintonian verbal errors of George W. Bush (or "Dubya"), which earned their own term: "Bushisms." His grammatical perversions were legendary ("You teach a child to read, and he or her will be able to pass a literacy test"), as were his neologisms such as "misunderestimated" and "the internets." While some, including Noam Chomsky, suggested his mispronunciations may have been faked to appeal to a working-class base (Polychroniou 2016), his blunders suggested to others that he might be easily controlled by the keener manipulative minds in his cabinet. Yet his style also held what anthropologist Michael Silverstein (2003: 70–71, 124) calls a "posture of earnestness that has got to make our hearts go out to the guy"; a sincere message that implied something like, "Hey, I'm not perfect, but I'm *really trying*!" All in all, linguist John McWhorter (2017) suggests that the Dubya era presaged Trump's "semi-articulate" language: Evidently, "being well spoken was a much lower priority for Americans in choosing a president than it once was." The next step toward an inarticulate head of state was the selection of Sarah Palin, "blithely unconcerned with her swivel-tongued syntax and yet revered by millions" (ibid.), as a Republican vice-presidential nominee.

But before America arrived at Trump, there were two preconditions in the 2000s: an African American president whose election stoked a White supremacist backlash, and a sea change in the mass mediation of communication between politicians and the populace. Obama's grassroots campaign team used Facebook, Twitter (founded only in 2006, but rapidly relevant to political campaigning), and other forms of social media. These mechanisms reached voters at their laptops and cell phones, sometimes striving to appeal to young people – a prime example being Obama's uplifting "Yes We Can" slogan and its celebrity-laced music video. Before a podium, Obama also managed to "remix" the inspirational structures of both White and Black jeremiadic traditions (Alim and Smitherman 2012: 87). Educated liberals swooned over his erudition and verbal dexterity. Depending on the moment, too, he could toggle between a Black discursive style and a "white Mainstream way of speaking," sounding "Black, but not *too* Black" and "White, but not *too* White" (ibid. 20–22), while endearing himself to many, including younger generations, with his verbal indicators of "cool." Such versatility gave him broad demographic appeal, and was particularly important since American verbal culture, if there's any one such thing, had become more casual and informal; less rigid about old grammatical rules and more enthusiastic about "relatability" in authority figures.

Any remaining expectations of presidential language have been shattered by Trump's ascendancy, which was partly propelled by yet more rapid change in the mass mediation of communication. In the decade leading up to Trump's campaign, the Internet and other digital technologies upended the way professional media handled their reporting and deadlines (Cotter 2015), while social media created millions of new channels for the public to generate and transmit political sentiment. One result has been that people's existing political opinions are more likely to be stoked than challenged. Social network algorithms are designed to feed consumers the very news stories they are likely to click on based on their browsing history. Trump's campaign received a boost from professional "trolls" hired by Russia, who promulgated supportive memes and often falsified stories by way of Facebook, 4chan, and Reddit (Davlashyan and Titova 2018). And the rocketing popularity of Twitter furnished Trump with a platform in many respects perfectly suited to his style.

Trump thrives on Twitter's character limit (140 words before 2017, now 280 words) for his compulsive provocations and claims, many of which he seems unable to elaborate on anyway. Twitter's cursory form is perfect for the man seeking what linguistic anthropologists call a "zero-evidential" speech style; that is, a mode in which the speaker furnishes no grounds for their claims. Tweets scroll away as new ones come in, easily drowned by public responses, giving them an ephemeral quality that facilitates Trump's ability to escape long-term consequences of his words (Stolee and Caton 2018: 160). And he can pipe his conspiracy theories, insults, and threats to tens of millions of followers while lying in bed with his cell phone.

Though his tweets have been characterized as "official" presidential statements, Trump has used Twitter to issue erratic and contradictory policy promises, gestures of alarming international (un)diplomacy, and hateful, disruptive pronouncements. Many are ungrammatical and peppered with spelling errors and exclamation points – though aides sometimes correct his errors later in a kind of verbal mop-up. Critics fulminate while diplomats and policy makers scramble to understand the implications of and the level of commitment behind any given tweet. Though some Trump voters chose him in spite of his style, others enjoy the experience of someone so unmediated by conventional political packaging, as though it gives him "authenticity" (Stolee and Caton 2018: 157). Meanwhile, supporters have the option of issuing their own (anonymous, and therefore disinhibited) cheers for Trump and snide rejoinders to his detractors.

With the easy replication social media offers, Trump can guarantee that his attention-getting phrases will be widely disseminated. Spam accounts and automated internet "bots" have also created the simulacrum of larger masses of Twitter users than actually exist, including thousands, potentially millions, of Trump's "supporters" (Fishkin 2018; see also Kakutani 2018). By seeming to echo one another and establishing solidarity, a community that might have once seemed fringe picks up steam and adherents (cf. Jaworska and

Sogomonian 2019). In this new digital era, the work of journalism has been jarred as conventional news media struggle to compete and keep up with social media. The news media's former function as a sort of "jury" to politicians (van Hout and Burger 2017: 471) seems to have little purchase on the opinions of Trump's base.

Social media, in combination with Trump's exceedingly tight relationship with the conservative *Fox News* channel, has created a rhetorical feedback loop between Trump and his cheerleaders, who sometimes mutually amplify catchy political phrases. A few Trump supporters, for instance, were the first to promote the image of left-wing protesters as irrational, unhinged "mobs" on Twitter around October 11, 2018. They soon juxtaposed these baying mobs with the job growth Trump has taken credit for, coining the phrase "jobs, not mobs!" Prominent supporters endorsed the slogan on Twitter and Reddit, stating their strategy: "The brain interprets rhymes as persuasive" (Collins and Roose 2018). The catchy meme, which condensed a political worldview in three syllables (a popular pattern among Trump supporters), was soon chanted at Trump rallies and widespread on the web. On October 18, 2018, Trump himself tweeted "#Jobsnotmobs!" for the first of several times, and the meme became a nationwide device of persuasion in the run-up to the midterm elections (ibid.).

Twitter's casual immediacy has a stylistic resemblance to the very political architecture Trump promised. Rather than electing an image-mongering traditional politician, America would get a self-proclaimed "transparent" populist leader who would overturn the old political ways and bring an expeditious toughness to the White House. Rather than appealing to urban "coastal elites" with their polished oration and long words, the president would appeal to the guts, the heartland, and the South, as well as some in suburbia. I return below to the matter of Trump's verbal style and its disparate reception by the political right and left, but to pave the way, I also provide more context about a pre-eminent language ideology in his campaign and presidency.

On "Political Correctness" and Mutual Minorityhood

The resurgence of the right wing's "anti-politically correct language" stance helped to bring Trump into office. Over the course of a couple of decades, the USA had seen a rapid rise in progressive norms of linguistic sensitivity around historically marginalized groups. The ideology driving this shift holds that language is a kind of social action, and word choice can wound, marginalize, perniciously stereotype, and outright oppress (Cameron 1995). Many have reached for new and more careful terminology, eschewing language deemed racist or sexist while opting for phrases like "differently abled" rather than "disabled" to avoid an implicit judgment about worth, or phrases such as "enslaved people" rather than "slaves" to underscore the humanity of those locked into structural violence. In recent years, too, many academics and college students have put a fine point on "microaggressions," those passing verbal and non-verbal slights, often unwitting, that may communicate hostile or offensive assumptions to marginalized group members.

But those who scorn what they call politically correct (or PC) language ideology refuse the notion that word choice creates problems, arguing instead that linguistic care stokes oversensitivity, or that it evades harsh realities that harsh language merely describes. The anti-PC stance sometimes seems informed by the ideology that speakers' intentions should determine what they "really" mean when they say something, which is sometimes called the "personalist" theory of meaning in the study of language ideology (Duranti 1993). In this perspective, the PC police are unfair in holding speakers accountable for unintended effects of what they say, such as offending the hearer. To be clear, this issue has attracted concern from some on the left as well. It is undoubtedly the case, as Mikhail Bakhtin (1983) emphasized, that words carry some "taste" of the socially charged contexts in which they have already lived, but at their most extreme, PC defenders might not make much moral distinction between *using* and *mentioning someone else's use of* a slur, or might call the police on an eleven-year-old boy for "sexually harassing" when using a term he doesn't fathom the meaning of (an actual instance I heard about from an anthropologist colleague in the Boston area). Anti-PC crusaders, meanwhile, may let the most powerful man in the nation off the hook when he talks about "grabbing women by their pussies."

Both the political left and right have complained of being besieged by language in what has sometimes felt like a hothouse of mutual recrimination. Anthropologist Elise Kramer (2012) offers a salient framework for such moments by defining "mutual minorityhood" as a social context in which "each side of a debate perceives itself as a victimized minority and its opponent as a hegemonic majority." During the Obama years in particular, conservatives seethed that the PC shift had gone too far, propelled by "liberal elites," academics, and other coastal urban culture-makers.

The scorn for PC language is driven in part by a reluctance to cede power to formerly marginalized groups, but in some cases, too, it's driven by the fact that PC speech politics have sometimes come across as classist. Those with access to higher education, including some members of the "professional-managerial class" who play a key role in cultural production (Ehrenreich and Ehrenreich 1977), are more likely to scold others for insensitive language. It is often through discussions on university campuses or at other institutions, for instance, that one is likely to learn new conventions for talking about enslaved peoples, gender-neutral pronouns (using "they" as a singular pronoun, for instance), or vigilance for microaggressions. Learning these new linguistic prescriptions can feel as peculiar to the uninitiated as trying to master a prescriptive grammar rule, such as not splitting an infinitive. In some cases, those who scold them suffer from what I call "structural oblivion" (McIntosh 2016); that is, a failure to recognize the reasons for the resentment of those with relatively less power. Those who don't know the new lingo and haven't cultivated exquisite verbal sensitivity are sometimes judged as prejudiced by (hyper-)educated liberals, an assumption that in some contexts may impose what Richard Sennett and Jonathan Cobb (1972) call a "class injury."

Anti-PC ideology may be even more intimately linked to class politics than this. Those on the receiving end of accusations of bigotry have sometimes felt their economic grievances or fears of losing upward mobility are being side-lined by overly precious identity politics. Although a demographic range of voters supported Trump (including successful entrepreneurs from many ethnic groups), and while plenty of working-class Americans would never dream of voting for him (see Walley 2017 for a discussion of other class complexities in Trump's election), Trump had vital support from White Americans without college degrees, many of whom feel disenfranchised by global free trade and the loss of blue-collar jobs in the USA (Tyson and Maniam 2016).[3] Many expressed frustration at the fact that their wage insecurity and egregious work-ing and housing conditions did not seem to be on the radar of liberal politicians like Hillary Clinton. And for those who worry their jobs may be imperiled by immigrants, PC language has come across as if defending or cosseting the very groups who supposedly threaten the nation's economy. After all, some jobs are given to undocumented immigrants who can be paid below minimum wage, and, as many Trump supporters see it, tax money is being squandered to "undeserving" people – often, minorities – supposedly mooching off various welfare programs. From these voters' point of view, liberals were ignoring the way the (White) working class was being starved of economic opportunity, while putting them down for using the "wrong words."

For a while, it looked as if conservatives were losing the "culture war" (Kakutani 2018: 49), including navigating the PC language issue. But Trump has swung language around him like a medieval mace, delivering satisfaction to constituents who feel he is rescuing their pride or preserving their power. In fact, Trump frames PC language politics as not only silly, but also dangerous. During the August 6, 2015 GOP debate, he said: "I think the big problem this country has is being politically correct. I've been challenged by so many people and I don't, frankly, have time for total political correctness. And to be honest with you, this country doesn't have time, either" (Kilgore 2018). Selecting a word only takes milliseconds, but Trump's implication seems to be that PC energy is in a zero-sum game with other political urgencies, however ill-defined in this statement; perhaps its considerations detract from a certain expediency, a Nietzschean will-to-power. Or maybe, Trump's use of "time" really means "empathy," and all its implications for care and liberal compassion in policy formulation. In his 2017 Commencement Address at Notre Dame, Vice President Mike Pence focused on a different danger, arguing that politically correct "tone policing" on college campuses constitutes an attack on free speech (Stack 2017). Some have framed the PC peril as threatening an entire (conventional, Christian) way of life, as seen when *Fox News* claimed that under the Obama administration, saying the word "Christmas" was considered "politically incorrect" (Starnes 2017) and when a pro-Trump "super PAC" thanked President Trump in a commercial for "letting us say 'Merry Christmas' [as opposed to 'Happy Holidays'] again" (Butler Bass 2018).

Occasionally, supporters have even portrayed PC ideology as a mortal threat of sorts, such as the woman from Woodstock, Georgia who told *CNN* that before Trump's election, "the country was going on a near-death experience collision. Political correctness was about to strangle us all" (Enda 2017). In her phrasing, sensitive and inclusive language becomes a kind of vise, constraining speakers to the point where they cannot breathe. A software developer from Windham, New Hampshire framed the issue in terms of a dangerously weak foreign policy: "The Obama administration was preoccupied with not offend-ing people, [and] some nations that normally would not try some things are seeing how much they can get away with ... Sometimes, you have to smack them across the jaw" (ibid.). In such rhetoric, PC language is positioned as if in denial of harsh realities, with its opposite having a vital, near-physical force important even to national security. In spite of his prevarications, then, Trump's hostility to political correctness has been taken as a sign of his realism as well as his strength.

But beyond all this, some feel Trump's anti-PC language ideology – and its valorization by his election – has allowed his supporters to emerge from the moral doghouse. True, some Trump voters profess embarrassment or disap-proval when Trump comes across as racist or sexist, but many have gloried that their leader has brought their true feelings in front of the curtain. Consider Clint Eastwood's words to *Esquire* in August 2016: "Secretly everybody's getting tired of political correctness, kissing up ... When I grew up, those things weren't called racist" (Hainey 2016). To Eastwood, Trump is "just saying what's on his mind," and claiming one's verbal freedom – no matter who feels offended or oppressed by it – is framed as a traditional American value, beyond reproach. Jerry Falwell Jr. connects Trump's direct speech almost tenderly to his supposed emotional earnestness: "One of the reasons I support him is because he doesn't say what's politically correct. He says what's in his heart" (Zink 2017). Steve Tobak (2016) of *FoxBusiness.com* adds financial and legal alarmism to the arguments against PC language: "People are sick and tired of having to filter everything they say and do because they're afraid of being labeled a racist or a sexist and being sued or losing their jobs. In the minds of many Americans, political correctness is a real threat to 'Life, liberty, and the pursuit of happiness.'" The core value of the Trump movement, he adds, is to "live our lives without fear of prosecution again" (Tobak 2016).

Mutual minorityhood comes into clear focus, here. Historically marginalized people wish for greater consideration in language, and feel their own "life, liberty, and pursuit of happiness" may be imperiled by verbal denigration. But opponents of PC language claim they feel oppressed themselves, making Trump's anti-PC language practices feel, to them, like justice.

Anxieties about Style: Classist Judgments or Cognitive Incompetence?

The importance of speech style to voters' perceptions can be heard in the words of Carolyn Sharp, who works as a cashier at a restaurant in Johnstown, Pennsylvania. "I feel like maybe somebody who has a little more power and has a big mouth can actually get some words across," she says of Trump (Inskeep 2017). But Trump's big mouth, so well received by many of his fans, has been one reason his detractors have felt in crisis. In this section and the next, I focus on the form rather than the content of what Trump says, exploring why responses to his style have been so polarized. Here, I suggest aspects of Trump's style offer grounds for reasonable critiques of his intellect and character, but some of the attacks on his style are blighted by classism of the sort that indirectly helped to propel him into office. There isn't always a clear line to be drawn between mocking Trump's linguistic style because it lacks polish, and sounding the alarm when it suggests a genuine danger to the nation, but it's worth being aware of the potential distinction.

For Trump's detractors, his speech style exudes the "unpresidential" quali- ties they deride as inappropriate to his station. He has given relatively few formal addresses or press conferences, and his most extensive public utterances have been at rallies and on Twitter, where he routinely adorns his tweets with exclamation points, randomly capitalized words, and all caps lettering. His steady ping of spelling, punctuation, and grammatical errors began with one of his first Presidential tweets, on Jan 21, 2017: "I am honered to serve you" (Smilowitz 2017). Under Trump's tweeting thumbs, "heal" becomes "heel" (Wootson 2017); "whether" is "wether" (Nakamura 2018); the "Marine Corps" becomes "Marine Core" (Thomsen 2018); the "Prince of Wales," the "Prince of Whales" (Dallison 2019). His staff, too, has been implicated: "Air Force Once"; a "lasting peach" in the Middle East; the "State of the Uniom" address (*BBC News* 2018). Even Trump's official inauguration poster included a common spelling error over a beaming image of the new President: "No dream is too big, no challenge is to great" (Calfas 2017). A close-up photo of Trump's notes for a May 2019 press conference revealed new goofs in his own handwriting: "achomlishments" and "intentially" (Cummings 2019). When Trump issued a nonsensical typo late one night on Twitter – "Despite the constant negative press covfefe" – Trump's verbal incompetence seemed to have frolicked into absurdity. Sean Spicer, the then-press secretary, told a gathering of journalists with a straight face: "The president and a small group of people know exactly what he meant" (Nelson 2017), but those present snickered audibly at the attempt to save face. Trump's critics immediately generated memes, mugs, and T-shirts overflowing with mirth and dismay.

A stylistic companion to Trump's spelling difficulties has been his limited vocabulary. Linguists have concluded that most of Trump's favorite words are monosyllabic (Atkin 2015), and that, compared to the past fifteen presidents, his vocabulary and other linguistic metrics rank the lowest (Frischling 2018). He sprinkles his language with empty intensifiers ("very, very") and puffery, as when he dictated his own bill of clean health to his doctor, reporting "astonishingly excellent" laboratory results (McCarthy 2018). Things he likes, such as the wall he aspires to build between the US and Mexico, or various letters he received from Vladimir Putin and Kim Jong-un, are "beautiful" (Reichmann 2019). His (ultimately impeachment-worthy) phone call with Ukrainian President Volodymyr Zelensky was "perfect" (Diamond 2019). People and things Trump doesn't favor get a single, hyperbolic predicate: "crooked," "stupid," "sad," "weak," "pathetic," or "dumb" (Hodges 2019a, Stuart 2016). And Trump's grammatical errors are so legion that if one tried to compile a book of them the way Reagan's critics did, there would be little to exclude.[4]

Then, there is the word-salad effect of how Trump concatenates his phrases and non sequiturs. Teddy Wayne of the *New York Times* characterizes his speech stream as "bob-and-weave," with "the appearance of continued communication being more important than what's actually being said" (Wayne 2017). International translators have wrung their hands over the embarrassing challenges of representing Trump's words; if they are to be true to his tone and style, the translators themselves come across as inarticulate (Viennot 2016), yet if they try to present his most "disjointed and meandering" statements as if intelligible, they may be doing a political disservice by masking his incoherence (Taylor 2019). Charles Blow (2017) suggests Trump's "gibberish … stitched together with arrogance and ignorance" is downright damaging, not only to Trump, but "to language itself." To millions of Americans accustomed to more presidential polish, it has seemed as if Trump can barely hold his words together with Scotch tape.[5]

For Trump's detractors, small linguistic cues have served as indexes of – semiotic pointers to – all kinds of deficits: lack of education, lack of intelligence, lack of care, lack of competence, lack of civility, lack of fitness for office, and a generally untrammeled president without common sense or staff to corral him. Here is where the linguistic anthropologist, looking on at these judgments, has a tricky task. Across societies and history, fairly or not, the form of a person's speech (their accent, the musical lilt of their speech, the structure of their sentences, and so forth) or writing (e.g. spelling or handwriting) tends to be perceived as an index of deeper qualities of the speaker. In fact, it is a truism for those who study language ideology that judgments about linguistic styles are commonly proxies for judgments about speakers themselves. Often, linguistic anthropologists find these judgments take the form of "iconization," a semiotic dynamic where qualities of language, such as the minutiae of speech style, are assumed to mirror or resemble supposed inner attributes of the speaker themselves (Irvine and Gal 2000).

Sometimes this extrapolation from form is justifiable and correct. Sometimes, for instance, rapid speech *is* an indicator of rapid thought and brilliance (just think of the late actor and comedian Robin Williams). Sometimes, though, such judgments are downright unfair, driven by bias. When southerners in the US speak more slowly than northerners or Native Americans speak more slowly than native New Yorkers, it's prejudicial to imagine this slow speech is an index of stupidity. When Americans hear the consonants in German language as reflections of a harsh or domineering national character, they are projecting the sins of mid-twentieth-century German political regimes onto millions of contemporary German citizens. Nevertheless, our snap linguistic judgments tend to resonate in our very bones, as if we have located the essence of the speaker.

There's little question that Trump neither speaks nor thinks in sophisticated paragraphs, but it's not always easy to know how much to extrapolate from the form of his language. At least some of the disdain shown toward Trump's style has been bound up with the notion among the highly educated that (for instance) poor spelling is a direct mirror of poor thinking, yet consider the brilliant, accomplished colleague of mine at a world-class university who confessed to me (sotto voce) that he "saw himself" in Trump's spelling difficulties. In some cases, problems with verbal form reflect specific deficits such as dyslexia, rather than poor overall intellect. More persuasive evidence of Trump's intellectual limits can be found in places like Trump's relationship to briefing memos. By his request, apparently, they include about a quarter of the amount of information of those of Obama's, while excluding both nuance and dissenting views (Dejean 2017). Michael Wolff (2018: 97) further describes Trump refusing to read even the shortest pieces of writing. Even if dyslexia or some other domain-specific processing issue is a culprit, here, this pattern means the Commander-in-Chief is perfectly happy to suffer a critical information deficit.

As for Trump's attenuated words and disorganized speech, their implications for his fitness for office are hotly contested. It's hard for this critic not to feel that the chaos in his linguistic form mirrors a contradictory and stunted thought process. Some hear a deeper derangement in his style. Psychiatrists such as John Gartner, David Reiss, and Steven Buser (the latter being a member of the "Duty to Warn" group of mental health practitioners who believe Trump may have a dangerous mental illness) have argued that Trump's declining vocabulary, repetitions, and difficulties "reading, listening, and comprehending" might point to pre-dementia (Gartner et al. 2018). Before impeachment was on the table in 2019, the ultimate fantasy of Trump's critics was that he might be ousted for mental incompetence based on the 25th Amendment to the Constitution, which allows for the removal of a President "unable to discharge the powers and duties of his office." Yet *Fox News* and other conservative backers deem Trump "stone cold sane" (Ablow 2017), while Trump famously characterizes himself as a "very stable genius." Using one of Trump's favorite deflections, "I know you are but what am I," his defenders have argued that liberals and Democrat politicians such as Nancy Pelosi and Joe Biden (an admittedly easy target) are the ones who are "incoherent," "unhinged," or "losing their minds" (Harwell 2019), suffering from what the right jokingly calls "Trump Derangement Syndrome."

Yet even some Trump critics see the possibility of his dementia as a red herring. Former FBI Director James Comey has tried to reframe the issue by saying that rather than seeing cognitive impairment, "I think he is *morally* unfit to be president" (Shear 2018; emphasis added). Some have suggested Trump may use sloppy speech by design, to appeal to his base. And one of the most vocal critics of the dementia theory has been the linguist John McWhorter. McWhorter (2018a) closely reads Trump's speech style in excerpts such as the following, from 2015: "My uncle was a great professor and scientist and engineer, Dr. John Trump at MIT, good genes, very good genes, OK, very smart, the Wharton School of finance, very good, very smart." According to McWhorter, Trump's sentence fragments, repetition, and tendency to string simple clauses together (formally called "parataxis") are characteristic of rapid, spontaneous talk; in other words, examples of "casual speech as it has always existed." Although it's true that Trump's language has grown less polished over the years, perhaps Trump is now simply taking "the path of least resistance"; after all, he's "learned that he can just show up and run his mouth, and he'll be adored regardless" (ibid.). When people suspect Trump of being linguistically abnormal, in McWhorter's argument, they are drawing on an older language ideology that politicians should use formal, high prestige speech, and forgetting how sloppy ordinary talk can be. With his White masculine privilege, he adds, Trump doesn't have to try as hard as others do to polish his self-presentation. (Obama would have been judged on racial grounds – probably as less intelligent or educated – for such careless speech, while Hillary Clinton would have risked being seen as "trivial.")

It is possible Trump will ultimately be diagnosed with dementia, and the very fact that the nation has had a protracted debate over it signals how deeply

Trump has plunged us into uncertainty. But some of the hype surrounding Trump's sentence fragments and misspellings suggests that bourgeois verbal propriety and conventional notions of professionalism may sometimes divert the focus from a deeper understanding of what Trump has been up to, both verbally and politically.

Abrasive "Authenticity"

To be sure, some Trump voters have admitted they find his tweets and his style petty and rash (Enda 2017). Yet many fans see in his verbal style grounds for optimism that America is in the hands of a great leader. How can Trump's supporters have such a different reading of his style from his critics? What linguistic elements are Trump supporters picking up on, and what language ideologies inform their conclusions? If Trump's detractors are placing too much inferential burden on his spelling and sloppiness, I contend his supporters are extrapolating too much about the man's supposed merits from his abrasive and direct style. And while I don't underestimate the racial animus that motivates at least some of Trump's supporters, nor dismiss the fact that plenty of well-to-do Whites voted for him, I again suggest class-related experiences of economic precarity and frustration with politics-as-usual have inflected some of these judgments about his style.

Sclafani (2018) has examined Trump's stylistic appeal to his supporters through a close reading of the debates leading up to the 2016 election. Trump's opening salvos as he responds to debate questions, for example, are telling. Politicians typically launch their responses with what linguists call "discourse markers"; ostensibly extra words like "well," "now," and "so," that can buy a little time, orient a listener, and perhaps refocus the politician's answer away from the question asked so they can land a point favorable to them. Trump instead tended to start his answers with "I." While his blunt openings could be disorienting to those seeking more rhetorical elegance or careful consideration of the questions, Sclafani suggests that putting his opinions front and center may have implied a decisive style of governance. Meanwhile, his catchphrase "believe me" – which often preceded factually dubious claims – suggested an authoritative voice of "direct experience," building Trump's image as a man who knows better (George Lakoff, quoted in Sclafani 2018: 37). Trump's open-palmed gestures may have suggested to some an appealingly "big" personality, in contrast to Obama with his intellectual "precision grip" (Lempert 2011), potentially alienating to blue-collar voters. All in all, Sclafani suggests Trump's rhetorical style conveys attitude more than content, but this is true to the politician's requirement that their "message" be constituted in part by what Lempert and Silverstein (2012) call a "biographical aura."

And the aura in question, nourished in Trump's campaign rallies and tweets, tacked wildly away from conventional political speak. After all, one of Trump's campaign promises was to "drain the swamp" – a chantable three-word rallying cry (another one, about Hillary Clinton, being "Lock her up!"), suggesting Trump would rid Washington of the supposedly insincere, inefficient beltway insiders. Within his stylistic forms, Trump's supporters saw clues to, even diagrams of, the new political order they hoped for. And because their ideological starting points were so different from those on the left, so too were their interpretations of his verbal style. If Trump's talk was structurally disorganized or fragmented, this was not a sign of a cognitive deficit, but of his hostility to conventionally scripted (and thus manipulative) performances of ordinary politicians. If his clauses and word choices were simple and repetitive, these did not reflect a dearth of education or intelligence, but a mirror of his inner clarity of purpose and an antidote to the slick, alienating jargon wielded by academics and corporate elites. If he flouted politeness with profanity, this did not stand for a mean or emotionally unreconstructed soul, but a satisfying symbolic revenge against liberal niceties (a theme to which I return below). After the primaries, the uptake was clear: Trump scored particularly well on measures of "authenticity" (Sclafani 2018: 5; see also Jamieson and Taussig 2017: 620).

Trump's style was also taken as an indication of his supposed class affiliations. Although stylistic fragmentation cuts across class divisions, and Trump himself comes from wealth as well as an "academy" education, his language has sometimes been interpreted as a sign that he has a communicative pipeline to the working class. In fact, when Trump's staff tweet in his name, some have deliberately imitated his choppy ideation, malapropisms, and random capital letters, "relish[ing] the scoldings Trump gets from elites shocked by the Trumpian language they strive to imitate," while "believing that debates over presidential typos fortify the belief within his base that he has the common touch" (Linskey 2018). One might add that if linguistic style tends to be selected to accommodate one's audience, as argued by sociolinguist Allan Bell (1984), Trump and his team's style may equally be selected as a deliberate means to aggravate his more hypereducated and smug detractors.

As the political left has nitpicked Trump's language, many Trump supporters have relished the occasion to contrast his masculine brand of clarity with the left's feminized elitists and "snowflakes" (see McIntosh, "Crybabies and Snowflakes," this volume). While Obama's multi-clausal hedging, for instance, may have been read as a sign of sophistication to his fans, Trump and other detractors framed it as indicative of an egghead's political paralysis and diplomatic weakness. And with a threat to patriarchy, Hillary Clinton, as his ultimate opponent, Trump could only stand to gain by invoking what Robin Lakoff (2005, quoted in Sclafani 2018: 8) called a "No More Mister Nice Guy" persona. Even his mob-like verbal stylings – so-and-so's a "rat," a lawyer might "flip," etc., possibly picked up from his father's associates – distance him from the appearance of class snobbery while fortifying his tough image (Landler 2018). Trump's very rudeness thus comes across to some like a sign of masculine vigor in a world where conventional politicians (their critics say) so often fail to "get things done."

Between his promises to help the working-class victims of globalization and the minutiae of his rhetoric, Trump secured the loyalty of a critical base and inspired former Communications Director Anthony Scaramucci to title his 2018 encomium *Trump: The Blue-Collar President*. Trump's supporters are viscerally convinced that his simple formulations make him a "man of the people." Never mind the tax cut that overwhelmingly favors the wealthy, continued threats to healthcare for all, tariffs that have caused financial chaos for farmers, and many more policies that imperil the working class. In spite of his millions, the man with golden toilets came to be framed as speaking truth to power.

Both the right and the left have thus turned to Trump's verbal style to seek evidence for their deeper beliefs about who he is, but style is always interpreted through the lens of ideology, rather than being a reliable index of deeper essences. Trump's lousy spelling doesn't in itself make him a bad leader, any more than his simple language suggests he's an honest man.[6] While some of Trump's stylistic fragmentation does seem to merge messy form with confused content, an abiding question is just how much one can legitimately extrapolate from Trump's linguistic style without overextending what it can tell us. In some of the chapters within, the authors imply that we might do well to focus on more complex and impactful ways in which Trump's language has created real emergencies, from collective delusions to violent divisions.

What *can* be said, however, is that Trump's raw and harsh language has turned out to be an accurate mirror of harsh policies that bring the hammer down upon those he frames as social threats – immigrants, Muslims, people of color, LGBTQ+ individuals, and more – while also (ironically) imperiling even many of his supporters in the working class through conservative measures on healthcare, labor legislation, and beyond. What is also clear is that the Trump administration has changed some of the deepest expectations about presidential language, not just when it comes to style, but also the relationship between words and reality.

Lies and Language Control

> Power is in tearing human minds to pieces and putting them together again in new shapes of your own choosing.   George Orwell, *1984*

A major element of the Trumpian linguistic emergency has been the unprecedented depth and breadth of his prevarication. Kakutani (2018: 79) notes that this political trend picked up speed around the time that Lee Atwater, consultant to George Bush senior, declared that "perception is reality" in 1988. But Trump has lied and bullshitted his way across the political landscape with new velocity, repeatedly "dismissing discernable reality" (Jamieson and Taussig 2017: 632; see also Skinnell 2018a, Jacquemet this volume). By mid-October 2019, the *Washington Post* had documented more than 13,000 lies or misleading statements (Kessler et al. 2019). Trump has lied about matters both trivial (e.g. claiming it didn't rain during his inaugural address [Dale 2017]) and profound (e.g. claiming the United States has the world's cleanest air and water [Meyer 2019], or tweeting, in late February 2020, that "the Coronavirus is very much under control in the USA"; Trump 2020b). When confronted by a threat, such as Robert Mueller's report about the Russia investigation, Trump responds with a new flurry of patent falsehoods.[7] When accused, during the late 2019 impeachment proceedings, of pressuring the President of Ukraine to investigate Joe Biden before receiving further military aid, Trump calls the proceedings a "hoax" and a "witchhunt" while feigning ignorance of the communicative norms that clearly locate bribery in his implied meaning (Hodges 2019b, Pinker 2019). When news outlets call Trump out, he repeatedly discredits them as "fake news" backed by Democrats, a smear that has sown mistrust of journalists while being enthusiastically taken up by fascists across the world (Davis and Sinnreich 2018, Jamieson and Taussig 2017, Kakutani 2018: 101). Spokespeople such as Kellyanne Conway and Sarah Huckabee Sanders have enhanced the confusion with verbal fog and artful dodges; fans on social media and *Fox News* spin information in his favor; and his detractors follow entirely different sources of information, all of which widens the divide between the nation's communicative "silos" or "bubbles" (see Slotta, this volume).

Trump's perverse relationship with truth has done a huge amount of political and social work. Many of the chapters in this volume discuss how Trump's distorted claims stoke fear and hatred. But even setting aside its content, Trump's prevarication sometimes follows a reliable structure that controls the political narrative, while enthralling, even entertaining, swathes of the public. Amanda Carpenter (2018), a former Ted Cruz campaign advisor and Republican *CNN* commentator, has described the patterned stages of one such technique. First, Trump stakes out shocking political territory by advancing a fringe claim, such as the birtherist notion that Obama was not born in the US. Next, he uses a strategy that Carpenter calls "advance and deny," in which Trump states something like, "I'm not saying it [e.g. that Obama was born outside the US], but other people are." This move prompts the media to debate the fabricated issue on his terms. Trump may opt to hold attention through a suspenseful announcement about an imminent lawsuit, revelation, or leaked tape (e.g. Obama's grandmother says on tape he was born in Kenya! [Farley

2011]), none of which ever materialize. Sometimes he'll choose a detractor to scapegoat, projecting the identity of "liar" onto them. Finally, he may hold a press conference to proclaim victory over the issue, as in his much-hyped 2016 statement to the press that the birther controversy was started by Hillary Clinton, and Trump had heroically "finished it" (Obama was born in the USA after all, he said; Haberman and Rappeport 2016).

The media ecosystem and public attention alike have been repeatedly co-opted by this pattern, which has kept Trump front and center while discombobulating his detractors. Some onlookers feel "gaslit" by the shenanigans; made to question evidence that feels obvious, and feeling a little crazy for it. For his supporters, though, the veracity of Trump's statements often seems beside the point, being eclipsed by the moments that feel true to them. One of Trump's biggest champions, Tucker Carlson of *Fox News*, concedes that Trump is a "full-blown BS artist," but that the "reality-avoiding" left *really* hates Trump when he tells the "truth," as in his scathing assessments of the condition of inner cities and sub-Saharan African nations (Folley 2019a). And beyond his racist aversions, Trump's glistening, confident, employee-firing biographical aura – the man who declares himself the "winner" no matter what – is a bigger player than his lies.

Indeed, Trump's appeal may be enhanced by the fact that the "experts," including beltway politicians, educated elites, scientists, journalists, and other members of the professional-managerial class, so often challenge what he says. If the political establishment has a crisis of legitimacy and coastal intellectuals have patronized blue-collar America for too long, outrageous statements that flout their verbal norms may have an enticing, even an empowering quality. (Not incidentally, anti-intellectual, anti-fact frameworks are also widespread among right-wing populist politicians across Europe, a dynamic Ruth Wodak [2015: 2] calls the "arrogance of ignorance.") Rebellion against dominant narratives may have special appeal when Trump's "alternative facts" are framed as if they are "common sense" prevailing over oppressive snobbery, or when they tender the goal of uplifting those Americans who have felt lost in a globalized economy and threatened by accusatory identity politics (see Hahl et al. 2018). As an added bonus, Trump's lies repeatedly piss off the left, and after years of leftists seemingly winning the "culture wars," his statements may have a pleasurable element of "trolling" and *schadenfreude* (pleasure in others' misfortune).

Precisely how much Trump's base believes of what he claims is an open question, and there's surely internal diversity among his voters on this score. That said, the sheer repetition of Trump's lies might give him a certain cognitive sway over those who listen faithfully. Linguist George Lakoff, with Gil Duran (2018), notes that the repetition of language activates and reinforces the brain structures called "frame-circuits" used to understand experience. In this model, Trump's repetition of lies, or even mocking aliases ("Crooked Hillary" being an old favorite), circulated continuously on social media and some press outlets, can literally change how his followers view the social world (Lakoff and Duran 2018).

George Orwell predicted that authoritarian lies can stick for a different reason: They simply wear you down. As Adam Gopnik phrases Orwell's conclusions, after a while, "fighting the lie becomes not simply more danger-ous but more exhausting than repeating it" (Gopnik 2017; see also Snyder 2017, Kakutani 2018: 143). The sheer volume of lies can help the cause. The news media can hardly keep up with fact-checking, the newsworthy implica-tions of any one lie are rapidly eclipsed by the next one, and important lies are concealed in swarms of trivial ones. For individuals trying to keep pace, there's simply too much cognitive load to track it all. Based on the prescient theory of historian Daniel Boorstin (1962), we might say that Trump's lies constitute one extended "pseudo-event," fabricated precisely for the purpose of being reported, and all part of the Trump spectacle that diverts attention from actual changes to policy and the judiciary, many of which have dismal implications for human rights, international relations, and climate change. After one week's worth of particularly rambling public appearances in 2019 – during which Trump claimed that his father was born in Germany (he was not), argued that noise from wind turbines causes cancer (it does not), and then backed off from his threat to close the southern border – *CNN* political analyst Julian Zelizer neatly summed up his impression: "Chaos is the strategy" (Zelizer 2019).

One aspect of the confusion for onlookers is simply interpretive. Many citizens recognize that presidents engage in a degree of verbal theater to burnish their personal brand (see Hill 2000), but there's also been an expecta-tion that high-stakes presidential claims about the world will map onto empiri-cal reality in some fashion. Political comedian John Oliver described the new disorientation: "This is what makes covering Donald Trump so difficult. What does he mean when he says words?" (Prakash 2017). Some, like Trump's former campaign manager Corey Lewandowski, suggest that the mainstream media has erred when it takes Trump "literally," given that (Lewandowski claims) his supporters don't (Kakutani 2018: 60). Similarly, spokeswoman Kellyanne Conway tells us we should judge him on "what's in his heart" – the content of which appears to be up for anyone's projection – rather than "what's come out of his mouth" (Benen 2017). It's an ingenious way of deflecting the power of a lie.

But many of Trump's supporters *do* have concern for truth, or some version of it. Partly, the matter baffles because people locate their political truths in different places, or focus on truth at different scales. Some of Trump's suppor-ters seem to read him as engaged in what could be called truthful hyperbole; as rhetorician Ryan Skinnell puts it, "Hyperbole brings an underlying truth to the surface that factual truth can't quite describe" (Skinnell 2018a: 80). The same might be said about metaphor in the Trump era. Consider the back-and-forthing among commentators concerning the question of whether Trump's much-vaunted "wall" between the US and Mexico should be taken literally, or as a metaphor. There is ongoing enthusiasm for a physical wall; in anthropological parlance, it seems to be a concept that's been good to think with for many of his supporters. Trump even staged a government shutdown in early 2019 in (vain) hopes of securing more funding for it. Yet some of Trump's backers have told journalists the wall may not literally take shape but stands for his commitment to blocking immigrants from the South. When "build that wall" slides the speaker and hearer effortlessly between a visual image of a barrier and a feeling that one's hostility toward immigrants will be satisfied one way or another, perhaps the wall-as-metaphor still feels "literal" in some sense, because it emerges from and is addressing what feels like an underlying truth.

Much of that underlying truth may be connected to what sociologist Arlie Hochschild (2018) calls the "deep story" of the American right. Hochschild conducted fieldwork among right-wing Louisianans in the years just before Trump emerged on the political scene, and found she could understand their political choices with reference to their "deep story," that is, an account that's not necessarily literally true but it "feels-as-if" it's true. One deep story for at least some of Trump's base is that the White working class has been marginalized globally (by economic forces) and nationally (by coastal elites and Democrats who are coddling underrepresented groups and helping them to cut in line for handouts). Hyperbole might be recognized as hyperbolic and metaphor as not strictly accurate in every detail, but they gesture at this deeper *emotional* truth. The details of Trump's claims and stated plans may not be factual, but the big picture he paints may *feel* real. (Anecdotally, some years ago when I sent an evangelical acquaintance a dozen links debunking the many falsified news articles she had sent me about Obama bringing sharia law to the US, she replied with, "Some of these claims may be exaggerated, but I still find them very convincing." This confounded me at the time.) And if facts can't really be used to loosen the power of hyperbole or metaphor, no wonder conservatives have been charged with "epistemic closure": operating in a contained universe of assumptions, where challenging information is considered false *a priori*.

Finally, one might argue at least some of Trump's lies function to breathe life into their own ideas, a gambit that flips conventional ideas about the relationship between representation and reality in political speech (though it is more common in talk than we realize). As Patricia Williams (2017) writes in *The Nation*, phrases such as "immigration must be controlled" create a kind of "grammatical neediness": a sense of a challenge to be met that creates its own sense of urgency. In a related vein, Carole McGranahan (2017: 244), following Hannah Arendt (1972), has noted that some of Trump's lies have "aspiration," like "calls to action" that create "new realities for which contradictory facts need to be eliminated." If Trump falsely claims, as he did in November 2015, that "thousands and thousands of people were cheering" (Fang 2018) as they watched the devastation of 9/11, he emboldens a community whose hostility toward Muslims might feed into a cycle of mutual bad feeling. Some claims may be lies when they're made, but they have a self-fulfilling potency. In linguistic anthropology, we sometimes talk about the distinction between "constative" language, which describes a true or false state of affairs, and "performative" language, which does something and brings states of affairs into being. Perhaps many of Trump's lies are performatives concealed as constatives. All of this tilts toward Russian-American journalist Massa Gessen's (2016) observation: Trump's lies are designed, like those of Vladimir Putin, "to assert power over truth itself." Whether Trump is attempting to steer action, to impress (cf. Jacquemet this volume), or to invert the conventionally understood relationship between signifier and signified, he asserts supreme authority over world-making.

Indeed, beyond contradicting the facts with their statements, Trump and his administration have tinkered with word meanings and word use. This goes beyond the opposite-day goofiness of Trump saying, for instance, "nobody knows" something, when just about everybody does (e.g. what a community college is, or that healthcare could be so complicated), or that "everybody knows" something, when in fact that something is profoundly controversial (e.g. that we need his wall, or that he didn't obstruct justice) (Bump 2019, Liptak 2017, Wong 2018). Trump's administration has dipped into the Orwellian maneuvers Victor Klemperer (1957: 56) described in the language of the Third Reich, where the term "special treatment" substituted for "murder," and the word "fanatical" was twisted into an accolade rather than a slur. Every time Trump has used phrases like "the enemy of the people" to characterize the mass media, "fake news" to ding a report he doesn't like, or "suppression polls" to suggest poll results unfavorable to him have been tampered with to discourage his voters, he twists the meaning of the words (Kakutani 2018: 80). Similarities to the Third Reich became eerily plain when Steve Bannon, former top advisor to President Trump, issued the following directive in his March 2018 speech to a group of hard-right National Front Party members in France: "Let them call you racists, let them call you xenophobes ... Let them call you nativists. Wear it as a badge of honor" (Stanley 2018a).

Beyond such inversions of moral terminology, the Trump administration has systematically gone after the verbal building blocks of science. Starting in

December 2017, the CDC, among other federal agencies, was instructed that certain words should be "avoided" in their 2018 budget documents: "diversity," "fetus," "transgender," "vulnerable," "entitlement," "science-based," and "evidence-based." While the guidance was not framed as a strict "word ban," it was pitched as a crucial means of avoiding the conservative political biases of those sitting in the White House and Congress, and thus had the force of a directive (Cohen 2018). At the US Environmental Protection Agency, meanwhile, several allusions to "climate change" have been removed from their website. What seems to be happening under the Trump administration, as its draconian conservatism meets its anti-Enlightenment hostility to science, is what might be called "word discouragement."

Trump's Department of Health and Human Services has also been working toward a redefinition of "gender" in the language associated with Title IX, the law enforced by the US Department of Education's office of civil rights that ensures no Americans will be discriminated against in terms of their sex. The proposed redefinition would assign male or female identity based on one's genitals at birth, defining gender in terms of something biological and immutable. Not only does this maneuver conflate biological sex and gender identity, in ignorance of decades of gender studies; it also stands in contradiction to current biological science, which recognizes a much more complex spectrum of intersex possibilities than the male/female binary opposition recognizes (see Fausto-Sterling 2000). And the proposed redefinition attempts to deny the reality of transgender identity, with breathtaking implications for the rights of transgender people.

And then there's the Trump administration's fascistic verbal obfuscation of brutal policy. In March 2019, for instance, then-Homeland Security chief Kirstjen Nielsen was questioned about the detention facilities along the Mexican border, where thousands of children, deliberately separated from their parents as a supposed deterrent to undocumented immigration, have been kept in enclosed chain-link rectangles on concrete floors. "Are we still putting children in cages?" Mississippi representative Bennie Thompson asked Nielsen, continuing, "I've seen the cages; I just want you to admit that they exist" (Edwards 2019). Nielsen replied, "Sir, they're not cages. They are areas of the border facility that are carved out for the safety and protection of those who remain there while they're being processed" (ibid.). Anderson Cooper called the evasion as he saw it: "It's Orwellian" (Cooper 2019).[8]

How ironic that even as the right wing attacks the "PC" left for using careful, decorous words, here Nielsen appears to paper something over verbally herself. The motives, however, are vastly different. The left polices language in hopes of diminishing the pain inflicted by bigotry. The right has begun to police language, it seems, in hopes of covering up the pain its bigoted policies inflict or contribute toward.

The Loosening of Tongues: Profanity and Hate Speech

It's hard to imagine any time in the past when a serious book on presidential language would have such words as "bullshit" and "shithole" in the chapter titles, but Trump has upended presidential convention with regard to profanity. During the campaign, Americans overheard Trump use the word "pussy" while bragging on a bus to other men (see Cameron, Mannheim, this volume), but more norm-shattering has been his public word choice, as when he boasted that he'd "beat the shit out of" Republican rivals in 2016, nicknamed Democratic Congressman and Chair of the House Intelligence Committee Adam Schiff "Adam Shitt," or said, "Wouldn't you love to see one of these NFL owners, when somebody disrespects our flag, to say, 'Get that son of a bitch off the field right now. Out! He's fired'" (Baker 2019, Gleeson 2018). Supporters at his rallies have joined the party of bravado, wearing "Donald Fuckin' Trump" t-shirts (ibid.). The man who served as his Communications Director for ten profane days, Anthony Scaramucci, infamously told a reporter from the *New Yorker* that he wanted to "fucking kill all the leakers" (Lizza 2017). When former Campaign Manager Corey Lewandowski was called to answer questions before Democrats on the House Intelligence Committee in April 2018, he repeatedly swore that he wasn't going to answer their "fucking" questions (Herb and Raju 2018). By the time the impeachment hearings arrived in late 2019, few viewers could have been shocked to hear of EU Ambassador Gordon Sondland telling Trump that "[Ukraine President] Zelensky loves your ass" and was therefore likely to comply with Trump's hoped-for investigation of rival Joe Biden (Wade 2019).

Trump's detractors have joined the profanity game, too. Media outlets tabulate the abundant uptick in the use of the f-word by politicians, many of them outraged Democrats (Hughes 2017). When in October 2017, Trump fallaciously claimed that Obama had failed to call the families of service members killed in action, former Obama staffer Alyssa Mastromonaco tweeted: "That's a fucking lie . . . he's a deranged animal" (Mastromonaco on Twitter, October 16, 2017). After Trump called again for a travel ban on those from Muslim nations, *CNN* host Reza Aslan called him a "piece of shit . . . an embarrassment to humankind" (Olson 2017). A 2018 *Mother Jones* headline read: "Our President is an Asshole" (Drum 2018), while a distinguished writer for *The Root* deemed Trump the "fucktard-in-chief" (Harriot 2017). The May 11, 2018 issue of Germany's respected *Der Spiegel* published an op-ed about Trump's capricious foreign policy, featuring a cover image of a bright orange hand flipping the bird, the middle finger dressed to look like Trump (Brinkbäumer 2018). Evidently, the semiotic gloves are off.

The *New York Times* reporter Frank Bruni lamented the trend, chalking our "coarser" language up to the mass and social mediated hubbub of political opinions: "To be seen in a thicket of hashtags and heard above the din, people screech. Passion and provocation blur" (Bruni 2017). Bruni frets that such verbal patterns are "a path away from high-minded engagement." But while Bruni's explanation surely captures part of the dynamic, profanity in the Trump era seems to do a lot more social, political, and psychological work than mere "screeching" or attention-getting.

Profane and obscene words take "offstage" topics – usually to do with sex, excretion, and oral, anal, and genital functions – and bring them onstage through speech. Unlike the insulting language that PC ideology objects to – racist, sexist, homophobic, ableist, and so forth – profanity speaks to deep and common elements of the human embodied experience. Many Americans subscribe to the language ideology that profanity is more deeply connected to feeling than other language, being almost pre-verbal or pre-cognitive, and there may be an element of truth to this; when people stub their toe, for instance, they may automatically utter an obscenity, suggesting these words help externalize pain or excess emotion. There is no question that intense emotion is at stake with Trump's rise, from the fury and fear some Trump supporters evince toward (for instance) "illegal immigrants" and "Muslim terrorists," to the laments among Trump detractors at the suffering and anxiety his policies and words have wrought.

But even if profanity can be unwitting or emotional, it can have a vital strategic or performance element, adopting a stance that does social work for the speaker, such as indexing alignment, antagonism, enthusiasm, and more. So, for instance, Trump's infamous "grab 'em by the pussy" remark became another reason for many on the left to dismiss him as a sexist vulgarian, but did not deter millions of voters – in fact, Cameron and Mannheim (both in this volume) suggest it may have helped him align with his male interlocutors and, ultimately, with his base. At least some profanity from Trump's camp has seemed to advertise his manic political boundary-pushing; during Trump's attacks against Robert Mueller's investigation in February 2018, for instance, a "Trump friend" reported his mood to journalists as "fucking excited and jubilant . . . He was like, everything's great and these fuckers in the media are beside themselves" (Sherman 2018). If Trump said "fuckers," here, and didn't mind if the public heard it through his "friend," he may have been stoking his supporters' thrill at one-upping the mass media and the Mueller investigation. Profanity is an index of Trump's willingness to flout politics-as-usual. And, the documentarian Errol Morris has argued, for voters sick of being talked down to by smug liberals, sick of hearing that White men are the problem, sick of being asked to empathize with people they don't even know, Trump became the "fuck you" president (Wilkinson 2019).

Class is surely at stake, as part of this. Of the many American social divides exacerbated by Trump, one is between those who feel his use of profanity denigrates political life and national principles of civility, and those who feel it's a healthy reaction against bourgeois masks of good taste, adding a much-needed dose of affective sincerity and grit. Trump's foul mouth may be perceived as a conduit of earthy "truth" lying beneath the surface of all the fancy verbal niceties of the Obama administration and cultural elites. Who knows; maybe some Democrats have switched registers into a new profanity habit partly because Hillary Clinton's measured, educated tones – and her seemingly oblivious amplification of professional-managerial class values at the expense of understanding blue-collar concerns – attracted more antipathy than they'd expected.

Profanity has historically been associated with men more than women, and Trump may benefit from this. Its shocking, "indecent," and insolent qualities may bring with them a certain covert masculine prestige, while women have been expected to maintain polite, face-saving behavior. Linguistic anthropologists might locate iconization in this aspect of profanity; hard language supposedly reflects a hardened speaker able to deal with harsh realities, as when Trump blasts that he's going to "knock the shit out of ISIS" (Gonyea 2016). Our head of state is comfortable with the shocking social edgework of profanity; this in itself is an enactment of masculinized power.

Finally, profanity mirrors depth of conviction. It's a way of indicating that ordinary semantics won't do the job; the speaker has almost run out of words, and to express their extreme enthusiasm or dismay they need to do a verbal end-run. Bruni's (2017) appeal for "high-minded engagement" thus may sound like a chat around teacups when people feel that livelihoods or lives are at stake. Consider how inadequate the ordinary semiotics of presidential opinion polls feel at the moment; while they deliver approval rating by percentages, profanity bespeaks the depth of voters' conviction ("hell yes" or "fuck no"). Profanity also signals what the speaker might be willing to put on the line in the future to defend the strength of this conviction. If some see the nation as being dragged into the gutter with the profanity, another way to look at it is as an indicator of how high the political stakes feel to many, and how deep the conflict. It's perhaps not a coincidence that language looks like this – profane, enraged – among soldiers in combat.

The Trump rise has emboldened another kind of formerly taboo language: aggressive and hateful speech. Trump has indulged in unprecedented levels of name-calling and snark to incite the disdain, anger, and fear that galvanize some in his base. When the New York Times gathered a corpus from Trump's Twitter feed, it found about one in every eight tweets was an insult (Hodges 2017), and with public and press exhaustion, many of these now go by with barely a ripple. (It took about a day, in October 2018, for the nation to forget that Trump referred to his alleged former lover Stormy Daniels as "horseface.") In Trump's rhetoric,

Mexican immigrants are "not people," but "animals" (see Santa Ana et al., this volume), while "Black people," Trump informed his personal lawyer, "are too stupid to vote for me" (Fox 2018; see Hall et al., Alim and Smitherman, Santa Ana et al., Mendoza-Denton, Williams, Boum this volume for more on Trump's insults and distortions of fact about immigrants, Muslims, Mexicans, African nations, and beyond).

The divided body politic in America seems to have vastly different language ideologies when it comes to the question of whether hate speech is fitting to the presidency. Chants of "Lock her up!" (Samuels 2018), whether referring to Hillary Clinton in 2016 or Diane Feinstein in 2018, apparently strike Republican crowds as fair retribution for transgressive Democratic women, while to Democrats these chants feel like atavistic baying, striking a fear of violence. Some fear there's been a disintegration of verbal "shame"; of shared and communally enforced ethics of what can and can't, should and shouldn't be said. More importantly, according to Yale philosopher Jason Stanley (2018b), Trump's hateful speech parallels the propaganda of some of the most reviled twentieth- and twenty-first-century fascists, expressing nostalgia for a mythic past of White male hegemony destroyed by liberals, feminists, and immigrants (see also Steudeman 2018). Indeed, Trump's rhetoric has striking similarity to that documented by Ruth Wodak (2015) among European right-wing populists, especially the tendency to stoke fear and scapegoat, pushing rhetorics of exclusion and nativist notions of citizenship.

There's little question Trump's discourse has inspired mimicry among some of his supporters. At Democratic candidate Bernie Sanders' rallies in early 2020, some protesters waved Trump flags and flashed the White nationalist "OK" sign with their hands, while another unfurled a swastika banner (Neiwert 2020). (Sanders, whose extended family from Poland was killed in the Holocaust, later told Jake Tapper of *CNN*, "I got to tell you, I never expected in my life, as an American, to see a swastika at a major political rally. It's horrible" [Cole 2020].) Organizations such as the Southern Poverty Law Center have documented a spike in hate speech corresponding with Trump's rise, some of it in schools and universities, including anti-Muslim and anti-Mexican sidewalk chalking, swastikas, n-word graffiti, homophobic language, and chants of "build the wall" or "go home" to students of color (Pollock 2017). Many of us can attest to witnessing the changes ourselves; in 2017, for instance, I overheard a middle-aged White man telling a group of Hispanic parking attendants that they'd "better speak English or Trump would send them back." This enabling effect has surely been shaped by the psychology of norm-shifting: People tend to extrapolate the views of other people from the views expressed by authority figures, and when authority figures express things once unexpressible, the masses feel they have social license to follow suit (Konnikova 2017). And while hate speech in schools has been reported as traumatic for countless children (Pollock 2017), his defenders will guard it in the name of freedom of speech.

There have been hot debates about whether Trump's rhetoric can be considered a causal force in violence such as the mass shootings in Black churches, mosques, and synagogues, or in the case of the "MAGA bomber" who, in October 2018, sent (nonviable) bombs to CNN offices and numerous prominent Democrats (Derysh 2019). The MAGA bomber's van and social media accounts were plastered with Trump ads and hostility against Trump's enemies. But few of Trump's supporters are inclined to see Trump's language as dangerous. After the MAGA bomber was apprehended, Geraldo Rivera argued that "crazy people can do crazy things; they don't need the president's words ... [we can't] start blaming the speech rather than the perpetrator" (Moye 2018). This ideology, common among Trump's supporters, treats hateful speech a bit like gun culture; the rise of each in the environment may correspond with the rise in murderous crimes, but rather than seeing a cultural shift that facilitates vicious behavior, the conservative model puts the onus on individual responsibility alone. Another way of seeing the situation, though, is that the language endorsed by those in power helps create the force field within which people learn their behavioral parameters.[9]

In late 2018, an argument that Trump's speech translated into violence emerged from unexpected parties: the defense lawyers of three Kansas militia group members convicted for taking part in a conspiracy to kill Muslim refugees just before the 2016 election. The lawyers used Trump's words and tweets as evidence, asking for leniency on grounds that Trump's stoking of Islamophobia through "rough-and-tumble verbal pummeling" (Orr 2018) had made some feel justified in committing violence against supposed enemies. They bolstered their argument with the fact that anti-Muslim violence had been on the rise since his election (ibid.). Perhaps in the future there will be other such cases brought before the courts. What remains unknown is whether a critical mass of the American public will come to share the language ideology that repeated aggressive speech about other groups can increase the risk of violence against them.

Still, at least some right-wing groups are aware that they're playing with fire in their use of language. American fascists sometimes strategically claim that their dangerous speech is not intended to be taken seriously. After infamously ending a speech by shouting "Hail Trump! Hail our people! Hail victory" into an of Nazi salutes, the White supremacist Richard Spencer contended he had done so in a "spirit of irony and exuberance" (Barajas 2016). Some Neo-Nazi websites urge those who are posting comments to use a light tone so that the "unindoctrinated" reader can't tell whether they're joking (Kakutani 2018: 158–59). These techniques use a similar strategy to the president himself when he engages in "plausible deniability" (as explored by Hodges in this volume) to wiggle away from his own controversial words. But even if there is peril in extremist rhetoric, it hasn't turned away all the prospective voters who might dislike Trump's language. Some Trump supporters say they find his language distasteful, but they overlook it in order to secure what they consider more important prizes, such as tax relief for corporations or conservative Supreme Court justices.

One can learn a lot about the antagonism Trump has fomented by noticing the use of his own name, which has come to condense so much that he stands for. For his supporters, merely chanting his name has become one means of intimidating the vulnerable. The Southern Poverty Law Center reports some children use the single word "Trump" as a taunt while ganging up on members of the social groups Trump has attacked (Costello n.d.). Around the time of the 2016 election, there were reports that White men would sometimes approach a person of color on the street, utter the word "Trump," and then walk away in a supremely condensed semiotic act of intimidation (Mazzarella n.d.).

No wonder Trump's critics have been so tempted to take the stuffing out of his name. Some have decided to treat it orthographically as a profanity, spelling it "Tr*mp." (I have heard it said that some authors offer a substitute such as "45" so that Trump's name does not appear as often in searches, especially in conjunction with their own.) The fluorescence of Trump nicknames also provides playful delight for his detractors in a dark time: Orange Hitler, Adolf Twitler, Hair Fuhrer, Mango Mussolini, the Short-Fingered Vulgarian, Mrs. Putin, Fake President, President Spanky McLiarface, Impotus, Cadet Bone Spurs, Dolt 45, Agent Orango, Chancellor Cheeto, Tweeto, the Orange Ringmaster, the Angry Creamsicle, Cheeto Jesus, Barbequed Brutus, Vanilla Isis, Creep Throat. After Trump mistakenly tweeted that Scotland had voted to leave the European Union, the Scots joined in the fun with an even freer hand: Utter Cockwomble, Rug Wearing Thunder Nugget, Mangled Apricot Hellbeast, Witless Fucking Cocksplat, Rotten Orange Fucknut, Degenerate Corned Beef Face Syrup Wearing Wankstain, and Gerbil-headed Woodstained Haunted Spunktrumpet (Mitchell 2016).

If you don't like Trump, these are fun. But the verbal processes discussed in this chapter remind us of how serious the times are, for they collectively feed a sense of chaos and growing polarization in the US and beyond. We have seen messages of hatred and anger; the rise of combative profanity; aggressive disagreements about truth; dissent about what kinds of language are acceptable; Orwellian re-working of meaning; a disregard for conventional spelling and grammar (amusing to some, outrageous to others); and a sense that social media has staged an upheaval of our political structure. All of these are set to the backdrop of conflicting red-vs-blue language ideologies among the public, with the result yielding the current mass confusion about circulating meanings. Is Trump in the early stages of dementia, or an evil genius, able to manipulate and calibrate his speech to exactly the minimal education level some believe he imputes to his core base? Is he a man of the people, who will make Americans into winners, or a bigot whose deeds will disadvantage not only the vulnerable, but also, ultimately, his own voters?

Summary of Chapters, Possible Futures

Many of the early chapters in this volume engage in a close, novel reading of Trump's language and that of his supporters to understand the role language has played in his rise. Part I examines the ways in which Trump and his supporters have divided public constituencies with language. Slotta, for instance, examines how Trump's seeming inscrutability is, in fact, perfectly intelligible for some Americans, partly through coded "dog whistles" (provocations that are superficially not about race, but still communicate negative messages about non-Whites; Haney López 2014), and also because some of his words and phrases are "abbreviations for stories and other forms of cultural knowledge" that circulate among his right-wing followers. This verbal pattern enlists the rest of the public and the media to scramble to decipher him, while reinforcing the sense that the nation is divided into communicative bubbles. Sidnell describes how Trump used his repeated call of "Get 'em out!" at campaign rallies to enlist his followers' aggression toward those symbolically framed as interlopers – whether protesters at the rallies or foreigners at the level of the nation. And in my chapter, "Crybabies and Snowflakes," I examine why those insults were hurled *en masse* at Trump protesters after his election and inauguration, and argue that they have surprising resonance with the ritualistic language used by Drill Instructors in the military to toughen up recruits, who must dull their semiotic sensitivities for the sake of national security. This verbal stance carved out thus shuts down conversation, while suggesting the American left needs to "grow up" by abandoning its empathic ways and hypersensitive language ideology.

In Part II, authors explore themes of Trump as a dramatist and Trump's falsehoods. Goldstein, Hall, and Ingram examine Trump's mocking gestural imitations of vulnerable groups, and how through these gestures he indirectly performs part of his intended political message for his base. Jacquemet explores the thesis that at least some of Trump's prevarication should count not as "lying," in which a speaker knows the truth but tries to conceal it from his audience, but rather as "bullshit," in which the speaker has no particular commitment to what's true or not. For Trump, bullshit is highly functional, just one of many verbal tools he uses to create spectacle, self-aggrandize, and otherwise manage impressions. Finally, Hodges explores Trump's recurrent ability to "plausibly deny" some of his most outrageous statements. Since many people presume that words in and of themselves convey all of the meaning in an interaction. Trump exploits this language ideology by focusing on the literal or contextually narrow meaning of what he's said, and pretending that the implied elements of his statements simply don't exist. It's an ingenious way to evade his critics while holding his base.

Part III focuses on how Trump manages to construct and uphold hierarchy, including gender hierarchy, through interactional routines and dynamics. Cameron's and Mannheim's chapters respectively focus on Trump's infamous "grab 'em by the pussy" remark to explore how Trump reproduces fratriarchal male dominance through a conversational routine he waves away as mere "banter." Cohn argues that in representing the prospect of nuclear war as a kind of phallic competition, Trump engages in a classic genre of militaristic language that delights in nuclear power by distracting from the prospect of actual human suffering. Van Over examines how Trump can enlist those around a conference table into a kind of routine, constructing his identity as "boss" in part by coaxing his conversational interlocutors into obsequious verbal roles while seizing the role of "evaluator" for himself. Sierra and Shrikant examine how Trump uses deft frame shifts to create a veneer of agreement with African Americans by way of a putatively common enemy, "fake news."

Part IV includes five chapters discussing the verbal dynamics surrounding Trump's racism and ethnonationalism, as well as some international responses to him. Alim and Smitherman examine an incident in which Trump praises the "perfect English" of a Latinx Border Patrol Agent, exceptionalizing one individual, and in doing so, reinforcing a negative stereotype of his ethnic group. Santa Ana et al. discuss the many speech acts in which Trump portrays the nation as a fortress that is being overrun and invaded by "criminals" from the South, constructing a powerful metaphor to justify his and his supporters' fixation on his "wall" concept. Mendoza-Denton explores how Trump's insulting stances toward Latin America have begotten a series of narrative strategies of compensatory masculinity on the part of Latin American leaders. Williams explores how Trump draws on age-old metaphors of pollution to besmirch sub-Saharan Africa, as well as classic verbal strategies of denial and deflection of his own racism. Southern African political leaders and culture-makers have called him out in strategically parodic or dignified tones. And, finally, Boum explores how Trump neatly cuts the Arab world into two segments with his verbal stance-taking: those who are wealthy (and thus worthwhile) "friends," and those who are more-or-less dismissible terrorists.

Reading such chapters about the pernicious verbal ideologies and mechanisms underpinning Trump's ascendancy and tenure, the reader who is a Trump critic would be forgiven for feeling dispirited. His formulaic "Lock her up" and "Build that wall" chants still have legs at his rallies as I write this chapter. Of course, his detractors continually speak back, but persuading a critical mass of

Trump supporters to vote otherwise has proven a substantial challenge. While some of the problem lies in the Democratic candidates' difficulty addressing the grievances of Trump supporters, voters are also perpetually digitally looped back to websites, memes, tweets, and the like that reaffirm the allegiances they already had. Trump's political opponents have also not been savvy about their verbal appeal; in late 2017 Republican strategist Evan Siegfried aptly noted that "The problem with the argument that Democrats are making . . . is that [it] takes longer than a bumper-sticker slogan to make" (Peters 2017). And while one might have imagined that Trump would crack his own enamel by continuing to editorialize on Twitter outside the official controls of party politics, so far, his fans and many in the GOP have been forgiving of a multitude of contradictions. Former Republican Representative Charlie Dent told news outlets during the impeachment inquiry of late 2019 that GOP lawmakers were "absolutely disgusted and exhausted" by the President's behavior, but kept their disdain private to cater to their base (Folley 2019b).

However the Trump era winds down, however voters come to their disen-chantment (if they do), it doesn't appear that it will happen in the same way that anthropologist Alexei Yurchak (2005) describes the end of the former Soviet state. A critical semiotic theorist, Yurchak argues the rapid collapse of the Soviet system was simultaneously unthinkable yet not altogether surprising, and that a close look at how state discourse was used and then dismantled furnishes one key. Under Stalin's thumb, communist discourse such as ideolo-gical slogans were to be rigidly copied and their semantics taken literally. Over the decades, however, many citizens became more invested in copying the forms to engage in a kind of social performance than in subscribing to their content. This decoupling of form from meaning, Yurchak argues, resulted in a destabilization of the system, destabilization that was largely invisible until the political system abruptly imploded and the citizenry adjusted to its fall with startling speed. But "state discourse" under Trump isn't nearly as monolithic or tightly controlled as it was under the Soviet system, and, as described above, it has never been taken altogether literally. The very bagginess of Trumpian meaning – Is his claim truly true in the details? Or just emotionally resonant? – means it can accommodate an awful lot of counterargument before it pops.

If nobody can count on Trump's supporters to question their emotional truths, another domain to examine is the approach of his detractors. While the American left shouldn't be held responsible for Trump, it is also the case that – as discussed above – some leftist language ideologies and verbal practices have been more alienating than they may have realized. Perhaps greater lay understanding of the linguistic dynamics underpinning mutual minorityhood could be helpful, including, at least, *recognition* of the feeling that liberal language crusaders can sometimes come across as patronizing, sanctimonious, even disdainful, as well as ignorant about the economic hardships of some of the very people they are accusing of being verbally oppressive. If one wants language to respect the humanity of others, then this consideration may need to expand to some liberals checking their classism as they promote empathy.

And perhaps overcoming Trumpism is going to require a transnational lens as well as a domestic one, for sadly, the problem extends far beyond the United States. Recent years have seen the global rise of leaders with violent, fascistic leanings, driving for ethnic, racial, religious, and/or heteronormative nationalism with a brutal, emotionally volatile verbal style. These include Duterte in the Philippines, the re-elected Narendra Modi in India, Jair Bolsonaro in Brazil, and politicians across Latin America. Numerous European nations, too, have been rocked by hard-right, White nationalist movements in recent years, a situation aggravated by the influx of refugees fleeing unrest and hunger in the global South and Middle East. And plenty of these right-wing leaders seem to be feeding on Trump's discourse. What was once unspeakable has become speakable, and detractors across the world are aghast. Our worst fears cast our minds back to the ugly fascistic genocides and wars of the past, and to Mark Twain's reputed statement that "History doesn't repeat itself, but it often rhymes." One can only hope that closer attention to the role of language in recent political developments can help shed light on them and ultimately, in some fashion beyond the scope of this volume, be used to counteract them.

Notes

1. David A. Graham, Adrienne Green, Cullen Murphy, and Parker Richards. 2019. "An Oral History of Trump's Bigotry." *The Atlantic*, June 2019. https://bit.ly/2WRRSY1.
2. Trump sent that tweet on March 8, 2020, when there were roughly 500 diagnosed cases of COVID-19 in the US. As this book goes to press on March 17, that number has grown to well over 5,000, entire cities and states are shutting down, and the economy is in a nosedive as we face months of tragedy and uncertainty. America's low rate of COVID-19 testing has drawn worldwide criticism. Trump has nonsensically blamed Obama. www.cnbc.com/2020/03/13/coronavirus-trump-says-i-dont-take-responsibility-at-all-for-lack-of-tests.html.
3. It is worth noting that 60 percent of "working-class" Trump voters were located in the top half of the national income distribution (Carnes and Lupu 2017). This figure emerges from the fact that "class" here is defined in terms of a four-year education; many middle-class small business owners (for example) don't have a four-year degree.
4. Some suspected her husband's clunky influence in First Lady Melania Trump's "Be Best" slogan, which not only smacks of one-upmanship but also "plainly doesn't hold up to the laws of English grammar" (see, for instance, Hill 2018).
5. Trump has been capable of more conventional presidential dignity, as during his 2017 Joint Address to Congress when he gravely read from a teleprompter to commend a Navy Seal – William "Ryan" Owens – killed in a risky raid Trump had

approved in Yemen. ("Ryan died as he lived: a warrior and a hero, battling against terrorism and securing our nation … Ryan's legacy is etched into eternity.") Following Reagan's playbook, the camera focused on Owens' weeping widow looking heavenward as Trump spoke, and lengthy applause affirmed Trump's effort to orchestrate reverential patriotic affect. Van Jones of CNN, who until then had been a staunch Trump critic, said in his post-address commentary, "This was the moment Trump became president" (Kurtz 2017). Jones thought he glimpsed a leader of inspiring solemnity, but Trump was soon back to his fractured and informal tweeting. It had been a fleeting mirage.

6. As an analogy, consider the analyses of Trump's handwriting that look more like soothsaying than political analysis. Graphologists have said Trump's signature shows signs of arrogance and megalomania (Edevane 2018) and a ruthless lack of empathy (Gomes 2017). But can't we extrapolate these simply from his political maneuvers?

7. In the latter case, such falsehoods included exaggerating the cost of Mueller's investigation, alleging conflicts of interest, claiming Mueller would have brought charges if he had evidence against Trump, and wishfully stating Russian meddling had "disappeared" from national debate (Cohen 2019).

8. Some administration officials, such as Jeff Sessions and John Kelly, admitted that the separation policy was implemented to "deter" immigration. When asked if it was intended thus, however, Nielsen retorted that the question was offensive (Cooper 2019).

9. To skirt the difficulties of defining "hate speech" while clarifying that speech can encourage harmful acts, Benesch et al. (2018) have developed a category they call "Dangerous Speech." They define dangerous speech as "Any form of expression (e.g. speech, text, or images) that can increase the risk that its audience will condone or commit violence against members of another group. Importantly, the definition refers to increasing the risk of violence, not causing it. We generally cannot know that speech caused violence … To say that speech is dangerous, then, is to make an educated guess about the effect that the speech is likely to have on other people" (Benesch et al. 2018).

References

Ablow, Keith. 2017. "Relax, Trump Is Stone Cold Sane." *Fox News* article, February 15, 2017. https://fxn.ws/2PbWOUO.

Alim, H. Samy, and Geneva Smitherman. 2012. *Articulate While Black: Barack Obama, Language, and Race in the US*. Oxford University Press.

Arendt, Hannah. 1972. *Crises of the Republic: Lying in Politics; Civil Disobedience; On Violence; Thoughts on Politics and Revolution*. Mariner Books.

Atkin, Emily. 2015. "What Language Experts Find So Strange about Donald Trump." *Think Progress*, September 15, 2015. https://bit.ly/33atf9k.

Baker, Peter. 2019. "The Profanity President: Trump's Four-Letter Vocabulary." *The New York Times*, May 19, 2019. https://nyti.ms/2EdFHtG.

Bakhtin, Mikhail. 1983 *The Dialogic Imagination: Four Essays*. Edited by Michael Holquist. Translated by Caryl Emerson and Michael Holquist. University of Texas Press.

Barajas, Joshua. 2016. "Nazi Salutes 'Done in a Spirit of Irony and Exuberance', Alt-Right Leader Says." *PBS News Hour*, November 22, 2016. https://to.pbs.org/34Cp2v7.

BBC News. 2018. "Air Force Once and Other White House Typos." *BBC News* article, May 1, 2018. https://bbc.in/2KmEK3x.

Bell, Allan. 1984. "Language Style as Audience Design." *Language in Society* 13, no. 2: 145–204.

Benen, Steve. 2017. "Conway: Look at Trump's Heart, Not 'What's Come Out of His Mouth.'" *MSNBC*, January 9, 2017. https://on.msnbc.com/2jv9zJu.

Benesch, Susan, Cathy Buerger, Tonei Glavinic, and Sean Manion. 2018. "Dangerous Speech: A Practical Guide." *Dangerous Speech Project*, December 31, 2018. https://dangerousspeech.org/guide/.

Blow, Charles M. 2017. "Trump's Degradation of the Language." *The New York Times*, May 1, 2017. https://nyti.ms/2p1LhpJ.

Boorstin, Daniel J. 1962. *The Image: A Guide to Pseudo-Events in America*. Harper & Row.

Brinkbäumer, Klaus. 2018. "Trump and Iran: Time for Europe to Join the Resistance." *Spiegel Online*, May 11, 2018. https://bit.ly/334ersA.

Bump, Philip. 2019. "All of The Things That 'Everybody Knows,' According to Trump." *The Washington Post*, April 20, 2019. https://wapo.st/2Nybo6H.

Bruni, Frank. 2017. "I'm O.K. – You're Pure Evil." *The New York Times*, June 17, 2017. https://nyti.ms/2LY66kO.

Butler Bass, Diana. 2018. "Thank Trump, or You'll Be Sorry." *The New York Times*, April 22, 2018. https://nyti.ms/2YaSYiS.

Calfas, Jennifer. 2017. "Trump's Official Inauguration Poster Has Glaring Typo." *The Hill*, February 12, 2017. https://bit.ly/341rhbJ.

Cameron, Deborah. 1995. *Verbal Hygiene*. Routledge.

Carnes, Nicholas, and Noam Lupu. 2017. "It's Time to Bust the Myth: Most Trump Voters Were Not Working Class." *The Washington Post*, June 5, 2017. https://wapo.st/2YAiXQa.

Carpenter, Amanda. 2018. *Gaslighting America: Why We Love It When Trump Lies to Us*. Broadside Books.

Cohen, Elizabeth. 2018. "The Truth about Those 7 Words 'Banned' at the CDC." *CNN Digital*, January 31, 2018. https://cnn.it/2W1N8dJ.

Cohen, Marshall. 2019. "Fact-Checking Trump's Flurry of Falsehoods and Lies after Mueller Declined to Exonerate Him." *CNN Digital*, May 30, 2019. https://cnn.it/2OvxDw7.

Cole, Devan. 2020. "Bernie Sanders Says He Never Expected to See a Nazi Flag Waved at a Major Political Rally." *CNN Politics*, March 8, 2020. https://cnn.it/2vcXsZ8.

Collins, Keith, and Kevin Roose. 2018. "Tracing a Meme from the Internet's Fringe to a Republican Slogan." *The New York Times*, November 4, 2018. https://nyti.ms/2Dqkr5o.

Cooper, Anderson. 2019. "Cooper Stunned by Trump Official's 'Orwellian' Response." *CNN* video, 10:04. March 7, 2019. https://bit.ly/2yB7fq5.

Costello, Maureen B. n.d. *Teaching the 2016 Election: The Trump Effect; The Impact of the Presidential Campaign on Our Nation's Schools*. Southern Poverty Law Center. https://bit.ly/25fcbgv.

Cotter, Colleen. 2010. *News Talk: Investigating the Language of Journalism.* Cambridge University Press.

—— 2015. "Discourse and Media." In *The Handbook of Discourse Analysis*, edited by Deborah Tannen, Heidi E. Hamilton, and Deborah Schiffrin, pp. 795–821. 2nd edn. Wiley-Blackwell.

Cummings, William. 2019. "'Achomlishments': Photographer Snaps Look at Trump's Notes in Rose Garden News Conference." *USA Today*, May 23, 2019. https://bit.ly/2W2T1Mw.

Dale, Daniel. 2017. "The 5 False Things Donald Trump Has Already Said as President." *The Star*, January 23, 2017. https://bit.ly/2kdXaXz.

Dallison, Paul. 2019. "Trump Makes Splash with 'Prince of Whales' Tweet." *Politico*, June 13, 2019. https://politi.co/2HFBwZN.

Davis, Dorian Hunter, and Aram Sinnreich. 2018. "Tweet the Press: Effects of Donald Trump's 'Fake News!' Epithet on Civics and Popular Culture." In *President Donald Trump and His Political Discourse: Ramifications of Rhetoric via Twitter*, edited by Michele Lockhart, pp. 149–69. Routledge.

Davlashyan, Nyra, and Irina Titova. 2018. "Ex-Workers at Russian 'Troll Factory' Trust US Indictment." *The Washington Post*, February 20, 2018. https://wapo.st/2PIK1Xb.

Dejean, Ashley. 2017. "Exclusive: Classified Memo Tells Intelligence Analysts to Keep Trump's Daily Brief Short." *Mother Jones*, February 16, 2017. https://bit.ly/337Qr80.

Derysh, Igor. 2019. "'MAGA Bomber' Cesar Sayoc Was Radicalized by Trump and Fox News Before Terror Plot, Lawyer Says." *Salon*, July 23, 2019. https://bit.ly/2T7dgnI.

Diamond, Jeremy. 2019. "Trump Focuses on 'Perfect' Ukraine Call Despite Allegations of Broader Pressure Campaign." *CNN Politics*, November 4, 2019. https://cnn.it/2DSn8Lk.

Drum, Kevin. 2018. "Our President is an Asshole." *Mother Jones*, November 10, 2018. https://bit.ly/2OCYbvD.

Duranti, Alessandro. 1993. "Intentions, Self, and Responsibility: An Essay in Samoan Ethnopragmatics." In *Responsibility and Evidence in Oral Discourse*, edited by Jane H. Hill and Judith T. Irvine, pp. 24–47. Cambridge University Press

Edevane, Gillian. 2018. "What Does Donald Trump's Handwriting Say about Him? Author J. K. Rowling Has an Answer." *Newsweek*, May 11, 2018. https://bit.ly/2MqUlD5.

Edwards, David. 2019. "Kirstjen Nielsen Accused of Misleading Congress after Claiming Migrant Kids Are Not Kept in 'Cages.'" *Salon*, March 6, 2019. https://bit.ly/2UbNn6Q.

Ehrenreich, Barbara, and John Ehrenreich. 1977. "The Professional-Managerial Class." *Radical America* 11 no. 2: 7–32.

Enda, Jodi. 2017. "These Republicans Didn't Like Trump at First. They Do Now." *CNN Digital*, February 21, 2017. https://cnn.it/2LRDtGc.

Fang, Marina. 2018. "A History of Donald Trump's Tasteless Comments about 911." *The Huffington Post*, September 11, 2018. https://bit.ly/2Pgn2FW.

Farley, Robert. 2011. "Trump Said Obama's Grandmother Caught on Tape Saying She Witnessed His Birth in Kenya." *PolitiFact*, April 7, 2011. https://bit.ly/2PvPRyj.

Fausto-Sterling, Anne. 2000. *Sexing the Body: Gender Politics and The Construction of Sexuality.* Basic Books.

Fishkin, Rand. 2018. "We Analyzed Every Twitter Account Following Donald Trump: 61% Are Bots, Spam, Inactive, or Propaganda." *SparkToro*, October 9, 2018. https://bit.ly/2RDiVki.

Folley, Aris. 2019a. "Tucker Carlson Calls Trump 'Full-Blown BS Artist' in Segment Defending Him from Media Coverage." *The Hill*, November 28, 2019. https://bit.ly/2DI1cCB.

2019b. "Ex-GOP Lawmaker: Former Colleagues Privately Say They're 'Disgusted and Exhausted' by Trump." *The Hill*, November 29, 2019. https://bit.ly/2R9dax2.

Fox, Emily Jane. 2018. "Michael Cohen Says Trump Repeatedly Used Racist Language Before His Presidency." *Vanity Fair*, November 2, 2018. https://bit.ly/2P7ybrQ.

Frischling, Bill. 2018. "'Stable Genius' – Let's Go to the Data." *Factbl.og*, January 8, 2018. https://bit.ly/31ctzCo.

Gartner, John, David Reiss, and Steven Buser. 2018. "Trump's Troubling Behavior Raises Questions His Medical Exam Didn't Answer." *USA Today*, January 22, 2018. https://bit.ly/2n1a9hv.

Gessen, Masha. 2016. "The Putin Paradigm." *The New York Review Daily*, December 13, 2016. https://bit.ly/31dV0vQ.

Gleeson, Scott. 2018. "Donald Trump vs NFL Players." *USA Today*, May 24, 2018. https://bit.ly/34CKZtY.

Gomes, Luke Henriques. 2017. "'I Was Quite Alarmed': Handwriting Expert Analyses Trump's Signature." *The New Daily*, February 1, 2017. https://bit.ly/2MpNVnz.

Gonyea, Don. 2016. "F-Bomb on a T-Shift: At Trump Rallies, Profanity Comes Onstage and Off." *National Public Radio*, June 17, 2016. https://n.pr/31eTFoe.

Gopnik, Adam. 2017. "Orwell's '1984' and Trump's America." *The New Yorker*, January 27, 2017. https://bit.ly/2zY09i4.

Green, Mark J., and Gail MacColl. 1983. *There He Goes Again: Ronald Reagan's Reign of Error.* Pantheon Books.

Haberman, Maggie, and Alan Rappeport. 2016. "Trump Drops False 'Birther' Theory, But Floats a New One: Clinton Started It." *The New York Times*, September 16, 2016. https://nyti.ms/322iep0.

Hahl, Oliver, Minjae Kim, and Ezra W. Zuckerman Sivan. 2018. "The Authentic Appeal of the Lying Demagogue: Proclaiming the Deeper Truth about Political Illegitimacy." *American Sociological Review* 83, no. 1: 1–33.

Hainey, Michael. 2016. "Clint and Scott Eastwood: No Holds Barred in Their First Interview Together." *Esquire*, August 3, 2016. https://bit.ly/330LiP5.

Haney López, Ian. 2014. *Dog Whistle Politics: How Coded Racial Appeals Have Reinvented Racism and Wrecked the Middle Class.* Oxford University Press.

Harriot, Michael. 2017. "Maybe the Earth Is Flat." *The Root*, February 21, 2017. https://bit.ly/2MBIrqa.

Harwell, Drew. 2019. "Faked Pelosi Videos, Slowed to Make Her Appear Drunk, Spread across Social Media." *The Washington Post*, May 23, 2019. https://wapo.st/2LUrhEF.

Herb, Jeremy, and Manu Raju. 2018. "Lewandowski to Democrats: I'm Not Answering Your 'F–ing' Questions." *CNN Digital*, April 7, 2018. https://cnn.it/2JmMYZa.

Hill, Jane H. 2000. "'Read My Article': Ideological Complexity and the Overdetermination of Promising in American Presidential Politics." In *Regimes of Language: Ideologies, Politics, and Identities*, edited by Paul V. Kroskrity, pp. 259–92. School of American Research Press.

2008. *The Everyday Language of White Racism*. Wiley-Blackwell.

Hill, Tim. 2018. "'Be Best': Does Melania Trump's Oddly Named Initiative Break the Laws of Grammar?" *The Guardian*, May 8, 2018. https://bit.ly/3cNxdJu

Hochschild, Arlie Russell. 2018. *Strangers in Their Own Land: Anger and Mourning on the American Right*. The New Press.

Hodges, Adam. 2017. "Trump's Formulaic Twitter Insults." *Anthropology News*, January 18, 2017. https://doi.org/10.1111/AN.308.

2018. "Government of, by, and for the Trolls." *Anthropology News*, December 20, 2018. https://bit.ly/2KhvQ8N.

2019a. *When Words Trump Politics: Resisting a Hostile Regime of Language*. Stanford University Press.

2019b. "Trump's Metaphorical Drug Deal and Lynching Fallacy." *Stanford University Press Blog*, October 30, 2019. https://bit.ly/38HlAR3.

Hughes, Kyle. 2017. "Lawmaker's Increasing Use of 'F-Word' Concerns Some Political Observers." *Daily Freeman*, June 14, 2017. https://bit.ly/2ORXQp5.

Inskeep, Steve. 2017. "How's the New President Doing? Voters in One Trump County Talk." *NPR*, February 3, 2017. https://n.pr/2LQacvc.

Irvine, Judith T., and Susan Gal. 2000. "Language Ideology and Linguistic Differentiation." In *Regimes of Language: Ideologies, Politics, and Identities*, edited by Paul V. Kroskrity, pp. 35–84. School of American Research Press.

Jackson, Jennifer. 2013. *Political Oratory and Cartooning: An Ethnography of Democratic Processes in Madagascar*. Wiley-Blackwell.

Jamieson, Kathleen Hall. 1998. *Eloquence in an Electronic Age: The Transformation of Political Speechmaking*. Oxford University Press.

Jamieson, Kathleen Hall, and Doron Taussig. 2017. "Disruption, Demonization, Deliverance, and Norm Destruction: The Rhetorical Signature of Donald J. Trump." *Political Science Quarterly* 132, no. 4: 619–50.

Jaworska, Sylvia, and Tigran Sogomonian. 2019."After We #VoteLeave We Can #TakeControl: Political Campaigning and Imagined Collectives on Twitter before the Brexit Vote." In *Reference and Identity in Public Discourses*, edited by Ursula Lutzky and Minna Nevala, pp. 181–202. John Benjamins Publishing Company.

Kakutani, Michiko. 2018. *The Death of Truth: Notes on Falsehood in the Age of Trump*. Tim Duggan Books.

Kessler, Glenn, Salvador Rizzo, and Meg Kelly. 2019. "President Trump has made 13,435 false or misleading claims over 993 days." *The Washington Post*, October 14, 2019. https://wapo.st/2suJUX3.

Kilgore, Ed. 2018. "'Political Incorrectness' Is Just 'Political Correctness' for Conservatives." *Intelligencer*, July 17, 2018. https://nym.ag/30vJhbX.

Klemperer, Victor. [1957]2000. *The Language of the Third Reich. LTI: Lingua Tertii Imperii*. Translated by Martin Brady. Athlone Press.

Konnikova, Maria. 2017. "How Norms Change." *The New Yorker*, October 11, 2017. https://bit.ly/2yAeazM.

Kramer, Elise. 2012. "Interview with Elise Kramer on 'Mutual Minorityhood.'" By Daniel Salas. *The Wenner-Gren Blog*, April 12, 2012. https://bit.ly/331ZrLS.

Kurtz, Jason. 2017. "Van Jones on Trump: 'He Became President of the United States in That Moment, Period.'" *CNNPolitics*, March 1, 2017. https://cnn.it /2UbsZCQ.

Lakoff, George P., and Gil Duran. 2018. "Trump Has Turned Words into Weapons. And He's Winning the Linguistic War." *The Guardian*, June 13, 2018. https://bit.ly /2GD3YKZ.

Landler, Mark. 2018. "White House Memo: With a Vocabulary From 'Goodfellas,' Trump Evokes His Native New York." *The New York Times*, August 23, 2018. ht tps://nyti.ms/2PzYbZK.

Lempert, Michael. 2011. "Barack Obama, Being Sharp: Indexical Order in the Pragmatics of Precision-Grip Gesture." *Gesture* 11, no. 3: 241–70.

Lempert, Michael, and Michael Silverstein. 2012. *Creatures of Politics: Media, Message, and the American Presidency*. Indiana University Press.

Lim, Elvin T. 2003. "The Lion and the Lamb: De-mythologizing Franklin Roosevelt's Fireside Chats." *Rhetoric and Public Affairs* 6, no. 3: 437–64.

Linskey, Annie. 2018. "Inside the Trump Tweet Machine: Staff-Written Posts, Bad Grammar (On Purpose), and Delight in the Chaos." *The Boston Globe*, May 22, 2018. https://bit.ly/3361BtT.

Liptak, Kevin. 2017. "Trump: 'Nobody Knew Health Care Could Be So Complicated.'" *CNNPolitics*, February 28, 2017. https://cnn.it/2PvU2dt.

Lizza, Ryan. 2017. "Anthony Scaramucci Called Me to Unload about White House Leakers, Reince Priebus, and Steve Bannon." *The New Yorker*, July 27, 2017. htt ps://bit.ly/2vNo12x.

Lockhart, Michele, ed. 2018. *President Donald Trump and His Political Discourse: Ramifications of Rhetoric via Twitter*. Routledge.

Mastromonaco, Alyssa (@AlyssaMastro44). 2017. "That's a fucking lie. To say president Obama (or past presidents) didn't call the family members of soldiers KIA – he's a deranged animal." Twitter, October 16, 2017. https://bit.ly/2ZuhrfF.

Mazzarella, William. n.d. "Brand(ish)ing the Name, or Why Is Trump So Enjoyable?" *Academia*. https://bit.ly/2OuIZjZ.

McCarthy, Tom. 2018. "Trump Dictated Note Saying He Was 'Astonishingly' Healthy, Doctor Says." *The Guardian*, May 2, 2018. https://bit.ly/2LsRKar.

McGranahan, Carole. 2017. "An Anthropology of Lying: Trump and the Political Sociality of Moral Outrage." *American Ethnologist* 44, no. 2: 243–48.

McIntosh, Janet. 2016. *Unsettled: Denial and Belonging among White Kenyans*. University of California Press.

McWhorter, John. 2017. "How to Listen to Donald Trump Every Day for Years." *The New York Times*, January 21, 2017. https://nyti.ms/2jkAK67.

2018a. "What Trump's Speech Says about His Mental Fitness." *The New York Times*, February 6, 2018. https://nyti.ms/2GVcZgY.

2018b. "The Best Words: Trump and the Future of English." *The American Interest*, April 23, 2018. https://bit.ly/2HYAqqF.

Meyer, Robinson. 2019. "The Air Really Was Cleaner under Obama." *The Atlantic*, July 19, 2019. https://bit.ly/2XVAXnR.

Mitchell, Hilary. 2016. "24 Times Scottish Twitter Roasted the Fuck out of Trump." *BuzzFeed*, October 7, 2016. https://bzfd.it/2dVU9Il.

Moye, David. 2018. "Geraldo Rivera Tells 'The View': 'I Was a Right-Wing Lunatic' about Bomb Threat Conspiracy." *The Huffington Post*, November 1, 2018. https://bit.ly/2YDnRMk.

Nakamura, David. 2018. "Donald Trump May Have 'Best Words,' but Spelling Mistakes Are Commonplace among President and Team." *The Independent*, March 22, 2018. https://bit.ly/2MCjdso.

Neiwert, David. 2020. "Neo-Nazi's Swastika Flag Stunt at Sanders Rally in Phoenix Just the Latest Far-Right Event Attack." *Daily Kos*, March 6. 2020. https://bit.ly/2ILLs45.

Nelson, Louis. 2017. "Spicer Refuses to Say Trump's 'Covfefe' Tweet Was a Typo." *Politico*, May 31, 2017. https://politi.co/2MDQ1RF.

Olson, Kyle. 2017. "CNN Host Calls Trump 'Piece of Sh*t' over Renewed Call for Travel Ban." *The American Mirror*, June 3, 2017. https://bit.ly/2roE32M.

Orr, Caroline. 2018. "Convicted in Mass Murder Plot, Extremists Blame Trump's Anti-Muslim Rhetoric." *The National Memo*, November 2, 2018. https://bit.ly/2MypEvD.

Peters, Evan. 2017. "Fox News Had a Good Segment." *Slate*, October 18, 2017.https://bit.ly/2rnMXQA.

Pinker, Stephen. 2019. "A Linguist's Guide to Quid Pro Quo." *The New York Times*, October 7, 2019. https://nyti.ms/352mPJE.

Pollock, Mica. 2017. "Three Challenges for Teachers in the Era of Trump." *Educational Studies* 53, no. 4: 426–27.

Polychroniou, C. J. 2016. "Trump in the White House: An Interview with Noam Chomsky." *Truthout*, November 14, 2016. https://bit.ly/2SWZpjJ.

Prakash, Nidhi. 2017. "'What Does He Mean When He Says Words': Watch John Oliver's Searing Takedown of Trump's Lies." *Splinter News*, February 13, 2017. https://bit.ly/2YnxnDQ.

Reichmann, Deb. 2019. "Trump Said He Got a Beautiful Letter from North Korea's Kim Jong Un." *PBS News Hour*, August 9, 2017. https://to.pbs.org/2ZfF5QU.

Samuels, Brett. 2018. "Trump Rally Crowd Erupts with Chants of 'Lock Her Up' about Feinstein." *The Hill*, October 9, 2018. https://bit.ly/3346Ri9.

Sclafani, Jennifer. 2018. *Talking Donald Trump: A Sociolinguistic Study of Style, Metadiscourse, and Political Identity*. Routledge.

Sennett, Richard, and Jonathan Cobb. 1972. *The Hidden Injuries of Class*. Knopf.

Shear, Michael D. 2018. "James Comey's Interview on ABC's '20/20': Annotated Excerpts." *The New York Times*, April 15, 2018. https://nyti.ms/2IYqOLQ.

Sherman, Gabriel. 2018. "'Now I'm F–ing Doing It My Way': Jubilant and Self-Liberated, the President Prepares for War with Mueller." *Vanity Fair*, March 22, 2018. https://bit.ly/2pxFTMh.

Silverstein, Michael. 2003. *Talking Politics: The Substance of Style from Abe to "W."* Prickly Paradigm Press.

Skinnell, Ryan. 2018a. "What Passes for Truth in the Trump Era: Telling It Like It Isn't." In *Faking the News: What Rhetoric Can Teach Us about Donald J. Trump*, edited by Ryan Skinnell, pp. 76–94. Imprint Academic.

Skinnell, Ryan, ed. 2018b. *Faking the News: What Rhetoric Can Teach Us about Donald J. Trump.* Imprint Academic.

Smilowitz, Elliot. 2017. "Trump Deletes Misspelled Tweet Saying He's 'Honored' to Serve." *The Hill*, January 21, 2017. https://bit.ly/2Lbd5Ee.

Snyder, Timothy. 2017. *On Tyranny: Twenty Lessons from the Twentieth Century.* Tim Duggan Books.

Stack, Liam. 2017. "Notre Dame Students Walk Out of Mike Pence Commencement Address." *The New York Times*, May 21, 2017. https://nyti.ms/2qOfWbv.

Stanley, Jason. 2018a. "Bannon's Deviant 'Badge of Honor.'" *The New York Times*, March 13, 2018. https://nyti.ms/2LZVYYL.

 2018b. *How Fascism Works: The Politics of Us and Them.* Random House.

Starnes, Todd. 2017. "Thank You, Mr. Trump for Bringing 'Merry Christmas' Back to the White House." *Fox News* article, November 29, 2017. https://fxn.ws /2LQ6vpE.

Steudeman, Michael J. 2018. "Demagoguery and the Donald's Duplicitous Victimhood." In *Faking the News: What Rhetoric Can Teach Us about Donald J. Trump*, edited by Ryan Skinnell, pp. 1–14. Imprint Academic.

Stolee, Galen, and Steven Caton. 2018. "Twitter, Trump, and the Base: A Shift to a New Form of Presidential Talk?" *Signs and Society* 6, no. 1: 147–65.

Stuart, Tessa. 2016. "Donald Trump's Meanest Twitter Insults." *Rolling Stone*, March 10, 2016. https://bit.ly/2Zn7T5m.

Suk Gersen, Jeannie. 2018. "Donald Trump's Brain Is a Catch-22." *The New Yorker*, January 28, 2018. https://bit.ly/2GIX473.

Taylor, Lenore. 2019. "As a Foreign Reporter Visiting the US I Was Stunned by Trump's Press Conference." *The Guardian*, September 20, 2019. https://bit.ly /2DJO3bU.

Thomsen, Jacqueline. 2018. "Twitter Users Mock Trump for 'Marine Core' Misspelling." *The Hill*, March 13, 2018. https://bit.ly/349sQEy.

Tobak, Steve. 2016. "Donald Trump's War on Political Correctness." *Fox Business* article, August 9, 2016. https://fxn.ws/2K8e1bS.

Todd, Sarah. 2017. "21 Unexpected Things That Donald Trump Thinks Are Beautiful." *Quartz*, September 26, 2017. https://bit.ly/2wPdyb0.

Trump, Donald. 2015. "Donald Trump Campaign Rally in Hilton Head, South Carolina." C-SPAN video, 00:24. March 7, 2017. www.c-span.org/video/?c4659 877/trump-words.

 2017. "Remarks by President Trump in Joint Address to Congress." *Whitehouse.gov*, February 28, 2017. https://bit.ly/2rPz9xG.

Trump, Donald.(@realDonaldTrump). 2020a. "The Coronavirus is very much under control in the USA. We are in contact with everyone and all relevant countries. CDC & World Health have been working hard and very smart. Stock Market starting to look very good to me!" Twitter, February 24, 2020. https://bit.ly /2TEj61y.

 2020b. "We have a perfectly coordinated and fine tuned plan at the White House for our attack on CoronaVirus. We moved VERY early to close borders to certain areas, which was a Godsend. V.P. is doing a great job. The Fake News Media is doing everything possible to make us look bad. Sad!" Twitter, March 8, 2020. htt ps://bit.ly/2IxJmo7.

Tyson, Alec, and Shiva Maniam. 2016. "Behind Trump's Victory: Divisions by Race, Gender, Education." *Fact Tank*, November 9, 2016. https://pewrsr.ch/2IrtQex.

van Dijk, Teun Adrianus. 2005. Racism and discourse in Spain and Latin America. John Benjamins Publishing.

Van Hout, Tom, and Peter Burger. 2017. "Text Bite News: The Metapragmatics of Feature News." *Text and Talk* 37, no. 4: 461–84. https://doi.org/10.1515/text-2017–0015.

Viennot, Bérengère. 2016. "Pour les traducteurs, Trump est un casse-tête inédit et désolant." *Slate (France)*, December 14, 2016. https://bit.ly/2LlaEjj.

Wade, Peter. 2019. "Embassy Official Confirms Overhearing Trump's Damning Ukraine Phone Call." *Rolling Stone*, November 16, 2019. https://bit.ly/365SwSC.

Walley, Christine J. 2017. "Trump's Election and the 'White Working Class': What We Missed." *American Ethnologist* 44, no. 2: 231–36.

Warzel, Charlie. 2019. "Epstein Suicide Conspiracies Show How Our Information System Is Poisoned." *The New York Times*, August 11, 2019. https://nyti.ms/2qaNeGa.

Wayne, Teddy. 2017. "What We Talk about When We Talk about and Exactly Like Trump." *The New York Times*, September 8, 2017. https://nyti.ms/2xU5Qbp.

Wilkinson, Alissa. 2019. "Errol Morris Thinks He May Have 'Assumed Too Much' with His Steve Bannon Documentary." *Vox*, November 5, 2019. https://bit.ly/2ONuKow.

Williams, Patricia J. 2017. "How Donald Trump's Words Create Emergencies: A Linguistic Political Analysis." *The Nation*, May 18, 2017. https://bit.ly/2GJhZab.

Wodak, Ruth. 2015. *The Politics of Fear: What Right-Wing Populist Discourses Mean*. SAGE Publishing.

Wolff, Michael. 2018. *Fire and Fury: Inside the Trump White House*. Little Brown. https://bit.ly/2YmB0dm.

Wong, Alia. 2018. "Donald Trump Doesn't Understand Community Colleges." *The Atlantic*, March 30, 2018. https://bit.ly/33YmiIF.

Wootson Jr., Cleve R. 2017. "Trump Mistakenly Tweeted That the Country Needs 'to Heel.' The Internet Gave Him Hell." *The Washington Post*, August 20, 2017. https://wapo.st/327DnOO.

Young, Anna M. 2018. "Rhetorics of Fear and Loathing: Donald Trump's Populist Style." In *Faking the News: What Rhetoric Can Teach Us about Donald J. Trump*, edited by Ryan Skinnell, pp. 21–38. Imprint Academic.

Yurchak, Alexei. 2005. *Everything Was Forever, Until It Was No More: The Last Soviet Generation*. Princeton University Press.

Zelizer, Julian. 2019. "Donald Trump's Week of Utter Chaos Sends a Message." *CNN Digital*, April 5, 2019. https://cnn.it/2T0VBxS.

Zink, Nicki. 2017. "Trump Has 'Inside Information' on Who Protested in Charlottesville, Says Falwell Jr. in President's Defense." *ABC News*, August 20, 2017. https://abcn.ws/2MpMTYJ.

Part I

Dividing the American Public

1 Part I Introduction: "Ask the Gays": How to Use Language to Fragment and Redefine the Public Sphere

Norma Mendoza-Denton

What does it mean to have a breakdown of the body politic; of the bonds that unite us? Donald Trump's commemorative presidential challenge coin (customarily given to military service members) overturns tradition by replacing the official motto of the United States, *E Pluribus Unum* (Out of Many, One), with his own image, and no fewer than three engravings of his name, alongside his official Republican campaign committee slogan, "Make America Great Again." Although many have attributed this numismatic self-aggrandizement to Trump's obsession with quasi-military paraphernalia (tanks, parades, medals, etc.), this change parallels the large and small verbal actions of the Trump presidency in which the unity of the whole is lost to a carver's knife, resulting in social rupture and the re-parceling of groups along strategically decided fault lines.

Slotta's contribution in this section offers one example of this fragmentation. Slotta suggests that what looks like incoherence in Trump's referents in speech is actually strategically restricted communication ("dog whistles") understandable to specific parts of his audience; namely, those who are familiar with right-wing websites and television media such as *Fox News*. As we take in Slotta's account of the need for mainstream journalism to decipher and explain Trump's tweets and statements, we are reminded that the public sphere is more divided than ever.

1.1 Using "The" to Marginalize

But how can a powerful figure slowly create division among subgroups, and what are we to make of the mechanisms through which this happens? One of the principal ways divisiveness is managed is through language, in even the smallest of features. Linguistic anthropologists argue that we create and perform our personae and our politics through the accretion of small speech acts. Take, for example, the determiner *the* as it may be used before a noun. Acton (2014, 2019) has investigated Trump's usage before nouns denoting subgroups such as *blacks*, *gays*, and *women*. Consider the following examples:

"Ask the gays what they think . . ."
"I will be phenomenal to the women."
"You look at what the women are looking for – they want to have security."
"I have a great relationship with the blacks. I've always had a great relation-
ship with the blacks."

This feature of Trump's speech has been frequently noticed in the media and by linguists (Liberman 2016, Parker 2016). Acton argues that it not only delineates the groups in question, but also pigeonholes them, with the determiner serving both to homogenize the group and to distance the speaker from the referent, making members of the group into an undifferentiated "other." Now, it's true that some decades ago just about everyone tended to use the word "the" in this fashion, so maybe one could argue Trump is just an older speaker for whom this type of determiner + noun construction is more acceptable. Certainly laypeople have noted it as an anachronism, such as Twitter user Catherine Rampell, who observed, "Why does putting 'the' in front of demog group often sound so dated (or bigoted)? The blacks, the Jews, the gays, etc." (Rampell on Twitter, June 15, 2016). Still, an additional linguistic fact emerges which argues for this construction as a pejorative or put-down: Acton (2019) also investigated determiner + noun usage among present-day Democrats and Republicans, and found that when referring to their own party, members of Congress by and large used the noun without determiner, whereas in referring to the other party, they used the determiner. In other words, for Republicans, the other party is "THE DEMOCRATS," while for Democrats, more often than not, the other side of the aisle is designated as "THE REPUBLICANS." There's a certain amount of "othering" that seems built into the way American politicians are using this construction. But it's not just the other side of the aisle that Trump designates with a determiner. It's "the blacks," "the gays," "the Hispanics," "the women," and in a famous Trumpian turn of phrase, "I love the poorly educated!" (Gambino 2016). In sum, usage of even small bits of language makes a difference in how we think of ourselves and other groups, whether we embrace them as part of the body politic or hold them at a distance.

In Slotta's contribution, the strategic calling forth of specific "publics" – fragmentary but internally unified portions of the general public – recalls what has been a strong focus for linguistic anthropologists. To understand the background of this work, we refer to Habermas' ([1962]1991) book, *The Structural Transformation of the Public Sphere*, widely influential in contemporary understandings of the development of Western-style democracy. An idealized public sphere is characterized by principles derived directly from the European Enlightenment: A rational individual freely participates with others in discussions of common problems, and in these discussions the best way to settle an argument is not with force but through the use of reason. In Habermas' idealization of communication in the public sphere, people from all walks of life and all demographics at least share reason and a common language so that they can communicate and understand each other. But Slotta's material suggests that in the Trump era, there's so much silo-ing of information that we can't even understand each other's references. It's almost as if different political groups are using different language. And as a result, America doesn't even feel like it *has* a shared "public sphere."

Many linguistic anthropologists would argue that even the original idealization of a public sphere was a failed project in the first place, since it deliberately excluded women (who were thought to lack reason) and oppressed groups (they lacked the standing to be heard in public). More often than not, in fact, the putative "public sphere" created counterpublics (i.e. a parade of pink pussy-hats: self-aware subordinated groups responding to the ideologies of the larger publics, as per Warner 2002). If this is the case, we can argue that Trump has cleaved his knife along already pre-existing sinews in the body politic, hailing new publics as well as exacerbating the divisions between existing publics and counterpublics.

1.2   The Making of a Battle Cry

Another way in which Trump uses language to interpellate or call forth portions of the public is through interactional routines. Sidnell's chapter, centered around the refrain *Get them out!* traces the emergence of one such routine: a gradual evolution in Trump's way of calling out disruptive protesters. The development of this call-out as a Trumpian slogan and battle cry arose both through (1) intertextuality with the second-person exhortation *You're fired!* (intertextuality is a recognizable reference to a prior discourse; in this case, from Trump's appearance on the show *The Apprentice* [*NBC* 2004–2015]), and (2) Trump's reaction to Bernie Sanders' handling of his own protesters. By overtly drawing a contrast with Sanders (who was portrayed as having had his microphone taken away by "two young girls," see Sidnell's chapter), Trump tried to make himself seem tougher and more masculine, and perhaps at first unwittingly, but then very much purposefully, imbued his utterance with violent overtones and encouraged his followers to rough up protesters. Once the pattern of the imperative use in his rallies was established, Trump solidified it through occasioned repetition and slight variation, rendering it recognizable as slogan, catchphrase and formula, partially because it was uttered in the same context (as the apex of a crescendo to get rid of undesirables), and partially because it was uttered with the same intonational contour.

As a slogan, the exhortation-turned-chant "Get Them Out!" emerged more or less contemporaneously with "Lock Her Up" (Parton 2019), which has the same tripartite structure observed by Sidnell. It is issued by Trump, the militaristic, tough-guy disciplinarian (in the subject position); it's directed at his followers, his army of sorts (in the indirect object position), and talks about the target of the possibly violent action (in the direct object position). Crucially, there's the possibility of ambiguous attribution in these distributed, multi-authored chanted repetitions. Suddenly, in the process of repeating Trump's directives, the indirect object becomes the subject, the army cadet becomes the general, and the private becomes public (Gal 2002). The person uttering the chant "Lock Her Up," or "Get Her Out," has been fully incorporated and momentarily realized into Trump himself; they now inhabit the heady position of being the one giving orders to those around them. In this way, as Sidnell writes, "supporters [both] embody and enact the political project that Trump advocated."

1.3   Sanctioned Insensitivity

If the army cadet has become the general, and Trump gives full rein to our self-aggrandizing impulses in the "Get Them Out" discourse described above, the "Crybaby" discourse hurled at liberals and described by McIntosh is the other side of the same Trump-inscribed coin. Hurling insults at "snowflakes," advocating for the toughening up of buttercups, and proclaiming not to care about coddled liberal feelings places the speaker in the gendered role of the military Drill Instructor, the layered interdiscursivity of which McIntosh has excavated through her ethnographic work on Marine Corps Drill Instructors. In this case, interdiscursivity means that as the Drill Instructors use discourses of sanctioned insensitivity, so are they paralleled by Trump supporters. The structure of the armed services condones this type of language for the purpose of breaking down recruits, while Trump ("No more Mr. Nice Guy" [Robin Lakoff 2005]) himself sanctions his followers' efforts to use the same language to break down opponents. As noted by McIntosh, this discursive stance is consistent with a dynamic noted by George Lakoff (1996) where the Republican party fashions itself as the party of the stern father figure, while the Democrats are more akin to a protective and indulgent mother. By verbally nudging his supporters in the direction of pre-established discursive divisions in society, and by creating new patterns through which the groups can attack each other, Trump works publics and counterpublics to his advantage.

References

Acton, Eric. 2014. "Pragmatics and the Social Meaning of Determiners." Ph.D. diss., Stanford University. https://stanford.io/2m1BNhu.
    2019. "Pragmatics and the Social Life of the English Definite Article." *Language* 95, no. 1: 37–65.
Gal, Susan. 2002. "A Semiotics of the Public/Private Distinction." *Differences: A Journal of Feminist Cultural Studies* 13, no. 1: 77–95.

Gambino, Lauren. 2016. "'I Love the Poorly Educated': Why White College Graduates Are Deserting Trump." *The Guardian*, October 16, 2016. https://bit.ly/35krqqF.

Habermas, Jürgen. 1991. *The Structural Transformation of the Public Sphere: An Inquiry into a Category of Bourgeois Society*. Translated by Thomas Burger. MIT Press.

Lakoff, George. 1996. *Moral Politics: What Conservatives Know That Liberals Don't*. University of Chicago Press.

Lakoff, Robin T. 2005. "The Politics of Nice." *Journal of Politeness Research* 1, no. 2: 173–91.

Liberman, Mark. 2016. "The NOUNs." *Language Log*, September 5, 2016. https://bit.ly/2m3bfwt.

National Broadcasting Corporation. 2004–2015. *The Apprentice*. Television show.

Parker, Kathleen. 2016. "Donald Trump and 'The Blacks.'" *The Chicago Tribune*, August 31, 2016. https://bit.ly/2kt2US7.

Parton, Heather Digby. 2019. "The Trump Administration Drained the Swamp – Into the White House." *Truthout*, June 24, 2019. https://bit.ly/2ziSgkT.

Rampell, Catherine (@crampell). 2016. "Why does putting 'the' in front of demog group often sound so dated (or bigoted)? The blacks, the Jews, the gays, etc." Twitter, June 15, 2016. https://bit.ly/2ktJ7lH.

Warner, Michael. 2002. *Publics and Counterpublics*. Zone Books.

2   The Significance of Trump's Incoherence

James Slotta

Donald Trump's rhetoric has been a regular topic of media reports from the moment he announced his campaign for the presidency. It has been labeled "violent," "heated," "anti-Muslim," "misogynist," and "racist," and generally taken to be conspicuously different from that of other presidential candidates, past and present. Not only is the content of his rhetoric criticized, but so is the linguistically unsavory delivery of it. Among other linguistic sins, Trump's oratory has been held up as a model of incoherence. "His spelling and grammar are disastrous, he contradicts himself, trails into incoherence, never sounds dignified or recognisably presidential – but none of it does him any harm. In fact, it seems to help," marvels an article headlined "Trump's rhetoric: a triumph of inarticulacy" (Leith 2017).

A variety of explanations have been offered. Trump's rhetorical style is an indication of his mental abilities, according to linguist Geoffrey Pullum, who compares Trump's use of language unfavorably to the complex syntax used by "more sophisticated thinkers and speakers (including many past presidents)":

> You get no such organized thoughts from Trump. It's bursts of noun phrases, self-interruptions, sudden departures from the theme, flashes of memory, odd side remarks ... It's the disordered language of a person with a concentration problem. (Golshan 2016)

Others see Trump's incoherence as a residue of the privilege he has enjoyed his entire life, which according to media scholar Todd Gitlin (2017) has given rise to a belief that "[h]is power is such that he is not subject to laws of ordinary grammar."

Whatever the motive, there is a cunning effectiveness in Trump's "word stroganoff" in *Slate* staff writer Katy Waldman's view:

> Ironically, because Trump relies so heavily on footnotes, false starts, and flights of association, and because his digressions rarely hook back up with the main thought, the emotional terms take on added power. They become rays of clarity in an incoherent verbal miasma. (Waldman 2016)

In fact, Trump's "incoherent verbal miasma" may be a key part of his message. Contemporary electoral politics in the US, as Michael Lempert and Michael Silverstein (2012) have argued, is centered on conveying "message": a set of values, character traits, and social affiliations embodied in a candidate, crafted through stylized public behaviors, and set within political, religious, and other narratives salient to voters.

As part of "message politics," verbal incoherence is not necessarily a liability. According to linguist Jennifer Sclafani, "[Trump's] unique rhetorical style may come off as incoherent and unintelligible when we compare it with the organized structure of other candidates' answers ... On the other hand, his conversational style may also help construct an identity for him as authentic, relatable and trustworthy, which are qualities that voters look for in a presidential candidate" (Pappas 2016). One might say that Trump's positioning as a political outsider who promised to "drain the swamp" is signaled by a lack of the verbal skills characteristic of the managerial and professional class, epitomized in particular by the former lawyer and president of the *Harvard Law Review*, Barack Obama. In this, Trump resembles former President George W. Bush, for whom incoherence and ungrammaticality were not bugs, but features of his message (Silverstein 2003).

But I'd like to suggest that Trump's speech is not as incoherent as it may appear at first. Rather, Trump's "bursts of noun phrases" and "odd side remarks" are often coherent enough, though not in a way that some audiences can detect. That is to say, for some audiences, Trump makes a great deal more sense than for others. This, as we'll see, is a significant feature of Trump's rhetoric, one that highlights communicative divisions in the American public and undermines a vision of the United States as a political community forged through participation in a common national conversation.

2.1   Who Is Sidney Blumenthal?

In the first presidential debate, moderator Lester Holt asked Trump why he had finally accepted that Obama was born in the United States after claiming for five years that he was not. Trump responded:

I'll tell you very – well, just very simple to say. Sidney Blumenthal works for the campaign and close – very close friend of Secretary Clinton. And her campaign manager, Patti Doyle, went to – during the campaign, her campaign against President Obama, fought very hard. And you can go look it up, and you can check it out.

And if you look at CNN this past week, Patti Solis Doyle was on Wolf Blitzer saying that this happened. Blumenthal sent McClatchy, highly respected reporter at McClatchy, to Kenya to find out about it. They were pressing it very hard. She failed to get the birth certificate.

When I got involved, I didn't fail. I got him to give the birth certificate. So I'm satisfied with it ... (Blake 2016)

In her analysis of the debate, Amy Davidson Sorkin (2016) described Trump's response as "an undiagrammable sentence structured around the name Sidney Blumenthal." And that name does not help much to clarify what appears to be a typical example of Trump's incoherence. After all, who is Sidney Blumenthal?

In the first two debates of the 2016 US presidential campaign, Donald Trump mentioned the name "Sidney Blumenthal" five times. One can identify when the debates happened simply by looking at a timeline of searches for the name *Sidney Blumenthal* on Google Trends (Figure 2.1).

One finds people asking on Twitter (@AmandaBecker, September 26, 2016: "Who is Sidney Blumenthal? – Most of America about 30 minutes ago"; @shansquared, October 9, 2016: "Serial Season Three: Who is Sidney Blumenthal"), and on the live blogs of the debate (Marcus Wohlsen: "Two debates in a row, Trump brings up Sidney Blumenthal. Two debates in a row, nearly every American says, "Who?" [WIRED Staff 2016]).

For those unfamiliar with its bearer, the name may still carry certain connotations which help to clarify its coherence in this context. The Jewish-sounding name *Blumenthal* could be seen as a "dog whistle," a political message that has an innocuous meaning for a general audience and a coded meaning for a different audience (Haney López 2014). In this case, the ethnic overtones of the name *Blumenthal* may be inaudible to much of the audience, but they are undoubtedly heard by anti-Semites and White supremacists.

But that is not all there is to this name. *Sidney Blumenthal* is a name familiar to anyone attuned to right-wing media outlets: as an advisor to Bill Clinton from 1997 to 2001, he earned the nickname "Sid Vicious" for his no-holds-barred defense of President Clinton during the lead-up to his impeachment. More recently, as a close friend and confidant of Secretary of State Hillary Clinton, he featured as a major figure in the 2015 Benghazi hearings, which centered on Secretary of State Clinton's handling of an attack on the US diplomatic mission in Benghazi, Libya and which were heavily hyped by right-wing media outlets. And, most salient in this context, Trump and right-wing media circulated the claim that, back when Blumenthal was a senior advisor to Hillary Clinton during her presidential primary campaign in 2008 against Obama, he had been among the first to push the Birther claim that Obama was not born in the United States.

Let me suggest that *Sidney Blumenthal* and many of Trump's other seemingly incoherent noun phrases and inscrutable side remarks serve as something like titles of artistic works. In his "Theory of Entitlement," literary theorist Kenneth Burke (1962) notes that words often function like titles. As

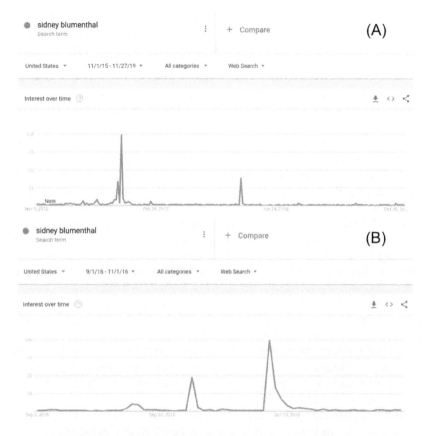

Figure 2.1 "Sidney Blumenthal." Screenshots of Google Trends graphs depicting search requests to Google for the name *Sidney Blumenthal* over periods of time that include the first and second presidential debates (September 26, 2016 and October 9, 2016). Graph (A) charts trends between November 1, 2015 and November 27, 2019, with the highest spike the week of the second presidential debate (October 9–15, 2016); (B) narrows the timeframe for searches of the name *Sidney Blumenthal* to the days between September 1, 2016 and November 1, 2016, showing peaks on September 27 and October 10, the days after the first and second presidential debates. Source: Google Trends, www.google.com/trends.

titles, they not only serve as labels for things in the world, but as summaries and abbreviations of complex situations and narratives. For instance, *Romeo and Juliet* can be used to refer to a play by Shakespeare or to the two main characters in it, but it has also come to stand for a situation involving star-crossed lovers whose families are at odds with one another. When Kanye West describes his relationship with Kim Kardashian as "a Romeo and Juliet kind of thing" (Dawn 2013), he is referencing the complex scenario of true loves who come from two different worlds (in Kanye's case, "she's a reality star and I'm a rapper"; ibid.).

Similarly, the name *Sidney Blumenthal* considered as a title serves as an abbreviation of a whole Zelig-like set of appearances Blumenthal has made in the reporting of the right-wing media, in which he is not so much a person as he is a character: the Clintons' evil henchman. Once one is familiar with right-wing media and its narratives, it becomes much easier to recognize the relevance of the name *Sidney Blumenthal* to Lester Holt's question.

In this respect, Trump's apparent incoherence recalls Keith Basso's (1996) account of a Western Apache speech genre called "speaking with names" (*yałti' bee'izhi*). In the example Basso provides, friends of a woman named Louise "speak with names" in an effort to console her, after she informs them that her younger brother had been taken to the hospital early that morning after coming down with a serious illness. This, Louise suspects, is likely because her brother rejected advice to see a "snake medicine person" after he had stepped on a snakeskin several months before. Lola responds to the news, and Louise's worry, by speaking with names: "It happened at Line of White Rocks Extends Up and Out, at this very place!" After a long period of silence, another woman, Emily, adds: "Yes. It happened at Whiteness Spreads Out Descending to Water, at this very place!" More silence. Lola: "Truly. It happened at Trail Extends Across a Red Ridge with Alder Trees, at this very place!" Louise laughs softly, and Lola's husband begins to wrap up this intervention: "Pleasantness and goodness will be forthcoming."

Basso's presentation is deliberately puzzling. What do these place names have to do with each other, or with Louise, her brother, and his predicament? In Basso's words, "We are unable to place a construction on the text that invests it with *coherence*" (1996: 80). Basso translates the place names into English for us, but though we know what the words mean we do not understand what they mean in this context. The text remains incoherent.

The key to the puzzle, it turns out, are the historical tales associated with these places. Line of White Rocks Extends Up and Out is the place where, in a historical tale, a girl who disobeys her grandmother's warnings gets bitten by a snake. The girl heals physically and is morally improved as a result of the experience. The story, interpreted as a kind of allegory of Louise's brother's predicament, is at once obliquely critical of him and consoling for Louise.

Historical tales among the Western Apache are, in a sense, titled with the names of places. A story begins and ends with the name of the place where it occurred: "It happened at Line of White Rocks Extends Up and Out" is the first and last sentence of the historical tale. And once we grasp the stories associated with the place names, the act of "Speaking with Names" gains coherence. For the Western Apache participants who know the stories associated with these place names, there is nothing incoherent about the genre. But for readers who do not know the stories, it appears inscrutable.

There are two points in Basso's essay that are particularly relevant to an understanding of Trump's rhetoric. First, names are more than labels for people and places; they serve as abbreviations for stories and other forms of cultural knowledge, entitling complex situations in the way that Kenneth Burke described. Second, knowledge of names and their associated stories circulates from person to person, group to group along what Asif Agha (2007) has called "speech chains." Not everybody is exposed to the stories associated with particular names. Until Keith Basso shares the story that happened at "Line of White Rocks Extends Up and Out" with us, Lola's remark appears incoherent. But once we become participants in the "speech chain" through which the historical tale circulates, the comment makes perfect sense.

Similarly, until we encounter right-wing media narratives, Trump's "bursts of noun phrases" and "odd side remarks" can appear completely incoherent. Once we know the stories, Trump's titles for them make a great deal more sense. We return, then, to the theme of Trump's incoherence, but now with the recognition that what may be incoherent to some in Trump's audience is perfectly coherent to others. It all depends on whether or not you are part of right-wing media speech chains.

2.2   From Speaking with Names to Living in Bubbles

For those unfamiliar with right-wing media narratives, the incoherence of Trump's speech has had an interesting effect: It has drawn attention to the speech chains through which stories circulate, and to the limits of that circulation. The name *Sidney Blumenthal* leaves some viewers of the presidential   debates   wondering   and   googling: "Who's   Sidney Blumenthal?" That, in turn, points them toward a world of right-wing media discussion that they never knew existed and had never, until that moment, been a part of.

Even more, Trump's noun phrases and odd side remarks draw mainstream media attention to the circulation of stories in the right-wing media, which has become a focus of reporting in the Trump era. Trump's perplexing statements consistently flummox the mainstream media, which each time note the lack of evidence for Trump's claims and send reporters in search of their source. There are a number of exemplary instances we might look at: there's Trump's claim that 96 million are looking for work, his assertion that the media does not cover terrorist attacks, his remark about "what's happening last night in Sweden." There's his tweet about Obama tapping his wires. His mentions of the Uranium One deal and

South Africa land seizures. There's his comment that Google search results are rigged, that the Kurds did not help us with Normandy, and on and on.

See if you can identify all of the "stories" Trump gives titles to in this tweet from February 17, 2018. In it, Trump refers to his national security advisor at the time, General H. R. McMaster, who had said that there was "incontrovertible" evidence of Russian meddling in the US election:

General McMaster forgot to say that the results of the 2016 election were not impacted or changed by the Russians and that the only Collusion was between Russia and Crooked H, the DNC and Dems. Remember the Dirty Dossier, Uranium, Speeches, Emails and the Podesta Company! (Trump on Twitter, February 17, 2018; my thanks to Bruce Mannheim for calling this tweet to my attention)

The search for the sources of these titles again and again points back to the realm of right-wing media, where Trump's apparently inscrutable messages turn out to be often canny or highly abbreviated titles for well-known storylines in circulation. Consider Trump's allegation that President Obama had had Trump's "wires tapped" in Trump Tower, which Trump tweeted early in the morning on March 4, 2017. The tweet was met with the usual response from the mainstream media and left-wing outlets, which described the accusations as "explosive" and "wild," repeatedly noting they were "unsubstantiated" and "offered without evidence to back them up." The source of the claims – an article in *Breitbart* from March 3 (Pollak 2017) – was relatively quickly identified by the *Washington Post*'s Robert Costa (Costa on Twitter, March 4, 2017), and widely reported by mainstream media outlets. Over the next few days, the mainstream media reported on the circulation of wiretapping claims in the right-wing media going back to January 2017 (e.g. Bloomberg: "Trump Calls for Probe into Wiretap Report He Read on Breitbart"; BuzzFeed: "Trump Repeats Talk Radio Rumor That Obama Wiretapped Him During Election"; see Olorunnipa et al. 2017 and Melville-Smith and Mack 2017).

This is just one example of a genre of reporting that has arisen in response to the incoherence and inscrutability of Trump's remarks: we might call it "the annotated Donald Trump," a genre in which reporters annotate Trump's words with their sources in right-wing media. This journalistic account of the circulation of messages through the right-wing media ecosystem and out of Trump's Twitter feed takes a variety of forms, some quite elaborate. For instance, a *CNN Business* article, "From Conservative Media to the White House: Anatomy of Trump's 'Diversity Visa' Tweet" (Kludt 2017), examines the history of right-wing media reporting behind a Trump tweet on "Diversity Visas," which followed a deadly vehicular assault in New York City that killed eight and injured twelve on October 31, 2017. The article reports how the suspect in the attack got linked to Democratic Senator and Minority Leader Charles Schumer as the story circulated through right-wing media outlets over a twelve-hour period, starting with right-wing websites *Breitbart* (Binder 2017) and *Gateway Pundit* (Caplan 2017) before migrating to Tucker Carlson, Sean Hannity, and Laura Ingraham's programs on *Fox News* the evening of the attack and finally to *Fox and Friends* the next morning. That is likely where Trump learned of the connection between the suspect in the attack, the Diversity Visa Program, and Charles Schumer. While *Fox and Friends* was still airing, Trump tweeted: "The terrorist came into our country through what is called the 'Diversity Visa Lottery Program,' a Chuck Schumer beauty."

This sort of reporting on the speech chain leading up to Trump's comments is now quite common. In a real-time version of the Annotated Donald Trump genre, journalists now keep one eye on *Fox and Friends* and another on Trump's Twitter feed to more easily track the speech chains behind his pronouncements. For instance, Trump tweeted: "Ungrateful TRAITOR Chelsea Manning, who should never have been released from prison, is now calling President Obama a weak leader. Terrible!" (Trump on Twitter, January 26, 2017a). Brian Stelter noted on Twitter (via @brianstelt) that fourteen minutes earlier, *Fox News* aired a segment on Chelsea Manning that labeled her as an "Ungrateful Traitor," during which *Fox News* commentator Abby Huntsman described Obama "as a weak leader with few permanent accomplishments" (Wright 2017). Later that year, Trump tweeted: "Going to the White House is considered a great honor for a championship team. Stephen Curry is hesitating, therefore invitation is withdrawn!" (Trump on Twitter, September 23, 2017b). Stefan Becket of cbsnews.com noted (via @becket) that twenty minutes earlier, *Fox and Friends* reported that "Curry wants to skip white house visit" (Becket on Twitter, September 23, 2017). Examples like these are plentifully documented on Twitter and in the mainstream media.

I highlight this genre of reporting – and Trump's incoherent and inscrutable speech that has given rise to it – because together they have helped to reshape a vision of political communication in the contemporary United States. In this vision, the US populace is increasingly divided along the lines of media ecosystems, living in separate echo chambers and information cocoons (Sunstein 2018) isolated by their filter bubbles (Pariser 2011). Public intellectuals, media commentators, and members of the public alike lament this communicative condition as a cause of increasing polarization and the decline of what Jürgen Habermas (1991) called the public sphere. For Habermas, the public sphere is where citizens in a democracy engage in debate over issues of broad public concern, supporting their arguments with reasons and evidence. Ideally, debate in the public sphere provides a way for all citizens to become informed, to have a voice, and to reach a consensus about future action. In that respect, public sphere debate is essential to a vision of democratic governance in which all citizens have the opportunity to shape public opinion and, ultimately, law and government policy.

Bubbles, echo chambers, and cocoons fall short of Habermas' ideal of an all-inclusive public sphere. They are less-than-public spheres, in which people interact only with the like-minded, not the public at large. Commentators worry that in echo chambers, citizens are not exposed to different views, to new information, or to counter-arguments, giving rise to increased polarization. Citizens not only fail to reach a consensus, they do not even participate in a common discussion. Less-than-public spheres, then, pose a danger to democratic governance.

Though these sorts of concerns about bubbles are likely as old as democracy itself, in the past two years they have become a regular part of discussions about the nature of public discourse in the United States. And all sorts of remedies have been proposed that are designed to encourage a more fully public debate, including curated reading lists (e.g. *Burst Your Bubble*: "The Guardian's weekly guide to conservative articles worth reading to expand your thinking" [The Guardian 2019]), browser extensions (e.g. *PolitEcho*: "Is your news feed a bubble?" [PolitEcho 2019]), and apps (*Read Across the Aisle*: "Break out of your social media filter bubble with Read Across The Aisle!" [BeeLine Reader, Inc. 2019]).

Of course, for right-wing media outlets, bubbles are nothing new; they have been decrying the biases and blinders of the mainstream media bubble for years. But in the mainstream media, talk of bubbles has largely accompanied the emergence of Donald Trump as a national political figure. Indeed, the day after his election – November 9, 2016 – media discourse about "filter bubbles," "online bubbles," and "information bubbles" peaked (Leetaru 2017).

Trump's campaign and election have induced a sense among many in the mainstream media and its audience that we live in a communicative dystopia of bubbles, echo chambers, and cocoons that threaten American democracy. And Trump's incoherence and media annotations of it have nurtured this vision of a country divided into less-than-public spheres. As the mainstream media and its audience trace the circulation of stories around the right-wing ecosystem and out of the West Wing, they trace the outline of the bubble the president inhabits. And in doing so, they discover that they too inhabit a bubble. In this way, a bubble-filled vision of the US populace springs from Trump's rhetoric and, particularly, its apparent incoherence.

References

Agha, Asif. 2007. *Language and Social Relations*. Cambridge University Press.
Basso, Keith H. 1996. *Wisdom Sits in Places: Landscape and Language among the Western Apache*. University of New Mexico Press.
Becket, Stefan (@becket). 2017. "Fox & Friends, 20 minutes before Trump's tweet." Twitter, September 23, 2017. https://tinyurl.com/y65ljsy5.

Bee Line Reader, Inc. 2019. "Read across the Aisle." Accessed November 4, 2019, https://tinyurl.com/yxajcd7o.

Binder, John. 2017. "Report: NYC Foreign Terror Suspect Entered U.S. with 'Diversity Visa' Trump Wants to End." *Breitbart*, October 31, 2017. https://tinyurl.com /y33sd6vy.

Blake, Aaron. 2016. "The First Trump–Clinton Presidential Debate Transcript, Annotated." *The Washington Post*, September 26, 2016. https://wapo.st/2dms94f.

Burke, Kenneth. 1962. "What Are the Signs of What?: A Theory of 'Entitlement.'" *Anthropological Linguistics* 4, no. 6: 1–23.

Caplan, Joshua. 2017. "Manhattan Terrorist Sayfullo Saipov Entered U.S. on Chuck Schumer's 'Diversity Visa' Program." *Gateway Pundit*, October 31, 2017. https:// tinyurl.com/ycs93784.

Costa, Robert (@costareports). 2017. "Per an official, I've confirmed that several people at the White House have been circulating this Breitbart story." Twitter, March 4, 2017. https://tinyurl.com/y44s56cq.

Dawn, Randee. 2013. "Kanye West Compares Relationship with Kim Kardashian to 'Romeo and Juliet.'" *Today*, November 27, 2013. https://on.today.com/2kW2bck.

Gitlin, Todd. 2017. "The Bad Art of the Non Sequitur: Gibberish Is the White House's New Normal." *Salon*, March 27, 2017. https://bit.ly/2mpgjeA.

Golshan, Tara. 2016. "Donald Trump's Strange Speaking Style, as Explained by Linguists." *Vox*, October 19, 2016. https://bit.ly/2Qw9NMM.

The Guardian. 2019. "Burst Your Bubble." Accessed November 4, 2019, https://tinyurl .com/hoh3len.

Habermas, Jürgen. 1991. *The Structural Transformation of the Public Sphere: An Inquiry into a Category of Bourgeois Society.* Translated by Thomas Burger. MIT Press.

Haney López, Ian. 2014. *Dog Whistle Politics: How Coded Racial Appeals Have Reinvented Racism and Wrecked the Middle Class.* Oxford University Press.

Kludt, Tom. 2017. "From Conservative Media to the White House: Anatomy of Trump's 'Diversity Visa' Tweet." *CNN Business*, November 1, 2017. https://cnn.it /2mmDXs7.

Leetaru, Kalev. 2017. "Why 2017 Was the Year of the Filter Bubble?" *Forbes*, December 18, 2017. https://bit.ly/2ktuJK6.

Leith, Sam. 2017. "Trump's Rhetoric: A Triumph of Inarticulacy." *The Guardian*, January 13, 2017. https://bit.ly/2jcFAD5.

Lempert, Michael, and Michael Silverstein. 2012. *Creatures of Politics: Media, Message, and the American Presidency.* Indiana University Press.

Melville-Smith, Alicia, and David Mack. 2017. "Trump Repeats Talk Radio Rumor That Obama Wiretapped Him during Election." *BuzzFeed News*, March 4, 2017. https://bit.ly/2kYwRcX.

Olorunnipa, Toluse, Jennifer Jacobs, and Margaret Talev. 2017. "Trump Calls for Probe into Wiretap Report He Read on Breitbart." *Bloomberg*, March 4, 2017. https:// bloom.bg/2kwTpBy.

Pappas, Stephanie. 2016. "Trump's Broken Speech Appeals to the Masses." *Live Science*, March 14, 2016. https://bit.ly/2mohvPj.

Pariser, Eli. 2011. *The Filter Bubble: What the Internet Is Hiding from You.* Penguin Press.

PolitEcho. 2019. "Is Your News Feed a Bubble?" Accessed November 4, 2019, polite cho.org.

Pollak, Joel B. 2017. "Mark Levin to Congress: Investigate Obama's 'Silent Coup' vs. Trump." *Breitbart*, March 3, 2017. https://tinyurl.com/y6kch2k8.

Silverstein, Michael. 2003. *Talking Politics: The Substance of Style from Abe to "W."* Prickly Paradigm Press.

Sorkin, Amy Davidson. 2016. "Donald Trump, A Failed Bully in His Debate with Clinton." *The New Yorker*, September 27, 2016. https://bit.ly/2muEad1.

Sunstein, Cass R. 2018. *#Republic: Divided Democracy in the Age of Social Media.* Princeton University Press.

Trump, Donald (@realDonaldTrump). 2017a. "Ungrateful TRAITOR Chelsea Manning . . ." Twitter, January 26, 2017. https://bit.ly/2kYz2x8.

   2017b. "Going to the White House is considered a great honor for . . ." Twitter, September 23, 2017. https://bit.ly/2Geolw3.

   2018. "General McMaster forgot to say . . ." Twitter, February 17, 2018. https://bit.ly /2mu3Bve.

Waldman, Katy. 2016. "Trump's Tower of Babel." *Slate*, November 2, 2016. https://bit .ly/2ktL0ih.

WIRED Staff. 2016. "Wired Live Blog: Fact-Checking the Second Presidential Debate." *WIRED*, October 9, 2016. https://bit.ly/2dCFrdS.

Wright, David. 2017. "Trump Calls Manning 'Ungrateful TRAITOR.'" *CNN Digital*, January 26, 2017. https://cnn.it/2kwEes7.

3   "Get 'Em Out!": The Meaning of Ejecting Protesters

Jack Sidnell

During the course of his campaigns for the Republican nomination and then for president, Donald Trump repeatedly instructed his supporters and event security staff to eject protesters from his rallies by memorably snarling such phrases as: "Get 'em out!" The news media gave these ejections extensive coverage, while the expression "get 'em out!" was celebrated and memorialized in various internet memes and YouTube video remixes. Was it just another display of belligerence from a candidate trying to assert his alpha-male status? Masculinity was surely at stake, but I suggest that at the same time, the activity of removing protesters became a tool of interactional messaging which not only allowed Trump to signify his own self-image, but also created opportunities for supporters to embody and enact the political project that Trump advocated.[1]

In what follows, I will suggest that the ideas of Charles Sanders Peirce, the influential American pragmatist philosopher of signs and signification, and, in particular, his notion of iconicity, provide a key to understanding these events. For Peirce, icons are signs that represent by virtue of a resemblance or similarity with their objects or, as he puts it, "serve to convey ideas of the things they represent simply by imitating them" (Peirce 1998: 5). In an extremely terse passage, Peirce (1998: 274) went on to distinguish three kinds of iconic signs.[2] Those which share qualities with their objects, and so represent them in this capacity, he terms *images*. Those which represent "the parts of one thing by analogous relations in their own parts" he calls *diagrams*. And, finally, simplifying somewhat, "those which represent ... a parallelism in something else, are *metaphors* [emphasis added]." On this analysis, (and to take examples from linguistic communication) onomatopoeia (e.g. "ribbit") is an image; a sentence, such as "Mary gave Jane the flowers," is a diagram; and an expression, such as "to wallow in self-pity," is a metaphor.[3]

Trump's ejecting protesters was in part a matter of practical utility; protesters interrupted his talk, threatened to detract from his political message, and at the same time publicly rejected his claim to be a viable candidate for the office of president. Still, these events and the particular way they unfolded had communicative import; they served as the vehicles for messages of broad political significance. More specifically, we can see the activity of ejecting protesters as involving a complex set of iconic signs through which Trump communicated an image of strong, masculine leadership, while diagramming aspects of his proposed immigration policy, and, at the same time, metaphorically alluding to a large-scale redistribution of power and agency, a new morally righteous populism, that his leadership would bring about.

3.1   The Image of a Strong Leader and the Making of a Catchphrase

In his earliest campaign encounters with protesters, Trump did not issue the instruction to "get them out." Indeed, in these early appearances, when protesters confronted him, Trump simply watched them being removed, sometimes indicating that they should "not be hurt" or even proposing that they were, in interrupting his address, exercising a right to free speech. But by October 2015, he was starting to more directly involve himself in their ejection, and by November "get them out" had emerged as a standard practice and catchphrase. So, for instance, at a rally in Miami on October 23, 2015, Trump was talking about making a deal to buy the Doral resort when someone in the audience began shouting and other audience members subsequently started booing. Trump looked in the direction of the disturbance, saying, "That's all right" (Trump 2015c) while momentarily pausing.[4] The crowd began to chant "U-S-A" and Trump joined in briefly, maintaining a wide, zippered smile, until flinching and saying, "Don't hurt him, don't hurt him. Don't hurt him. You can get 'im out but don't hurt him. We don't want anybody getting hurt" (Trump 2015c). His approach had become more aggressive by the time of the rally in Birmingham, Alabama on November 21, 2015. When a protester, Mercutio Southall, began shouting "Black Lives Matter" during his address, Trump interrupted his own talk about how many states he was winning in, asking, "Do I hear somebody over there?" (Trump 2015e). He paused, looking in Southall's direction, and began shaking his head. Trump then instructed, "Yeah get 'em the hell out of here would you please? Get 'im outta here! Throw 'im out!" After mentioning an incident at an earlier rally in Worcester, MA, Trump started repeating similar instructions, "Yeah you can get him out. Yeah get him out. Get 'im the hell outta here. Get him outta here! GET OUT! Get him outta here."

What might account for this significant change in Trump's rhetoric in mid-to-late 2015, from invoking ideas about free speech to instructing others to remove protesters? The pivotal event appears to have been a confrontation between Bernie Sanders and Black Lives Matter activists in Seattle on August 8, 2015. There are multiple strands of evidence that converge to suggest that this catalyzed the shift in Trump's rhetorical strategy. First, at a press conference before his rally in Birch Run, Michigan on August 11, just three days after the Sanders confrontation, Trump said that what happened to Sanders would never happen to him (Trump 2015b). And, two months later, in Springfield, Massachusetts, a protester holding a "Feel the Bern!" sign inspired Trump to yell, "Get outta here!" and to recount his version of the encounter between Sanders and the activists. "A couple of young women took over the microphone from Bernie a month ago," he said, then re-enacted a gaping-mouthed Sanders retreating from the podium, seemingly dumbfounded (Trump 2015d; see Hall, Goldstein, and Ingram 2016, and Goldstein, Hall, and Ingram in this volume). Returning to the microphone, Trump impugned his political efficacy, remarking, "He is not stopping ISIS" (Trump 2015d). And, finally, in late November 2015, when Trump was questioned about Mercutio Southall's claim that he had been "roughed up" at the rally in Birmingham, Trump suggested that the situation "was not handled the way Bernie Sanders handled his problem, I will tell you that" (CNN 2015). We can see then that Trump's practice of instructing supporters and security personnel to "get them out" emerged through an explicit comparison with Bernie Sanders who, by virtue of having relinquished the microphone to people Trump repeatedly described as "two young girls" (e.g. Trump 2016e, 2016g), was characterized as weak, ineffective, effeminate, and incapable of stopping ISIS.

Trump's rhetorical strategy crystallized between the summer of 2015 and the spring of 2016, and became, eventually, remarkably consistent. Across a collection of more than sixty instances of ejecting protesters from sixteen different rallies held between July 2015 and April 2016, Trump's instruction most often took the form of a grammatical imperative to "get them out," sometimes with additional commentary addressed either to the protester (e.g. "Go home to mommy" [Trump 2016i], "Go home and get a job" [Trump 2016i]), or to the assembled supporters (e.g. "I don't want anybody to get hurt, maybe" [Trump 2016a], or "[I'd] like to punch him in the face" [Trump 2016d]). Variations of the imperative portion included, "Get them out of here," "Get them the hell out of here" (Trump 2016f), "Throw them out" (Trump 2016a), and on occasion, simply, "Out! Out! Out!" (Trump 2016e). For example, while talking about his competitors in the race for the Republican nomination at a rally in Cadillac, Michigan, on March 4, 2016, Trump was interrupted by a protester chanting "NO TRUMP, USA, NO TRUMP, NO KKK!" (Trump 2016g). Trump initially competed with the protester for the floor by repeating the word he'd just said, but abruptly abandoned this course of action and issued the instruction, "Get 'im outta here." This was met by much cheering from the audience. Trump repeated the instruction several times and then, after briefly shaking his head and looking away, addressed the audience by saying:

Are these rallies the most fun of everybody, do we have the most fun. Do we have the most fun? Yeah, get him out of here. Get him out. Get him out. So disruptive. Remember when Bernie Sanders, they took the mic away from him. That's not gonna happen with us folks. ((*circling, making a pointing gesture*)) That's not gonna happen. Remember that? He walked away from the mic and he stood back. And he watched these two young girls talking to the audience. And they said we came to listen to him. And he was standing in the back as two women took the mic away. Now that doesn't happen to us.

He then turned to look in the direction of the protester and, pointing, reissued the instruction to remove him with, "Get that guy outta here. Get 'im out. Get that guy outta here." And while the audience responded with cheers, he repeated one more time, with a clear increase of amplitude, "GET 'IM OUTTA HERE."

As was the case in Cadillac, the episodes in which protesters were removed typically began when Trump noticed a disturbance, whether due to the efforts of a protester to disrupt his talk, as above, or because a conflict had started to emerge among audience members (e.g. supporters sometimes attempted to grab or destroy protesters' signs). Once the disturbance had been detected, Trump often made a show of watching it by, for instance, raising his hand above his brow (Trump 2016h). At this point he might direct the attention of security staff or begin instructing supporters to "get him out." Alternatively, in some cases, he simply said, "Get out," directly addressing the protesters. Either way, these occasions involved Trump suspending his "campaign talk" (whether this was scripted or not) and turning his attention to the business of ejecting protesters.

The practice of ejecting protesters by the issuance of instruction transformed an activity that was meant to detract from Trump's political message into one that tended to enhance it. Trump's direct involvement in this activity became a central piece of his political message, channeled through his practice of instruction-giving (on "message" in this sense; see Lempert and Silverstein 2012). On March 13, 2016, an article in the *New York Times* reported that "The phrase 'Get 'em out' has replaced 'You're fired' in Mr. Trump's vernacular, offering him an air of iron-fisted authority to buttress the image of toughness he projects" (Rappeport and Haberman 2016). The preceding discussion suggests additional ways in which this message was specified. By pitching his own practice through explicit comparison with Bernie Sanders, Trump conveyed an image of masculine, patriarchal authority that, he suggested, would be required to stand up to political adversaries. Returning to the Peircean notion of an image, a sign that shares qualities with that which it represents, we can see that various features of the instruction to "get them out" including its putative "directness" and the "tough" vernacular in which it was articulated served to convey something about the speaker and about the kind of presidency he promised.

3.2   Diagramming Immigration Policy

Beyond what the activity of ejecting protesters communicated about Trump as a person, it also served as a kind of portrait in miniature of his promised immigration policy, with ejected protesters standing in for those Trump labeled "illegals." This interactional message involved another kind of icon: diagrams, or signs that represent "the relations ... of the parts of one thing by analogous relations in their own parts" (Peirce 1998: 274).[5]

This message was never far from the surface of the events themselves, but at times was realized in quite specific ways. For instance, early on in his campaign on July 11, 2015, in Phoenix, Arizona, Trump's discussion of his proposal for immigration reform was interrupted when protesters held up a banner and Trump supporters attempted to pull it down. After security removed the protesters Trump said, "I wonder if the Mexican government sent them over here," and continued, "Don't worry, we'll take our country back" (Trump 2015a). Eight months later, during a rally in Radford, Virginia (February 29, 2016), Trump was talking about how he would prevent plant closures and layoffs at Carrier, which had proposed to move some of its operations to Mexico, when he was interrupted by a protester and yelling from the Trump supporters who had begun to respond. Trump instructed, "All right get him out of here please. Get him out. Get 'em out," then, pausing, looked back in the direction of the protester and asked, "Are you from Mexico? Are you from Mexico?" at which point the crowd began chanting "USA, USA, USA" (Trump 2016e).

In the course of ejecting protesters from the campaign rally, Trump thus often drew an explicit parallel between the people being ejected and Mexicans, whom he cast as illegal immigrants. Moreover, he often characterized protesters as "trouble makers" (Trump 2016b) and even sometimes as "animals" (Trump 2016d), both of which are terms he also routinely used to describe undocumented persons living in the United States. And Trump often made the relations of "division" within the event stand proxy for divisions within the country as a whole, suggesting, in Radford for instance, as protesters were being removed, that, "Believe it or not we're gonna unify this country. This is not a unified country. We're gonna bring this country together" (Trump 2016e).

We can see this diagrammatic construal from the other direction as well. During the final presidential debate on October 19, 2016 Trump used the very same words, "get them out," not to direct his supporters to eject protesters from the building, but rather to describe his own government's future action if he were to be elected president. The candidates were addressing the issue of immigration, and Trump, who had been invited to speak first, mentioned four mothers in the audience whose children had been "brutally killed by people that came into the country illegally" (Politico Staff 2016). He went on to discuss the drug trade, suggesting that the single biggest problem in New Hampshire "is heroin that pours across our southern borders." Trump concluded:

> One of my first acts will be to get all of the drug lords, all of the bad ones, we have some bad, bad people in this country that have to go out. We're going to *get them out*. We're going to secure the border. And once the border is secured, at a later date, we'll make a determination as to the rest. But we have some bad hombres here and we're going to *get them out* [emphases added].

The prosodic realization of the second "get them out" is unmistakably the same as the frequent instruction to his supporters, "Get 'em out." It is a token of that type and as such marks a connection between the two groups to which it refers: protesters, on the one hand, and illegal immigrants *qua* Mexican drug lords, on the other.

3.3   We the People: A Metaphor for a New America

In the vast majority of cases collected, Trump addresses *not* the protester, but rather the police, the event security staff, or the supporters whose agency he seeks to mobilize. Thus, while Trump does, occasionally, say, "Get out," most often he says, "Get *them* out" (emphasis added), in this way establishing a triadic relation between himself, the protester(s), and the persons to whom his instruction is directed. In other words, Trump's distinctive way of handling protesters often involved harnessing and directing the agency of his supporters, getting them to carry out actions he authored. At the same time, such instructions effected a redistribution of agency, authorizing and emboldening his supporters to act on Trump's behalf and under his authority. In this respect, the activity of ejecting protesters served as a metaphorical icon, one in which the redistribution of agency in the local, here-and-now context of the rally stood for a broad scale reorganization of the political landscape, a return of power to the people, a rejection of elite influence and the ideology of political correctness with which it is, according to Trump, allied. True, there is also a diagrammatic aspect to this icon which is incorporated into and partially constitutive of the metaphorical meanings conveyed. In this case, however, it is not just that one set of relations diagrams another. Rather, there's the implicit suggestion of equivalence between the act of ejecting (or otherwise harassing) protesters and participation in large-scale political processes involved in "taking the country back" and in "making America great again."

To convey this message, Trump first had to bring into existence the group, the "we" to whom power was to be returned. The rhetoric used to do this made extensive use of the first person, plural pronoun. For instance, in Burlington, Vermont (January 7, 2016), he suggested: "I don't think *we* can be beaten. There's a momentum that *we* have. There's a momentum that *we* have. That is so unbelievable" (Trump 2016a, emphases added). And in the case from Cadillac already discussed, Trump, speaking of the incident involving Bernie Sanders and Black Lives Matter activists in Seattle, promises, "That's not going to happen with *us* folks" (Trump 2016g). As Trump says, "With us folks," he produces a circling pointing gesture which suggests a delimitation of the group referred to. At the same time, using "folks" as an address term (admittedly a commonplace of US political talk) conveys the ordinariness of his intended addressee (and referent).

Trump's instructions suggested a redistribution of agency among a reconstituted "we" and the manner in which many of his supporters responded indicated not only their recognition of this message but also their acceptance of the new duties that were being handed down. This is particularly obvious in the events that took place at a rally held in Louisville, Kentucky on March 1, 2016, during which Trump four times issued an instruction to "get them out." On the fourth and final occasion, Trump was in the course of talking about Hillary Clinton when, apparently noticing a disturbance in the audience, he began addressing a protester directly saying, "Ohhhh get outta here. Get outta here. Look at these people. Get outta here. GET OUT. OUT. OUT. OUT. GET OUT" (Trump 2016f). As can be seen in various audience-perspective video recordings, a few of Trump's supporters took a lead role in ejecting the person to whom he was pointing (*CNN* 2017). Specifically, a man later identified as Matthew Heimbach can be seen yelling "get out" at the protester. Another man, identified as Alvin Bamberger, can be seen leading/pushing her through the crowd.

Further evidence for this analysis comes from events that took place at a rally in Fayetteville, North Carolina on March 9, 2016. As the police were escorting Rakeem Jones from the stadium, seventy-eight-year-old Trump supporter John McGraw elbow-punched him in the face, forcing him to scramble up the stairs whereupon he was wrestled to the ground by police deputies and subsequently handcuffed (Conroy 2016, Vitali 2016). McGraw returned to his seat, where he was met with cheers from members of the audience who had seen what happened. When interviewed upon exiting the rally he said, "Next time *we* see him, *we* might have to kill him. *We* don't know who he is. He might be with a terrorist organization" (*Inside Edition* 2016). He continued: "*We* don't know if he's ISIS. *We* don't know who he is, but *we* know he's not acting like an American."

When asked about the incident during an *NBC Meet the Press* interview, Trump suggested, "I do want to see what that young man was doing because he was very taunting, he was very loud and very disruptive and from what

I understand he was sticking a certain finger up in the air and that is a terrible thing to do in front of somebody that, frankly, wants to see America made great again, and so we'll see" (Drum 2016). Although he in this way contextualizes the events in relation to interactional norms of politeness, when pressed to say whether giving the finger would "condone" being sucker-punched, Trump insisted, "No, as I told you before, nothing condones, but I want to see. The man got carried away, he's 78 years old, *he obviously loves his country and maybe he doesn't like seeing what's happening to the country*" (emphasis added, Drum 2016). Trump then went on to indicate that he would possibly help with McGraw's legal fees.

As is well known, at a rally in Cedar Rapids on February 1, 2016, Trump encouraged his supporters to "knock the crap" out of anyone throwing toma-toes. "If you see somebody getting ready to throw a tomato, knock the crap out of them, would you? Seriously. Okay." He went on, "I promise you, I will pay for the legal fees. I promise" (Trump 2016c).

So, Trump's instructions not only directed the actions of others, they also implicitly deputized them. Supporters like John McGraw certainly appeared to recognize this, explaining their own actions with reference to a collective "we" who were somehow responsible for protecting Americans from any potential threat. In promising to pay for the legal fees of supporters who took matters into their own hands by "knocking the crap out of" protesters, or those who, like McGraw, don't "like seeing what's happening to the country," Trump himself acknowledged the sense in which such people were acting as his agents.

These events involved then a redistribution of agency on the ground in such a way as to metaphorically represent a broader political transformation in which power would be wrestled from the elites and returned to the people, the ordinary folks, "the silent majority."

3.4   Conclusion

A number of scholars have written about the way in which Trump manages to tap into affective currents that range from anger and resentment to excitement and fun through his use of speech and gesture (see Hall, Goldstein, and Ingram 2016, Anderson 2017, Mazzarella 2019). Anderson (2017), for instance, remarks of his campaign rallies:

People laughed at the exaggeration and perhaps at his outrageousness, but they also laughed at his insults, at his verbal and gestural impressions, at his name calling. Sometimes, it was the fun of not being serious in a world of responsibilities, the fun of being with other people in a shared situation, the fun of not being weighed down, for a time, by all the impediments to action that block, thwart, and frustrate . . . Often, it was a terrifying fun inseparable from violence.

As the example with which I began attests, these were moments within the campaign rally that were explicitly marked off as "fun" and as "entertaining." Part of that fun was an effect of what Anderson (2017) refers to as "action without limit" or "unimpeded action." Trump routinely contrasted his own conduct with that of his adversaries, which he characterized as "politically correct." Political correctness according to the Trumpian worldview involves norms and expectations that constrain, frustrate, thwart, and ultimately negate action. In demanding that protesters "get out" or be "thrown out," in saying that he'd like to punch a protester in the face (Trump 2016d), he challenged this supposed tyranny of political correctness. And in the case from Louisville, Trump waxed nostalgic about "the old days," "when we were less politically correct" and "that kind of stuff wouldn't have happened" (Trump 2016f).

And yet the preceding analysis suggests that the activity of ejecting protesters came to take on a more specific significance over the course of Trump's campaign. The occasion of ejecting protesters provided an opportunity for a distribution of agency such that supporters were simultaneously recruited but also emboldened and brought into the fold of power. Moreover, supporters who participated in the activities of ejecting protesters diagrammed, no doubt unconsciously, the very immigration policies that Trump advocated, policies by which he proposed to unify the country by expelling those whom he characterized as a threat to it. Finally, the very words used to instruct supporters (i.e. the phrase "get 'em out!") came to stand not as index but as icon of the speaker, serving as a sign of Trump's masculine and aggressive character or essence and in this way contributing to his political message. I have argued that a pivotal moment, upon which this entire complex semiotic process was to hang, came when Trump characterized his own method of dealing with protesters as standing in opposition to that of Bernie Sanders, as exemplified in a confrontation between Sanders and Black Lives Matter activists in Seattle, Washington. Trump used this contrast to define his own conduct, and ultimately himself, as direct, effective, powerful, and strong, in contrast to Sanders as weak and ineffective. These activities of ejecting protesters thus came, in various ways, to stand for an anticipated and explicitly promised social formation, one in which ordinary persons, "who love their country," might, under Trump's leadership, participate in the job of "taking it back."

Notes

1. My use of "message" here derives from the work of Lempert and Silverstein (2012, see also Silverstein 2017). As Silverstein (2017: 408) notes, message in this sense "has nothing inherently to do with positions on issues of public policy," which are at most "useful ingredients for or components of creating a message." Rather, message is akin to brand in the commercial marketplace: "a semiotic composite, a projectable

distinctive (and thus differential) narrative or biography" (Silverstein 2017: 408). Message is a matter of communicating the politician's persona, and "issues" are merely one of several means by which this is achieved (see Lempert and Silverstein 2012).

2. This passage, in which Peirce first introduces and then distinguishes among three kinds of "hypoicon," has inspired significant debate among specialists. Peirce suggests that a true icon can only be what he calls a "qualisign," or pure possibility, but that a "sinsign" (an existing thing or event that represents) may nevertheless be said to be "iconic" insofar as it represents its object in virtue of some likeness with it. Such iconic signs (which, given that that they are embodied sinsigns, are not, strictly speaking, icons) he terms hypoicons.

3. The argument structure of the sentence "Mary gave Jane the flowers" diagrams the relations it purports to represent. An expression like "to wallow in self-pity" involves a parallelism between pigs in mud on the one hand and persons and their emotions on the other.

4. Video recordings of all the rallies from which Trump's talk is quoted are in the author's possession and may or may not be available on YouTube. These can be located by searching for "Trump rally" with the appropriate place and date.

5. See also Irvine and Gal's (2000: 36) notion of "fractal recursivity."

References

Anderson, Ben. 2017. "'We Will Win Again. We Will Win a Lot': The Affective Styles of Donald Trump." *Environment and Planning D: Society and Space* (open site). https://bit.ly/2ktQlpH.

CNN. 2015. "Trump: Maybe Protester 'Should Have Been Roughed Up.'" *CNN*, November 22, 2015. https://cnn.it/2spLNnR.

2017. "Protester Pushed at 2016 Trump Rally." *CNN*, April 2, 2017. https://cnn.it/2R5KTr1.

Conroy, Scott. 2016. "Donald Trump Says He Might Pay Legal Fees for Man Who Sucker-Punched a Protester." *Huffington Post*, March 13, 2016. https://bit.ly/2syiUGf.

Drum, Kevin. 2016. "Donald Trump Is Basically Encouraging Violence Now." *Mother Jones*, March 13, 2016. https://bit.ly/35HesTU.

Hall, Kira, Donna Meryl Goldstein, and Matthew Bruce Ingram. 2016. "The Hands of Donald Trump: Entertainment, Gesture, Spectacle." *HAU: Journal of Ethnographic Theory* 6, no. 2: 71–100.

Inside Edition. 2016. "Trump Supporter Who Punched Protester: Next Time, We Might Have to Kill Him." *Inside Edition*, March 10, 2016. www.youtube.com/watch?v=DzU3FLZglhc.

Irvine, Judith, and Susan Gal. 2000. "Language Ideology and Linguistic Differentiation." In *Regimes of Language: Ideologies, Polities, and Identities*, edited by Paul V. Kroskrity, pp. 35–84. School of American Research Press.

Lempert, Michael, and Michael Silverstein. 2012. *Creatures of Politics: Media, Message, and the American Presidency.* Indiana University Press.

Mazzarella, William. 2019. "Brand(ish)ing the Name, or Why Is Trump So Enjoyable?" In *Sovereignty, Inc.: Three Inquiries in Politics and Enjoyment*, edited by William Mazzarella, Eric L. Santer and Aaron Schuster, pp. 113–160. University of Chicago Press.

Peirce, Charles Sanders. 1998. *The Essential Peirce: Selected Philosophical Writings: Volume 2 (1893–1913)*. Indiana University Press.

Politico Staff. 2016. "Full transcript: Third 2016 Presidential Debate." *Politico*, October 20, 2016. https://politi.co/34A2VW9.

Rappeport, Alan, and Maggie Haberman. 2016. "For Donald Trump, 'Get 'Em Out' Is the New 'You're Fired.'" *The New York Times*, March 13, 2016. https://nyti.ms/34CzuTB.

Silverstein, Michael. 2017. "Message, Myopia, Dystopia." *HAU: Journal of Ethnographic Theory* 7, no. 1: 407–13.

Trump, Donald. 2015a. *Trump Campaign Rally*, Phoenix, AZ. July 11, 2015.

   2015b. *Trump Press Conference*, Birch Run, MI. August 11, 2015. www .youtube.com/watch?v=Gh4Xpv9P78A.

   2015c. *Trump Campaign Rally*, Miami, FL. October 23, 2015.

   2015d. *Trump Campaign Rally*, Springfield, IL. November 9, 2015.

   2015e. *Trump Campaign Rally*, Birmingham, AL. November 21, 2015.

   2016a. *Trump Campaign Rally*, Burlington, VT. January 7, 2016.

   2016b. *Trump Campaign Rally*, Iowa City, IA. January 26, 2016.

   2016c. *Trump Campaign Rally*, Cedar Rapids, IA. February 1, 2016.

   2016d. *Trump Campaign Rally*, Las Vegas, NV. February 22, 2016.

   2016e. *Trump Campaign Rally*, Radford, VA. February 29, 2016.

   2016f. *Trump Campaign Rally*, Louisville, KY. March 1, 2016.

   2016g. *Trump Campaign Rally*, Cadillac, MI. March 4, 2016.

   2016h. *Trump Campaign Rally*, Fayetteville, NC. March 9, 2016.

   2016i. *Trump Campaign Rally*, St. Louis, MO. March 11, 2016.

Vitali, Ali. 2016. "Man Charged with Assault after Punching Protester at Trump Event." *NBC News*. March 10, 2016. https://nbcnews.to/2rKlrwo.

4   Crybabies and Snowflakes

Janet McIntosh

When Barack Obama won the 2008 election, he attracted unprecedented venom from the American political right, not only on grounds of his political orientation and race, but also because of gender anxiety. Even in 2019, googling "Obama gay rumors" yields more than twenty-eight million hits – just one element of what Neal Gabler (2012) has identified as a persistent Republican pattern of hyper-masculine "posturing" against Democrats. The notion that Obama was "weak" and "wimpy" when it came to the military and national security was a recurrent trope. His detractors framed him as a "butt-kissing liberal" (Chapman 2018) wearing "mom jeans" (Bump 2014) – this, in spite of his dictator-toppling maneuvers, military escalations, and numerous ethically dubious drone strikes in the Middle East. Bound up with their military critiques, Republicans also saw Obama as encouraging a kind of verbal femininity by way of so-called "politically correct" (or PC) language. Over the last decade, the right has excoriated Democrats for stoking gender- and race-based grievances among "coastal elites" and on college campuses, where the so-called "speech police" enforce new norms of verbal sensitivity. These new norms see moral inferiority in what many consider ordinary designations. They also come across to their critics as problematically feminine and childishly sensitive (McQuillan 2017).

Donald Trump's election on November 9, 2016 initiated one of the most dramatic campaigns of verbal backlash America has ever seen. While millions of Trump's critics mobilized to march against him, conservative websites, meme creators, and public figures – Rudy Giuliani, *Fox News* host Sean Hannity, and political commentator Tomi Lahren, to name just a few – flooded the airwaves and Internet to lambast these protesters as "liberal crybabies" and "snowflakes." Trump's former Campaign Manager Kellyanne Conway was a particular fan of these insults. A few days after the election she appeared on Hannity's show dismissing protesters and politicians who "whine and cry over Donald Trump's election" (Lima 2016), and arguing that student demonstrations on university campuses were staged by "precious snowflakes" (Flood 2016). A couple of weeks later, Conway appeared on "Meet the Press" to pooh-pooh the vote recounts Democrats had requested, saying Dems were "interfering" like "a bunch of crybabies" (*NBC News* 2016). It wouldn't be long before White House Chief Strategist Steve Bannon would mock those protesting Trump's travel ban against citizens of seven majority-Muslim countries, deeming them laughable "snowflakes" (Wolff 2018: 65).

The Google Trends website, which tracks "interest" (i.e. volume of web searches) over time, confirms that the phrases "liberal crybabies" and "liberal snowflakes" spiked sharply around the time of Trump's election and inauguration (see Figures 4.1 and 4.2). Trump protesters, meanwhile, were sometimes bewildered by the mismatch between the right's insults and their own understanding of what they were up to. Trump's detractors shed tears, to be sure, but from law professors to workaday Americans alarmed by his bigotry, they were also mustering a wide array of stances and strategies: erudite argumentation about his politics, anger inflected by shades of wit, strategic mobilization in well-organized marches, and so forth. Why would the right converge again and again on words and phrases so implacable and so dramatically mismatched to the actions and experiences of the left? And just what were they trying to achieve with them?

The crybaby/snowflake discourse serves as a stark reminder of a linguistic-anthropological truism: people don't just use language to communicate information about the world. In fact, sometimes language is of only incidental referential value. Language *does* things, and it can be mobilized to reshape

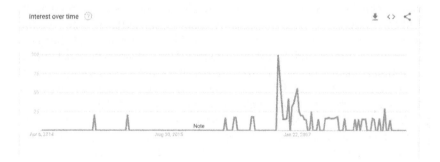

Figure 4.1 "Liberal crybabies." Screenshot of google trends, showing "interest over time" in the phrase "liberal crybabies" from April 2014 to April 2018. The highest spike dates to November 6–November 12, 2016, the week after the election, when Trump's detractors wrung their hands and his supporters went on the verbal attack. The second highest spike dates to January 22–January 28, 2017, the week after the inauguration. (Precise dates are only visible when the user interacts with the chart online.) Source: Google Trends, https://trends.google.com/trends/explore?date=2014–04-01% 202018–04-01&geo=US&q=%22liberal%20crybabies%22.

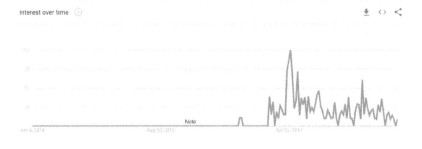

Figure 4.2 "Liberal snowflakes." Screenshot of Google Trends, tracking "interest over time" of the phrase "liberal snowflakes" from April 2014 to April 2018. The flat line first shows signs of life on November 5, 2016, the eve of the election, followed immediately by a cluster of spikes, with the two highest points of interest taking place over a three-week window surrounding Trump's inauguration. (The related phrase "special snowflake" also peaks in January 2017.) Source: Google Trends, https://trends.google.com/trends/exp lore?date=2014–04-01%202018–04-01&geo=US&q=%22liberal%20snow flakes%22.

social relations. Understanding how words can have this world-shaping significance requires looking to broader context. The crybaby/snowflake discourse obtains some of its meaning through what linguistic anthropologists call "interdiscursive" (sometimes called "intertextual") effects. When we talk about interdiscursivity, we mean that the significance of words and utterances doesn't just come from inherent word meaning or the immediate situation, but also from a history of use and from relationships with speech events in other contexts (Agha 2005: 2). Put another way, words have a social life, and carry baggage with them from one context to another (Bakhtin 1983).

In the case of the crybaby and snowflake insults, for instance, their significance played on a long-standing cleavage in "language ideology" – that is, in value-laden ideas about language. The main ideological gap concerns PC language, a gap that widened during the Obama years. After conservatives' electoral defeat to Obama, lashing out verbally against sensitive liberals who claimed to be on the moral high ground seemed like satisfying retribution. But in this chapter, I also suggest that with their linguistic grenades, the right has borrowed a semiotic weapon from a context where a regime of overt linguistic insensitivity has long flourished; namely, the United States military. Based on my recent fieldwork among Army and Marine Corps veterans and Marine Corps Drill Instructors (both active duty and retired), I suggest the most potent interdiscursive resonance for the right wing's current crybaby/snowflake discourse – and what pushes it in the direction of social action more than reference – can be found in the rites of passage that take place during basic training, or "boot camp."

By looking at this interdiscursivity, we can see that the crybaby/snowflake discourse is more complex in its agenda than mere "trolling," in the sense of "comment[ing] and debat[ing] for the sole purpose of agitation" (Smith 2019: 132). I suggest that once we grasp the loose resonance between pro-Trump insults and boot camp insults, we are better poised to understand why the crybaby/snowflake discourse has had such appeal to the right; what broader ideological visions it brings with it; and what, exactly, these utterances are supposed to *do* in the world, in terms of their social effects. I should be clear, too, that the interdiscursive resonance is not just a matter of similar words such as "crybaby" and "snowflake," but also the similar *stances* that accompany those words. "Stance," a concept in linguistic anthropology and sociolinguistics (Jaffe 2009), describes the relational attitude a speaker takes up, including the speaker's relationship to their interlocutors and, sometimes, to their utterance itself. When we recognize the military cousins of the crybaby/snowflake discourse, it is easier to understand that the stance it carves out is hierarchical, gendered, and ritualistic (the ritual part will become clearer below), designed to rebuke and possibly even school the interlocutor.

Below, I discuss four kinds of social action implied by the crybaby/snowflake discourse. First, although right-wingers indulging in the crybaby/snowflake discourse probably wouldn't imagine themselves to be staging a rite of passage, they adopt a stance with uncanny resemblance to the structural role of a Drill Instructor – or, in terms of ritual theory, a "ritual elder" who will school their interlocutor. Second, the crybaby/snowflake discourse tries to shut down the back-and-forth of standard conventions for political discussion, framing Trump's detractors as callow neophytes whose protestations are unworthy of deliberative verbal exchange. Third, the discourse sends the message that the left's empathy – the emotional root of some leftist policy preferences – is misplaced and that part of "growing up" means setting it aside. And finally, more subtly, the crybaby/snowflake discourse may be asserting a message (a *meta*-message, perhaps) that Trump's critics are too sensitive to language itself. All of these effects, in military contexts and Trumpian ones, are tied to the ostensible goal of making the nation stronger and harder, in a pugilistic, zero-sum model of the political world.

4.1   Crybabies and Semiotic Callousing in Boot Camp

So how does the crybaby/snowflake stance play out in military contexts? As many people know, basic military training – perhaps most famously in the Marine Corps, where most of my examples come from – consists of a multi-week rite of passage that breaks down the recruit (roughly 90 percent of whom are male in the Marines, so I opt for male pronouns, here) and builds him back up in line with an ideal of military masculinity. Drill Instructors, or DIs, assume the role of the "ritual elder" and subjugate their initiates (recruits) to physical demands and psychological stress. Language is crucial to the process, by way of a dynamic I call "semiotic callousing." In semiotic callousing, the DI deploys signs, especially terms of address, designed to berate and wound and, in so doing, to habituate the recruit to such wounding, dulling the recruit's interpretive sensitivity. (One could say that the process involves numbing *by way of* words, but also numbing the interlocutor *to* words.)

Exactly how semiotic callousing shakes out varies from one branch and unit to the next. In the post-Vietnam era, for instance, the Recruit Training Order at Parris Island, SC (one of two Marine Corps Training Depots), has stated that DIs are not supposed to use profanity or disrespectful language, but my own interviews with post-9/11 veterans suggest this official dictum is variably applied. Plenty of DIs have a florid vocabulary of lacerating put-downs. Collecting these, I've come across "crybabies," "snowflakes," "whiners," "weaklings," "wusses," "lazy bastards," "maggots," "hogs," "crayon-eaters," "clowns," "retards," "shit-bags," "shit-birds," and a raft of gender-troubled insults, including "ladies," "little girls," "faggots," "pussies," "pansies," "but-tercups," "cupcakes," and "sweethearts." One former Marine Corps Drill Instructor (in an unpublished interview; I withhold his name for confidentiality)[1] told me that during his service in the 1980s, he would first allow a seemingly level-headed DI to address recruits before he would "charge in, yelling and screaming, and spit's foaming out of [my] mouth. Actually, I used to put an Alka-Seltzer tab in my mouth so that when I was yelling and screaming, the foam would come out." This is not talk-as-usual. Initiates are startled as they realize that rationality, and certainly the possibility of a retort, have gone out the window. Already we might begin to see some similarities with the tidal wave of insults aimed at Trump's detractors after the election, when conventional political discussion and debate seemed to be impossible.

Of course, the daunting insults listed above do not accurately describe groups of young people striving and sometimes struggling to meet the exhaust-ing and bewildering demands made of them during boot camp, any more than the word "crybaby" neatly characterizes a legal scholar mobilizing an argument for a vote recount. Insults like these aren't meant to function with referential accuracy. Rather, in the military context – and, just maybe, in the context of a shocking political turnaround – they function in the way that so many rites of passage do: in the words of anthropologist Victor Turner ([1969]2017: 95), they "[grind] down [the initiate] to a uniform condition to be fashioned anew." In the case of the Marine Corps, the tender young person is being made into a Marine who will function well in a combat situation and obey orders at all cost. Drill

Instructors and veterans alike tell me that the berating of basic training helps accustom recruits to stress, while shucking off the self-centered quality they were raised with and habituating them to the notion that sensitivity is unwelcome in this hardened context. Complaints are not tolerated. When anyone feels upset or defeated, such soldiers or vets are often met with the military catchphrase, "Suck it up."

Plenty of veterans vociferously defend this mode of training when it comes under attack, as it occasionally does when, for instance, recruits report being abused or even take their own life. A number of veterans have told me of the importance of learning to "let the words roll off you."[2] In the comments section of an article about a recruit who complained about his treatment, one veteran likened (anti-PC) military language directly to the importance of strict parenting: "As a parent when raising kids I used a few words to my kids that perhaps were not politically correct and smacked them when the need was there and their little egos did not get damaged and they have gone on to become responsible adults. This little crybaby should be sent home to his Mama so she can cut his meat for him" (Dodd 2004). What Marines and service members from other branches learn over time is the fundamental military axiom that if you are going to be considered not merely a responsible adult, but what anthropologist Catherine Lutz (2002) calls a "super-citizen," a person armed to save the very nation, your language ideology should align with the old maxim: "Sticks and stones may break my bones, but words will never hurt me." If you can't handle verbal slights, how can you handle the rigors of combat? Semiotic callousing is thus construed by military insiders as a positive moral act of salvation or re-education; it's for the recruit's own good, and in turn, good for the strength of the nation.

4.2 Interdiscursive Influence: From Boot Camp to Trumpist Triumphalism

The notion that boot camp dynamics have some alignment with conservative attitudes toward left-leaning Americans may sound far-fetched, but occasionally one can witness the connections being drawn. Take my 2019 conversation with a retired Drill Instructor while we ate breakfast at a mess hall at the Parris Island Recruit Training Depot. He was griping that the current generation of young recruits are overly sensitive compared to those in generations past, and that the winds of change during the Obama era had pressured some DIs to be more careful with their insults. "What are they going to give these Marines at graduation," he asked with a rhetorical flourish. "A dress? But then," he went on, "It's a whole generation of entitled liberal snowflakes." Such words and concepts – snowflakes, crybabies, whiners, and any number of slurs depicting hapless childishness or femininity – circulate among DIs and Republicans alike; a grab bag of signifiers that call up a raft of ideological assumptions about those who are problematically weak, be they recruits, sensitive young people, or liberals.

Some of the clearest interdiscursive bridges can be found in the internet memes that draw direct lines between Trump's rise, military authority, and the crybaby/snowflake discourse. Consider, for instance, one meme that appeared online shortly after the election, when Trump announced that he would nominate career Marine General James Mattis for Secretary of Defense. In the image (Figure 4.3), Mattis stares implacably in uniform, framed by words that would seem to address Obama's supporters or the left more broadly: "IT'S OVER SNOWFLAKES . . . THE ADULTS ARE BACK IN CHARGE."

Another meme (Figure 4.4) features R. Lee Ermey, the Parris Island Drill Instructor who was famously hired to play a Marine Corps Drill Instructor in Stanley Kubrick's 1987 film *Full Metal Jacket*. In the meme, Ermey confronts the viewer as if they were ambiguously suspended between being a Marine Corps recruit and a Trump critic. Some of the following phrases are lifted directly from his Drill Instructor lines in the film: "LISTEN HERE SNOWFLAKE . . . YOU BETTER FLUSH THAT LIBERAL SEPTIC TANK THAT SITS BETWEEN YOUR TWO SHOULDER BLADES. AND SAY TRUMP IS MY PRESIDENT, OR I WILL GOUGE OUT YOUR EYES AND SKULL FU*K YOU!"

Figure 4.3 "IT'S OVER SNOWFLAKES." Digital Image. Twitter Page. February 7, 2017. https://bit.ly/2qU8rVh.

Figure 4.4 "LISTEN HERE SNOWFLAKE." Digital Image. *Meme.*
January 26, 2017. https://bit.ly/2rLHG5a.

Another Ermey meme (Figure 4.5) features a different image of him pointing
aggressively at the camera. It reads: "SUCK IT UP BUTTERCUP! IT'S
TRUMP TIME AND WE DON'T GIVE A SHIT ABOUT YOUR FEELINGS!"

Consider, too, the connections drawn by an Air Force Veteran in his video
response to the protests after Trump's election. On November 14, 2016, *Fox
News* posted his clip under the title "You Crybabies Are Why Donald Trump
Won" (Fox News Insider 2016; the clip now has over twenty-four million
views).[3] As the veteran faces the camera to address Trump's detractors, he
rants: "That's the problem with this country. You can't always get your way!
Everybody wants to be politically correct! . . . We're tired of you crybabies! . . .
None of you put on a uniform, but you're quick to disrespect the flag . . . you
didn't fight for anything, but you want it! . . . This ain't your damn country!
Leave!" Trump's critics, he suggests, are "crybaby" military avoiders and PC-
enthusiasts, who between their softness and failure to sacrifice haven't earned
the right to be full citizens.

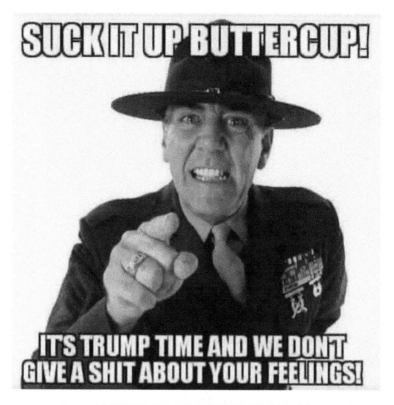

Figure 4.5 "SUCK IT UP BUTTERCUP!" Digital image. Pinterest. n.d. www.pinterest.com/pin/471118811012099164/.

4.3   Trumpist Insults as Social Action

To be sure, many Trump supporters who have used the crybaby/snowflake discourse may not be consciously aware of its interdiscursive resonance in the United States military. But in spite of any individual's intentions, words circulate within and take their meaning from broader ideological fields that some speakers will recognize, however dimly; interdiscursivity often works through loose understanding and partial recognition. Of course, the aims of the crybaby/snowflake discourse in the military are rigidly goal-oriented, intended to bring the majority of recruits into the club (as it were) of combat-ready service members, while the discourse of Trump supporters is not as clear in its aims. Nevertheless, I suggest the overlap furnishes an instructive framework. The vaguely military stances of the crybaby/snowflake discourse steep these communicative acts, these *kinds* of insults, in meaning, giving them more force as a kind of social action.

First, in both the military and the political cases, Victor Turner's ([1969] 2017) insights about the structure of rites of passage seem relevant, for the insulter adopts the role of masculinized ritual elder who is in a position to pummel and school the initiates through what I've called semiotic callousing. Surely being in a position to adopt such a role has been gratifying for the part of Trump's base that have framed themselves as long-silenced underdogs vis-à-vis the hypereducated "liberal elites" feared to be winning the "culture war." The crybaby/snowflake discourse allows the right to frame liberals as infantilized and spoiled, requiring maturation. After all, "crybabies" whine, fuss, and go into the fetal position when they don't get what they want, while "snowflakes" insist on their delicate uniqueness (a common complaint about leftists from the right), and shrivel and melt the instant things get heated. (The earliest documented appearance of the term "snowflake" as an insult – an origin that underscores its pugilism and nihilism – comes from Chuck Palahniuk's [2005-[1996]: 134] novel *Fight Club*: "You are not special. You're not a beautiful and unique snowflake. You're the same decaying organic matter as everything else. We're all part of the same compost heap.") The stance of the doctrinaire ritual elder meshes well, incidentally, with what George Lakoff (1996) has long said about conservative politics; namely, that it is underpinned by what he calls a "strict father" model, emphasizing authoritarian masculinity, punitive discipline, and personal responsibility in contrast to a progressive "nurturant parent" model of the state. If those on the right have been feeling threatened, even fearful, of the influence of the left, they have their moment now in which to adopt a paternalist and punitive stance. It's worth noting that Trump himself lacks strong military masculine credentials – although he attended the New York Military Academy in his teens, he famously dodged the Vietnam draft by way of his supposed "bone spurs" – but even so, his supporters' insults seem to give them a grip on masculine power over Democrats.

Second, the stance adopted by the speaker (or yeller) – the proverbial ritual elder – is one of domination, denigration, and de-ratification that shuts down communication, in the sense that the recruit or the protester is not able to speak back or respond in any way. Protesters may mobilize a carefully reasoned objection to some aspect of Trump's political stances, but they are met with a semiotic punch. In her discussion of insulting speech acts, Judith Butler (1997: 4) notes how socially disorienting they can be: "[When] addressed injuriously," she writes, "one can be 'put in one's place' by such speech, but such a place may be no place." Injurious speech can strip the target of recognition, rendering them not an interlocutor so much as a non-entity. Accordingly, many of the right-wing "snowflake" memes concern the idea that the left has had difficulty accepting a world in which they "lost" and Trump and supporters "won," as if "losing" an election means losing a voice. Again, this stance makes sense if one considers that the repetitive cudgeling of the crybaby/snowflake discourse has no resemblance to a communicative exchange, but instead the whiff of rite-of-passage dynamics. Not only are Trump supporters in the role of ritual elder, but Trump's detractors are placed into the role of what Victor Turner calls the "liminal" neophyte, who is often symbolically denigrated to the point of being a social non-entity, a person in-between their former social role and their future one. And when their objections are reduced to childish whining, they don't deserve to be heard (they deserve to be spanked, in fact, if one goes with a retrograde model of the strict father). The crybaby/snowflake discourse thus clarifies the stance of the speakers toward their targets: *We are not in conversation, and unless and until you change you are not worth listening to.*

Third, like Drill Instructors' insults, and arguably beyond typical internet trolling, the right-wing's crybaby/snowflake discourse has a hint of a pedagogical dimension. In many rites of passage, when the initiates are at their most vulnerable, they are presented with teaching tools (Turner calls them *sacra*) that instruct neophytes explicitly or implicitly in what their new social role ought to be as they "grow up." In military basic training, the semiotic callousing of insults functions simultaneously to grind down the recruits and, as *sacra*, to inculcate the vital lesson that military strength, "national security," is contingent on attenuating both personal sensitivity and empathy for the vulnerable (cf. Cohn and Ruddick 2004). This is a lesson many Trump supporters would approve of; indeed, the United States is in the midst of a major ideological disagreement when it comes to the question of whether it is morally appropriate to extend empathic feeling far and wide. The "crybabies" at anti-Trump rallies have expressed their dismay on behalf of the many historically vulnerable groups Trump's rise imperils. Yet, as part of their "anti-PC" stance, many Trump supporters feel that women's rights and LGBTQ+ rights imperil a strong traditional patriarchy; that Muslims and immigrants threaten both national security (supposedly via terrorism and crime) and Christian hegemony; and that ethnic and racial minorities have weakened a strong economy by "cutting in line" for "handouts" (see Hochschild 2016 for ethnographic discussion of the political predecessors of this stance, the "tea partiers"). Blasting away at the hand-wringers who object to Trump, an unofficial campaign slogan started appearing on T-shirts at Trump rallies in 2015 reading: "TRUMP ***2016*** FUCK YOUR FEELINGS."[4] Perhaps a hidden script in the "crybaby/snowflake" discourse is that the right wing wishes its own callousness could serve as a model of "growing up," and the left would follow suit, hardening their own stance toward the huddled masses. If they did, the right seems to believe, the nation would be better off – no coddling or "handouts" for minorities, no sympathy for those locked out of the gates, no tears for those who feel oppressed by Trump's patriarchal White nationalist agenda. Just "America" – narrowly defined, patently racialized, and patriarchally heteronormative – "first."

Finally, perhaps another element of the *sacra* in the verbal cudgeling from the right is the message that liberals shouldn't be so sensitive *about language itself*. We know Trump and many of his supporters have refused the liberal language ideology that sensitivity in word choice is morally right and good. After all, Trump was elected partly by dint of his identity as a "straight talker" who doesn't care who he offends – a gratifying stance for supporters who feel the "PC" language movement has gone too far. Many on the right have expressed their disgust at being told they are ignorant, immoral, or both for the way they use language. The stance adopted in their crybaby/snowflake discourse includes a relational attitude toward these very utterances, one that resonates with military insults. The attitude seems to be: If you can't handle an insult, if you're going to wither whenever someone hurts your feelings, how will you handle the harsh realities of the world, or get anything done in politics, for that matter? This message is an extension of the right's attack on political correctness. It cleverly turns the left's put-down ("you Republicans are ignorant and immoral in your verbal disregard for others") into something no one wanted to be associated with; namely, being pathetically sensitive to language, and out of touch as a result. The messaging further aggravates the split in politics between overly educated elites (Obama, Hillary Clinton, and beyond) with their painstaking parsing of word meaning, and the voters who see them as snobbish and distant compared to Republican candidates such as Trump who try to frame themselves as "straight shooters" and "everyday guys."

The discourse has also helped clear a path for a president who excels at insults, and exacerbates a political climate that, instead of being centered around democratic discussion and mutuality, divides the nation into winners and losers. Unlike military recruits, however, those on the left don't "learn to let the words roll off," accept their silencing, or curtail their empathy. What they've done, sometimes, is to try to flip the script against their would-be ritual elders, with protest signs and memes reading: "Damn right we're snowflakes. WINTER IS COMING" (which happens to be an interdiscursive reference to the popular 2011–2019 HBO series about succession wars, *Game of Thrones*). And in a proliferating discourse, many have decided to lob the crybaby discourse right back in the direction of the (ironically, notoriously) thin-skinned president himself. The Internet and news media are teeming with caricatures and memes of Trump in a onesie, Trump having a tantrum, Trump sucking on a binkie. The diapered "Trump blimp" has made appearances at demonstrations across the world, while broadcasters and journalists have taken to calling Trump "President Snowflake."[5] It's fun, a bit gratifying, but boomeranging the right's insults back in their direction also smacks of the schoolyard, when there are so many difficult but constructive political conversations that need to be had (and that indeed many of Trump's critics are striving for). In order to create a space for such conversation, we will need a national communicative framework that resists the temptation of the silencing maneuvers I have described.

Notes

1. I engaged in personal conversation with retired and active duty Marine Corps Drill Instructors over the course of several months in 2018–2019, both remotely and in person. Due to the ethical requirement to protect the identities of those I spoke to, I do not furnish their names, and in some cases opt to withhold details of when or where a conversation took place. Some conversations took place on Parris Island, and others via Skype with far-flung respondents.
2. Over the course of 2018–2019 I interviewed several dozen American veterans who served in the Marine Corps or Army during the Vietnam War or the Global War on Terror. The particular statement quoted here, or variations of it, encapsulates a language-ideological stance I heard from at least ten veterans.
3. It is tempting to imagine that *Fox News* was capitalizing not only on the "crybabies" title, but also on the fact that the veteran is Black, a tokenism that they may have hoped gives support to the argument that Trump has legitimate appeal to minorities.
4. The sentiment has been echoed in various other memes, such as the bumper sticker I have seen around Massachusetts reading "TRUMP 2020: MAKE LIBERALS CRY AGAIN."
5. In Van Jones' case, it was based on Trump's response to the FBI's Russia probe in May 2017 (CNN 2017; see also Schneider 2017).

References

Agha, Asif. 2005. "Introduction: Semiosis across Encounters." *Journal of Linguistic Anthropology* 15, no. 1: 1–5.
Bakhtin, Mikhail. 1983 *The Dialogic Imagination: Four Essays*. Edited by Michael Holquist. Translated by Caryl Emerson and Michael Holquist. University of Texas Press.
Bump, Philip. 2014. "Obama Is a Horrible Dictator Who Is Also a Wimp." *The Atlantic*, March 4, 2014. https://bit.ly/2nGpdFp.
Butler, Judith. 1997. *Excitable Speech: A Politics of the Performative*. Routledge.
Chapman, Steve. 2018. "Trump the Wimp." *The Chicago Tribune*, March 16, 2018. https://bit.ly/2nHnfVe.
CNN. 2017. "Van Jones: Trump Is 'President Snowflake.'" *CNN* video, May 18, 2017. https://bit.ly/35VVUPZ.
Cohn, Carol, and Sara Ruddick. 2004. "A Feminist Ethical Perspective on Weapons of Mass Destruction." In *Ethics and Weapons of Mass Destruction: Religious and Secular Perspectives*, edited by Sohail H. Hashmi and Steven P. Lee, pp. 405–35. Cambridge University Press.

Dodd, Matthew. 2004. Reply to "Has Marine Corps Training Gone Soft?" *LeatherNeck*, October 10, 2004. https://bit.ly/2m8rBnK.

Flood, Brian. 2016. "'What's the Worst That Can Happen to These Millennials?' Donald Trump's Campaign Manager Asks Sean Hannity." *The Wrap*, November 17, 2016. https://bit.ly/2majbMN.

Fox News Insider. 2016. "You Crybabies Are Why Trump Won! See Fed-Up Vet's Message to Protesters." *Fox News* article, November 14, 2016. https://bit.ly /2mrauxf.

Gabler, Neal. 2012. "What's Behind the Right's 'Obama Is Gay' Conspiracy." *The Nation*, October 23, 2012. https://bit.ly/2mUnyfd.

Hochschild, Arlie Russell. 2016. *Strangers in Their Own Land: Anger and Mourning on the American Right*. The New Press.

Jaffe, Alexandra, ed. 2009. *Stance: Sociolinguistic Perspectives*. Oxford University Press.

Lakoff, George. 1996. *Moral Politics: What Conservatives Know That Liberals Don't*. University of Chicago Press.

Lima, Cristiano. 2016. "Conway: Anti-Trump Protesters 'Degrade' Presidency." *Politico*, November 16, 2016. https://politi.co/2mLGblH.

Lutz, Catherine. 2002. "Making War at Home in the United States: Militarization and the Current Crisis." *American Anthropologist* 104, no. 3: 723–35.

McQuillan, Karin. 2017. "Obama's Snowflakes." *American Thinker*, March 9, 2017. https://bit.ly/2nHoUtW.

NBC News. 2016. "Meet the Press, November 27, 2016." Online video clip, November 27, 2016. https://nbcnews.to/2orHy9w.

Palahniuk, Chuck. 2005[1996]. *Fight Club*. W. W. Norton.

Schneider, Christian. 2017. "Donald Trump Is America's Snowflake in Chief." *USA Today Opinion*, October 12, 2017. https://bit.ly/2yijCb3.

Smith, Erec. 2019. "Habitat for Inhumanity: How Trolls Set the Stage for @realDonaldTrump." In *President Donald Trump and His Political Discourse: Ramifications of Rhetoric via Twitter*, edited by Michele Lockhart, pp. 131–46. Routledge.

Turner, Victor. [1969]2017. *The Ritual Process: Structure and Anti-Structure*. Routledge.

Wolff, Michael. 2018. *Fire and Fury: Inside the Trump White House*. Little Brown.

Part II

Performance and Falsehood

5   Part II Introduction: The Show Must Go On: Hyperbole and Falsehood in Trump's Performance

Norma Mendoza-Denton

5.1   A Super Stable Genius

"Super Genius Stuff!" is the way that Donald J. Trump has described his natural intellect and his ability to get into "the hardest school in the world," Wharton Business School at the University of Pennsylvania. An in-depth article in the *Washington Post* (Kranish 2019) investigates both of these claims. Was Wharton the hardest school in the world? Not exactly. What is today a 7.4 percent acceptance rate hovered above 40 percent in 1980, and was likely even more generous when Trump attended school in the mid-sixties. Was Trump a (super) genius? Not according to his classmates, nor according to James Nolan, the only University of Pennsylvania admissions officer to have interviewed him before acceptance. Even though Trump has since 1973 claimed (or allowed it to be claimed) that he graduated at the top of his class, his name was nowhere to be found in his graduating class' honorees, nor in the top fifty (Dean's list) of the nearly 400 students who graduated with him that year. But Trump himself is evasive about the veracity of the claim, occasionally implying that it's someone else's assertion that he is merely letting stand (ibid.). It is precisely his couldn't-care-less attitude toward facts and the willingness to use these may-or-may-not-be-facts to manipulate impressions that makes Trump a Frankfurtian bullshitter (in the technical sense of Frankfurt 1986), as Jacquemet points out in his chapter, "45 as a Bullshit Artist" (in this section).

Language scholars in this section of the book elucidate aspects of Trump's behavior that verge on or cross into falsehood, including innuendo, gaslighting, and plausible deniability. Much has been observed about Trump's ever-increasingly tenuous relationship to truth, with commentary from both scholarly and popular writers. In her book *The Death of Truth*, Michiko Kakutani (2018) makes a careful comparison between the linguistic and symbolic practices of Nazi Germany and Trump's administration. She quotes Viktor Klemperer in observing that the "splendor of the banners, the parades, garlands, fanfares, and choruses" was an advertisement for the Führer and served to conflate him with the majesty of his imagined state (Klemperer, quoted in Kakutani 2018: 92). This over-the-top quality also extended to language, where superlatives and hyperbole were so exaggerated that they took on, according to Klemperer, a "fairy tale quality," with Nazis lying about the number of enemies killed, prisoners taken, attendance at rallies, and even how cold the weather was on the fighting field, where Hitler claimed to have outdone Napoleon in Russia by fighting not in minus twenty-five but in minus fifty-two degrees centigrade (ibid.: 93).

5.2   Why Use Hyperbole?

Trump's penchant for hyperbole is strategic and self-aware. In his (ghost-written) book *The Art of the Deal*, he states:

> The . . . key to the way I promote is bravado. I play to people's fantasies. People may not always think big themselves, but they can still get very excited by those who do. That's why a little hyperbole never hurts. People want to believe that something is the biggest and the greatest and the most spectacular. I call it truthful hyperbole. It's an innocent form of exaggeration – and a very effective form of promotion. (Trump 1987: 36)

The classical definition of hyperbole, as advanced by Aristotle ([350 BCE] 2018), has as its domain political speech and is predicated not only on the form but on the content of the speech. Aristotle identified three modes of rhetorical persuasion: *ethos* (credibility established by the good character of the speaker as evidenced in their words and manner), *pathos* (the arousal of emotions in the hearer), and *logos* (the logical construction of proofs by means of argument; Claridge 2010: 217). Although hyperbole is technically possible in all the modes, it is most common in pathos (at a cost to both ethos and logos); Aristotle thought hyperbole juvenile and most likely to be used by angry people. Bringing our consideration of this rhetorical device up to the present time, linguist Claudia Claridge conducted an extensive study of hyperbole in English using corpora – large collections of texts, speeches, and conversations (Claridge 2010). She found that hyperbolic expressions can be used to influence people's opinions, and this is well borne out in the psycholinguistic literature. For instance, in a famous study from the 1970s, it was shown that having an accident described as "one car smashed into another" versus "one car hit another" causes experimental subjects to estimate the speed at which the accident happened as being much greater (Loftus and Palmer 1974), a result that bears tremendous importance in the courtroom and beyond.

Claims that something is the fastest, biggest, best, the most *superlative* in all of history are the kinds of exaggerations to which President Trump is prone.

But why is it important for us to know this? It is because through these exaggerations and turns of phrase, vociferously asserted, Trump manipulates the truth. In his chapter for this volume, Jacquemet contends that Trump does not actually care whether most statements that he makes are technically true or not, as long as they serve his image-building, performative purposes. For the sake of creating an impression in the mind of the public, he can time and again claim that his father was born in Germany (though a birth certificate shows him to have been born in the Bronx [Smokinggun.com 2019]), or he can insistently assert that he had the biggest inauguration crowds, despite both of these claims being debunked every single time they are issued.

Public image is also addressed in the other two chapters in this section. Trump's interactional routines, as Goldstein, Hall, and Ingram remind us, unfold beyond the domain of spoken language. Even in the previous section, we saw how Trump's supporters have a chance at embodying *him* through the "Get Them Out" and crybaby and snowflake discourses (see McIntosh's "Crybabies and Snowflakes" and Sidnell's "'Get 'Em Out!'" chapters, this volume). By pantomiming and caricaturing his opponents, Trump creates spectacles, embodying *his opponents* in a way that is laughable, inviting viewers to mock said opponents with him. These spectacles are squarely in the domain of hyperbole, this time gestural as well as linguistic. These hyperbolic gestural moves share an element with Trump's use of nicknames. By functioning as bodily metonyms (in which some small aspect of the person comes to represent the whole of them), the Food-Shoveling Governor and the Choking Presidential Candidate (Goldstein et al., this volume) share a semiotic space with Little Marco Rubio and Low-Energy Jeb. Through this strategic use of hyperbole, bodily metonyms, and actual nicknames, Trump whips up humor, passion, and the allegiance of his base, structuring both truth and feeling.

5.3   Reactive Reversal

How do people react to Trump's hyperbole? Do they always suspend disbelief and buy what he is selling? How long can he get away with it? Here I identify a discourse sequence that I term "reactive reversal," which hinges on the plausible deniability discussed by Hodges (this volume; see also Carpenter's 2018 description of Trump's "gaslighting" techniques), and which played out in Trump's impeachment proceedings in late 2019. If Trump leaves himself enough room that deniability is plausible, Trump is able to pull back and reverse himself on his claims. Reactive reversal occurs upon public negative reaction or fallout after Trump stakes a hyperbolic claim, which he often follows up by logical extensions, each one staking further territory. Consider the following sequence:

(1) Trump stakes a (hyperbolic) claim, optionally followed up by logical extensions.
(2) A public outcry follows, growing enough to become problematic for administration.
(3) Trump uses plausible deniability and reacts by reversing his claim, pleading total innocence and optionally blaming others or even the listener for the inference.
(4) Trump may triumphantly declare victory over whoever "really" claimed/did what he originally claimed.

This is one of Trump's ways of gauging reaction from the public. Will they go with his claims? If the statement is allowed to stand (perhaps because the news narrative is cacophonous and attention cycles so short), then the statement enters into Trump's stock of agreed-upon assertions. If the first statement gets a strong counter-reaction, then he'll reverse himself and deny the implications of the statement, and sometimes the denial goes so far as to question that the statement was even uttered in the first place. Either way, Trump has gained important information about how far the public is willing to go in supporting his assertions. Reactive reversals are a classic part of Trump's arsenal, and they can be further seen in Hodges' chapter on plausible deniability.

A recent example occurred in an interview between Donald Trump and Fox News, where he stated, of the North Korean leader Kim Jong-un: "He's the head of the country. And I mean he's the strong head. Don't let anyone think anything different. He speaks and his people sit up at attention, I want my people to do the same." Trump then chuckled and made reference to how Kim had fired three of his generals, adding, "Fired may be a nice word" (Stracqualursi and Liptak 2018). Here, Trump is alluding to the fact that Kim Jong-un doesn't merely dismiss his staff, but also reportedly has them executed. Later on, Trump and his press secretary claimed that he was joking (ibid.). George Lakoff calls the first part of this routine sending out a "trial balloon" (Lakoff on Twitter, January 3, 2018). In the press, the disclaimer is sometimes called a "joking-not-joking routine," and is widely thought to be a hallmark of Trumpian humor. Walking back assertions such as these, branding his own press conferences "fake news," or blaming the interpretation of "blood coming out of her wherever" (*CNN* 2015) on the listening public are all examples of reactive reversals. The idea is to risk, to go out on a limb to see how much one might get away with, and when there is a revelation of a response, to retreat into plausible deniability, rank ignorance, or "just joking."

The path leading to reactive reversal has not been Trump's alone, though. In the spring of 2010, Sarah Palin's PAC television spot put rifle sights on a number of Democrats whose districts Republicans were hoping to overturn. While on the campaign trail, Palin followed up these ads with sayings such as,

"Don't retreat, reload!" (CBS 2010). Gabrielle Giffords, whose Arizona district she had pinpointed, had the following to say in a prescient MSNBC March 2010 interview: "[W]e're on Sarah Palin's targeted list, but the thing is that the way that she has it depicted has the crosshairs of a gun-sight over our district, and when people do that, they've gotta realize there are consequences to that action" (MSNBC, *The Daily Rundown*, March 25, 2010).

In January 2011, Giffords was shot in the head by a disgruntled constituent at a meet-your-congressperson event at a grocery store in Tucson, AZ. While Palin's advertisements were widely blamed for stoking the rage of the gunman, both her campaign and supporters replied that the symbols were not crosshairs but a surveyor's symbol, and in any case the gunman's problem was mental illness and not politics (*The Atlantic* 2011). Even before the appearance of Trump as political candidate, aspects of the Trump playbook began to take shape.

As political actors, we the public must remain vigilant when we identify routines such as reactive reversals, the crybaby and snowflake discourse (McIntosh, preceding section), the plausible denials, and the comedic gestures. They represent the typology of public manipulation.

References

Aristotle. [350 BCE]2018. *Aristotle: Rhetoric*. Translated by C. D. C. Reeve. Hackett Publishing Company.

The Atlantic. 2011. "Tragedy in Arizona: The Shooting of Congresswoman Gabrielle Giffords." January 8, 2011. https://bit.ly/2EgwL6H.

Carpenter, Amanda. 2018. *Gaslighting America: Why We Love It When Trump Lies to Us*. Broadside Books.

CBS. 2010. "Palin: Don't Retreat! Reload!" April 9, 2010. https://bit.ly/2RPgeP9.

Claridge, Claudia. 2010. *Hyperbole in English: A Corpus-Based Study of Exaggeration*. Cambridge University Press.

CNN. 2015. "Donald Trump on Megyn Kelly: 'There was Blood Coming out of Her Wherever.'" August 7, 2015. https://bit.ly/2rLCyhN

Frankfurt, Harry. 1986. "On Bullshit." *Raritan* 6, no. 2: 81–100.

Kakutani, Michiko. 2018. *The Death of Truth: Notes on Falsehood in the Age of Trump*. Tim Duggan Books.

Kranish, Michael. 2019. "Trump Has Referred to His Wharton Degree As 'Super Genius Stuff.' An Admissions Officer Recalls it Differently." *The Washington Post*, July 8, 2019. https://wapo.st/2JosRfn.

Lakoff, George (@GeorgeLakoff). 2018. "Trump Uses Social Media as a Weapon to Control the News Cycle." Twitter, January 3, 2018. https://bit.ly/2PNIUoS.

Loftus, E. F., and J. C. Palmer. 1974. "Reconstruction of Auto-Mobile Destruction: An Example of the Interaction between Language and Memory." *Journal of Verbal Learning and Verbal Behavior* 13: 585–89.

MSNBC. 2010. "Dangerous Backlash." *The Daily Rundown*, March 25, 2010.

Smokinggun.com 2019. "Why Has Donald Trump Been Saying That His Father Was Born in Germany?" April 2, 2019. https://bit.ly/38Giltf.

Stracqualursi, Veronica, and Kevin Liptak. 2018. "Trump Says He Wants 'My People' to Sit Up 'At Attention' Like the North Koreans, Later Says He's 'Just Kidding.'" *CNN*, June 15, 2018. https://cnn.it/35jckSl.

Trump, Donald. 1987. *The Art of the Deal*. Ballantine.

6   Trump's Comedic Gestures as Political Weapon

Donna M. Goldstein, Kira Hall, and Matthew Bruce Ingram

6.1   Introduction

This chapter, adapted from Hall, Goldstein, and Ingram (2016),[1] argues that Trump's campaign to become the Republican nominee was successful because it was, in a word, entertaining – not just for his alleged white rural working-class voting bloc,[2] but also for the public at large, even those who strongly opposed his candidacy. Whether understood as pleasing or offensive, Trump's ongoing show was compelling. Our analysis refrains from defining segments of the population as economically, socially, or psychologically vulnerable to Trump's messaging and instead explores why we are all vulnerable. Many good analyses offer insights on Trump's popular appeal, and we draw on some of these discussions here. But we believe it is important to consider the specifics of Trump's entertainment value – that is, how Trump's comedic media appearances over the course of the Republican primary season, and indeed continuing into his presidential term, built momentum in a celebrity and mediatized culture.

Specifically, we consider how Trump elevated his entertainment value by crafting comedic representations of his political opponents as well as himself. These representations take the form of a kind of bodily performance primarily discussed by scholars studying embodied communication. Characterized by several interrelated terms that include *bodily quoting* (Keevallik 2010), *transmodal stylizations* (Goodwin and Alim 2010), *full-body enactments* (Mittelberg 2013), *gestural reenactments* (Sidnell 2006), *pantomime* (Streeck 2008a), *demonstrations* (Clark 1996), and *ventriloquizing* (Tannen 2010), these performances involve the dramaturgical replaying of an actual or imagined event, action, or behavior (cf. Goffman 1974), often by assuming another's alleged subjectivity. Trump's impersonations of political opponents are most clearly seen in his campaign rallies. Through the use of gestural methods, Trump reduces others to laughable portrayals while elevating himself. During the Republican primaries, some of Trump's more notorious gestural enactments (as we call them here) included contorted wrist and facial movements when rebuking a disabled reporter (Trump 2015a); downward hand chops and sidewise throat slices to convey how ISIS has treated American citizens (Trump 2015b); and a slumped torso with closed eyes to depict Republican competitor Jeb Bush (Trump 2015b). Many of these enactments were repeated across multiple campaign speeches and became emblems of the political persona that Trump presented to his electorate. The media's conflicted response to the social meaning of these bodily displays, together with Trump's easy deniability of what he intended by them, suggests that comedic gesture may accomplish ideological work that exceeds even what can be conveyed in the already protected category of verbal humor.

The electoral allure of Trump's "grotesque body" – to borrow a phrase used by Mikhail Bakhtin (1984) to describe the subversive humor of the medieval marketplace – suggests that scholarship on society as well as gesture may benefit from a deeper consideration of comedic entertainment as an effective persuasive strategy at this transitional moment in US political history. Trump's enactments received unprecedented attention during the campaign by inspiring countless news discussions, video compilations, and comedy skits, many of which we reviewed for the writing of this chapter. Together we observed twenty-seven hours of video data to make the claims expressed here, with nineteen of those hours coming from campaign speeches delivered in sixteen different locations. We argue that Trump's humor worked because it incorporates that central Bakhtinian trope of vulgarity. In Trump we find a Rabelaisian character that deploys bawdy humor to entertain his audience. He provides carnivalesque moments as he pokes fun at other candidates, at their bodies, at their fluids, at their stiffness. Like Rabelais, Trump understood that crude humor has the power to bring down the princely classes – aka, the political establishment – as well as anyone who opposed him. He used it to advance the "antipolitics politics" that has been building in the US public sphere since at least the early 1990s. Viewers stayed amazed by Trump's expressions of physical disgust regarding the embodiment of others, whether in reaction to Megyn Kelly's menstruation, Hillary Clinton's toilet behaviors, or Marco Rubio's sweating. By reducing his opponents to exaggerated bodily behaviors and habits, Trump assumed the position of a Rabelaisian clown, bringing down the old guard by exposing the grotesque body beneath. This strategy is key to understanding the political effectiveness of Trump's gestural enactments in the 2016 presidential campaign and beyond.

6.2   Trump's Gestures as Comedic Entertainment

Trump's gestures during the Republican primaries deviated from the gestural rules and constraints that have dominated the American political arena by bringing to politics a bodily style more prominently seen in entertainment venues. Consider Trump's use of the pistol hand during his stump speeches. In a speech in Raleigh, North Carolina, Trump abruptly interrupts a woman as she asks, "I was wondering what you would say to President Obama . . ." with the reply, "You're fired!" (Trump 2015b). The performative has a vulgar emphasis on the [f] as he throws his index finger forward (see Figure 6.1) to make the shape of a gun. The crowd gets the allusion to Trump's role as an entertainer and irrupts explosively into cheers, whistles, and screams.

Trump's use of this gesture can be traced back to his boardroom executive persona on *The Apprentice* (see Figure 6.2), and before that to his involvement with professional wrestling, an entertainment genre in which competitors craft a persona through a particular move that is packaged for fan consumption through staged comedic routines of violence. When Trump used the pistol hand on *The Apprentice* to fire unworthy contestants (where producers called it "the Cobra"; Grynbaum and Parker 2016), it conveyed arrogance, sovereign power, and commanding force. Trump is the kind of guy who will never admit to his own failures and rarely gives others a second chance. In his Raleigh stump speech, Trump brings this meaning to the realm of competitive politics. The gesture is understood through the iconicity of its production (that is, its physical resemblance to what it stands for), where swiftness and precision accompany a gun shape in the striking down of an unworthy opponent. Yet the gesture is

Figure 6.1 Trump's Pistol Hand gesture. AP Photo/Ted Richardson.

Figure 6.2 Trump's Pistol Hand gesture, *The Apprentice* 2006. AP Photo/ Stuart Ramson.

also playful: When Trump thrusts his hand forward to mimic the firing of a gun, he converts the sovereign force behind the performative "you're fired" into comedic appeal. He brings a child's pantomime of shooting an enemy – the use of hands to imitate the action of killing – to the firing of an adult in an entrepreneurial battle. The repeated image of a grown man using the pantomime of a child's gun-hand to dismiss contestants ("Bang! You're dead") functions as comedy. Celebrity businessman and politician are brought together in a playful image of executive power.

   A comparison between this highly emblematic gesture and those normatively used by presidential candidates reveals the semiotic limitations of politics-as-usual. Trump's pistol hand is depictive, a show move, flashy. Typical gestures used by presidential candidates are didactic and emphatic, used as accompaniments to speech to promote clarity. Jürgen Streeck (2008b) observed in his analysis of gestures used in the 2004 Democratic presidential primary that candidates avoid pictorially oriented depictive gestures (also called *iconics* in McNeill's [1992] taxonomy). He notes that even as early as the first century CE, the Roman orator Quintilian was critical of these gestures, viewing them as theatrical and lacking rhetorical gravitas. Instead, presidential candidates tend to use *interactive* or *pragmatic gestures* (Bavelas et al. 1992, Kendon 2004), hand movements such as beats or points that do not depict the social world but rather accentuate or illustrate the rhetorical structure of a speech. Pragmatic gestures are now the subject of a growing body of research on political style, which includes analyses of Barack Obama's precision-grip (Lempert 2011) and Howard Dean's indexical point (Streeck 2008b). But the depictive gestures deployed by Trump – especially the type that caricatures opponents by embodying a behavior or activity associated with them – rarely surface in the same literature. How do we explain the success of Trump's divergence from what appears to be normative gestural behavior for politicians seeking the Oval Office?

We make sense of Trump's gestural repertoire by viewing it as part of a comedic political style that accrues entertainment value as it opposes the usual bodily habits expected of US presidential candidates (cf. Jamieson and Taussig 2017 on Trump's rhetorical signature). When used in coordination with verbal strategies similarly designed to lampoon opponents, Trump's enactments craft stereotyped and reductive characterizations of identity categories – essentialized representations – that simultaneously cast their members as problematic citizens, whether Democrat, disabled, lower class, Mexican, Black, or female. These depictive gestures operate across a range of contexts to signal that he challenges what is widely viewed by Trump's base as the political establishment's debilitating rhetoric of political correctness. When Trump promises to tell the "truth" (e.g. Muslims are terrorists; some women are uglier than others; Mexicans are rapists), he aligns himself with an increasingly well-organized right-wing opposition to political correctness, rejecting rhetorical caution regarding minority religions, genders, and ethnicities. Yet as entertainment, his gestures intensify the force of his words, attracting and holding the attention of the wider public as they dominate the news cycle.

6.3   Trump's Gestures as Political Ideology

Depictive enactments are formed by incorporating bodily knowledge of the social world, abstracting qualities exhibited by the targeted object such as height, weight, shape, and speed (LeBaron and Streeck 2000, Mittelberg and Waugh 2014, Streeck 2008a). Because this incorporation is selective, such bodily acts may produce a kind of social meaning that is ideological (see also Bucholtz and Hall 2016). For instance, Trump's use of a firing squad gesture (see Figure 6.3) does not merely resemble the action of execution; it also unites moral and material worlds to critique Obama as losing ground, being weak in confronting terrorism, and making poor deals. When imitating a firing squad in a campaign speech in Greensboro, North Carolina (Trump 2016a), Trump registered a critique against the US government for exchanging five Guantanamo prisoners for Sergeant Bergdahl, a US army soldier captured in

Figure 6.3 Trump's Firing Squad gesture. Johny Louis/Film Magic via Getty Images.

Afghanistan and thought by some to be guilty of desertion if not treason. "In the old days," Trump says, "you know what would have happened to him, right?"; then he pauses to enact the sideways firing of a rifle as if part of a firing squad. When performing this same routine in a campaign speech in Doral, Florida (Trump 2015c), he repeats the gesture twice before professing his love for the Second Amendment. The gesture materializes both a time period and a moral position that preceded political correctness, when corporal punishment for betrayal was acceptable practice. In this way, gestural enactments have much in common with what linguistic anthropologists and sociolinguists such as Niko Besnier (1993) and Deborah Tannen (1986) have identified for reported speech: They are citations disguised as quotes that "leak" the citer's own imagining of social life and the ideologies that constitute it. Even the most conventionalized of depictive gestures map broader societal discourses onto movements of the body, transforming these discourses into an action.

For many viewers, the exaggerated displays that we outline in this chapter recall a moment-to-moment reality television star whose character role is built on spontaneity. Linguist Jennifer Sclafani has observed that Trump is "turning political discourse into reality TV," noting in particular the way he uses large gestures to remind viewers of his "big personality" (cited in Atkin 2015; see also Sclafani 2018). Sclafani is not alone in noticing an iconic relationship between Trump's gestures and Trump's personality: Certainly, widely circulating metacommentary on the meaning of Trump's gestures play off this reading (Taylor-Coleman and Bressanin 2016, Bloomberg Politics 2016, Civiello 2016, Rozzo 2016). Donald Trump has done for presidential campaigns what Jerry Springer did for tabloid talk shows: he has inserted a level of lowbrow drama, humor, and violence into the genre through exaggerated appeals to the body. Trump's body matters to advocates as well as opponents. To advocates, Trump's gestures suggest a man who is spontaneous and real instead of scripted. He is an unplanned man, even an honest man, who tells it how he sees it. To opponents, Trump's gestures suggest a man who is vulgar if not offensive. They reveal a different sort of spontaneity: a buffoon, even a fake, who only poses as a politician.

Trump exploits both kinds of attention when he uses bodily performance to characterize the less competent behaviors of political opponents. This strategy is an important one for an entertainer new to politics; above all, it enables Trump to reposition the job experience of his opponents as a drawback instead of a qualification. Tellingly, the most common enactments used by Trump for established politicians involve the performance of small or restricted gestural space. Although gesture scholars often discuss gestural space (the personal space appropriated in the execution of gesturing) as a matter of individual, cultural, and contextual concerns (McNeill 1992, Sweetser and Sizemore 2008), Trump's essentializing poses, repeated multiple times across campaign speeches, make it clear that gestural space can also be a matter of ideology (Hoenes del Pinal 2011, Lakoff 1992). They include the performance of a hunched body reading from a script for Hillary Clinton (see Figure 6.4), a stiff upper body for Mitt Romney (see Figure 6.5), and a huddled sleeping body for Jeb Bush (see Figure 6.6).

With depictions like these, Trump uses gestural space to drive home his critique of the political establishment. The discourse goes something like this: Politicians are people who do not act, who are not business people, and who do not know real risk. When mapped onto a restricted torso, an elite political class materializes as bookish, stiff, lackluster, and – perhaps most critically to Trump's identity as an entertainer – boring. The mimicked gestural spaces of his opponents contrast sharply with the gestural space Trump inhabits in his own persona. Excessive gestural space is often negatively associated with recurring representations of social groups (e.g. the flamboyant gay man, the sassy Black woman), but Trump uses gestural excess to convey the impression he is a new kind of politician, unconstrained by petty rules and competent at accomplishing daunting tasks. His performance of a large gestural space thereby becomes acceptable, if not politically desirable. In effect, Trump has expanded the space allowed for political gesture (at least for outsider politicians like himself).

Figure 6.4 Script-Reading Hillary. AP Photo/Ted S. Warren.

Figure 6.5 Stiff Mitt Romney. AP Photo/Chris O'Meara.

Figure 6.6 Low-Energy Jeb. AP Photo/Alan Diaz.

Trump's gestural enactments function similarly to nicknames, crafting a reductive representation of the referent that purportedly captures some essential truth. In the early anthropological literature, nicknames were discussed as part of the brick and mortar of local social systems (Pitt-Rivers [1954]1961, Cohen 1977, Gilmore 1982, McDowell 1981). But nicknames also form part of an oblique naming system that belongs to comedic insult and "can be understood as a play upon form: that is, as a joke, or rather, the punchline of a joke" (Blok 2001: 157). In other words, the purpose of a nickname is not just to mock but also to entertain. In the new political process orchestrated by a comedic billionaire, the public watched as Trump rolled out nicknames for each successive opponent. The gestural enactments were initially coarticulated with verbal nicknames such as "Low-energy Jeb" (Trump 2015d) but later took on their own independence as detachables (cf. Spitulnik

1996) that could recall the verbal nickname independently of speech. In Bakhtinian perspective, this naming process accomplishes something important: Nicknames connect the subject to the grotesque body, thus becoming comic and provoking hilarity. By mocking the subject and making the named person look foolish, nicknames give special powers to the provider. After all, the one who is the master of nicknaming is the person declaring the public secret.

6.4   Trump's Gestures as Political Weapon

We turn now to five widely mediatized gestural enactments that display Trump's antagonism to political correctness by invoking discourses of disability, class, immigration, race, and gender, respectively. As we would expect for nicknames waged in the modality of gesture, these enactments reduce a target perceived as an opponent to an action of the body: the Wrist-Flailing Reporter, the Food-Shoveling Governor, the Border-Crossing Mexican, the Choking Presidential Candidate, and the Wobbling Democratic Nominee. Trump's bodily parodies deliver the message that he rejects progressive social expectations regarding how minority groups should be represented. In each case, the media responded by moving away from an initial critical stance to a discussion of the meaning conveyed by Trump's body.

6.4.1   *The Wrist-Flailing Reporter*

One of the most cited of Trump's gestural spectacles involves a full-body enactment of the *Washington Post* reporter Serge Kovaleski. Trump quoted Kovaleski on the campaign trail as saying fourteen years earlier that Muslims were celebrating in response to 9/11 (Trump 2015e), an allegation Kovaleski denied. At a rally in Myrtle Beach, South Carolina (Trump 2015a), Trump responded to this denial by framing Kovaleski as one of many "incompetent dopes" together with the president, politicians, and journalists. The theme of the speech is thus about incompetence. As with the firing squad example, Trump's speech is particularly focused on the ineptitude wrought by political correctness, which in his view keeps politicians from speaking the truth and doing the right thing. But Kovaleski also happens to be afflicted by a muscular condition that involves contracture of the body muscles and joints. In his full-bodied depiction of Kovaleski (AP Television 2016), Trump transforms a discourse of incompetence into the action of flailing, limp wrists (see Figure 6.7a–c) and produces a multimodal image depictive of disability. (Owing to space constraints, the images included in Excerpts 1–3 capture only a single frame of the extended depictive gestures used in these enactments; Trump also uses a number of pragmatic gestures that we do not notate in the transcripts. In addition, we have selected a few transcription conventions to represent the sound of Trump's speech, among them underlining for emphasis [e.g. 'y<u>ea</u>rs'] and letter repetition for vowel lengthening [e.g. 'smaaall']).

Excerpt 1 The Wrist-Flailing Reporter

Figure 6.7a Wrist-Flailing Reporter. AP Television.

Figure 6.7b Wrist-Flailing Reporter. AP Television.

Figure 6.7c Wrist-Flailing Reporter. AP Television.

Written by a nice reporter. Now the poor guy, you gotta see this guy. ((*Mimics Kovaleski's voice and actions.*)) ["Uhaaaaaaaaaaaa I don't know what I said uhaaaaaa!][6.7a] [I don't remember!"][6.7b] He's going like ["I don't remember uh doh, maybe that's what I said."][6.7c] ((*He returns to his own voice, shouting.*)) This is fourteen years ago he still – They didn't do a retraction? Fourteen years ago, they did no retraction.

In this excerpt, a perceived opponent is represented by a flailing body (uncontrolled, limp-wristed movements), facial contortions (rounded o-lip), and incoherent speech (loud elongated vocalizations produced in the back of the throat). The depiction thus produces a recognizable emblem in US popular culture of physical and mental disability. Gestures may sometimes be used in place of speech to displace responsibility for taboo topics (see, e.g. Brookes' 2011 discussion of a three-finger gesture used in South Africa for "HIV"), but the highly negative public response to Trump's enactment suggests that this gesture cannot easily escape its performative associations. Yet Trump was nevertheless able to deny this interpretation in a follow-up statement: "I have no idea who Serge Kovaleski is, what he looks like, or his level of intelligence. I merely mimicked what I thought would be a flustered reporter trying to get out of a statement he made long ago. I have tremendous respect for people who are physically challenged" (BBC News 2015). Trump thus retroactively characterizes his act as "mimicry," but he denies the public interpretation of that mimicry as a biographically specific impersonation targeting a category of disabled persons. Although the media response was initially condemning, Trump's defense transformed the critique into an interpretive discussion.

Regardless of the relationship between the performance and the object depicted, Trump moved political discourse to a new place by highlighting gestural ambiguity through comedic routine.

6.4.2   The Food-Shoveling Governor

A second gestural enactment that caught the attention of the media is Trump's depiction of Ohio governor John Kasich shoveling a pancake into his mouth (see Figures 6.8a–d), which was performed at a rally in Warwick, Rhode Island (Trump 2016b) in response to widely circulated images of Kasich eating at a New York restaurant (e.g. Tani 2016). The depiction invites comparison with the Wrist-Flailing Reporter, except that it draws from discourses of social class instead of disability. (Again, the images below, taken from The Free Beacon 2016, are provided as single-frame examples of the main gestural depictions used in the excerpt.)

Excerpt 2 The Food-Shoveling Governor

Figure 6.8a Food-Shoveling gesture. MSNBC.

Figure 6.8b Small Bites gesture. MSNBC.

Figure 6.8c Big Pancake gesture. MSNBC.

Figure 6.8d Food-Stuffing gesture. MSNBC.

Now you look at Kasich, I don't think he knows what – you know, did you see him? He has a news conference [all the time when he's eating.]⁶·⁸ᵃ ((*Crowd laughs.*)) I have never seen a human being eat in such a disgusting fashion. ((*Crowd laughs and cheers.*)) I'm always telling my young son Barron, I'm saying – and I always with my kids, all of 'em – [I'd say, "Children, smaaall little bites,]⁶·⁸ᵇ small." ((*Crowd laughs.*)) This guy [takes a pancake]⁶·⁸ᶜ and he's [shoving it in his mouth]⁶·⁸ᵈ you know. ((*Crowd laughs and cheers.*)) It's disgusting. Do you want that for your president? I don't think so. ((*Crowd boos "no!"*)) I don't think so. It's disgu – honestly, it's disgusting.

In this dramatization of Kasich's table manners, we are again confronted by a display of discomfort with "nonnormative" bodies. It is well known that Trump avoided the fray of vernacular embodiment on the campaign trail by rarely eating with locals, even though this activity is expected of presidential candidates. In fact, Trump is famous for eating even fast food with a knife and a fork (e.g. Zaru 2016). Anthropologists familiar with the work of Norbert Elias (1982) and Pierre Bourdieu (1984) on the importance of table manners to class distinction would recognize Trump's enactment as a veiled class assault:

Kasich is a slob, a lowlife, a "sub-human" who would have difficulty being presidential. Trump, in contrast, is a man who teaches his children to exhibit good manners and eat politely in "small bites." When returning to this same routine later in the speech, Trump illustrates that even his youngest child (named Barron) knows that Kasich's behavior is wrong: "He said, 'Daddy, look!' I said, 'Don't watch. Little bites, little bites'" (Trump 2016b). Trump performs versions of this routine in several campaign venues (e.g. Trump 2016c). Each time, as in the above excerpt, the crowd's laughter, cheers, and boos suggest alignment with Trump's perspective, even as he portrays Kasich as eating like a pig.

We again turn to the power of entertainment to understand the rhetorical effects of Trump's display. His stint on Kasich incorporates recognizable techniques from impromptu stand-up comedy: He performs the voices of others as prompts for mockery (his young son), involves the audience through call-and-response ("Did you see him?" "Do you want that for your president?"), and uses a repetitive verbal refrain to thematize a mocking stance toward his target ("disgusting"). Perhaps most critically, he employs the method of abjection (Kristeva 1982) by characterizing a fellow candidate's eating habits as a kind of corporeal "horror" that betrays unfitness for presidential office. Trump creates the caricature of Kasich by assuming the roles of punishing father and naughty son, with Kasich in the role of the latter. In sum, these cross-modal stylizations provide the ground for the rhetorical call-and-response that comedic routine relies on while also signaling the inability of Kasich to perform competently as president.

6.4.3   The Border-Crossing Mexican

Trump has developed a series of depictive gestures that coordinate with his promise to build a wall at the Mexican border. These depictions work together to construe Mexicans as bodies out of place. The "huuuge" wall that Trump performs in several campaign speeches (e.g. Trump 2016d) – wide out-stretched arms to illustrate width, tall upright arms to illustrate height, a sharp L-shaped drawing pattern to illustrate strength – positions Mexicans as migrating invaders who need to be stopped. In a campaign rally in Harrisburg, Pennsylvania (Trump 2016d), Trump even performed a gestural enactment of Mexicans as "candy grabbers" when discussing outsourcing (with fingers pulling toward the palm), again suggesting a greedy people who put their hands in places they do not belong ("Mexico has been taking your companies like it's candy from a baby, right?"). With these and related gestures, Trump expresses disdain for individuals whose lives are structured around migration.

A prominent media spectacle during the Republican primary season was a video broadcast of Trump disembarking from his car, climbing through a fence to cross over a concrete structure, and walking across a field to enter the back door of a stadium surrounded by protesters in San Francisco, California (NBC Bay Area 2016). When he finally arrives at the podium of the California GOP convention, knowing that his actions are being followed in real-time on cable news, Trump leads his audience in laughter by comparing his trek to "crossing the border" (Trump 2016e). His darkly satirical portrayal draws its humor from the absurd image of Trump the billionaire in the role of a border-crossing Mexican immigrant. This enactment differs from the previous two examples in that it is a reinterpretation of Trump's own bodily movements televised earlier. Yet the performance has all the elements of comedy. It turns something tragic and deadly for so many who attempt the crossing into something funny, and even absurd (Goldstein [2003]2013). A privileged well-dressed body is reimagined in the role of impoverished migrant: Trump-the-immigrant crossing dangerous regions filled with protesters in order to get to his podium.

6.4.4   The Choking Presidential Candidate

The three preceding examples reveal the rhetorical strength of Trump's gestural enactments. A stylistics of comedy shrouded Trump's movements in ambiguity, enabling supporters to position his actions as humor instead of cruelty. And in each case, the media responded by putting Trump's movements on trial, recirculating the offending videos while commentators debated Trump's "true" intentions. Sociocultural linguists using the method of ethnography have amply shown that social meaning is never singular. The determination of what a sign "means" in the social world is cultivated diversely across social groups as speakers engage in everyday practice.

Our fourth example illuminates how the 2016 presidential election, perhaps more than any other, exposed the disunity in American society with respect to semiotic interpretation, particularly across racial lines (see also Rosa and Bonilla 2017). This became acutely apparent in divergent interpretations of a choking gesture performed by Trump in Rome, New York on April 12, 2016 (Trump 2016f; see Figure 6.9a). In the preceding month at a campaign rally in Portland, Maine (Trump 2016g), Trump had characterized Mitt Romney, the Republican presidential candidate who lost to Obama in 2012, as a "choke artist." This attack surfaced shortly after Romney, in a widely publicized speech at Utah's Hinckley Institute, identified Trump as a threat to the country's future and

Figure 6.9a Choking Mitt Romney, Rome, New York 2016. LesGrossman News Video 2016.

Figure 6.9b Choking Republican Competitors, Oklahoma City, Oklahoma 2015. AP Photo/J Pat Carter.

urged Republicans to choose a different candidate. In Portland, Trump explained his choice of the term "choke artist" with characteristic hyperbole: "Mitt is a failed candidate. He failed. He failed horribly. He failed badly." The use of a choking metaphor to illustrate losing – or in this case, political death – was not new to Trump. He had used it at a 2015 Oklahoma City rally (Trump 2015f; that time accompanied by a choking gesture) when characterizing his Republican competitors as "losers" (see Figure 6.9b).

But for audiences who had been attentive to the death of Eric Garner at the hands of New York City police in 2014, there was something newly sinister about Trump's use of this gesture at his campaign rally in New York. Garner, a Black cigarette salesman, was killed on the street in 2014 by a police officer who used an illegal chokehold and ignored Garner's pleas. Garner's final words, "I can't breathe," repeated eleven times in the video recording that later emerged from a friend's mobile phone (*The Guardian* 2014), came to stand for the incident. The expression was thus well known to New Yorkers by the time Trump's rally took place. In fact, the global network Black Lives Matter had adopted Garner's final words as a slogan against police violence and as a call to action. Yet in spite of the phrase's notoriety, Trump introduced it into his New York routine when describing how Romney had "choked like a dog" in the previous election. Wrapping his hands around his neck, sticking out his tongue, and bobbing his head, Trump added the words "I can't breathe, I can't breathe" to his routine – allegedly imitating what an imaginary Romney would have said when losing the election to candidate Obama. Many progressive viewers, and especially African Americans, understood the gesture as a thinly veiled attempt to attract New York supporters who would hear the racist dog whistle connecting Romney's choking to Garner's choking (Roland 2017; see also Goldstein and Hall 2017, Maskovsky 2017). Here again, the ambiguity of a comedic gestural form incited debate regarding the form's "true" meaning (e.g. The Young Turks 2016). For some audiences, the performance benignly positioned Trump as a winner, as someone who, unlike Romney, doesn't lose – or "choke." For others, the performance was a mocking reference to Garner's death, calling out to racist supporters behind the disguise of political theater.

6.4.5   The Wobbling Democratic Nominee

The final gestural enactment we analyze in this chapter, performed by Trump just five weeks before the national election, was perhaps his most effective. Exploiting stereotypes surrounding aging women (see also Bordo 2017), the impersonation caricatured the Democratic presidential candidate Hillary Clinton as physically weak. "She has been a disaster," Trump states at an early October campaign rally in Manheim,

Pennsylvania (Trump 2016h). "Here's a woman, she is supposed to fight all these different things, and she can't make it 15 feet to her car. Give me a break." In the performance that follows (see Figure 6.10a–c), Trump teeters side to side, mocking Clinton as unable to be stable on her feet. He continues this mimicry as he moves out from behind the podium, slowly hunching over while walking and fading downward as if to exit the stage. "Give me a break," he says again to a cheering crowd as he stands back up and tosses his wrists outward in dismissive gesture, bonding with an audience who could now visualize the lack of stamina he had projected onto Clinton throughout his campaign. Trump had been using the gendered term "stamina" in reference to Clinton since at least 2015 ("No strength, no *stamina*, she cannot lead us"; Trump 2015b). In late September 2016, just one week before his Manheim performance, Trump brought this term with him to the nationally televised First Presidential Debate: "She doesn't have the presidential look. She doesn't have the stamina … To be president of this country, you need tremendous stamina." But it was not until Trump upgraded this evaluation to pantomime in the Manheim rally that Trump's rhetoric fully caught the attention of the broader public.

Excerpt 3 The Wobbling Democratic Nominee

Figure 6.10a Swooning Hillary Clinton. AP Television.

Figure 6.10b Swooning Hillary Clinton. AP Television.

Figure 6.10c Swooning Hillary Clinton. AP Television.

As with many of these impersonations, the source of Trump's display was a video recording that this time featured Clinton in the distance wobbling to her van after a ceremony commemorating the fifteenth anniversary of 9/11 (BBC News 2016). Clinton's physician later revealed that she had been diagnosed with pneumonia shortly before this event (Martin and Chozick 2016). Her wobbling body – or the "worrisome wobble," as some commentators came to call it (Warnke 2016) – was a highly citable form, casting doubt on her ability to be president while affirming for many the sexist stereotype that Trump had already built into his comedic routines. In the end, Trump's performance drew broad attention to a video that may have otherwise faded from the public's notice, with news outlets circulating Trump's impersonation alongside the video that inspired it. By aligning Clinton with weakness and illness (Neville-Shepard and Nolan 2019), Trump's unsteady feet and hunching back fed the fears of an electorate who already had doubts about electing a female president. But even as Trump called attention to Clinton's gender by connecting her to physical weakness, the sexism behind this representation could be plausibly denied as simply a "fact" about the health of a presidential contender. Five weeks later, propelled by the gestural insults analyzed in this chapter, Donald Trump became the forty-fifth president of the United States.

6.5   Conclusion

Trump's one-upmanship form of humor reinforces his superiority to those he critiques, a process noted by laughter theorist Henri Bergson (1921) almost a hundred years ago. His gestural enactments produce the comedic callousness that is central to his political persona. The emblematic gesture that accompanies "You're Fired!" lacks the power to have any effect on the status of Trump's political competitors, making it all the more comical for its absurdity. This explains why commentators posting about Trump's pistol hand on video sharing platforms, such as YouTube, indicate a playful enjoyment of the gesture even when they do not necessarily agree with its message ("Not a fan of him at all. But honestly, that was actually funny"; Live Satellite News 2015). It also explains why audience members at a campaign rally in Madison, Alabama (Trump 2016i), break into uproarious laughter when Trump fires his pistol hand three times at a random plane flying overhead ("What is that? Oh. Uh oh, it's ISIS, get them down!"), and why audience members laugh in Manchester, New Hampshire (Trump 2016j), when Trump points to another plane and suggests it might be carrying Mexicans. These are packaged comedy routines, cliché gags, and shticks. If Trump brags about his ability to deliver a speech without a teleprompter ("I don't really need those notes because I don't need notes. Aren't I lucky?"; Trump 2016j), it is because he knows how to exploit what is unfolding in the world around him as a comedic prompt. Specifically, he incorporates the immediate environment into the performance of his own comparative competence. Trump's gestural enactments, as with parody more generally, exhibit a dual social meaning that points to the teller of the joke as much as to its target (Hill 1998; cf. Hall 2005). They may denigrate a social group by linking them to stereotyped body movements, but they also point back to him as a fun-loving guy who breaks the rules to enjoy a good joke. In short, Trump's body becomes a spectacle that resembles stand-up comedy, where politically correct language and sensitive topics are breached for entertaining effects.

Throughout the 2016 presidential campaign cycle, circulating videos of the verbal and gestural enactments discussed in this chapter kept Trump at the forefront of national attention. As each day of the campaign passed, news consumers wanted to know: Who did Trump offend this time? The question we pursue in this chapter is a relatively uncharted area for gesture studies: How do Trump's bodily acts keep supporters as well as adversaries coming back for more? Scholars working on conversational interaction provide one possible answer by illustrating how gestural enactments elicit heightened displays of attention, build a form of shared common ground, enlist coparticipation, and provoke laughter (Sidnell 2006, Thompson and Suzuki 2014). This body of research offers empirical support to Bergson's early characterization of gesture as "something explosive, which awakens our sensibility when on the point of being lulled to sleep and, by thus rousing us up, prevents our taking matters seriously" (1921: 144). Perhaps it is true that Trump has become America's newest "guilty pleasure" (Grossman 2015), dominating newsrooms, comedy sketches, social media, classrooms, and everyday conversation. Through these bodily per-formances, Trump creates a spectacle to be consumed. It does not matter whether the spectacle is respected, simply tolerated, or even abhorred, the outcome remains the same: *We keep on watching.*

Notes

1. We have adapted this chapter from an essay published by *HAU: Journal of Ethnographic Theory* shortly before the 2016 presidential election (Hall, Goldstein, and Ingram 2016). Some sections of this chapter are taken directly from the original publication, but we include a new analysis of two additional gestural enactments performed by Trump during the primaries that we believe respectively embody discourses of race and gender: a choking gesture to caricature Mitt Romney and a wobbling gesture to caricature Hillary Clinton.
2. Although scholars, journalists, pollsters, and the media have repeatedly referred to Trump's "white rural working-class voting bloc," there is more complexity to Trump's enduring base than suggested by this simple reduction. See, for example, Goldstein and Hall (2017), Smith (2017), and Walley (2017).

References

AP Television. 2016. "Trump Appears to Mock Reporter." Online video. November 26, 2016. https://bit.ly/34myFNA.

Atkin, Emily. 2015. "What Language Experts Find So Strange about Donald Trump." *Think Progress*, September 15, 2015. https://bit.ly/33atf9k.

Bakhtin, Mikhail. 1984. *Rabelais and His World*. Translated by Helene Iswolsky. Indiana University Press.

Bavelas, Janet Beavin, Nicole Chovil, Douglas A. Lawrie, and Allan Wade. 1992. "Interactive Gestures." *Discourse Processes* 15, no. 4: 469–89.

BBC News. 2015. "Donald Trump Denies Mocking Disabled Reporter." November 27, 2015. www.bbc.com/news/world-us-canada-34940861.

2016. "Hillary Clinton 'Stumbles' at 9/11 Event." Online video. September 12, 2016. https://www.youtube.com/watch?v=Onb88xnMlo8.

Bergson, Henri. 1921. *Laughter: An Essay on the Meaning of the Comic*. Translated by Cloudesley Brereton and Fred Rothwell. The Macmillan Company.

Besnier, Niko. 1993. "Reported Speech and Affect on Nukulaelae Atoll." In *Responsibility and Evidence in Oral Discourse*, edited by Jane H. Hill and Judith T. Irvine, pp. 161–81. Cambridge University Press.

Blok, Anton. 2001. *Honour and Violence*. Polity Press.

Bloomberg Politics. 2016. "Donald Trump's Hand Gestures: A Huge List." *Bloomberg* video, April 19, 2016. https://bloom.bg/2kVYovJ.

Bordo, Susan. 2017. *The Destruction of Hillary Clinton*. Melville House Publishing.

Bourdieu, Pierre. 1984. *Distinction: A Social Critique of the Judgment of Taste*. Translated by Richard Nice. Harvard University Press.

Brookes, Heather. 2011. "*Amangama Amathathu* 'The Three Letters': The Emergence of a Quotable Gesture (Emblem)." *Gesture* 11, no. 2: 194–218.

Bucholtz, Mary, and Kira Hall. 2016. "Embodied Sociolinguistics." In *Sociolinguistics: Theoretical Debates*, edited by Nikolas Coupland, pp. 173–200. Cambridge University Press.

Civiello, Mary. 2016. "The Brilliance behind Donald's Trump's Wild Hand Gestures." *Fortune*, April 30, 2016. http://fortune.com/2016/04/30/donald-trump-hands/.

Clark, Herbert H. 1996. *Using Language*. Cambridge University Press.

Cohen, Eugene N. 1977. "Nicknames, Social Boundaries, and Community in an Italian Village." *International Journal of Contemporary Sociology* 14: 102–13.

Elias, Norbert. 1982. *The Civilizing Process, Volume 1: The History of Manners*. Translated by Edmund Jephcott. Pantheon Books.

The Free Beacon. 2016. "Trump Rips Kasich Eating Style: 'I Have Never Seen a Human Being Eat in Such a Disgusting Fashion.'" Online video. April 25, 2016. www.youtube.com/watch?v=kDOWzQGu8Oc. (Fair Dealings, Transformative Use.)

Gilmore, David D. 1982. "Some Notes on Community Nicknaming in Spain." *Man* 17, no. 4: 686–700.

Goffman, Erving. 1974. *Frame Analysis: An Essay on the Organization of Experience*. Harvard University Press.

Goldstein, Donna M. [2003]2013. *Laughter out of Place: Race, Class, Violence, and Sexuality in a Rio Shantytown*. University of California Press.

Goldstein, Donna M., and Kira Hall. 2017. "Postelection Surrealism and Nostalgic Racism in the Hands of Donald Trump." *HAU: Journal of Ethnographic Theory* 6, no. 4: 397–406.

Goodwin, Marjorie Harness, and H. Samy Alim. 2010. "'Whatever (Neck Roll, Eye Roll, Teeth Suck)': The Situated Coproduction of Social Categories and Identities

Through Stancetaking and Transmodal Stylization." *Journal of Linguistic Anthropology* 20, no. 1: 179–94.

Grossman, Seth. 2015. "Donald Trump, Our Reality TV Candidate." *The New York Times*, September 26, 2015. https://nyti.ms/2kWstLH.

Grynbaum, Michael, and Ashley Parker. 2016. "Donald Trump the Political Showman, Born on 'The Apprentice.'" *The New York Times*, July 16, 2016. https://nyti.ms/38BkoA6.

The Guardian. 2014. "'I Can't Breathe': Eric Garner Put in Chokehold by NYPD Officer – Video." Online video. December 4, 2014. www.theguardian.com/us-news/video/2014/dec/04/i-cant-breathe-eric-garner-chokehold-death-video.

Hall, Kira. 2005. "Intertextual Sexuality: Parodies of Class, Identity, and Desire in Liminal Delhi." *Journal of Linguistic Anthropology* 15, no. 1: 125–44.

Hall, Kira, Donna M. Goldstein, and Matthew Bruce Ingram. 2016. "The Hands of Donald Trump: Entertainment, Gesture, Spectacle." *HAU: Journal of Ethnographic Theory* 6, no. 2: 71–100.

Hill, Jane. 1998. "Language, Race, and White Public Space." *American Anthropologist* 100, no. 3: 680–89.

Hoenes del Pinal, Eric. 2011. "Towards an Ideology of Gesture: Gesture, Body Movement, and Language Ideology Among Q'eqchi'-Maya Catholics." *Anthropological Quarterly* 84, no. 3: 595–630.

Jamieson, Kathleen Hall, and Doron Taussig. 2017. "Disruption, Demonization, Deliverance, and Norm Destruction: The Rhetorical Signature of Donald J. Trump." *Political Science Quarterly* 132, no. 4: 619–50.

Keevallik, Leelo. 2010. "Bodily Quoting in Dance Correction." *Research on Language and Social Interaction* 43, no. 4: 401–26.

Kendon, Adam. 2004. *Gesture: Visible Action as Utterance*. Cambridge University Press.

Kristeva, Julia. 1982. *Powers of Horror: An Essay on Abjection*. Translated by Leon S. Roudiez. Columbia University Press.

Lakoff, Robin T. 1992. *Talking Power: The Politics of Language; From Courtroom to Classroom, from Summit Talks to Small Talk: How What We Say – and How We Say It – Influences Every Aspect of Our Lives*. Basic Books.

LeBaron, Curtis, and Jürgen Streeck. 2000. "Gestures, Knowledge, and the World." In *Language and Gesture*, edited by David McNeill, pp. 118–38. Cambridge University Press.

Lempert, Michael. 2011. "Barack Obama Being Sharp: Indexical Order in the Pragmatics of Precision-Grip Gesture." *Gesture* 11, no. 3: 241–70.

LesGrossman News Video. 2016. "Donald Trump Rome NY Rally." April 12, 2016. www.youtube.com/watch?v=yQWdE9n2tD8. (Fair Dealings, Transformative Use.)

Live Satellite News. 2015. "Donald Trump Tells President Obama 'You're Fired.'" Comments section. www.youtube.com/watch?v=RPfxyFMUd1k. Link no longer available; accessed August 2015.

Martin, Jonathan, and Amy Chozick. 2016. "Hillary Clinton's Doctor Says Pneumonia Led to Abrupt Exit from 9/11 Event." *The New York Times*, September 11, 2016. https://nyti.ms/2Pitt9m.

Maskovsky, Jeff. 2017. "Toward the Anthropology of White Nationalist Postracialism: Comments Inspired by Hall, Goldstein, and Ingram's 'The Hands of Donald Trump.'" *HAU: Journal of Ethnographic Theory* 7, no. 1: 433–40.

McDowell, John H. 1981. "Toward a Semiotics of Nicknaming: The Kamsá Example." *The Journal of American Folklore* 94, no. 371: 1–18.

McNeill, David. 1992. *Hand and Mind: What Gestures Reveal about Thought.* University of Chicago Press.

Mittelberg, Irene. 2013. "Balancing Acts: Image Schemas and Force Dynamics as Experiential Essence in Pictures by Paul Klee and Their Gestural Enactments." In *Language and the Creative Mind*, edited by Mike Borkent, Barbara Dancygier, and Jennifer Hinnell, pp. 325–46. University of Chicago Press.

Mittelberg, Irene, and Linda Waugh. 2014. "Gestures and Metonymy." In *Body-Language-Communication*, Vol. 2, edited by Cornelia Müller, Alan Cienki, Ellen Fricke, Silva H. Ladewig, David McNeill, and Jana Bressem, pp. 1747–66. De Gruyter Mouton.

NBC Bay Area. 2016. "RAW VIDEO: Trump Jumps Wall to Get Past Protesters." Online video. April 29, 2016. https://tinyurl.com/yapwcggh.

Neville-Shepard, Ryan, and Jaclyn Nolan. 2019. "'She Doesn't Have the Stamina': Hillary Clinton and the Hysteria Diagnosis in the 2016 Presidential Election." *Women's Studies in Communication* 42, no. 1: 60–79.

Pitt-Rivers, Julian A. [1954]1971. *The People of the Sierra*. University of Chicago Press.

Roland, L. Kaifa. 2017. "How Bodies Matter: Yesterday's America Today." *HAU: Journal of Ethnographic Theory* 7, no. 1: 441–47.

Rosa, Jonathan, and Yarimar Bonilla. 2017. "Deprovincializing Trump, Decolonizing Diversity, and Unsettling Anthropology." *American Ethnologist* 44, no. 2: 201–08.

Rozzo, Mark. 2016. "Was This Robert De Niro Role the Inspiration for Trump's Wild Hand Gestures?" *Vanity Fair*, April 18, 2016. https://bit.ly/2m1wrTy.

Sclafani, Jennifer. 2018. *Talking Donald Trump: A Sociolinguistic Study of Style, Metadiscourse, and Political Identity*. Routledge.

Sidnell, Jack. 2006. "Coordinating Gesture, Talk, and Gaze in Reenactments." *Research on Language and Social Interaction* 39, no. 4: 377–409.

Smith, Jessica. 2017. "Blind Spots of Liberal Righteousness." *Society for Cultural Anthropology*, January 18, 2017. https://culanth.org/fieldsights/blind-spots-of-liberal-righteousness.

Spitulnik, Debra. 1996. "The Social Circulation of Media Discourse and the Mediation of Communities." *Journal of Linguistic Anthropology* 6, no. 2: 161–87.

Streeck, Jürgen. 2008a. "Depicting by Gesture." *Gesture* 8, no. 3: 285–301.

2008b. "Gesture in Political Communication: A Case Study of Democratic Presidential Candidates during the 2004 Primary Campaign." *Research on Language and Social Interaction* 41, no. 2: 154–86.

Sweetser, Eve, and Marisa Sizemore. 2008. "Personal and Interpersonal Gesture Spaces: Functional Contrasts in Language and Gesture." In *Language In the Context of Use: Discourse and Cognitive Approaches to Language*, edited by Andrea Tyler, Yiyoung Kim, and Mari Takada, pp. 25–51. De Gruyter Mouton.

Tani, Maxwell. 2016. "GOP Candidate John Kasich Just Ate a Crazy Amount of Italian Food in the Bronx." *Business Insider*. April 7, 2016. www.businessinsider.com/john-kasich-italian-food-the-bronx-2016-4.

Tannen, Deborah. 1986. "Introducing Constructed Dialogue in Greek and American Conversational and Literary Narrative." In *Direct and Indirect Speech*, edited by Florian Coulmas, pp. 311–32. De Gruyter Mouton.

2010. "Abduction and Identity in Family Interaction: Ventriloquizing as Indirectness." *Journal of Pragmatics* 42, no. 2: 307–16.

Taylor-Coleman, Jasmine, and Anna Bressanin. 2016. "What Trump's Hand Gestures Say about Him." *BBC News* video, August 16, 2016. https://bbc.in/2kWFZyU.

Thompson, Sandra A., and Ryoko Suzuki. 2014. "Reenactments in Conversation: Gaze and Recipiency." *Discourse Studies* 16, no. 6: 816–46.

Trump, Donald. 2015a. *Trump Campaign Rally*, Myrtle Beach, SC. November 24, 2015.

2015b. *Trump Campaign Rally*, Raleigh, NC. December 4, 2015.

2015c. *Trump Campaign Rally*, Doral, FL. October 23, 2015.

2015d. *Trump Campaign Rally*, Dubuque, IA. August 25, 2015.

2015e. *Trump Campaign Rally*, Birmingham, AL. August 21, 2015.

2015f. *Trump Campaign Rally*, Oklahoma City, OK. September 25, 2015.

2016a. *Trump Campaign Rally*, Greensboro, NC. June 14, 2016.

2016b. *Trump Campaign Rally*, Warwick, RI. April 25, 2016.

2016c. *Trump Campaign Rally*, West Chester, PA. April 25, 2016.

2016d. *Trump Campaign Rally*, Harrisburg, PA. April 21, 2016.

2016e. *Trump GOP Convention Speech*, Burlingame, CA. April 29, 2016.

2016f. *Trump Campaign Rally*, Rome, NY. April 12, 2016.

2016g. *Trump Campaign Rally*, Portland, ME. March 3, 2016.

2016h. *Trump Campaign Rally*, Manheim, PA. October 1, 2016.

2016i. *Trump Campaign Rally*, Madison, AL. February 28, 2016.

2016j. *Trump Campaign Rally*, Manchester, NH. October 28, 2016.

Walley, Christine J. 2017. "Trump's Election and the 'White Working Class': What We Missed." *American Ethnologist* 44, no. 2: 231–36.

Warnke, Melissa Batchelor. 2016. "Opinion: Hillary Clinton's Worrisome Wobble." *Los Angeles Times*, September 11, 2016. https://lat.ms/2mv7bVZ.

The Young Turks. 2016. "Did Trump Dog Whistle 'I Can't Breathe' for Racist Votes?" Online video clip. April 14, 2016. www.youtube.com/watch?v=bYKe7fuHY4c.

Zaru, Deena. 2016. "Feathers Fly over Donald Trump Eating Fried Chicken with a Fork." *CNN*, August 2, 2016. www.cnn.com/2016/08/02/politics/donald-trump-eats-kfc-knife-fork/index.html.

7   45 as a Bullshit Artist: Straining for Charisma

Marco Jacquemet

"He's nothing but a bullshitter," President Barack Obama told two friends in November 2016 (Holloway 2017), describing an election night phone call with President-elect Donald Trump, in which the businessman suddenly professed his "respect" and "admiration" for Obama – after years of hectoring. In this chapter I heed the words of the former president, but when I call Trump a bullshitter, I don't mean it as invective. Rather, I mean it as a technical, linguistic description of his relationship with factual representations.

In the first 200 days of his presidency, Trump made roughly 560 false statements, according to Daniel Dale and Tanya Talaga of the *Toronto Star* (Dale and Talaga 2016). His pace accelerated, however, and by day 993, he'd made 13,435 false or misleading claims (Kessler et al. 2019). That's an impressive amount of misinformation. Trump says a lot of things that aren't true, often shamelessly so, and it's tempting to call him a liar. To be sure, a good portion of Trump's false claims do not have a direct correlation with factual references, which meets the basic definition of a lie. But calling Trump a liar, besides being a truism, does nothing to advance our understanding of how he uses language, through bullshitting, to portray himself as a charismatic autocrat. In fact, there are distinctions to be made between his various falsehoods. A statement such as, "I'll build the wall and Mexico will pay for it" (Qin 2019) seems to belong to an entirely different plane than Trump's tweeted claim that "3,000 people did not die in two hurricanes that hit Puerto Rico" (Sherman 2018), a claim that directly contradicts the figure published in late August by George Washington University's Milken Institute after extensive research (*BBC News* 2018). Whereas the second of these statements is clearly a lie, the first is more ambiguous, leading commentators to qualify it as "bullshit."

As the Princeton University philosophy professor Harry Frankfurt put it in a famous essay (2005), to lie presumes a kind of awareness of and interest in the truth – and the goal is to convince others that the false thing you are saying is in fact true. Trump, more often than not, isn't interested in convincing anyone of anything. He's a bullshitter who simply doesn't care about the veracity of his statements, as long as they boost his image.

While other commentators have remarked that Trump's statements comprise a spectrum ranging from "true" to "pants-on-fire" lies (McGranahan 2017, Snyder 2018), several scholars have converged on the claim that Trump is at least sometimes bullshitting (see, for instance, Carter 2018, Gavaler and Goldberg 2017, and Yglesias 2017 for contributions formulated more or less simultaneously with my own first iteration of this claim at the 2017 American Anthropological Association meetings, Jacquemet 2017). Going beyond their arguments, I would contend that lies and bullshit belong to two different, yet converging and at times overlapping, epistemological planes. These planes are shaped by different concerns: a need to deceive in the case of lies; a desire to impress in the case of bullshitting.

Trump's lies, furthermore, have been portrayed as tactical moves in his twofold strategy of, first, sowing confusion to create the conditions for an authoritarian regime and, second, creating aspirational communities and motivating them to act. Without denying the importance of these claims, in the following pages I analyze Trump's deceptive statements as part of a strategy of impression management to shape his image into the larger-than-life personality that is a necessary condition of all autocratic rulers. I will do so by breaking down bullshitting into its three basic elements: the speaker, the text, and the audience.

7.1   The Speaker

Frankfurt (2005) makes an important distinction between lying and bullshitting. Although both the liar and the bullshitter try to get away with something, the bullshitter says things not necessarily with the goal of lying but rather with no concern for their accuracy. This, according to Frankfurt, is the essence of bullshit (BS): it is spoken without any concern for the truth. It can be true or false, but the speaker does not really care. Still, though the bullshitter is indifferent to the truth of what he is saying, he does tell one kind of lie: he implicitly lies about what he is doing with his speech (generic "he" pronoun is intentional here). This is the thing most alike between liars and bullshitters: they both seek to deceive others about themselves. The liar seeks to make us believe that he believes his statement to be true (that is, he knows claim P is false, yet asserts P, and in so doing of course asserts that he believes P). The bullshitter seeks to make us believe that he is saying something that he knows (he makes claims like P, asserts P, and asserts that he believes P, but in fact he does not know or care if P is true or not). Furthermore, a lie is necessarily false, but bullshit is not – bullshit may happen to be correct or incorrect.

What a bullshitter cares about is accomplishing positive impression management through speech. The bullshitter's goal is not to convince others of any supposed facts. It is, rather, to shape his listeners' beliefs and attitudes about himself. The liar *knows* what the facts are and tries to mislead. The bullshitter may not presume he even knows what the truth is; bullshit is indifferent to the truth in ways that lies are not.

Trump's performance as a bullshitter has been an easy target for comedians over the past two years, precisely because of his transparent obsession with impression management. For instance, *The Daily Show* marked the first two years of Trump's presidency with a competition that asked viewers to vote for Trump's best "BS statement" (Noah 2018). More than three and a half million people participated in selecting the winner by voting online. Among the top statements were "We had the biggest inauguration crowd ever," "My response to Puerto Rico's hurricane was amazing," and "I'd personally run into a school unarmed to stop a shooter." All three clearly point to Trump's desire to shape American beliefs and attitudes about himself: He wants to be seen as a popular, courageous man always ready to respond to emergencies in "amazing" ways.

A more recent example of Trump's BS provides further evidence of his pre-occupation with his image. At a White House event on March 7, 2019, President Trump appeared to refer to Apple CEO Tim Cook as "Tim Apple" (Wang 2019). Video of the slip-up swiftly went viral, with social media users and late-night hosts piling ridicule on this slip of the tongue. Even Cook himself got in on the fun, changing his Twitter name to "Tim" followed by an icon of the Apple logo.

Trump responded by telling Republican donors at a subsequent event that he actually said "Tim Cook Apple" really fast, and that the "Cook" part of the sentence was pronounced softly. "But all you heard from the 'fake news,'" he said, "was Tim Apple." More ridicule followed. Then, in a tweet a few days later, Trump claimed, "At a recent round table meeting of business executives, & long after formally introducing Tim Cook of Apple, I quickly referred to Tim + Apple as Tim/Apple as an easy way to save time & words. The Fake News was disparagingly all over this, & it became yet another bad Trump story!" (Ross 2019).

This strenuous defense of a somewhat innocuous mistake must be understood in the context of the motivation at the basis of BS; namely, the bullshitter's general refusal to admit wrong (Carter 2018). This inability to let go of a gaffe (which Carter identifies as the first step of bullshitting) generates a feedback loop of increasingly dubious BS in an effort to save face and restore the authority of the speaker.

7.2   The Text

Numerous commentators on Frankfurt's work (in particular Fredal 2011 and Carter 2018) have pointed out that focusing exclusively on the bullshitter may produce a reification of the autonomous speaker at the expense of understanding the overall ecology of the bullshitting event. Frankfurt's approach also lodges us uncomfortably in the task of trying to understand a speaker's intention, when in fact we often detect bullshit without strictly knowing anyone's state of mind. Instead, we often infer BS, at least in part, from its semiotic features. And, I suggest below, some of the features that allow BS to succeed do so because of how they embed the interlocutors in the text, thus enlisting them in the BS event (see Eco 1979).

How is a bullshitter's indifference to truth expressed in textual and linguistic practices? Do BS statements share particular linguistic features? Although no scholar has yet produced a systematic textual analysis of this phenomenon, we can characterize BS as ego-centered discourse frequently (even if not always) marked by the use of repetitions, intensifiers, superlatives, and ellipsis. Non sequiturs and nonsensical statements also play a crucial role in this discourse (for Frankfurt, "nonsense" is seen as a foundation for BS).

Moreover, we may want to revisit, for bullshitological purposes, Grice's maxims for ideal conversation. Grice (1975: 45) argued that good communication follows what he calls the Cooperative Principle: "Make your conversational contribution such as is required, at the stage at which it occurs, by the accepted purpose or direction of the talk exchange in which you are engaged." The ideal speaker follows the Cooperative Principle by trying to do the following: to be as informative as possible, giving as much information as is needed and no more (i.e. Grice's "maxim of quantity"); to be truthful, not giving information that is false or unsupported by evidence (i.e. maxim of quality); to be relevant, saying things that are pertinent to the discussion (i.e. maxim of relevance); and to be as clear, as brief, and as orderly as possible, avoiding obscurity and ambiguity (i.e. maxim of manner).

According to Grice, when a speaker manifestly violates or "flouts" one or more of these maxims, they may be performing an "implicature," in which the flouting points to some underlying, non-literal meaning. On first being heard, in other words, an utterance may not appear to follow the Cooperative Principle, but it can still be understood as meaningful through implication. If Speaker A, for instance, says "Did you think my piano recital went well?" and Speaker B replies, "You looked great," Speaker B's response would seem to violate at least one maxim, primarily that of relevance. Speaker A will likely discern that an implicature is being made; speaker B is implicating that Speaker A didn't play especially well. Speaker B "means" to say this, but they opt not to state it outright.

Like all speakers, Trump engages in no shortage of implicatures. After one of the presidential debates in 2016, for instance, he criticized debate moderator Megyn Kelly of *Fox News*, telling *CNN*'s Don Lemon she had been unfairly aggressive and "ridiculous." "You could see there was blood coming out of her eyes, blood coming out of her wherever. In my opinion, she was off base" (Rucker 2015). The crucial maxim violation, here, is of quantity; Trump does not speak the name of the last of Kelly's body parts from which blood was supposedly coming out. This leaves the listener to infer there's some reason for which he didn't mention it, and an easy way to square Trump's meaning is to assume he's implicating a taboo part of the anatomy. Context informs the implicature, too; Trump's statements that Kelly's questions were "ridiculous" and "off base" tap into the widespread, sexist notion that women can be irrational, perhaps especially when influenced by their hormones. Many listeners thus took his underlying meaning, his implicature, to be that Kelly was menstruating. Trump, of course, took advantage of the fact that he didn't state this directly to deny he was referring to menstruation in a later interview. But at the time, it certainly behaved like an implicature.

Implicature is usually the first explanation for violation of maxims. But in some cases, maxims may be violated because the speaker is not following the Cooperative Principle – not trying to communicate seriously or well – and instead is simply bullshitting. If utterances convey not enough or too much information (maxim of quantity), lack evidence (maxim of quality), are irrelevant to any current topic or issue (maxim of relevance), or are obscure, ambiguous, unnecessarily wordy, or disorderly (maxim of manner), *and* if no clear implicature can be inferred, they may be candidates for being labeled BS. And some of Trump's BS seems bent on violating *all* of Grice's maxims.

Examples can be found from Trump's speech during his presidential campaign, which Jennifer Sclafani (2017) closely analyzed. She found much of his talk to be composed of simple words, asides, repetitions, non sequiturs, intensifiers, superlatives, and ellipsis. Many of these linguistic features can be understood as violations of Grice's maxims, but without following the Cooperative Principle (and, thus, not making sense by way of implicature). And much of his speech would seem to qualify as BS.

The following excerpt, a nonsensical rambling during a 2015 political speech, contains a clear example of how some of Trump's BS works:

Look, having nuclear – my uncle was a great professor and scientist and engineer, Dr. John Trump at MIT ... good genes, very good genes, OK, very smart, the Wharton School of Finance, very good, very smart – you know, if you're a conservative Republican, if I were a liberal, if, like, OK, if I ran as a liberal Democrat, they would say I'm one of the smartest people anywhere in the world – it's true! – but when you're a conservative Republican they try – oh, do they do a number – that's why I always start off: Went to Wharton, was a good student, went there, went there, did this, built a fortune – you know I have to give my like credentials all the time, because we're a little disadvantaged – but you look at the nuclear deal, the thing that really bothers me – it would have been so easy, and it's not as important as these lives are – nuclear is powerful, my uncle explained that to me many, many years ago, the power and that was 35 years ago, he would explain the power of what's going to happen and he was right – who would have thought, but when you look at what's going on with the four prisoners – now it used to be three, now it's four – but when it was three and even now, I would have said it's all in the messenger; fellas, and it is fellas because, you know, they don't, they haven't figured that the women are smarter right now than the men, so, you know, it's gonna take them about another 150 years – but the Persians are great negotiators, the Iranians are great negotiators, so, and they, they just killed, they just killed us. (Seven Generations 2017)

In this excerpt, we find both the violations of Grice's maxims and the basic features of Trump's BS identified by Sclafani. Trump began this ramble trying to criticize the nuclear deal the Obama administration had made with Iran, but seems derailed by his frenetic attempts to impress the audience with a cloud of bluster about his own credentials. In some cases, his garbled claims make it hard for critics to ascertain what he's even said in order to evaluate its truth or falsity (Yglesias 2017).

Yet, a simple reading of this same transcript of his speech does not convey the social effectiveness of Trump's spoken BS, achieved through prosody – that is, through paralinguistic features such as intonation, tone, stress, and rhythm. Prosody structures the interactional relationship between speaker and audience, cueing audiences on how to understand and respond to the speaker's words. Much spoken BS would not be successful without proper prosody. If we remove the prosodic features from this excerpt of BS, it falls flat, unable to convey the form and stance of the utterance. Hence, the transcript above immediately appears to be a piece of nonsense of surrealist heights rarely encountered in public life – although it may not have been perceived as such when heard by Trump's adoring audience. As he delivers his ramble, Trump enlivens it with impassioned lilting pitch, wry asides, and a sometimes-exasperated tone – he is clearly affecting the stance of a man sure of his opinions, even if the content of what he says is not entirely sensical. The exercise of stripping Trump's speech of prosody – of his "blindingly confident entertaining delivery" – was used to great comical effect by the comedian John Oliver in his show *Last Week Tonight* on November 12th, 2017, when he had the transcript above read aloud by a digitalized voice (*Last Week Tonight* 2017).

I'm not claiming every instance of BS has the textual features I describe above. When Trump said repeatedly that millions of "illegal voters" cost him the popular vote, for instance, he was indifferent to the truth of the claim and patently attempting a kind of impression management, yet his statements were mostly straightforward rather than florid violations of numerous Gricean maxims. But when Trump starts to stuff empty intensifiers, patent exaggerations, repetitions, non sequiturs, and the like into his claims, our bullshit-meters should be clanging.

7.3   The Audience

As the preceding discussion on prosody suggests, BS can be sustained through an interactional relationship between speaker and audience (Preti 2006). An analysis of Trump's BS solely focused on author and text is insufficient to explain how his BS appeals to such a sizeable audience – sizeable enough for him to win the presidency.

Social media serves as a dominant channel through which Trump develops an interactional relationship with his audience. Trump's BS is often delivered to his audience by the "evil mediation" offered by digital platforms – Twitter above all. Fuller and Goffey's (2012) concept of "evil media" refers to platforms where the format of a message is privileged over content, so that the preformatted nature of the interface (say, a limited number of characters and a limited way to interact with a message via emoticons, likes, and retweets) shapes how people can respond to it. Moreover, the need for immediacy in the current media environment means that misinformation (such as the majority of Trump's tweeted BS statements) is disseminated in a totally unfiltered fashion. In this environment, the step of fact-checking prior to publication (posting or tweeting) is typically skipped, and the scale of circulation is prioritized over the accuracy of content.

Twitter, in particular, possesses capabilities perfectly suitable for BS. As a broadcast medium, it provides the bullshitter with great reach in an interactive simulacrum, making the audience feel engaged directly in the conversation. It highlights the supremacy of the format and form over content through its 280-character limit. It imposes no editorial control over the quality of most messages. Finally, features such as the mention (i.e. @TwitterHandle; for example, @realDonaldTrump), the hashtag (e.g. #trumpbullshit), and particularly the retweet are ideally suited for amplifying BS.

Take for instance Trump's most retweeted tweet in 2018, a brazen threat against North Korea with his "bigger and more powerful" "Nuclear Button":

North Korean Leader Kim Un just stated that the "Nuclear Button is on his desk at all times." Will someone from his depleted and food starved regime please inform him that I too have a Nuclear Button, but it is a much bigger & more powerful one than his, and my Button works! (Trump on Twitter, January 2, 2018)

Here again, we see his braggadocio and desire to impress as expressed in his swaggering discourse and metaphorical implications. BS is a performance, and good performances echoed by others not only may give those who repeat them some reflected glory but also produce a multiplying effect that extends the reach of the initial performance, exposing in a viral manner more and more people to it, and consequently amplifying the bullshitter's seduction.

But retweeting can also happen by those who are appalled and fascinated by BS. As Richard Grusin (2017) pointed out, Trump's campaign, spearheaded by his tweets, weaponized formal and informal print, televisual, and networked media to produce a collective national mood that a Trump presidency was a legitimate, possible, and, for many, a desirable and inevitable future. In their endless coverage of his campaign, often telegraphing shock at Trump's outrageous claims, most mainstream media became amplifiers of Trump's political BS. They thus unwittingly but incessantly projected the possibility of a Trump presidency.

To explore Trump's use of evil media, Grusin focused on a passage from Félix Guattari's *The Three Ecologies* ([1989]2000), in which Guattari describes Trump's strategy as a real estate developer operating in the media environment of the late 1980s. This passage was gleefully quoted by many commentators opposed to Trump's campaign, for reasons that will be readily apparent.

Just as monstrous and mutant algae invade the lagoon of Venice, so our television screens are populated, saturated, by 'degenerate' images and statements. In the field of social ecology, men like Donald Trump are permitted to proliferate freely, like another species of algae, taking over entire districts of New York and Atlantic City; he 'redevelops' by raising rents, thereby driving out tens of thousands of poor families, most of whom are condemned to homelessness, becoming the equivalent of the dead fish of environmental ecology. (Guattari [1989]2000: 45)

Trump's ability to manipulate this environment for personal and political gain has been evident in the way in which he has used Twitter, both during the campaign and during his presidency, to control large swaths of media real estate. Political media watchers have demonstrated that many of his tweets come in response to *Fox News* reports. In many cases, Trump simply live-tweets his television viewing. But such tweets work to replicate themselves through a cascade of re-mediations in a kind of algal bloom in the media lagoon. His live-tweeting, like all his tweets, is remediated by other social media users through retweets, mentions, critiques, and likes, then remediated again by formal and informal media – blogs, print, televisual, networked, and "fake" news outlets. The end result of this process is that Trump uses tweets to redevelop media neighborhoods under his name and crowd out other competitors for as many news cycles as he can control, sometimes for a short time and sometimes for days, weeks, or even, in rare instances, months.

Trump's tweets (the most appealing ones, perhaps) pass successfully through this process because they have an orally performable dimension. As Jan Blommaert (2018) remarks, "Talk is tweet, and tweet is talk." When Donald Trump gives a public speech (such as the one quoted above), the units of his speeches are tweets – or at least, he produces chunks of performed rhetoric that can be effortlessly converted into the format of tweets. Some of his tweets appear as chunks of discourse that can be spoken by others. In fact, they contain pointers, such as exclamation marks or all caps, as to exactly how they can be delivered in speech. In other words, they are instructional, showing his followers how to speak like Trump and spread his word.

This mediatized BS then becomes a test of his audience's loyalty, both in terms of personal loyalty and political loyalty. *Vox* commentator Matthew Yglesias suggests that Trump's BS is a "loyalty test" precisely because it asks his followers and members of his administration to do something nutty; namely, sign on to his outrageous nonsense. "Trump not only keeps bullshitting, he tends to demand that his team offer a zealous defense of whatever bullshit he happens to spout on any given day – putting staffers and legislative allies in the untenable position of defending the indefensible" (Yglesias 2017: 2). But defend him they do. One thing that BS has in common with lying is its ability to create a community willing to believe (or at least perform belief in) the speaker, provide cover to his statements, and live in the world created by his words. In so doing, communities are glued together and people are incited to act, sometimes violently.

Moreover, Trump appears to customize his BS for the specific affordances of online and offline communication. While some of his confident BS tweets are not only repeatable, but also quotable, his offline communication is more susceptible to the slippery style analyzed above. We can see this in his follow-up to a tweet he produced in March 2017 to attack Obama for what Trump falsely claimed was his role in wiretapping then-candidate Trump:

How low has President Obama gone to tapp my phones during the very sacred election process. This is Nixon/Watergate. Bad (or sick) guy! (Trump on Twitter, March 4, 2017; also Schmidt and Shear 2017)

However, when confronted by CBS anchor John Dickerson, host of *Face the Nation*, on the meaning of this tweet, Trump took a conflict-avoiding (and cowardly) stance (as reported by John Oliver [*Last Week Tonight* 2017]):[1]

TRUMP:	well you saw what happened with surveillance
	and (.) I think that was inappropriate=
DICKERSON:	=what does that mean, sir?
TRUMP:	uuh:: you can figure that out yourself
DICKERSON:	well- the reason I ask is- you called him sick and BA:D
TRUMP:	look you can figure it out yourself
	he was very nice to me with words, but-
	and when I was with him, but after that-
	there has been (.) no relationship
DICKERSON:	but you stand by that claim about him=
TRUMP:	=I don't stand by anything
	I just- uh- you can take it the way you want
DICKERSON:	I just wanted to find it out that your-
	you are the president of the United States
	you said that he was sick and bad because he attempted=
TRUMP:	=you can take
	it any way, you can take it any way you want
DICKERSON:	but I'm asking you, because you don't want to do fake news, I want to
	hear it from president Trump=
TRUMP:	=you don't have to ask me=
DICKERSON:	=why not?

TRUMP:	because I have my own opinions, you can have your own opinions
DICKERSON:	but I want to know your opinions,
	you're the president of the United States
TRUMP:	that's enough, thank you, thank you very much.

This passage is fascinating for several reasons. Trump is clearly avoiding the issue of whether his tweet was true or false; indeed, his bizarrely relativistic repeated statement that "you can take it any way you want" almost seems an admission that the tweet wasn't really about truth or falsehood to begin with (a signature of BS). The exchange seems to concede his past BS, at the same time that it seems itself to qualify as another instance of BS. Trump doesn't care to follow the Cooperative Principle in this exchange, violating maxims of quantity (he repeatedly withholds information about what he was up to with the tweet) and relevance ("I have my own opinions, you have your opinions" – yet Dickerson's query was whether Trump would stand by his own claim that Obama was sick and bad). In its slipperiness, Trump's words again exemplify his indifference to truth, while, he hopes, sustaining his impression management as someone who can simply disregard these harassing journalists. His fans, encouraged by Trump to see mainstream media as "fake" and infected by "liberal bias," might have cheered as Trump evaded capture.

This discrepancy between the bellicose Tweeter-in-chief and the face-to-face slippery interlocutor points to the final characteristic of Trump's BS: It is one-sided discourse, arising in encounters characterized by Trump's arrogance and his desire to insult, becoming essentially the ultimate tool of the strong man:

Bullshit happens, more generally then, when one party in an encounter feels superior enough (in position, authority, or rhetorical skill, for example) to dispense with the rituals of cooperative interaction, leading the other to feel treated without due deference; when one participant in an exchange appears to have been undeservedly slighted; or when one side of a dialogue is unjustly disregarded. Bullshit arises from arrogant gestures of disregard. (Fredal 2011: 256)

What Fredal doesn't acknowledge is the possibility of multiple others: in Trump's case there is an audience that loves his self-presentation as a strong man, and others who feel disregarded, even dehumanized.

7.4   BS and Branded Despotism

As Frankfurt pointed out, bullshit is inevitable when someone speaks of something about which they are ignorant. Perhaps there are many such occasions arising from the demand for public figures to speak on everything. But in the case of Donald Trump, bullshitting becomes much more than a tool to cover his ignorance. It is part of his larger *strategy of branded despotism*: He uses bullshit interactionally (for self-aggrandizing and impression management), mediatically (to create the Trump spectacle), and politically (to test loyalty, both in terms of brand loyalty and political loyalty).

In Trump's attempt to deliver a charismatic performance, his total lack of constraint in bullshitting is framed as "authenticity," which supersedes sanity or competence, becoming the index of a politician who "tells it like it is." It's an approach that, like much of the rest of Trump's ideology and policy agenda, assumes (correctly, it appears) that his audiences care more about shock and entertainment value in their media consumption than almost anything else (Debord's 1969 work, *La société du spectacle*, comes to mind here). Trump supporters may wish for more jobs, fewer immigrants, and White supremacy (for instance), but they have gravitated toward his media output in part because of his style.

In promoting his brand, Trump makes false assertions, which he surely knows or could easily ascertain to be false. He also makes statements of whose truth he is uncertain – and he is indifferent to the fact that he doesn't actually regard them as true. In the first case, he is telling a lie. In the second case, it's BS.

Both lies and BS are about deception: in the first case the liar's deception is about facts and events in the world, while in the latter the deception is about the bullshitter himself, in particular his desire to be perceived in a positive light. In Trump's case, this light is somewhat more sinister: the glow of a would-be dictator.

As multiple commentators have mentioned, Trump's lies aim to rewrite or scramble history. His lies – "Obama was not born in the US" (Farley 2011) or "Arabs in New Jersey celebrated 9/11" (Kessler 2015) – glue communities together and spur them to action, whether at the ballot box or in the streets. His prevarication is highly strategic and functional, pointing to Trump's desire to rearrange society itself.

In this strategy, the use of BS stands out as a second rail, operating in conjunction with the destructive power of his lies to advance the image of a charismatic leader. All major modern dictators – Stalin, Mussolini, Hitler, and Mao – created cults of personality as the embodiment of their despotic policies, visible through their larger-than-life public image. Unable to win World War II, like Stalin, or go for a heroic swim in the Yangtze River, like Mao at seventy years old, Trump relies on the BS of self-flattery and self-praise to fashion his own image of an idealized, heroic, and worshipful superman. "Nobody knows politicians better than me," he brags. "Nobody knows the system better than me." "Nobody's bigger or better at the military than I am" (Blake 2016, Black 2016).

It is disturbing to find an important political figure who indulges freely both in lies and in bullshit. What is perhaps even more deeply disturbing is to discover an important portion of the American population responding to this dishonesty with such pervasive enthusiasm.

Note

1. Transcription conventions relevant to the analysis in this chapter include the use of CAPITALS to indicate talk spoken with special emphasis. A single period in parentheses (.) indicates a micropause of less than 0.1 seconds. A dash (-) marks the cut-off of the current sound. An equal sign (=) indicates "latching," where talk starts up in especially close temporal proximity to the end of the previous talk. Punctuation symbols are used to mark intonation changes rather than as grammatical symbols: a period indicates a falling contour; a question mark, a rising contour; and a comma, a falling-rising contour, as might be found in the midst of a list. Each line of text (without a hard return) indicates talk spoken within a single breath group.

References

BBC News. 2018. "Trump Disputes Puerto Rico Hurricane Death Toll." *BBC News* article, September 13, 2018. https://bbc.in/37RN07X.

Black, Eric. 2016. "Donald Trump's Breathtaking Self-Admiration." *MinnPost*, June 20, 2016. https://bit.ly/2Y7ehi6.

Blommaert, Jan. 2018. "Trump's Tweetopoetics." *Crtl+Alt+Dem*, January 19, 2018. https://bit.ly/34DfnV7.

Blake, Aaron. 2016. "Nineteen Things Donald Trump Knows Better Than Anybody Else, According to Donald Trump." *The Washington Post*, October 4, 2016. https://wapo.st/2ODd6DM.

Carter, Christopher. 2018. "The Paradox of Dissent: Bullshit and the Twitter Presidency." In *President Donald Trump and His Political Discourse: Ramifications of Rhetoric Via Twitter*, edited by Michele Lockhart, pp. 93–113. Routledge.

Dale, Daniel, and Tanya Talaga. 2016. "Donald Trump: The Unauthorized Database of False Things." *The Toronto Star*, November 4, 2016. https://bit.ly/2R9ffcg.

Debord, Guy. [1969]1994. *Society of the Spectacle*. MIT Press.

Eco, Umberto. 1979. *The Role of the Reader: Explorations in the Semiotics of Texts*. Indiana University Press.

Farley, Robert. 2011. "Trump Said Obama's Grandmother Caught on Tape Saying She Witnessed His Birth in Kenya." *PolitiFact*, April 7, 2011. https://bit.ly/2rJIrvE.

Frankfurt, Harry G. 2005. *On Bullshit*. Princeton University Press.

Fredal, James. 2011. "Rhetoric and Bullshit." *College English* 73, no. 3: 243–59.

Fuller, Matthew, and Andrew Goffey. 2012. *Evil Media*. MIT Press.

Gavaler, Chris, and Nathaniel Goldberg. 2017. "Beyond Bullshit: Donald Trump's Philosophy of Language." *Philosophy Now: A Magazine of Ideas*, no. 121. https://bit.ly/2mproNg.

Grice, H. Paul. 1975. "Logic and Conversation." In *Syntax and Semantics*, Vol. 3, *Speech Acts*, edited by Peter Cole and Jerry L. Morgan, pp. 41–58. Academic Press

Grusin, Richard. 2017. "Donald Trump's Evil Mediation." *Theory and Event* 20, no. 1: 86–99.

Guattari, Félix. [1989]2000. *The Three Ecologies*. The Athlone Press.

Holloway, Kali. 2017. "Obama Called Trump a Bullsh*tter." *AlterNet*, May 17, 2017. https://bit.ly/35Qn7mV.

Jacquemet, Marco. 2017. "45 as a Bullshit Artist." Paper presented at the Annual Meeting of the American Anthropological Association, Washington, DC. December 1, 2017.

Kessler, Glenn. 2015. "Trump's Outrageous Claim that 'Thousands' of New Jersey Muslims Celebrated the 9/11 Attack." *The Washington Post*, November 11, 2015. https://wapo.st/37XyfjW.

Kessler, Glenn, Salvador Rizzo, and Meg Kelly. 2019. "In 993 Days President Trump Has Made 13,435 False or Misleading Claims." *The Washington Post*, October 14, 2019. https://wapo.st/2OCBJRg.

Last Week Tonight. 2017. "The Trump Presidency: *Last Week Tonight with John Oliver* (HBO)." *Last Week Tonight with John Oliver* video. November 12, 2017. https://bit .ly/2rLJLy0.

McGranahan, Carole. 2017. "An Anthropology of Lying: Trump and the Political Sociality of Moral Outrage." *American Ethnologist* 44, no. 2: 1–6.

Noah, Trevor. 2018. "Third Month Mania: Bracket of Bullshit." *The Daily Show.* https:// on.cc.com/2sC7jWL.

Preti, Consuelo. 2006. "A Defense of Common Sense." In *Bullshit and Philosophy: Guaranteed to Get Perfect Results Every Time*, edited by Gary L. Hardcastle and George A. Reisch, pp. 19–32. Open Court Books.

Qiu, Linda. 2019. "The Many Ways Trump Has Said Mexico Will Pay for the Wall." *The New York Times*, January 11, 2019. https://nyti.ms/2q6ctt0.

Ross, Jamie. 2019. "Trump Claims He Only Called Tim Cook 'Tim Apple' to 'Save Time.'" *The Daily Beast*, March 11, 2019. https://bit.ly/35Pnka2.

Rucker, Philip. 2015. "Trump Says Fox's Megyn Kelly Had 'Blood Coming Out of Wherever.'" *The Washington Post*, August 8, 2015. https://wapo.st/35Qo8vf.

Schmidt, Michael S., and Michael D. Shear. 2017. "Comey Asks Justice Dept. to Reject Trump's Wiretapping Claims." *The New York Times*, March 5, 2017. https://nyti .ms/33JfHRf.

Sclafani, Jennifer. 2017. *Talking Donald Trump: A Sociolinguistic Study of Style, Metadiscourse, and Political Identity*. Routledge.

Seven Generations. 2017. "Donald Trump's Rambling Sentence on July 21, 2015." C-SPAN video. March 6, 2017. https://bit.ly/34HfY8y.

Sherman, Amy. 2018. "Donald Trump Wrong About Puerto Rico Death Toll from Hurricane Maria." *PolitiFact*, September 18, 2018. https://bit.ly/37RGCNL.

Snyder, Timothy. 2018. "The Cowardly Face of Authoritarianism." *The New York Times*, December 3, 2018. https://nyti.ms/2Le6lpU.

Trump, Donald (@realDonaldTrump). 2017. "How low has President Obama gone to tapp my phones during the very sacred election process. This is Nixon/Watergate. Bad (or sick) guy!" Twitter, March 4, 2017. https://bit.ly/2Pj5Hdl.

2018. "North Korean Leader Kim Jong Un just stated that the 'Nuclear Button is on his desk at all times.' Will someone . . ." Twitter, January 2, 2018. https://bit.ly /2oi4CHU.

Wang, Amy B. 2019. "Trump Called Tim Cook 'Tim Apple' and the Apple CEO Is Leaning into It." *The Washington Post*, March 7, 2019. https://wapo.st/2OXTnOg.

Yglesias, Matthew. 2017. "The Bullshitter-in-Chief." *Vox*, May 30, 2017. https://bit.ly /2qChu6P.

8   Plausible Deniability

Adam Hodges

According to James Comey's written testimony for the Senate Intelligence Committee in June 2017, these are the words President Donald Trump spoke to him during an Oval Office meeting less than a month after Trump was sworn into office: "I hope you can see your way clear to letting this go, to letting Flynn go. He is a good guy. I hope you can let this go" (Comey 2017a). "Flynn" was the then-National Security Advisor to Trump, under investigation for allegedly accepting money from foreign governments without the required approval; Comey at the time was the Director of the Federal Bureau of Investigation (FBI). When Comey heard Trump's remarks, he understood them to be a directive to "drop any investigation of Flynn" (ibid.). Yet a White House statement demurred: "While the President has repeatedly expressed his view that General Flynn is a decent man who served and protected our country, the President has never asked Mr. Comey or anyone else to end any investigation, including any investigation involving General Flynn" (Schmidt 2017). In the months to come, Trump's defenders would repeatedly deny that Trump was pressuring Comey or in any way obstructing justice, while his critics gnashed their teeth at the maddening slipperiness of his language.

Plausible deniability is a common world-shaping feature of political discourse that allows speakers to avoid taking responsibility for a controversial utterance by invoking possible counter-interpretations. To engage in plausible deniability, politicians invoke seemingly reasonable evidence to contest or refute that they meant what they said. What makes it often plausible to deny the meaning of political remarks is the ambiguity between what a speaker says in so many words (the literal semantic meaning) and how those words are interpreted in specific interactional contexts. To plausibly deny something, politicians will therefore suppress (or otherwise manipulate) context while foregrounding other elements of the meaning-making process more favorable to making their denial appear plausible.

Plausible deniability is helped along by a popular myth that claims that words – in and of themselves – convey all the meaning in a given interaction. Linguist Michael Reddy (1979) discussed this fallacy in his critique of the *conduit metaphor*. According to the conduit metaphor, speaking simply involves one person packaging their thoughts into words. These words supposedly act as containers of meaning that are then sent to another person who opens the package to find the meaning unproblematically revealed. By encouraging a context-free view of language, the conduit metaphor fails to account for the way social and cultural knowledge shapes the emergence of meaning in any given situation. Comey knew better; hence his interpretation of Trump's meaning.

Trump is hardly the first politician to lean on plausible deniability, but he pushes us to accept what many reasonable listeners would ordinarily find undeniably implausible. This chapter examines three cases where Trump attempts to plausibly deny what many interpreted to be controversial statements in situations that demanded the reassuring and unifying voice of a US president committed to democratic values.

First, I examine more deeply the case already invoked; namely, Trump's unusual conversation with then-FBI Director James Comey shortly after Trump took office. Despite the obvious interpretation that Trump was pressuring Comey to end an FBI investigation into his national security advisor, Michael Flynn, Trump denied he meant any such thing. Attempts at plausible deniability in this case were buttressed through an emphasis on the literal meaning of the word "hope" while erasing aspects of the context that contribute to the obstruction-of-justice interpretation.

In the second case, Trump attempts to revise the meaning of a statement he made in the aftermath of a violent White nationalist rally in Charlottesville in August 2017. Trump revisits his initial remarks in the context of a campaign-style rally with supporters, selectively choosing which words to ignore (i.e. the controversial ones) and which ones to highlight (i.e. the non-controversial ones). Here, plausible deniability hinges on the way Trump exploited the gap between the different contexts to imbue his initial statement with new meanings in the subsequent context.

In the final case, Trump attempts to focus attention on a single word – "would" vs. "wouldn't" (Trump 2018b) – while again ignoring the wider context in which that word (amongst others) was spoken: a joint press conference with Russian President Vladimir Putin after the two finished their summit in Helsinki in July 2018 (Trump 2018a). Trump's performance at the press conference managed to draw criticism once again from across the political spectrum after he stood next to Putin and refuted US intelligence findings on Russian meddling in the 2016 presidential election (*The New York Times* 2018). His subsequent attempt at plausible deniability seemed almost too transparent to take seriously. But the move characteristically (of Trump) denied obvious contextual evidence while retreating to the literal meaning (and pronunciation) of a single word. As the examples in this chapter illustrate, the political strategy of plausible deniability typically involves a narrow focus on semantics or grammar along with a grossly incomplete perspective on interactional context. It seems to be a recurrent mode of linguistic reasoning among Trump and his supporters, one that has apparently served Trump well.

8.1   "I hope you can let this go"

Comey testified before the Senate Intelligence Committee in June 2017, recounting his one-on-one meeting with Trump where the president expressed, "I hope you can see your way clear to letting this go, to letting Flynn go" (Comey 2017c). When Independent Senator Angus King of Maine asked whether Comey took Trump's expressed hope as "a directive," Comey responded with a medieval historical allusion: "Yes, yes. It rings in my ears as kind of, 'Will no one rid me of this meddlesome priest?'" (ibid.). This latter phrase has been attributed to Henry II of England; the utterance was supposedly interpreted as a command by the four knights who subsequently killed his political opponent Thomas Becket, Archbishop of Canterbury, in 1170 (Lipton 2017). With this allusion, Comey illustrates the way those in power can subtly communicate commands or directives without formulating them as explicit speech acts (e.g. "I hereby command you . . .").

But Republican Senator James Risch pressed Comey: "He [the president] said, 'I hope.' . . . Do you know of any case where a person has been charged for obstruction of justice or, for that matter, any other criminal offense, where they said, or thought, they hoped for an outcome?" Comey insisted that he "took it as a direction." He explained, "I mean, this is the president of the United States, with me alone, saying, 'I hope' this. I took it as, this is what he wants me to do." "You may have taken it as a direction, but that's not what he said," Risch averred (Comey 2017c).

The statement attributed to Trump (i.e. "I hope you can let this go") and Comey's understanding of it as a directive (i.e. "drop any investigation of Flynn") represents a classic example of what philosopher H. Paul Grice (1975) called *conversational implicature*. Grice formulated the concept to explain the way language can implicitly convey a meaning without stating that meaning in so many words. What is meant (in practical terms) may not always coincide with what is said (in literal terms). Nevertheless, savvy language users have little difficulty working out the meaning of indeterminate statements in specific contexts of situation.

The exchange between Risch and Comey illustrates the way a conversational implicature can be later plausibly denied due to the gap between what was literally said and what was meant.

On the one hand, as Risch points out, Trump said, "I hope." The verb *hope* denotes a feeling of expectation and desire for a certain thing to happen, but a speaker who *hopes* for something typically holds little control over the outcome. One can hope for rain, for example, but this is different than directing the sky to bring rain. In other words, the semantics of *hope* generally indicate a lack of agency on the part of the speaker to bring about what is hoped for. Risch emphasizes this strict semantic meaning of *hope* in his exchange with Comey.

On the other hand, Trump uttered "I hope" in a certain context. In everyday language use, we frequently encounter implicatures that require contextual knowledge to arrive at the generally recognized meaning of utterances. To use a textbook example, if I say, "It's cold in here," and you are sitting next to an open window, you are likely to shut the window. In this example, I have effectively communicated a request even though I didn't make a request in so many words (e.g. "I request that you close the window"). Contextual knowledge contributes to the meaning of my utterance.

In the Trump–Comey encounter, contextual factors included the power relationship between the two interlocutors – namely, that the Director of the FBI is subordinate to the President of the United States – and that the two were meeting alone for a one-on-one conversation in those roles. These contextual factors led Comey to interpret Trump's utterance ("I hope you can let this go") as a directive, or command. This interpretation arises from what philosopher J. L. Austin (1961) calls the *illocutionary force* of the utterance – the act performed in uttering the words "I hope you can let this go." The illocutionary force is independent of the semantic content of the utterance. The word *hope* may merely denote a feeling of desire, but the utterance made by the President of the United States within this particular context to a subordinate official carries the force of a directive, or command.

When we communicate, we draw not just upon the strict semantic meaning of words or propositional content of locutions, but also on sociocultural knowledge and contextually derived cues. We operate with a keen sense of both linguistic knowledge and sociocultural knowledge to make and interpret utterances. This includes an instinctive understanding of how power relations factor into the interpretation of utterances. Meaning making, in other words, is a contextually driven activity, a situated interactional accomplishment.

Plausible deniability in political discourse often relies upon a context-free view of language, as can be seen in this example. To suppress the directive force of Trump's utterance, Risch provides a context-free reading that emphasizes the narrow semantics of the word *hope* and erases salient contextual factors. Those contextual factors include a practical sense of the power dynamics between government officials meeting at the White House. The context-free interpretation of the utterance thereby attempts to block a conversational implicature from arising that imbibes the utterance with the force of a directive. To accept the denial that Trump meant to pressure Comey to drop the Flynn investigation requires ignoring the contextual factors of the interaction and the way we typically use language to make directives or requests. In Henry II's time, the pope refused to be so oblivious to the power dynamics at stake. Although Henry II tried to plausibly deny he had meant to incite murder, he was barred from church services and made to do penance (Lipton 2017).

8.2   "On many sides, on many sides"

On Saturday, August 12, 2017, after White nationalist groups gathered in Charlottesville, Virginia, to take part in what was billed as a "Unite the Right" rally, Trump made this statement: "We condemn in the strongest possible terms this egregious display of hatred, bigotry, and violence – on many sides, on many sides. It's been going on for a long time in our country. Not Donald Trump, not Barack Obama. This has been going on for a long, long time. It has no place in America" (Trump 2017a). As reported in the *New York Times* by Richard Fausset and Alan Feuer, "Many Americans watched trans-fixed as members of those groups marched down the street, barked out anti-Semitic chants and openly displayed the symbols of Nazi Germany and the secessionist South" (Fausset and Feuer 2017). Counter-protesters held their own rally to denounce hate and racism. Violence erupted and a car driven by a White nationalist sped into a crowd of counter-protesters, killing a young woman and injuring nineteen others (ibid.).

After learning of the violence, Trump read from a prepared statement in front of journalists at his golf club in Bedminster, New Jersey. But he apparently went off-script to adlib lines that included "on many sides, on many sides" (Trump 2017a). His emphasis on this repeated phrase ("on many sides") under-mined a condemnation of the White supremacist groups by effectively setting up a moral equivalence between those groups and the anti-racism protesters. Many across the political spectrum roundly criticized him, and members of his economic advisory councils began to resign (Bajaj and Thompson 2017).

In the days and weeks that followed, Trump engaged in what Mendoza-Denton ("The Show Must Go On," this volume) terms a "reactive reversal." He attempted to plausibly deny that he meant what most in the nation took him to mean when he spoke those words on the Saturday of the Charlottesville violence. On the Monday after the violence in Charlottesville, for instance, Trump read the statement again from the White House. This time he omitted the controversial "on many sides" qualification he made at the golf club: "As I said on Saturday, we condemn in the strongest possible terms this egregious display of hatred, bigotry, and violence. It has no place in America" (Trump 2017b).

However, the controversy followed him into a press conference the next day at the Trump Tower in New York City. Although Trump held the press conference to address infrastructure spending, journalists inevitably asked about his troubling response to Charlottesville. Trump responded by reiterating once again his original statement from the golf club – minus the controversial portion. "The statement I made on Saturday, the first statement, was a fine statement," Trump told reporters at the Trump Tower press conference (Trump 2017c). After further remarks and more attempted questions by journalists, he exclaimed, "I brought it. I brought it. I brought it" (ibid.). Trump pulled out a piece of paper from his suit pocket and spoke: "As I said on– Remember, this Saturday. 'We condemn in the strongest possible terms this egregious display of hatred, bigotry, and violence. It has no place in America.' And then it went on from there" (ibid.).

Trump's reiterations of Saturday's golf club statement at both the White House on Monday and Trump Tower on Tuesday illustrate the way that words spoken in one context can be recontextualized, giving them new meaning. However, the process of recontextualization introduces what linguistic anthropologists Richard Bauman and Charles Briggs (1992) call an *intertextual gap*: the inevitable opening that occurs when utterances are repeated in a new context.

As seen in the White House and Trump Tower performances above, Trump's recontextualization of his initial statement involves selective quoting and key omissions of his prior words. He attempts to plausibly deny the controversial meanings associated with his initial statement by expunging the damning contextual residues from that statement.

A week later, Trump addressed supporters at a campaign-style rally in Phoenix, Arizona. During the rally, he revisited his three prior appearances to further reshape his initial message. He again introduced a substantial intertextual gap between his initial statement made at the golf club and his recontextualization of that statement in Phoenix (omitting the controversial words "on many sides"). Then he worked to minimize or suppress the appearance of that intertextual gap by appealing to the authority of the written text and recharacterizing the criticisms of his initial statement (Trump 2017d).

In Phoenix, as he did a week earlier in his Trump Tower press conference, he pulled out a piece of paper that presumably contained his initial statement. This paper-as-prop physically represents that statement, seemingly fixing the text into an immutable object. This presumed immutability of the written text implicitly draws from popular beliefs and ideas about language that privilege the written word as an authoritative source of knowledge and transparent arbiter of truth.

Crucially, though, the textual model represented by the paper-as-prop harks back not to Trump's initial spoken statement at his golf club on the Saturday of the Charlottesville violence, but to the written statement he used as the model for that speech event – the one he started reading at the golf club before he adlibbed his "on many sides" line. Trump positions that prepared written text as the higher authority on what he supposedly communicated from the golf club, silently editing out the controversial words he spoke and the contextually derived implications of those words.

In Phoenix, he introduces his re-reading of his initial golf club statement: "So here's what I said, really fast, here's what I said on Saturday" (Trump 2017d). As he appeals to the authority of the written text in front of him, he repeatedly reminds the audience that he is the author of those words: "here's what I said," "so this is me," "this is my exact words," "that's what I said," "I said that," "these are my words" (ibid.). The implied expectation is that his re-reading involves verbatim replication of what he said at the golf club, thus minimizing the intertextual gap between then and now. As in any good theatrical performance, he encourages the audience to suspend disbelief and ignore questions of truth and accuracy when faced with the intertextual chasm between the two performances.

Trump positions his prior (decontextualized) words from the golf club as supposedly speaking for themselves. But, of course, this belies his active recontextualization that imbues those prior words with new meaning. Recall that at the golf club he expressed a condemnation of "this egregious display of hatred, bigotry, and violence – on many sides, on many sides" (Trump 2017a). This implied that anti-racism protesters exhibited the same type of hatred, bigotry, and violence as the White supremacists – promoting a moral equivalency between the two groups. In Phoenix, Trump deflects that criticism by first stripping away the words leading to that interpretation and then imagining different reasons for the criticism that ensued.

Trump constructs imaginary voices of critics to set up straw-man caricatures of their complaints as unjustified and ridiculous. For example, in a whiny voice, Trump pretends to be a journalist criticizing him for the initial statement he made about Charlottesville: "He didn't say it fast enough, he didn't do it on time, why did it take a day? He must be a racist. It took a day" (Trump 2017d). The main criticism ventriloquized by Trump is that he was merely late in issuing his response to Charlottesville. In fact, he delivered his controversial statement at the golf club on the same day of the violence in Charlottesville, so this is a specious claim that conveniently ignores the way his response lent tacit support to the White supremacists. On its own, the complaint of being late fails to adequately capture the kernel of the criticism. The complaint sounds almost absurd and even laughable, which, of course, is the point. This allows him to maintain the conceit that "I spoke out forcefully against hatred, bigotry, and violence" and to demonize "the very dishonest media" who he claims "don't report the facts" (ibid.). As he explains in Phoenix, "I'm really doing this to show how damned dishonest these people [the mainstream media] are" (ibid.).

In this case, Trump's denial of the initial meaning of his statement on Charlottesville may remain more implausible than plausible for most. But it represents another example of the way assumptions about words and meanings as they move across contexts allow Trump to avoid taking responsibility for a discreditable utterance by reshaping how that utterance is received by his most ardent supporters. Here, the context-specific meaning of Trump's initial response to Charlottesville is erased or at least minimized through the radical recontextualization of that statement in subsequent re-readings.

8.3   "I don't see any reason why it would be"

Standing next to Russian President Vladimir Putin at a joint news conference in Helsinki, Finland, on July 16, 2018, Trump said: "My people came to me, Dan Coats came to me and some others, they said they think it's Russia. I have President Putin; he just said it's not Russia. I will say this: I don't see any reason why it would be" (Trump 2018a). He spoke these words in response to a journalist's question about whether he accepted US intelligence agencies' findings on Russia's interference in the 2016 presidential election. These are just a few of the words representative of Trump's stance at the news conference where he decried Special Counsel Robert Mueller's investigation into Russian efforts to interfere in the 2016 presidential election as a "witch hunt" and passed up the opportunity to press Putin on the issue (ibid.).

Although the stance remained consistent with Trump's ongoing push to discredit the special counsel's investigation into election interference, the fact that he openly sided with Putin over US intelligence agencies while standing next to him in front of a world audience led to shock and condemnation from Americans across the political spectrum, including several prominent Republicans (*The New York Times* 2018). Senator John McCain, for example, called it "one of the most disgraceful performances by an American president in memory" (Landler 2018). Even vociferous Trump supporter Newt Gingrich tweeted, "It is the most serious mistake of his presidency and must be corrected – immediately" (Hirschfeld Davis 2018).

If ever there was a moment Trump needed to deploy a reactive reversal and plausibly deny controversial remarks, this was one of them. Back in Washington the day after the Helsinki summit, Trump spoke to the press before a meeting with lawmakers at the White House. He feigned surprise at the fuss over his news conference with Putin and told reporters, "I actually went out and reviewed a clip of an answer that I gave, and I realized that there is a need for some clarification. It should have been obvious, I thought it would be obvious but I would like to clarify just in case it wasn't" (Trump 2018b). Trump continued:

In a key sentence in my remarks, I said the word 'would' instead of 'wouldn't.' The sentence should have been 'I don't see any reason why I wouldn't' or 'why it wouldn't be Russia.' So just to repeat it, I said the word 'would' instead of 'wouldn't,' and the sentence should have been, and I thought I would be maybe a little bit unclear on the transcript or unclear on the actual video. The sentence should have been 'I don't see any reason why it wouldn't be Russia,' sort of a double negative. So you can put that in and I think that probably clarifies things pretty good by itself. I have on numerous occasions noted our intelligence findings that Russians attempted to interfere in our elections. (Trump 2018b)

As with the cases examined earlier, this one illustrates another narrow focus on an isolated segment of the initial controversial remarks, at the exclusion of the wider originating context in which those remarks were spoken. Here, Trump highlights a single word (i.e. "would") and claims a performance error in failing to adequately pronounce the negative contraction at the end of the word (i.e. "wouldn't").

Although Trump excuses the error by saying he meant to formulate "sort of a double negative," the locution ("I don't see any reason why it wouldn't be Russia") isn't really a double negative in the grammatical sense of using two negative elements in a single clause (e.g. "I don't see no reason"). Nevertheless, the excuse helps Trump shift attention onto an isolated line extracted from the totality of his remarks. Now, the focus revolves around a simple malapropism – that is, the mistaken use of a word in place of a similar-sounding one. Meaning to say "wouldn't" instead of "would" provides at least the appearance of a plausible defense – enough plausible deniability to provide upset congressional Republicans with some political cover to avoid taking substantial action against the president.

The problem with the defense, however, is that the narrow focus on this isolated line ignores the other words he spoke within the immediate context of the news conference and the broader context of his presidency. To accept Trump's excuse requires accepting the premise that the meaning most Americans drew from his performance hinged on a single word while ignoring Trump's track record of playing down the issue of Russian election interference. Indeed, Trump made several statements in the news conference that indicated a general lack of support for US intelligence assessments and law enforcement efforts to investigate Russian election interference (e.g. calling the special counsel investigation a "witch hunt") while giving credence to Russian denials (e.g. "I will tell you that President Putin was extremely strong and powerful in his denial today").

The wider context surrounding the news conference also mitigates against Trump's claim that he simply misspoke a single word. Before meeting with Putin, Trump had reaffirmed his stance against the special counsel investigation into Russian election interference in a tweet: "Our relationship with Russia has NEVER been worse thanks to many years of US foolishness and stupidity and now, the Rigged Witch Hunt!" (Trump on Twitter, July 15, 2018c).

Although, as he claimed the day after the Helsinki summit, Trump may have "noted our intelligence findings that Russians attempted to interfere in our elections" (Trump 2018b) on some past occasions, during the first two years of his presidency he typically accompanied such statements with the same type of equivocation expressed in Helsinki. Trump has a track record of contradictory statements – sometimes even within the same speech event – and the public record fails to support any claim that he has ever fully endorsed the intelligence community's assessment of Russian election interference without some equivocation.

Since Trump's lack of support for investigating Russian election interference is well known, the widespread negative reactions to Trump's Helsinki news conference have as much, if not more, to do with his speaking these remarks while standing next to Putin. After all, Trump has uttered similar conspiracy theories and disparaging remarks against US institutions investigating Russian election interference on Twitter and at campaign-style rallies. But doing so at a joint news conference with an American adversary contributes to the controversial reception his words received on this occasion.

Taking into account the full context of Trump's performance belies the implausible claim that a single word was the culprit for a supposed misunderstanding of what he meant. Trump argued the day after Helsinki that what he said "should have been obvious, I thought it would be obvious." Many Americans agreed that it was obvious, just not in the way Trump tried to assert after the fact.

8.4   Conclusion

As the examples in this chapter illustrate, the world-shaping political strategy of plausible deniability typically involves a narrow focus on semantics or grammar along with a grossly incomplete perspective on the interactional context. Whether by advocating for a context-free view of language or through recontextualization practices that replace prior words' contextual residues with new preferred meanings, plausible deniability attempts to sow enough doubt on the veracity of prior statements to allow politicians like Trump to avoid taking responsibility for them.

Feigning innocence in the face of controversial remarks is not new to the presidency of Donald Trump, but Trumpian discourse often pushes this language game to the limits of credulity – as evidenced by the examples examined here. To pretend along with Trump that he hasn't conveyed the objectionable ideas that he has spoken on many occasions is to enable his demagoguery. But countering this politics of division and fear can begin by calling out the faulty assumptions upon which much of his discourse is built. This requires a close look at the linguistic strategies and interactional contexts in which the discourse takes place.

References

Austin, J. L. 1961. "Performative Utterances." In *Philosophical Papers*, edited by
J. O. Urmson and G. J. Warnock, pp. 233–52. Oxford University Press.
Bajaj, Vikas, and Stuart A. Thompson. 2017. "Business Leaders Finally Walk Away
from Mr. Trump." *The New York Times*, August 16, 2017. https://nyti.ms
/2v1ppwX.
Briggs, Charles L., and Richard Bauman. 1992. "Genre, Intertextuality, and Social
Power." *Journal of Linguistic Anthropology* 2, no. 2: 131–72.
Comey, James. 2017a. "Statement for the Record." Hearings before the Senate Select
Committee on Intelligence, Senate, 115th Congress. June 8, 2017. http://bit.ly
/2ocoxYV.
  2017b. "Full Transcript and Video: James Comey's Testimony on Capitol Hill." *The
New York Times*, June 8, 2017. https://nyti.ms/2rZXsrn.
Fausset, Richard, and Alan Feuer. 2017. "Far-Right Groups Surge into National View in
Charlottesville." *The New York Times*, August 13, 2017. https://nyti.ms/2uTJK77.
Grice, H. Paul. 1975. "Logic and Conversation." In *Syntax and Semantics*, Vol. 3,
Speech Acts, edited by Peter Cole and Jerry L. Morgan, pp. 41–58. Academic Press.
Hirschfeld Davis, Julie. 2018. "Trump, at Putin's Side, Questions U.S. Intelligence on
2016 Election." *The New York Times*, July 16, 2018. https://nyti.ms/2Jp88Vz.
Landler, Mark. 2018. "Trump Sheds All Notions of How a President Should Conduct
Himself Abroad." *The New York Times*, July 16, 2018. https://nyti.ms/2Jsk6h3.
Lipton, Sara. 2017. "Trump's Meddlesome Priest." *The New York Times*, June 8, 2017.
https://nyti.ms/2s1PUUS.
The New York Times. 2018, July 17. "How Republican Lawmakers Responded to
Trump's Russian Meddling Denial." *The New York Times*, July 17, 2018. https://
nyti.ms/2Jqxi61.
Reddy, Michael J. 1979. "The Conduit Metaphor: A Case of Frame Conflict in Our
Language about Language." In *Metaphor and Thought*, edited by Andrew Ortony,
pp. 284–324. Cambridge University Press.
Schmidt, Michael S. 2017. "Comey Memo Says Trump Asked Him to End Flynn
Investigation." *The New York Times*, May 16, 2017. https://nyti.ms/2rnUb1z.
Trump, Donald. 2017a. "President Trump Signs Veterans Health Care Bill." C-SPAN
video, 14:42. August 12, 2017. https://cs.pn/2JglIx3.
  2017b. "Statement by President Trump." The White House, August 14, 2017. http://
bit.ly/32N8Oi8.
  2017c. "Trump Tower Press Conference." C-SPAN video, 34:01. August 15, 2017.
https://cs.pn/32IpAPb.
  2017d. "President Trump Rally in Phoenix, Arizona." C-SPAN video, 1:43:21.
August 22, 2017. https://cs.pn/2MH834w.
  2018a. "Joint News Conference by Trump and Putin: Full Video and Transcript." *The
New York Times*, July 16, 2018. https://nyti.ms/2Js0M3E.
  2018b. "Trump Addresses Criticism of Appearance with Putin: Full Transcript." *The
New York Times*, July 17, 2018. https://nyti.ms/2NX2vBp.
Trump, Donald. (@realDonaldTrump). 2018c. "Our relationship with Russia has
NEVER been worse thanks to many years of U.S. foolishness and stupidity and
now, the Rigged Witch Hunt!" Twitter, July 15, 2018. http://bit.ly/2N4Q9aN.

Part III

The Interactive Making of the Trumpian World

9   Part III Introduction: Collusion: On Playing Along with the President

Janet McIntosh

James Comey, Director of the Federal Bureau of Investigation until Trump fired him in May 2017, delivered a fascinating dollop of amateur language theory in his scathing May 2019 op-ed in the *New York Times* (Comey 2019). The op-ed focused on why the Trump-friendly Attorney General Bill Barr had downplayed the implications of the Mueller report about Russian interference in the 2016 general election. Barr's characterization was so misleading that even the usually taciturn Mueller publicly objected. Comey wonders whether Barr might have been mirroring Comey's own experience while in the White House: that of being caught in Trump's "web of alternative reality." Comey writes:

Proximity to an amoral leader reveals something depressing ... It starts with your sitting silent while he lies, both in public and private, making you complicit by your silence. In meetings with him, his assertions about what "everyone thinks" and what is "obviously true" wash over you, unchallenged ... Speaking rapid-fire with no spot for others to jump into the conversation, Mr. Trump makes everyone a co-conspirator to his preferred set of facts, or delusions. I have felt it – this president building with his words a web of alternative reality and busily wrapping it around all of us in the room ... From the private circle of assent, it moves to public displays of personal fealty at places like cabinet meetings. While the entire world is watching, you do what everyone else around the table does – you talk about how amazing the leader is and what an honor it is to be associated with him.

Comey furnishes a powerful testimonial to the way humans sometimes go along with others' words (particularly those of the powerful), fail to break the verbal spell being woven, and ultimately cooperate in jointly constructing a model of reality through their own utterances. His description of the displays of personal fealty Trump manages to elicit around a conference table, in fact, are observed in breathtaking detail in van Over's chapter in this section. "Mr. Trump," Comey concludes, "eats your soul in small bites."

Scholars of language have referred to dynamics like these as "collusion" (McDermott and Tylbor 1995). They don't mean "collusion" in the sense of a presidential campaign deliberately coordinating with the Russians to interfere in an election. Rather, "collusion" in language studies concerns the

151

often-unwitting ways in which people coordinate and synchronize aspects of what they are up to in a speech event, playing into one another's script while achieving a loose consensus about what is going on (ibid.: 218–19; see also Mannheim and Tedlock 1995). Conversational participants often don't even realize they're doing this; the dynamic emerges from organic qualities of our species, cooperativeness and impressionability, and it also preys on such impressionability to enlist people in social arrangements and hierarchies not directly of their own making and not necessarily in their interest. Who knows if Trump colluded with the Russians, but it seems clear that those in his circle collude with him verbally.

One implication of linguistic collusion is this: We like to imagine ourselves as free agents, especially in individualistic societies focused on personal choice, but the fact is that we operate within – and help to build – constraining social structures as we interact with others. By "structures" I mean not only clearly regimented institutional arrangements and forces, but also patterned behaviors loosely shared by groups of social actors, such as gendered roles and routines or habitual responses to individuals with power, as well as those invisible webs that interlocutors weave together on the fly in their embodied verbal minutiae (see Mannheim, this volume). A student goes to meet with a patronizing professor in office hours and, within a few minutes of conversation, finds himself acting like a subordinate. A woman meeting a courtly man finds herself adopting an unfamiliarly self-effacing role. An audience member ends up applauding a politician's forceful statement, even if they aren't quite sure what they think of it.

Collusion isn't quite the same thing as consent (McDermott and Tylbor 1995). It's hard to resist the role that is imposed upon or expected of you, particularly when the power dynamics aren't in your favor: when your interlocutor can hold sway over your career future; when the pressure to conform to gender roles tilts your contribution one way or another; or when your interlocutor speaks with the backing of a venerable institution – even if it is, as in the case of the presidency, besmirched. And as McDermott and Tylbor (1995: 232) argue, through collusion, much is swept under the rug. Deception and silence structure not only institutional life but also banal conversation. In Trump's world, there are countless "constraints on people telling the truth" (ibid.), and the chapters in this section explore how some of those constraints work, in speech events ranging from the formal to the casual.

9.1   Politicians, the Press, and Collusion

One of the many remarkable linguistic dimensions of Trump's rise is how he has ruptured traditional interactions with most journalists. Trump doesn't like the questions most media outlets ask of him, since they so often call him out on his falsehoods or confront him with the human rights implications of his tweets and policy efforts. He thus refuses to collude in the notion that such journalists are neutral, charging them with "liberal bias" and "fake news" even when they are speaking truth, and taking their questions as if they are personal criticisms. Many journalists, in turn, have grown more pointed and overtly aggressive in confronting him. To some extent, they seem to be realizing that although good journalism should be grounded in facts (as well as humans can know facts, anyway, with all our epistemological limitations) rather than Trumpian false-hoods, the question of how those facts are foregrounded or wielded has never been a matter of actual "neutrality."

However, when the Trump-friendly *Fox News* interviews him, everyone gets along. Not only that, but *Fox News* anchors somehow have to retain the journalistic illusion that they aren't merely a state TV outlet. Trump, too, is invested in the illusion that *Fox*, with all its flattery of him, is the only "objective" network. Consider the following exchange between Tucker Carlson and Trump in July 2019 (Schwartz 2019). The context was Trump's escalation of tensions with Iran since his 2018 abandonment of the 2015 nuclear deal, and his having come close to instigating another major Middle Eastern war (video excerpt starts at 1:53).[1]

CARLSON :   you came very close to sending the US military to strike Iran
            you pulled back at the last moment
            you were criticized by neo-cons in Washington for doing that- they wanted
            you to strike Ira:n
            why do you think they wanted [that]
TRUMP :   [A:ND] I was given a lot of credit by
            most people
            lotta people gave me a lotta credit=
CARLSON :   =the public was on your side.
            for sure=
TRUMP :   =lotta people said that was a great presidential moment which was
            you know
            rather shocking to hear

Carlson here confronts Trump with someone's criticism, a ploy that just might allow *Fox News* to retain its narrative of being hard-hitting and objective (cf. Clayman 1992). Trump never answers Carlson's question, instead launch-ing his self-defense with the word "and," as if he is completing a thought that Carlson began. Trump's focus? How much approval his act of restraint gar-nered (an act that sounds all the more heroic since Carlson has reminded viewers that neo-cons wanted Trump to follow through). Carlson quickly overlaps with him to say, in a bright, supportive-sounding tone, "The public was on your side. For sure." This sets up Trump for a moment of braggadocio; he was "shocked" to hear a "lotta people" deem it a "great presidential moment." (A sense of victimhood may underpin this remark, for Trump likes to complain that talking heads in the media undervalue him.)

In this exchange, Trump and Carlson share a world. *Fox* is hard-hitting because it confronts Trump with criticism, and Trump's calling-off of the strike was supposedly a triumphal moment. Throughout the interview, Carlson fixes Trump with a serious looking gaze, one that mirrors Trump's own, and sagely nods here and there. The body language alone signals a kind of acquiescence (see Mannheim and Tedlock 1995: 9), as collaborative agendas get weaved into each other turn by turn. Carlson retains the façade of journalism, and Trump retains the façade of greatness on the channel most favored by his supporters.

9.2   Coaching the Performance of Solidarity

A theme that recurs in the chapters that follow is how Trump sometimes guides and instructs his interlocutors to play along with him. We see this dynamic in van Over's discussion of how Trump coaches the participants in a Black History Month "listening session" to play into his hands as "evaluator in chief." We also see it in Cameron's and Mannheim's respective chapters about how Trump's "grab 'em by the pussy" conversation draws on long-standing, ritualistic routines of heteronormative male in-group talk, routines in which male interlocutors slot into pre-fabricated roles and collude to affirm a pernicious patriarchal solidarity. In several chapters, including that by Sierra and Shrikant, we see that laughter is vital to constructing the myth of widespread approval.

Indeed, collusive laughter, especially when in a widely televised event, can create the appearance of a popular president, even when those in the laughing group later report their own ambivalence. Consider Trump's infamous speech at Central Intelligence Agency (CIA) headquarters in Langley, Virginia, his first delivered after his inauguration (CNN 2017). Standing before TV cameras and an audience of about 400 self-selected CIA agents, employees, and cabinet members, Trump engaged in a rambling, self-centered speech. His words and sometimes-jocular affect flattered his audience and cued them to laugh about "out groups" (cf. Carty and Musharbash 2008: 214) – in this case, the mass media and anyone who didn't vote for him – as well as to applaud to affirm their mutual solidarity.

After being introduced, for instance, Trump said:

Well, I want to thank everybody. Very, very special people. And it is true, this is my first stop. Officially. We're not talking about the (inaugural) balls, or we're not talking about even the speeches – although they did treat me nicely on that speech yesterday. ((*laughter from crowd*)) I always call 'em the dishonest media, but they treated me nicely. ((*louder laughter from crowd*)) But I want to say that there is nobody that feels stronger

about the intelligence community and the CIA than Donald Trump. ((*applause begins*)) There's nobody. ((*continued applause, whooping*))
[Starting at 02:00] Probably almost everybody in this room voted for me, but I will not ask you to raise your hands if you did. ((*laughter from crowd*)) But I would guarantee a big portion, because we're all on the same wavelength, folks. ((*applause begins*)) We're all on the same wavelength, right? ((*continuing applause*)) (CNN 2017)

Audience members clapped, laughed, and ratified Trump at all the right moments, sounding perfectly entrained, in the sense of being interactively drawn in and carried along in synchrony. Later, those present gave mixed reviews, and some reported having found Trump's speech disrespectful, even appalling (Ignatius 2017). But like the "boys on the bus" described by Cameron and Mannheim, like the participants in the "listening session" described by van Over and Sierra and Shrikant, like all those members of the administration described by James Comey, those present allowed themselves to be swept along as the event unfolded. As McDermott and Tylbor (1995: 220) summarize it, collusion sometimes "amounts to a well-orchestrated lie that offers a world [participants] do not have to produce but can pretend to live by, a world everyone knows to be, at the same time, unrealizable, but momentarily useful as stated."

9.3   Colluding in Gendered Lies

The presidency furnishes a powerful social force field, but arguably, the socio-cultural force of gender expectations is just as powerful, perhaps more so because so often invisible. In conforming to gender roles, speakers collude in overarching models of and myths about the world, with powerful implications not only for male dominance, but also collective agreements about what even counts as real or important.

As Cameron and Mannheim emphasize in their chapters about Trump's *Access Hollywood* bus banter, the dynamics of gendered conversational routines produce a sense of what is normal and what is abnormal, with masculine routines tending to stigmatize femininity. Of course these patterns of speech pre-date Trump; one could argue, in fact, that not only did his interlocutors collude with him, but that he, in a broader sense, was colluding with these ambient ideas about gender.

Related to this, in Carol Cohn's chapter on the patterned speech of American national security professionals, we see them and commanders-in-chief collude in broad ideological frameworks that mark some stances as desirably "masculine" and others as undesirably "feminine," with war talk clearly steered in a masculine direction. Metaphors used in the defense industry – metaphors that sexualize weaponry, or that conceptually delete the human suffering of war – affirm the masculine status of speakers, while entraining them into patterns of talk and thought. As Cohn puts it, certain "ways of speaking and topics of conversation are ... pre-marked as masculine/legitimate or feminine/illegitimate," thus "short-circuiting" certain kinds of thinking and foreclosing certain kinds of conversation. Talking about empathy for casualties of war is off the table, or heavily policed if it makes an appearance. With his tweets turning nuclear arsenals into virtual pissing contests, Trump is caught in a web bigger than he is, and with his discourse he perpetuates this particular way of shaping "reality." These collusive patterns of speech influence those who make the biggest decisions about international violence.

Yet, as Comey's op-ed implies, not everyone has to collude with Trump. Sometimes his detractors boldly disrupt the conversational rhythm or violate protocol – as when Nancy Pelosi firmly cut into Trump's conversational tactics in the Oval Office to say "Please don't characterize the strength that I bring to this meeting" (Stolberg and Karni 2018), or when a bicyclist refused the typical show of deference and famously gave Trump's motorcade the finger, later paying the price by being fired from her job (though she went on to win a county supervisor seat in Virginia; Schwartzman 2019). Yet interactive collusion is often the easier path, being both unconscious and socially rewarded. And as Trump has demonstrated, not only can an entire administration be enlisted in collusion, but so too can nearly half a nation.

Note

1. Transcription conventions most relevant to the analysis in this chapter include the use of CAPITALS to indicate talk spoken with special emphasis. Colons after a vowel indicate an elongated vowel sound. A left bracket ([) marks the onset, and a right bracket (]) marks the offset of overlapping talk. A dash (-) marks the cut-off of the current sound. An equal sign (=) indicates "latching," where talk starts up in especially close temporal proximity to the end of the previous talk. Transcribers' comments and non-verbal action descriptors are italicized in double parentheses ((*like this*)); single parentheses, (like this), around talk indicate a problematic hearing. Punctuation symbols are used to mark intonation changes rather than as grammatical symbols: a period indicates a falling contour; a question mark, a rising contour; and a comma, a falling-rising contour, as might be found in the midst of a list. Each line of text (without a hard return) indicates talk spoken within a single breath group.

References

Carty, John, and Yasmine Musharbash. 2008. "You've *Got* to Be Joking: Asserting the Analytical Value of Humour and Laughter in Contemporary Anthropology." *Anthropological Forum* 18 no. 3: 209–17.
Clayman, Stephen. 1992. "Footing in the Achievement of Neutrality: The Case of News Interview Discourse." In *Talk at Work*, edited by Paul Drew and John Heritage, pp. 163–98. Cambridge University Press.

CNN. 2017. "Donald Trump's Entire CIA Speech." *CNN* video, January 21, 2017. https://bit.ly/2rI2yuk.

Comey, James. 2019. "James Comey: How Trump Co-opts Leaders Like Bill Barr." *The New York Times*, May 1, 2019. https://nyti.ms/2vuVwYp.

Ignatius, David. 2017. "CIA Officers Give Mixed Reviews of Trump's Strange Visit." *The Washington Post* video, January 22, 2017. https://wapo.st/2Dy3ZOn.

McDermott, R. P., and Henry Tylbor. 1995. "On the Necessity of Collusion in Conversation." In *The Dialogic Emergence of Culture*, edited by Dennis Tedlock and Bruce Mannheim, pp. 218–36. University of Illinois Press.

Mannheim, Bruce, and Dennis Tedlock. 1995. "Introduction." In *The Dialogic Emergence of Culture*, edited by Dennis Tedlock and Bruce Mannheim, pp. 1–32. University of Illinois Press.

Schwartz, Ian. 2019. "Full Trump Interview with Tucker Carlson: Not Striking Iran, Facebook, and Twitter, China, Afghanistan." *RealClear Politics* video, 01:53, July 1, 2019. https://bit.ly/2RavsOq.

Schwartzman, Paul. 2019. "Cyclist Who Flipped Off Trump Wins County Supervisor Seat Representing His Golf Club." *The Washington Post*, November 5, 2019. https://wapo .st/2P8FZXQ.

Stolberg, Sheryl Gay, and Annie Karni. 2018. "Pelosi vs. Trump: 'Don't Characterize the Strength That I Bring,' She Says." *The New York Times*, December 11, 2018. https://nyti.ms/2qblq4v.

10   Banter, Male Bonding, and the Language of Donald Trump

Deborah Cameron

In October 2016, just a few weeks before the presidential election, the *Washington Post* released a tape on which the Republican candidate Donald Trump could be heard engaging in what the newspaper called an "extremely lewd conversation about women" (Fahrenthold 2016). The *Post*'s report explained that the exchange had been recorded in 2005, on a bus taking Trump, along with Billy Bush, the host of the entertainment show *Access Hollywood*, to the set of a TV soap opera on which he was due to make a cameo appearance. The two men were not alone – there were several other people on the bus, and a third man's voice is heard on the tape – but they apparently assumed they were speaking privately and off the record. The flavor of the interaction is captured in the transcribed extract reproduced below, which begins when Billy Bush catches sight of Arianne Zucker, the actress Trump is about to meet (CBS News 2016; video excerpt starts at 0.30):[1]

Extract 10.1 "You can do anything"

BUSH:	sheesh your girl's hot as shit (.) in the purple
BUSH AND THIRD MAN:	WOAH YES WOAH
BUSH:	yes the Donald has scored woah my man
TRUMP:	look at you you are a pussy
	((*indecipherable simultaneous talk*))
TRUMP:	I better use some tic-tacs in case I start kissing her
	you know I'm automatically attracted to beautiful (.)
	I just start kissing them
	it's like a magnet kiss I don't even wait
	((*other men laughing*))
	and when you're a star they let you do it
	you can do anything
BUSH:	whatever you want
TRUMP:	grab em by the pussy ((*laughter*)) do anything

As commentators lined up to condemn him, Trump was compelled to issue an apology. "I said it," he admitted, "I am wrong. I apologize" (Jacobs et al. 2016). But he also sought to downplay the offense by describing the conversation as "locker-room talk" and "locker-room banter" (Gregory 2016). In this chapter, I want to take a closer look at the phenomenon of "banter." I will ask in general terms what banter is and what it does, both for the men directly engaged in it and in society at large. I will also consider more specifically what Donald Trump's participation in this highly publicized episode of banter contributed to his public image and his successful campaign for the presidency.

10.1   What Is Banter, and What Is It For?

The earliest recorded use of the word "banter" in English was as a verb meaning "to make fun of,"[2] and standard dictionaries still define it as good-humored joking or teasing.[3] When men in Trump's position dismiss offensive remarks as "just banter," they are trading on the idea that banter is a kind of verbal play, which therefore cannot be judged by the normal standards of public discourse. Whereas public discourse is expected to be serious, truthful, measured, and decorous, banter, by definition, is none of those things: It is light-hearted, humorous, full of untruths or half-truths (e.g. tall tales, joking, boasting), and often highly indecorous in both its content and its language. If you're offended by it, that only goes to show that you don't understand the rules of the game: You have taken the words out of their original context and misinterpreted their real (in)significance. The "just banter" defense also trades on our understanding of banter as a prototypically male speech genre – something men engage in casually among themselves, especially in all-male settings. Trump's description of the *Access Hollywood* tape as "locker-room" banter, and his subsequent claim that former President Bill Clinton had said worse things to him on the golf course (Jacobs et al. 2016), underscored the idea that this was just normal male behavior, of a kind that most men, from factory workers to presidents, would at some point have taken part in. As such, it said nothing about Trump's fitness for public office. It was just a harmless blowing-off of steam, an illustration of the truism that boys will be boys.

Though male banter is particularly associated with settings like the locker-room where men's behavior is not constrained by the presence of women, women often play a significant role in it by serving as its ostensible topic. The way men talk about women among themselves has been described in detail in research on adolescent male talk (e.g. Scott Kiesling's 2001 study of a college fraternity), and Extract 10.1, though the participants are much older, is a similar case. It begins with the men collectively passing judgment on the attractiveness of a particular woman and congratulating Trump on having "scored" with her, then continues with a sequence in which Trump brags about the license his celebrity gives him to "do anything" to women he finds attractive. The last part of this extract, containing the now-infamous reference to "grabbing women by the pussy," became a particular focus for criticism of Trump, much of it directed at what the tape allegedly revealed about his disrespectful attitudes and predatory sexual behavior. Some commentators evidently believed that he was admitting to acts of criminal sexual assault. But while it is possible Trump really has committed such acts (there have been several allegations to that effect), it is a mistake to treat exchanges like this one as straightforward factual reports. In the context of male banter, a man who brags about his exploits with women is like a fisherman telling tall tales about the size of his catch, or an old soldier exaggerating his heroic deeds on the battlefield. His companions understand that it's a performance: The laughter and other supportive responses they produce cannot be taken as an indication that they believe him, or even that they share the attitudes he expresses. I have studied several examples of sexist and homophobic male banter where the group included one or more men who were – and were known to be – gay. They were neither homophobic nor sexually interested in women, yet they still participated actively in conversations that mocked gay men and treated women as sexual objects. This behavior makes little sense unless we understand that the ostensible topic of men's banter is not its real subject: What it's really about is men's relationships with one another.

Though at one level Extract 10.1 is, as the *Washington Post* said, a "conversation about women," it is also a negotiation among the men. On one hand, they are bonding with one another around what they present as a shared interest in "scoring" with women who are "as hot as shit"; on the other, they are constructing a pecking order within the group, with Trump as the "alpha male" and Bush as his loyal sidekick. On sighting the actress Arianne Zucker, Bush immediately designates her as Trump's property (i.e. "your girl ... the Donald has scored"); in the following sequence he and the others actively encourage Trump to monopolize the floor, confining their own contributions to supportive laughter and other brief interjections designed to affirm Trump's dominant status. Some of the same features can be seen in the extract reproduced below, which comes from the first part of the tape. This sequence also begins with the men passing judgment on a particular woman's attractiveness: She has just been assessed by another speaker as "still very beautiful" when Trump embarks on a narrative about a personal encounter he had with her in the past (CBS News 2016: 0.00).

Extract 10.2 "I failed I'll admit it"

TRUMP: you know I moved on her actually
            you know she was down in Palm Beach and I moved on her and
            I failed I'll admit it
THIRD MAN: woah
TRUMP: I did try to fuck her she was married
THIRD MAN: ((*laughs*)) that's huge news there

TRUMP: and I moved on her very heavily in fact I took her out furniture shopping
she wanted to get some furniture and I said I'll show you where they have
some nice furniture I took her out furniture (.)
I moved on her like a bitch ((*other men laughing*)) but I couldn't get there
and she was married
then all of a sudden I see her and she's now got the big phony tits and
everything
she's totally changed her look

In this second extract, Trump is doing the opposite of bragging: He's telling
a story about an occasion when a woman he was interested in rejected his
advances. He's still subtly asserting his alpha-male status, assuming the right to
dominate the conversation and claiming to have superior knowledge about the
woman who is its current topic. Once again, his companions accept this, encouraging and supporting him with well-timed, sympathetic laughter. But something
else is going on here, too. By introducing the topic of what he explicitly describes
as a failed attempt at seduction, Trump positions the other men as trusted
confidants. He communicates that he feels comfortable sharing sensitive information with them, and that he trusts them to laugh with him rather than at him.

10.2   Banter and Gossip

Much of what I have said so far about male banter, and particularly about
Extract 10.2, would be equally applicable to another kind of talk we have
a generic label for in English: *gossip*. That might seem like a surprising claim,
given that in the popular imagination gossip is as strongly associated with
women talking in all-female settings as banter is with men talking in all-male
ones. But this stereotype is misleading. Research suggests that gossip, broadly
defined as informal peer-talk whose main subject is the personal lives of the
participants and other people they know, accounts for a significant proportion
of everyday talk among both sexes. According to the evolutionary scientist
Robin Dunbar (1996), the prevalence of gossip in everyday life across cultures
reflects the contribution it makes to the effective functioning of human social
groups. Three of the purposes it serves are particularly important in this respect.
    First, gossip is a conduit for disseminating socially valuable information: It
continually updates group members' knowledge about who is doing what with
whom, and how the community judges it. Second, it helps to regulate behavior
in accordance with community norms. Not only do people learn from gossip
what behaviors the community disapproves of, they also learn that being
gossiped about can have serious social consequences, which are an incentive
to avoid behaving in ways that attract disapproval. Because of that, gossip has
been seen as a "weapon of the weak" (Scott 1985), something relatively
powerless people can use against more powerful ones. This is one reason

why gossip has historically been depicted as a peculiarly female vice. The English word *gossip* originally denoted a woman's close female companion, and the intimacy of the relationship between "gossips" was often perceived by men as a threat: They feared that women talking among themselves would share damaging information or spread malicious rumors about their menfolk. In reality, of course, men also engaged in this kind of talk. Its ubiquity reflects the third important purpose it serves, which is reinforcing the social bonds among community members. One key feature of gossip is the exchanging of sensitive personal information: Participants share their own private experiences, secrets confided to them by others, and judgments on others' character or behavior which they might not want to be held accountable for in public. This sharing creates both intimacy and mutual dependence. If I tell you a secret, either about myself or someone else, that is a sign that I trust you and feel close to you, but in the longer term it also makes me dependent on your goodwill. You can show goodwill by reciprocating with a secret of your own, so that both of us have something to lose by betraying the other's confidence.

If we accept this account of what gossip is, and does, it becomes possible to view male banter as a subtype of gossip, one whose distinctive function is reinforcing homosocial bonds among men. By "homosocial bonds" I mean same-sex relationships with no overt sexual component – the kinds of relationships men are encouraged to cultivate in institutions like college fraternities, sports teams, street gangs, and the military services. Male homosocial relationships involve trust, loyalty, solidarity, and camaraderie, but not too much emotional display, and no explicit expression of sexual desire. Banter is a verbal enactment of these values. As with other types of gossip, the participants in banter constitute themselves as an in-group by talking about and passing judgment on an absent out-group (such as women or gay men); they may also share confidences or secrets (like Trump's story about his failure to seduce a woman) to create relationships of trust and mutual dependence. But male banter has other recurring features which are absent from, or less integral to, other kinds of gossip.

One of these features is the "lewdness" that was emphasized in media commentary on the *Access Hollywood* tape. Male banter is often deliberately and self-consciously transgressive: It revolves around acts, thoughts, and desires that would conventionally be judged offensive or shocking (common themes include sex, violence, crime, drugs/alcohol, and the expression of "politically incorrect" attitudes), and these are commonly discussed in markedly vulgar and explicit language. This serves two purposes. Like other forms of gossip, banter reinforces group norms, but in this case the norms are defined in opposition to mainstream social conventions: What's being asserted is men's freedom to transgress the normal rules of polite society. As well as being an expression of their masculinity, this contributes to the bonding process. Like the sharing of secrets, the sharing of transgressive desires, acts, and words is a token of closeness and trust. It says, "I am showing that I trust you by saying things, and using words, that I wouldn't want the whole world to hear." Affiliative responses, like the laughter the other men on the tape produce whenever Trump says something particularly crude, signal that the speaker's trust is not misplaced.

Another striking feature of male banter is its "light," non-serious or playful character. This can also be related to its homosocial bonding function. The pressure to avoid behavior that might be perceived as either feminine or gay limits men's options for expressing their feelings toward male peers (Way 2013); female friends (at least in cultures like the US) are freer to display both strong emotions and physical affection. Under these conditions, humor becomes an important vehicle for the expression of intimacy between men. Its importance is reflected in the regularity with which participants in male banter employ strategies such as joking, joshing, mock-insulting or verbal dueling, bragging, telling tall tales and embarrassing anecdotes.

As I will argue in more detail below, male homosocial banter also differs from other types of gossip in that it is not a "weapon of the weak." Though it may occur in situations where men feel insecure, or where they feel that their traditional privileges are under threat, banter is invariably a symbolic (re) assertion of their social and sexual dominance.

10.3   Male Banter, Solidarity, and Power

The account I have just given of male banter suggests that most public criticism of the *Access Hollywood* tape missed an important point: It focused too much on the content of the conversation and not enough on its interpersonal bonding function. But to say that is not to endorse the argument made by Trump and his defenders that "locker-room banter" is harmless. On the contrary, complaints about its "lewd" language and sexist sentiments completely bypass the deeper reasons why male banter is harmful – and why it remains harmful even when we know the participants are not describing real events or expressing their real beliefs. Banter is not just a window into the mind of the individual man who engages in it. It is a ritualized social practice that helps to maintain men's collective dominance over women.

The social system in which men dominate women is often referred to as "patriarchy," a term that literally means "the rule of the fathers." Some theorists have suggested, however, that the form of male dominance seen in modern societies might more aptly be called "fratriarchy," the rule of the brothers, or as the political theorist Carole Pateman (1988) puts it, "fraternal patriarchy." Whereas true patriarchies are organized around vertical relations of male power – both women and younger men are subject to the authority of the father who heads the household or the clan – modern fraternal patriarchy depends more on horizontal relationships of solidarity among men, who cooperate with one another to exclude and subjugate women. Male banter could be seen as this system's verbal glue. It strengthens the bonds among men while relegating women to much the same status as the fish in a fishing story or the faceless enemy in a war story: They do not matter for their own sake, they just provide the material for men's displays of fraternal solidarity. And while those displays may be symbolic, their consequences are real.

Though I have argued against interpreting Trump's boasting as a literal admission of sexual assault, that does not mean there is no connection between male banter and violence against women. In her classic study of fraternity gang rape, the anthropologist Peggy Reeves Sanday (2007) argued that what motivates men to commit rape in groups is their desire both to prove their manhood and to feel close to one another – which are also among the purposes served by banter. One former fraternity brother who was interviewed for Sanday's study recalled that banter was part of the fraternity's everyday life. For him, engaging in this "perpetual, hysterical banter" had served important purposes: Being included in the brothers' talk and their laughter helped to dispel the social and sexual anxieties he had felt when he first arrived on campus, making him feel "happy, confident and loved" (2007: 152). It is not a coincidence that banter is a common practice in the kinds of all-male groups (e.g. fraternities and sports teams) that are regularly implicated in cases of group rape. Sanday identified regular engagement in banter, along with homophobic attitudes, heavy alcohol consumption, and the use of pornography, as a significant factor producing "rape-prone" campus cultures. Of course, it is not inevitable that what the interviewee quoted above called "acting out on a verbal level" will lead those involved to commit acts of violence, but one can make the other seem more acceptable, or less unthinkable. The social and psychological benefits men derive from their membership of a tightly bonded group may also lead them to put their fraternal loyalties first, joining in with assaults that they would not have initiated, or remaining silent about behavior they have witnessed with horror.

But fraternal loyalties do not have to be expressed in such extreme ways to have negative consequences for women. In society as a whole, the most pervasive negative consequence of fraternal bonding is the way it shuts women out. Ritualized practices of fraternal solidarity are commonly used to exclude women, or consign them to second-class "interloper" status, in professions and institutions which no longer bar them formally. When bankers socialize with clients in strip clubs, or construction workers adorn the site office with pictures of topless models, they are communicating that women are Other: They do not belong to, and cannot participate on equal terms in, the fraternal networks men use to get things done. The link between fraternal solidarity and male dominance is particularly strong in politics, a domain from which women were historically excluded and where they continue to be heavily outnumbered.

To build and sustain successful political careers, men must be assiduous in forging fraternal bonds with other powerful men. And wherever there is fraternal bonding, there will also be male banter. This is why Trump's assertion that he had "heard worse from Bill Clinton on the golf course" was more believable (whether or not it was actually true) than the statements made by other politicians who claimed to be shocked by the *Access Hollywood* tape. It seemed unlikely that these senior political figures had got to where they were without at some point participating in similar conversations, and impossible that they had never heard this kind of talk before. Their public criticisms of Trump thus left them open to the charge of being hypocrites and political opportunists.

10.4   Banter, Authenticity, and the Trump "Brand"

What did his involvement in this episode of male banter do for Donald Trump as a public figure and a presidential candidate? When the tape was first released, it was widely assumed that the effect would be negative, causing many voters who had supported him thus far to turn away from him in disgust. In the event, though, that was not what happened. Undoubtedly there were people who listened to the tape and heard an unpresidential misogynist boor; but there were other audiences who heard something very different. In the context of an election in which his opponent was a woman (and was widely resented for that reason), it is likely that for some voters Trump's performance of masculinity, and indeed misogyny, only added to his appeal. As I noted earlier, Trump successfully positioned himself throughout the conversation as the alpha male of the group: Both his own behavior and the deference shown to him by the other men on the tape reinforced the impression that he possessed several qualities traditionally associated with strong male leaders, such as authority, aggressiveness, competitiveness, and high libido.

But Trump's behavior on the tape also reinforced another perception that was part of his appeal for many voters. Both the transgressiveness of his banter and the (hypo)critical responses it drew from other politicians tapped into the popular disaffection with conventional politics and politicians that his campaign had exploited from the outset. His political persona was that of the maverick outsider who was not afraid to offend the establishment in his quest to, as his campaign slogan put it, "make America great again." The release of the *Access Hollywood* tape – eleven years old and recorded without the participants' knowledge – seemed to confirm that this persona was not just cynically created for the purposes of the campaign; it was a consistent, transparent, and authentic expression of who Donald Trump really was.

Research in a number of contexts (discussed in Umbach and Humphrey 2018) suggests that "authenticity" – the perception of something or someone as genuine, honest and "real" rather than fake, insincere, and artificial – has become a quality people increasingly look for when choosing political leaders. We want to vote for someone who comes across as a "real person," someone whose public utterances reflect their own beliefs rather than the coaching of campaign strategists and party spin-doctors. The ironic but predictable result has been to make authenticity an important element of the successful politician's "brand," something the strategists and spin-doctors must try to ensure their candidate communicates. This posed a problem for Hillary Clinton. As a political insider whose independent career had followed a long period of supporting her husband's, Clinton was inevitably (and not inaccurately) seen as someone who had made compromises and switched positions: She could not project the same consistency as Trump, nor make the same claim to come from outside the political establishment. She based her campaign on the more traditional value of competence, having the skills and the experience for the job, and by any reasonable measure she was far more qualified than her opponent. But Trump's "authentic" persona, that of the maverick alpha-male business tycoon, is associated with competence by a large section of the American public. Though arguably Trump's image as a "good businessman" is entirely manufactured (he is not a self-made billionaire but someone who inherited his father's wealth, and many of his business dealings have been spectacularly unsuccessful), he has cultivated it over many years through his appearances on reality TV, and he has learned to perform it convincingly. His contribution to the banter heard on the *Access Hollywood* tape was in that sense completely "on brand" – simultaneously a display of authenticity, masculinity, and power.

In the end, then, the "unpresidential" quality of Trump's "locker-room banter" did not damage his political prospects; it may even have worked to his advantage, by reinforcing the message that a vote for him would be a vote against conventional politics. Yet from a feminist perspective there is something deeply ironic about that message. Though in many respects it would be fair to describe Donald Trump as an unconventional president, in one respect he has been anything but unconventional: His administration epitomizes the values and practices of traditional fraternal patriarchy. In Trump's White House, as in the locker-room, women continue to be excluded from conversations in which men discuss their bodies and make decisions about their lives.

Notes

1. Many versions of the tape are now publicly available, but I have chosen to cite this one, which *CBS News* used by courtesy of *The Washington Post*, because although – like all the most easily accessible versions I reviewed – it bleeps out the words deemed too "lewd" to broadcast (including *pussy* and *tits*), it has written captions that make clear what they were; it is also one of the better versions on YouTube in terms of its sound quality. Transcription conventions used for conversation analysis here include the use

of CAPITALS to indicate talk spoken with special emphasis. Colons after a vowel indicate an elongated vowel sound. A left bracket ([) marks the onset and a right bracket (]) marks the offset of overlapping talk. Numbers in parentheses – for example, (1.2) – note the length of silences in seconds, while a single period in parentheses (.) indicates a micropause of less than 0.1 seconds. A dash (-) marks the cut-off of the current sound. An equal sign (=) indicates "latching," where talk starts up in especially close temporal proximity to the end of the previous talk. Transcribers' comments and non-verbal action descriptors are italicized in double parentheses ((*like this*)); single parentheses, (like this), around talk indicate a problematic hearing. Punctuation symbols are used to mark intonation changes rather than as grammatical symbols: a period indicates a falling contour; a question mark, a rising contour; and a comma, a falling-rising contour, as might be found in the midst of a list. Each line of text (without a hard return) indicates talk spoken within a single breath group.

2. *Oxford English Dictionary Online*, s.v. "banter," accessed November 4, 2019. https://bit.ly/33h5FY2.
3. *Merriam-Webster Online*, s.v. "banter," accessed November 4, 2019. www.merriamwebster.com/dictionary/banter.

References

CBS News. 2016. "Trump Defends Crude Language from 2005 as 'Locker Room' Talk." Online video clip. www.youtube.com/watch?v=wFEqVARTYkY.

Dunbar, Robin. 1996. *Grooming, Gossip, and the Evolution of Language*. Harvard University Press.

Fahrenthold, David A. 2016. "Trump Recorded Having Extremely Lewd Conversation about Women in 2005." *The Washington Post*, October 7, 2016. https://wapo.st/2dSk1nD.

Gregory, S. 2016. "Trump Dismisses His 'Locker Room Talk' As Normal. Athletes Say It's Not." *Time*, October 11, 2016. https://time.com/4526039/donald-trump-locker-room-athletes/.

Jacobs, B., S. Siddiqui, and S. Bixby, 2016. "'You Can Do Anything': Trump Brags on Tape about Using Fame to Get Women," *The Guardian*, October 8, 2016. https://bit.ly/34uRUoQ.

Kiesling, Scott F. 2001. "Playing the Straight Man: Displaying and Maintaining Male Heterosexuality in Discourse." In *Language and Sexuality: Contesting Meaning in Theory and Practice*, edited by Kathryn Campbell-Kibler, Robert J. Podesva, Sarah J. Roberts, and Andrew Wong, pp. 249–66. Center for the Study of Language and Information Publications.

Pateman, Carole. 1988. *The Sexual Contract*. Stanford University Press.

Sanday, Peggy Reeves. 2007. *Fraternity Gang Rape: Sex, Brotherhood, and Privilege on Campus*. 2nd edn. New York University Press.

Scott, James C. 1985. *Weapons of the Weak: Everyday Forms of Peasant Resistance*. Yale University Press.

Umbach, Maiken, and Mathew Humphrey. 2018. *Authenticity: The Cultural History of a Political Concept*. Palgrave Macmillan.

Way, Niobe. 2013. *Deep Secrets: Boys' Friendships and the Crisis of Connection*. Harvard University Press.

11   On Social Routines and That *Access Hollywood* Bus

Bruce Mannheim

For D. E. D., whose ghost is haunting me from down the street.

Deborah Cameron's chapter in this volume identifies two themes that run through the now-infamous *Access Hollywood* video (Fahrenthold 2016): the creation of bonded male social space and an assertion – and performance – of dominance by Donald Trump, the latter likely enhancing his political prospects.[1] This video, in which Trump bragged about his sexual conquests (counterintuitively by admitting to a failure) and was affirmed by the laughter aboard a studio bus, is an instance of a social routine – a social ritual – so common in American culture that it is hiding in plain sight.[2] An Alpha individual establishes a superordinate position with respect to other participants (i.e. the In-group) by targeting an individual or group of individuals (i.e. Targets) outside the interaction, often by identifying the victim or victims with a social stigma (Goffman 1963b). The stigma extends beyond the duration of the routine, and so has consequences for the Target that extend well beyond the seemingly innocuous duration of the routine, often (but not always) violently threatening their physical well-being. The routine is familiar to the participants (it is occasionally named, as in "mean girls," after the film by Tina Fey of the same name, but so familiar as to be unnamed), and – as social routines do – recruits the Alpha and the In-group to their respective roles in an automatized way. There are significant social consequences for not participating as an In-groupie, including exclusion from the group of interactants (again, in an enduring way) or even becoming the next Target.

Such routines, out of which our social and political lives are built, rarely announce themselves in advance. Routines are interactional pre-fabs, embedded in the small spaces of everyday life (Canessa 2012, Pouillon 2015: 19–20), seemingly innocuous, and often effervescent (Durkheim [1912]1995), experienced as fun. Social routines frequently suck all the air out of an interaction; in this case, one of the few ways to avoid being drawn into the socially subordinate role is to take the social risk of challenging the routine in both its more horrific and its everyday guises. Because routines are both cumulative and specific to social surroundings, they might be understood differently by those who have experienced them repeatedly from those for whom they are relatively new and opaque. It is for that reason that I concur with Professor Cameron's observation that the *Access Hollywood* video may have actually enhanced Trump's election possibilities.

11.1   The Structure and Function of a Routine

Before returning to Trump's performance on the bus, I unpack here the dynamics of a social routine. My starting point is a high school in the northeastern United States in the late 1960s. While we like to think of adolescence and teenage years as being socially offstage, these are periods of intense and complex social interaction, in which linguistic routines, experienced and re-enacted, carry substantial social consequences. They sort people socially (often in ways that they neither intend nor understand), create affiliations and exclusions, and establish personal styles of interaction that follow them well beyond adolescence and youth. Adolescent and youth interactional sociolinguistics (ranging from language variation to very complex, interlocking interactional routines) have been an especially fruitful domain for understanding racism, ethnicity, class, and gender (Eckert 2000, Goodwin 1990, and Mendoza-Denton 2008 are milestones).

Consider the following example, from an urban high school late in the 1960s, with a student body that consisted overwhelmingly of English-speaking Whites. James, a high school student, went to the cafeteria, filled his tray, and went to sit at the same table with the same boys day after day. When he arrived one day, they were grouped around one of the boys, who was sketching while the others were laughing in near hysterics. As James recalled it, he looked down at the sketch, and it was of an African American woman singing a line from a recent Motown hit, musical notes around her head. She was drawn with stereotyped thick lips, and the microphone in front of her (an oversized, old-style microphone of the sort one saw in 1940s movies) had the call letters of a soul music radio station then popular in New York, changed ever-so-slightly into a racist slur. James didn't say anything but stood there, frozen for milliseconds longer than it would normally take to answer. His face turned a shade of green, as the artist looked up and said, "Don't worry, James. This is just what we White liberals do to let off steam." James still didn't say anything but took it as in invitation to put his tray down at another table, sitting by himself. James' high school memories from that point on have him hanging around with the burnouts at the corner.

What was that about? James walked into a social routine that is likely familiar to anyone who grew up – and went to high school – in the United

States, a social routine that the students in my classes today call "mean girls."
Everyone recognizes it, and many acknowledge having participated in one
version or another of the routine. Here is how it is structured. A focal individual – I'll call him or her an "Alpha" (the artist in the example) – makes
outrageous claims, which the other participants – the "In-group" – acquiesce to
in their laughter. The Alpha has broken the social conventions by which the In-
group – and the other denizens – of the high school lunchroom normally live.
These are conventions that normally go without saying, not conventions that
can be reduced to explicit rules. The conventions normally live in the background of everyday social interactions. The break in conventions is funny in the
same way that a waitperson balancing several dishes and then dropping them
all is funny. It is a frame breaker.

But laughter is as socially intricate as any other aspect of an interaction
(Glenn 2003). The other boys at the table were laughing *with* rather than
laughing *at* the Alpha, their laughter constituting a shared social alignment.
The timing of laughter, who laughs first, whether there is a break in the flow of
activity, whether the laughter is sequenced into or overlaps the rest of the
activity are all key to the ongoing interaction. The laughter does not reflect
the break in frame alone, nor the emotional energy of the shared activity alone,
but establishes a common ground or *shared public space* among the participants that builds a consensus about the relationship between the participants
and their Target. And while the joint activity is experienced as effervescent
(Durkheim [1912]1995: 220 and 313, Collins 2004), as a moment away from
the tight structures of everyday interaction, it is in fact tightly wound up and
closely tracks the relationship between the Alpha and the In-group. Here
Deborah Cameron's observation of the *Access Hollywood* video (this volume)
that "What it's really about is men's relationships with one another" rings
absolutely true. The Alpha sets up the conditions and the timing of the laughter.
The laughter in turn provides the "just banter" alibi that Cameron methodically
refutes.

Social routines (or "social rituals"), like all social interactions, involve
mutual entrainment among the interactants, an entrainment that coordinates
their expectations of each other's contributions to the interaction (Watson 1975:
53, Goffman 1979, Collins 2004: 47–101, Lempert 2014, Mannheim 2018).
The expectations of each interactant depend on other interactants interpreting
their contributions in particular ways. Social interaction, then, is more like
a dance than a series of soliloquies (Goffman 1976: 310, cf. Mannheim and
Tedlock 1995). When it is successfully established, coordination among interactants is indexed by a common rhythm, a rhythm that synchronizes all contributions to the interaction, be they verbal, gestural, gaze, or physical
positioning, each interactant unconsciously adjusting their individual behavior
to the broader situation with a microsecond swiftness, within a window of

about eighty milliseconds, just above the threshold of perception. (James' delayed response in the lunchroom is likely what the Alpha responded to when he made the comment.) A description of a social routine, therefore, must be holistic. All the participants in the interaction act in concert: The people seated at the table, the Alpha, and someone just happening upon the scene who is drawn into it (in this case, James) are part of the situation, but their behavior is only intelligible in the perspective of the whole.

But since situations like this are pre-choreographed, recognizable to a socially competent individual much as the sequence of events at a child's birthday party would be (Feldman-Savelsberg 2020), you don't simply decide to take on your prescribed role in the routine. Rather, the routine comes and gets you, particularly because it is a single all-encompassing engagement (Goffman 1963a: 154). McDermott and Tylbor (1995: 220–22) described this as "collusion." Regardless of your avowed beliefs, you are recruited into the routine, "stumbling toward the same ends," as they (1995: 222) wrote. Resistance is futile. The laughter ratifies the cohesion of the group – bringing with it emotional energy, as sociologist Randall Collins (2004) shows – but it also establishes a social hierarchy, in which the In-group validates the momentary power of the Alpha. The routine itself need not include a large In-group. Under the right circumstances it need only include one or two individuals, provided that they are able to establish a shared public space. So, collusion, power, and emotional energy.

So far, I have focused on two essential parts of the routine (the Alpha and the In-group), but not the third. The artist targeted a generic African American woman, though by the label on the microphone it was clear which of these two attributes was being singled out. The "mean girls" routine must have a Target, though that Target can be a stigmatized individual – someone singled out for almost any reason or none at all – as occurs in the movie, *Mean Girls*; or among faculty in a university Department of Geography targeting a female colleague who has achieved national recognition for her research; or a member of a group of people socially stigmatized for race, language, gender, religion, sexual preference, disability, past illness, and so on, one of the "categories of persons whose members pay a very considerable price interactionally" (Goffman 1983: 6). These need not be (and in my experience, often aren't) mutually exclusive. A stigma obtains, Goffman tells us, when "an individual who might have been received easily in ordinary social intercourse possesses a trait that can obtrude itself upon attention and turn those of us whom he meets away from him, breaking the claim that his other attributes have on us. He possesses a stigma, an undesired differentness from what we had anticipated" (1963b: 5). When Goffman refers to "us" and "we" he is referring to the non-stigmatized, which he (somewhat ironically) calls the "normals." Even nominally temporary stigmas are enduring; someone who has undergone psychiatric treatment, for example, continues to carry a stigma for their illness.

The issue here – and one relevance of the "mean girls" routine – is that the routine defines the boundary between a stigmatized individual or group and the normals. Not all exclusionary routines identify Targets as members of stigmatized groups. "He said, she said," a routine among African American adolescent girls in Philadelphia described by Goodwin (1990: 190–225), targeted individuals in order to rearrange the social hierarchy within a peer group, as does "talking shit" described by Mendoza-Denton (2008: 181–86). And there are no social parameters, such as the fratriarchy described by Cameron, that in themselves constitute normalcy. It is the routine itself, as a ritual, that defines "normalcy" (we might also call it the "unmarked" or default social status, or the shared public space) by exclusion of the Target, whether for an individual stigma (for example a birth defect), having been born into a particular ethnic or religious community, or being a woman who received a major research grant that a male colleague coveted.

Informal evidence suggests that sometimes the In-group includes an individual who is also identified as a Target, sometimes manifestly so, and sometimes because a stigmatized individual has worked to conceal their identity ("passing"), a move that has its own psycho-social consequences (Newheiser and Barreto 2014). A gay man might find himself among a group of men who are configuring the In-group around heterosexuality, and join in the by-talk and laughter that stigmatizes himself; sometimes a woman is invited to an otherwise all-male group as they take on individual Targets as generic stand-ins.

The production of "normalcy" is not restricted to routines like this. Jane Hill's (2008: 682–83) work on Mock Spanish, the jocular use of deliberately mangled Spanish such as "Hasta la vista, baby" as a mechanism for the production of White public space (that is to say, normative angloness) is an example. The marked use of stereotyped and grammatically mangled "Spanish" in English-language conversation marks English as doubly normative, first as the unmarked background to the Mock Spanish expressions, and second as the standard against which Spanish grammar and pronunciation is measured. It too is effervescent, producing solidarity among the interactants as first-language English-speakers, while excluding the speakers whose language is being mocked from shared interactional space. Its effervescent quality marks it as socially harmless when in fact the opposite is true. It remains to map these sociolinguistic mechanisms to understand how stigmas are socially reproduced through the society, in small – one might say "capillary" – ways. The identification of the Target, which may be generic or may be individual, is critical to the routine, and while individual members of the In-group might, when asked, profess no ill will to the Target, they still collude in both the stigmatization and in constituting themselves as "normals," enhancing their self-identification with the pleasure afforded the routine ("emotional energy" in the sense of Collins 2004: 102–40, equivalent to Durkheim's "effervescence"). The outcomes can be relatively private (e.g. default racism in the case of the lunch table), but can damage careers (e.g. professional "mobbing" [Harper 2013]) or inflict horrors beyond description (e.g. gang rape or lynching).

Because of the nature of social routines – that they conscript all participants in the interaction – there are very few options available to someone who wants to disable them on the fly (Jefferson et al. 1987: 169, Glenn 2003: 127–31). One can walk away, either literally or figuratively, with the social risk that one becomes the new Target. (In the earlier high school example, I have no idea whether James had become the new Target.) Or one can directly disrupt the interaction, by speaking up against it, for example. The consequences of the latter can be social but can also be physical.

11.2   Sucked into Trump's Male Routine

Trump, whom I'll refer to by his "Alpha" role in the routine described below, was a well-known television personality when he was contracted to make a guest appearance on the soap opera *Days of Our Lives* in September 2005. *Access Hollywood*, a program of celebrity features produced by the same television network, piggybacked on the appearance by recording a "behind the scenes" segment and interview. Alpha arrived on an *Access Hollywood* bus, along with *Access Hollywood* co-host Billy Bush, a nephew of then-President George W. Bush, and seven others, including a two-person film crew from *Access Hollywood*.[3] The crew audio-recorded the conversation on the bus on the record (both Bush and Alpha were wearing microphones), paused, set up a camera outside the bus and video-recorded Alpha and Billy Bush stepping off the bus to be met by an actress from *Days of Our Lives* (Fahrenthold 2016). There are two parts to the video recording of the event. The first part consists of the audio recording from inside the bus, while the video shows the outside of the bus arriving at the spot at which the camera is set up to record Alpha stepping off the bus. The second part begins with the traditional footage of the guest and co-host arriving, the door of the bus opening, and the guest stepping down to be escorted to the set. Both parts include offensive talk, but here I concentrate on the portion that instantiates the routine, which is to say, the one-minute, thirty-three-second audio from inside the bus (Fahrenthold 2016; video excerpt starts at 0.07).

In the transcription, the lines are numbered for ease of reference.[4] I use letters rather than names below because my analysis focuses on the roles these parties are playing in a social routine (as opposed to their identities as ordinarily understood).

A = Alpha, or Trump
B = Billy Bush
V = unidentifiable voice or voice of a third party
1 V: (indistinguishable) she's still very beautiful
   A: I moved on her, actually ((*aside*)) you know, she was down on Palm Beach
       I moved on her, and I failed.
       I'll admit it
5 V: whoa-ho ((*laughter*))
   A: I did try and fuck her (.) she was married.
   B: that's huge news, here
   A: no, no ((*name*)) no, this was ((*trails off*))
       and I moved on her very heavily in fact I took her out furniture shopping
10   she wanted to get some furniture
       I said I'll show you where they have some nice furniture
   B: ((*laughter, perhaps treating "nice furniture" as a double
           entendre*))
   A: I took her out furniture– ((*trails off*))
       I moved on her like a bitch
15   and I couldn't get there,
       and she was married.
       then all of a sudden I see her, she's now got the big phony tits and
       everything
       she's totally changed her look
   B: ((*looking at waiting actress*)) sheesh, your girl's hot as shit
20   in the purple
   A: ((*loudly*)) WHOA=
   B: =YES= ((*high five*))
   A: ((*loudly*))   =WHO::A=
   B: =YES ((*high five*)) the Donald has scored.
25   WHOA my MA:N ((*high five*))
       wait, you gotta look at her when you get outta– ((*crosstalk from the film
       crew*))
       you gotta give her the thumbs up.
   A: ((*to himself, describing the actress*)) look at you- you are a pussy
       ((*crosstalk from the film crew "Let me set this up"*))
30 B: all right you and I will walk out
       ((*background talk*))
   A: maybe it's a different one.
   B: it better not be the publicist-
       no it's- it's her it's-
35 A: yeah, that's her
       with the gold.
       I better use some Tic Tacs just in case I start kissing her
       you know I'm automatically attracted to beautiful- I just start kissing them
       it's like a magnet
40   just kiss
   B: ((*laughter*))

```
     A:  I don't even wait
         and when you're a star, they let you do it
         you can do anything=
45   B:                          =whatever you want
     A:  grab 'em by the pussy
     B:                   ((laughter))
     A:  you can do anything.
     B:  uh yeah those legs, all I can see is the legs
50   A:  oh it looks good
     V:  come on shorty (to Bush?)
     A:  oo:h nice legs, huh?
     B:  oof, get out of the way, honey
         oh, that's good legs
55       go ahead
```

((*The door to the bus opens again, A steps off the bus, followed by B. A addresses the waiting actress, his pitch rising about an octave*))

There are two sections to the interaction. In the first, lines 1–18, the Alpha narrates his fruitless effort to get the other co-host of Access Hollywood to sleep with him. He very deliberately controls the narrative by repeating phrases across the laughter and comments by Bush, and perhaps by a third party. Notice that he is discussing a specific individual but treating her as one example of a larger class (essentially that of women who might interest him). In the second, he sees the actress who is to escort him to the set of the soap opera, first commenting on her, "Look at you, you are a pussy" (line 28), again as an individual as an instance of a larger class, then seamlessly switching to a generic: "they let you do it" (line 43) and "you can do anything" (line 44) and "grab 'em by the pussy" (line 46), with Bush inserting himself into the "In-group" role through laughter and occasional counterpoint: "whatever you want" (line 45). Here again, Trump is using repetition to control the floor (Norrick 1987), establishing himself as Alpha in an interaction that is constructed jointly with Bush. For example, Trump repeats the phrase "I moved on her," three times between lines 1 and 9, resetting himself as the focus of the interaction. In less hierarchical interactions, parallelism and other forms of repetition frequently bleed across speaker turns (Silverstein 1984), but here Trump is largely flying solo, leaving Bush to play a subsidiary role in constructing male public space; it is the shift from specific to generic (lines 37–39) that is critical in establishing the interaction as male public space. The effervescence of the moment, reflected in Bush's laughter and intromissions (and in the laughter of others present on the bus) brought the fratriarchy into relief – both Trump's dominance and the exclusive maleness of the interaction. Bush was a perfect foil. At the same time, Bush avoided the immediate consequences of refusing the routine. But shortly after the *Access Hollywood* video became public, he "resigned" from a prestigious hosting position he'd just been promoted to, effectively ending his career.

The reactions to the release of the *Access Hollywood* video tended to treat it as the expression of a single individual in isolation – the Alpha – or, at best, the Alpha with Billy Bush acting as an accomplice. But beyond the politicians and the commentariat (as the film goes, "We're shocked, shocked") who systematically misread the interaction as improvised, it was one more instantiation of a familiar social routine, one which regimented power relations doubly: between the Alpha and the In-group (hence my conclusion that "shorty" referenced Billy Bush in line 51); and between the interactants as In-group, and the Target. As noted above, too, the Target is initially an individual as instantiation-of-generic women, then moves to a generic Target, and returns to an individual. The genericity of the Target is critical. Generic language constitutes a named category both as integral and as possessing a shared essence around which a secondary structure of stereotypes can be built (Nguyen and Gelman 2012) and is pivotal to the construction of social stigmas (Leslie 2014). Critical too, is that it is an interactional routine, which means that it is available to this end, ready to vacuum up any co-present individuals who have – up to that point – been interacting with each other. And it is its status as a social routine that made it – and its social consequences – transparent beyond the individual disavowals. Whatever it was, it was not some individuals just blowing off steam, not just "locker-room banter" (Cameron, this volume). The individuals are appropriated to the routine, not the other way around. Has this analysis let Billy Bush off the hook? No In-group, no routine; Bush was essential to its interactional success. And in the years that followed the release of the *Access Hollywood* video, an entire country has allowed itself to be appropriated as both In-group and foil.

Notes

1. This chapter was instigated by the brilliant analysis by Deborah Cameron (2016 and this volume) and presented for the first time to the Linguistic Anthropology Laboratory at the University of Michigan and to an informal, unscheduled session on pedagogy at the American Anthropological Association, both in 2016. It was completed at the Laboratoire d'Anthropologie Sociale, jointly supported by the École des Hautes Études en Sciences Sociales and the Collège de France. I am grateful to my audiences and co-conversationalists in these venues, especially to Alaina Lemon and to Jessica Lowen. Michael Lempert prodded me on pedagogical issues around this analysis. I wish to take this opportunity to acknowledge Professor Susan U. Philips, of the University of Arizona, who first encouraged me to think interactionally.

2. I am fairly certain that the routine I am describing here is intelligible to anyone who has grown up Anglophone in the United States. I don't know whether it holds anyplace else in the Anglophone world. The only place I know of with a routine of similar texture, Peru, has a superficially similar routine – *la raja* – but its interpersonal organization is distinctly different. There is an initiator, who does not establish a relationship of power with respect to the In-group. The Target is normally a member of the In-group; to be the Target of *raja* identifies the Target as sharing

social characteristics with the people involved in it, rather than a stigma. The virulent racism found in Lima is reproduced by other means (see Zavala and Back 2017).
3. I don't know the gender of the two-person film crew; the remaining passengers were all men.
4. Transcription conventions used in the chapter include the use of CAPITALS to indicate talk spoken with special emphasis. Colons after a vowel indicate an elongated vowel sound. A left bracket ([) marks the onset, and a right bracket (]) marks the offset of overlapping talk. Numbers in parentheses – for example, (1.2) – note the length of silences in seconds, while a single period in parentheses (.) indicates a micropause of less than 0.1 seconds. A dash (-) marks the cut-off of the current sound. An equal sign (=) indicates "latching," where talk starts up in especially close temporal proximity to the end of the previous talk. Transcribers' comments and non-verbal action descriptors are italicized in double parentheses ((*like this*)); single parentheses, (like this), around talk indicate a problematic hearing. Punctuation symbols are used to mark intonation changes rather than as grammatical symbols: a period indicates a falling contour; a question mark, a rising contour; and a comma, a falling-rising contour, as might be found in the midst of a list. Each line of text (without a hard return) indicates talk spoken within a single breath group.

References

Cameron, Deborah. 2016. "On Banter, Bonding, and Donald Trump." *Language: A Feminist Guide*, October 9, 2016. https://debuk.wordpress.com/2016/10/09/on-banter-bonding-and-donald-trump/.

Canessa, Andrew. 2012. *Intimate Indigeneities: Race, Sex, and History in the Small Spaces of Andean Life*. Duke University Press.

Collins, Randall. 2004. *Interaction Ritual Chains*. Princeton University Press.

Durkheim, Émile. [1912]1995. *Les formes élémentaires de la vie religieuse: le système totémique en Australie*. Presses Universitaires de France. Reprint, translated by Karen E. Fields as *The Elementary Forms of Religious Life*. The Free Press.

Eckert, Penelope. 2000. *Linguistic Variation as Social Practice: The Linguistic Construction of Identity in Belton High*. Blackwell Publishing.

Fahrenthold, David A. 2016. "Trump Recorded Having Extremely Lewd Conversation about Women in 2005." *The Washington Post*, October 7, 2016. https://wapo.st/2dSk1nD.

Feldman-Savelsberg, Pamela. 2020. "Class Performances: Children's Parties and the Reproduction of Social Class Among Diasporic Cameroonians." *Africa Today* 66, nos. 3–4.

Glenn, Phillip. 2003. *Laughter in Interaction*. Cambridge University Press.

Goffman, Erving. 1963a. *Behavior in Public Places: Notes on the Social Organization of Gatherings*. The Free Press.

1963b. *Stigma. Notes on the Management of Spoiled Identity*. Simon and Schuster.

1976. "Replies and Responses." *Language in Society* 5, no. 3: 257–313.

1979. "Footing." *Semiotica* 25, nos. 1–2: 1–30.

1983. "The Interaction Order: American Sociological Association, 1982 Presidential Address." *American Sociological Review* 48, no. 1: 1–17.

Goodwin, Marjorie Harness. 1990. *He-Said-She-Said: Talk as Social Organization among Black Children*. Indiana University Press.

Harper, Janice. 2013. *Mobbed. A Survival Guide to Adult Bullying and Mobbing*. Back Door Press.

Hill, Jane H. 2008. "Language, Race, and White Public Space." *American Anthropologist* 100, no. 3: 680–89.

Jefferson, Gail, Harvey Sacks, and Emanuel Schegloff. 1987. "Notes on Laughter in the Pursuit of Intimacy." In *Talk and Social Organization*, edited by Graham Button and John R. E. Lee, pp. 150–205. Multilingual Matters.

Lempert, Michael. 2014. "Imitation." *Annual Review of Anthropology* 43: 379–95.

Leslie, Sarah-Jane. 2014. "Carving Up the Social World with Generics." In *Oxford Studies in Experimental Philosophy: Volume 1*, edited by Tania Lombrozo, Joshua Knobe, and Shaun Nichols, pp. 208–31. Oxford University Press.

Mannheim, Bruce. 2018. "Preliminary Disciplines." *Signs and Society* 6, no. 1: 11–119.

Mannheim, Bruce, and Dennis Tedlock. 1995. "Introduction." In *The Dialogic Emergence of Culture*, edited by Dennis Tedlock and Bruce Mannheim, pp. 1–32. University of Illinois Press.

McDermott, Raymond P., and Henry Tylbor. 1995. "On the Necessity of Collusion in Conversation." In *The Dialogic Emergence of Culture*, edited by Dennis Tedlock and Bruce Mannheim, pp. 218–36. University of Illinois Press.

Mendoza-Denton, Norma. 2008. *Homegirls: Language and Cultural Practice among Latina Youth Gangs*. Blackwell Publishing.

Newheiser, Anna-Kaisa, and Manuela Barreto. 2014. "Hidden Costs of Hiding Stigma: Ironic Interpersonal Consequences of Concealing a Stigmatized Identity in Social Interactions." *Journal of Experimental Social Psychology* 52: 58–70.

Nguyen, Simone P., and Susan A. Gelman. 2012. "Generic Language Facilitates Children's Cross-Classification." *Child Development* 27, no. 2: 154–67.

Norrick, Neal R. 1987. "Functions of Repetition in Conversation." *Text* 7, no. 3: 245–64.

Pouillon, François. 2015. *L'Anthropologie des petites choses*. Le Bord de l'Eau.

Silverstein, Michael. 1984. "On the Pragmatic 'Poetry' of Prose: Parallelism, Repetition, and Cohesive Structure in the Time Course of Dyadic Conversation." In *Meaning, Form, and Use in Context: Linguistic Applications*, edited by Deborah Schiffrin, pp. 181–99. Georgetown University Press.

Watson, Karen Ann. 1975. "Transferable Communicative Routines: Strategies and Group Identity in Two Speech Events." *Language in Society* 4, no. 1: 53–72.

Zavala, Virginia, and Michele Back, eds. 2017. *Racismo y lenguaje*. Fondo Editorial de la Pontificia Universidad Católica del Perú.

12   "Cocked and Loaded": Trump and the Gendered Discourse of National Security

Carol Cohn

Donald Trump almost makes the job of a feminist political analyst too easy.[1] When the North Korean Supreme Leader Kim Jong-un alluded to the "nuclear button" on his office desk in his 2018 New Year's speech (Jong-un 2018), Trump's tweeted response on January 2 could not have been much more transparent: "I too have a Nuclear Button, but it is a much bigger & more powerful one than his, and my Button works!" (Trump on Twitter, January 2, 2018). That there *is* no nuclear button, that "nuclear button" is already a metaphor, only sharpens the point. Even for people not inclined to see the world through the lens of gender analysis, something seemed to click when Trump reduced the discussion of a nuclear war that would kill millions of people and leave millions more in horrific suffering down to the size of his and the North Korean president's buttons. The President of the United States' nuclear saber-rattling sounded a lot like, well, penis-measuring.

Sad. But significant? From most commentators, the response was an eye-rolling dismissal of Trump's tweet as "juvenile" and as yet one more impulsive, impolitic, dangerous, and unpresidential act by a president like no other. But those who dismissed his words may have missed their broader significance. The way we use language to frame things *matters*. I argue in this chapter that the metaphors we use and the gender discourse embedded in the ways we talk about war and weapons of mass destruction powerfully influence our understanding of them, or lack thereof. When I say "gender discourse," I mean not just language, but a system of meanings, ways of thinking, images, and words that first shape how we experience, shape, and represent our gender identities – but also do more than that; they shape many other aspects of our lives and culture. The ideas about masculinity and femininity that underpin Trump's tweets *matter*, not only in *his* understandings of the world, but also in international politics, in national security, and in nuclear strategic thinking more broadly.

While Donald Trump may in some ways appear exceptional – in the fragility of his ego; in his obsessive concern with his reputation for manliness

179

(exemplified in everything from the Billy Bush braggadocio to his defensiveness about the size of his digits); and in his apparent inability to do anything other than "let it all hang out," as it were, unscreened by a fig leaf of intelligence or prudence – it would be a grievous mistake to think that other political leaders and national security elites were not just as deeply affected by ideas about gender, albeit perhaps not always in such crude or lurid ways. Unspoken, unexamined ideas about gender are embedded in, and shaping of, the language used in national security paradigms, at the deepest levels. Trump's lack of diplomatic restraint and linguistic finesse may have brought these discursive gender dynamics to the surface, but they have been there all along.

12.1   Abstractions and Sexual Metaphors in Weapons Talk

These dynamics first became apparent to me over three decades ago, when I was working among civilian nuclear strategists, war planners, weapons scientists, and arms controllers. As I attended lectures, conversed with defense analysts, and interviewed graduate students in training, what first struck me was how removed they were from the human realities behind the use of the weapons they discussed. Nuclear weapons and nuclear warfare were discussed in abstract analytic tones, as games of strategy, without any graphic sense of the human suffering or environmental devastation they would wreak. Although my first reaction was to wonder, "How can they think this way?", my own experience of learning to speak in the language of the nuclear experts soon began to make it clear; their distancing from the human realities of nuclear war occurred in part through the professional discourse into which they (and I) were quickly enculturated. It was filled with bland, abstract phrases such as "first strikes," "counterforce exchanges," and "limited nuclear war," which in no way hinted at the concrete horrors of a nuclear holocaust. Suffering and devastating loss are erased through euphemism. When some (largely fusion) nuclear weapons are deemed "clean bombs" because they produce relatively less radioactive fallout than other (largely fission) nuclear weapons of the same yield, the impact on human bodies of the massive blast pressures and firestorms those "clean bombs" would unleash are sanitized away. Or, to choose another example, the women, men, and children who are killed by bombs targeting buildings, bases, ports, airports and weapons systems are completely invisible to the mind's eye when they are referred to in the now-familiar phrase "collateral damage" (Cohn 1987). The only way this erasure of humans from discussion of nuclear war does not seem completely incomprehensible is when you realize that the discourse used by nuclear experts is one that has as its subject the weapons themselves, abstractions of the weapons' relations to each other, and the geopolitical effects of those abstractions. Their language, then, has no words for the potential suffering of people in the targeted societies, and certainly none for grappling with the moral implications of possessing or using such weapons of massive, total destruction (Cohn and Ruddick 2004).

But the language I heard nuclear defense intellectuals using to discuss nuclear weapons wasn't only characterized by abstraction and euphemism. It was also saturated by a lively and troubling set of domestic and sexual metaphors, and it is in this gendered, sexualized discourse – evidently still very much alive – that Trump has found his comfort zone for talking about weaponry. The gendered metaphors I encountered evoked sexualized bodies through conversations about "vertical erector launchers," "thrust-to-weight ratios," "soft lay downs," "deep penetration," and the comparative advantages of "protracted" versus "spasm" attacks – or what one military advisor to the National Security Council called "releasing seventy to eighty percent of our megatonnage in one orgasmic whump." A former Pentagon target analyst once explained nuclear war to me in these terms: "You gotta understand that it's a pissing contest – you gotta expect them to use everything they've got." An academic referred to India's explosion of a nuclear bomb as "losing her virginity," while the question of how the United States should react was posed as whether or not we should "throw her away" (Cohn 1987: 693, 696).

While most of the men I met who used these metaphors would no doubt dismiss them as utterly trivial and insignificant, some linguists argue that metaphors like these are not just verbal window-dressing; they fundamentally shape our sense of reality. This basic claim has been elaborated over the decades by George Lakoff (1991; see also Lakoff and Johnson 1980), who argues that while metaphors are linguistic constructions on the surface, they are simultaneously conceptual constructions central to human thought. In a metaphor, one applies a domain of knowledge (A) to another (B), giving shape to one's perception and understanding of B. Often, domain A is more concrete and less abstract or conceptually elusive than B; the metaphor at hand thus makes domain B easier to think about, though the metaphor's simplifications may be terribly misleading or problematic.

Lakoff's claims about metaphor and thought have found support in cognitive science. A substantial body of empirical work has found that linguistic framing steers human reasoning, and that metaphors can give shape to the way people reason about abstract and complex ideas ranging from time to electricity to social dynamics. In a 2011 article, for instance, Paul Thibodeau and Lera Boroditsky examine whether metaphor can influence the way US Americans reason about the best social policy to address crime. They gave participants one of two paragraphs to read. Both paragraphs reported identical facts and figures about crime, but they diverged in their opening line: One described crime as "a wild beast preying on the city," the other as "a virus infecting the city" (ibid.: e16782). Then they asked subjects open-ended questions about the best way to address the crime problem. The subjects shown the "virus" metaphor were more likely to suggest social reforms that might help address the problem at its root and inoculate society against recurrences. Those shown the "beast" metaphor were significantly more likely to propose that law enforcement capture and punish criminals. Participants thus seem to build their mental representations of a phenomenon, and their reasoning about it, based on the metaphor used to frame it.

Needless to say, the stakes of metaphor are particularly high in discourse about politics and military conflict. Lakoff has written of metaphor's political implications, contending, for instance, that conservative American speech tends to work with a metaphor of the state as a "strict father" (2002), with many conservative political preferences springing from this conceptual model. In a related vein, I found that in discussions about international politics, defense intellectuals often framed the United States as a mature and powerful father figure who needed to set firm limits for immature countries who could not be trusted to know what was good for them (Cohn 1987: 697).

Lakoff has also argued that metaphors shape military decisions. In the run-up to the first Gulf War, he notes, American officials represented Kuwait as an "innocent ingénue" that had been "raped" by Iraq's occupation – one among several metaphors that justified the United States military coming to "rescue" it (1991: 25, 29). As Lakoff summarizes it, "Metaphors can kill" (1991: 32). When Trump's ego investment in always having the biggest and the best plays out in verbal assertions about the size, power, and efficacy of his "nuclear button," he taps into a broader set of gendered metaphors about masculine pride, power, and sexual prowess. This is probably useful for him politically, stirring the support of those who wish to feel identified with that version of manliness. But if Lakoff is right, it also has consequences in shaping Trump's own thinking about nuclear weapons. If "domain A" is contests over manliness, it is certainly more concrete and less abstract or conceptually elusive – as well as more familiar and more emotionally invested in – than "domain B," the specialized science and technology of nuclear weaponry and the arcane complexities of nuclear strategic theorizing. The danger, again, is that the metaphor at hand will not only make "domain B" easier to think about, but will also be terribly misleading or problematic. This may be especially so for Trump, who repeatedly shows his need to publicly portray himself as a manly, sexually powerful individual, while simultaneously, according to multiple sources from inside his administration, having absolutely no interest in or capacity to focus on reading or being briefed about topics about which he knows and understands little. Indeed, Trump has made statements which appear astonishingly ignorant about nuclear weapons; during his presidential campaign, he reportedly asked upon multiple occasions why if we have them we can't use them (Belvedere 2016). (Since becoming President he has taken actions to lower the threshold for their use, and also issued multiple, often self-contradictory, statements about them.)

12.2   Ideas about Gender as a Preemptive Deterrent

The role of gender in national security discourse, including Trump's talk, goes deeper than the role of not-so-subtle metaphors. Even more disturbing than what is said is what *cannot* be said, or even thought, within the confines of those male-dominated, professional spaces – the conversations that can't be had, the concerns seen as illegitimate or unprofessional to raise, the ideas which are never given serious consideration, the thinking that gets short-circuited. My argument is that ideas about gender have an ever-present role in national security and nuclear discourse, shaping and limiting the inputs which are considered valid, and the way actions and ideas are interpreted and valued. It happens in multiple ways: Some are overt, as in the name-calling that impugns the masculinity of men (or women) who don't conform, while some are much more subtle, as certain ways of speaking and topics of conversation are already, in a professional discourse, pre-marked as masculine/legitimate or feminine/illegitimate.

The gendered name-calling is startlingly rife. "What are you, some kind of wimp?" was an insult I frequently heard lobbed at anyone who urged restraint in responding to a provocation or attack. And I know from my own experience how effective it can be. I participated once in a war game sponsored by the RAND corporation. The players, nearly all of whom were men, were divided into opposing teams and then the teams were isolated from each other, so we could never be in dialogue with our opponents. We were given a "scenario," a situation of escalating tensions and military conflicts, starting in the Middle East and spreading to Eastern Europe. We were to make judgments about what military actions to take, and the game organizers would periodically ratchet up the tension by tweaking the scenario. Our team strategized with troop movements, attacking ground forces and at certain stages withdrawing troops from various sites such as Afghanistan, but the scenario gradually escalated until the other team decided to use tactical nuclear weapons against our troops. Our team decided against a hair-trigger use of nuclear weapons in retaliation.

In the debriefing after the game, a member of the opposing team described their impressions. Characterizing our team as a single, male individual (a common tic in discourse about the enemy in war, with profound implications beyond the scope of this chapter), he said: "When he took his troops out of Afghanistan, I knew he was weak and I could push him around. And then, when we nuked him and he didn't nuke us back, I knew he was just such a wimp, I could take him for everything he's got and I nuked him again. He just wimped out."

And it stung. Even as a woman, being called a wimp felt deeply cutting. It also functioned as a kind of catch-22 insult; we couldn't start explaining that our actions were not the result of wimpy-ness, but rather taken for other reasons, because the explaining and protesting itself would be taken as proof we were wimpy! In short, deploying the word "wimp" acts like a bath of sulfuric acid; it erases all other considerations. (For comparison, see McIntosh, "Crybabies and Snowflakes," this volume.) And the message for us, and for the others in the room who were watching this play out, was that the only way to avoid being seen as a wimp was to avoid advocating for anything other than military responses that are perceived as maximally aggressive and powerful (Cohn 1993: 234). The charge of being a "wimp," in other words, stops the processes of deliberation. Once an idea is gender-coded as insufficiently masculine, no one else in the room wants to give it serious consideration, because doing so means that they, too, would be considered wimpish.

But overt impugning of masculinity is still only the most surface level at which ideas about gender play out in strategic thinking. They work in deeper, more subtle ways, as well, to shape security discourse and habits of thought. This is because associations of masculinity with dispassionate distance, abstraction, toughness, and risk-taking, and of femininity with empathetic attention to others, bodily vulnerability, fear, and caution are culturally pervasive, and as such, they are already embedded within nuclear and national security discourse. And there they function to make some kinds of ideas seem self-evidently "realistic," hard-nosed and rational, and to make other ideas, inputs, thoughts, and feelings appear patently inadmissible, self-evidently inappropriate.

To offer an illustration: A national security analyst was walking me through the modeling he did of a hypothetical Soviet nuclear cruise missile attack in Western Europe and different scales of US responses. After listening to his account of what would be likely to happen in each scenario, I asked, "And what did it show would happen when the US did *not* respond militarily, at least initially?" He looked startled by the question, and replied, "We didn't model that – you just wouldn't model anything so passive." That is, even the thought-experiment was foreclosed, owing to its feminine-coded "passivity." How often does that form of cognitive self-censorship, whether conscious or not, result in both national security professionals and politicians not thinking through the full range of options when contemplating optimal policy responses?

Or perhaps even more seriously, how does it distort thinking about nuclear weapons altogether? A white male physicist at a nuclear strategic think tank described to me an experience that had disturbed him. When he and some colleagues were modeling a limited "counterforce" nuclear attack (i.e. an attack targeting the opponent's nuclear weapons systems, not purposefully targeting their civilian population), they found that by using slightly different assumptions, their projection showed that instead of thirty-six million immediate fatalities, there would "only be thirty million." He went on: "All of a sudden, I *heard* what we were saying. And I blurted out, 'Wait, I've just heard how we're talking – *Only* thirty million! *Only* thirty million human beings killed instantly?' Silence fell upon the room. Nobody said a word. They didn't even look at me. It was awful. I felt like a woman." He added that henceforth he was careful never to say anything like that again (Cohn 1993: 227).

What did the physicist mean when he said that he "felt like a woman"? One way to understand it is that communities have gendered linguistic behavior rules, and that he transgressed those of his community. That is, there are distinctive ideas about what is considered "normal" linguistic behavior for men and women. While in practice, there's tremendous flexibility in the linguistic behaviors people can adopt, and men and women violate prescriptive norms all the time, those violations do little to weaken what Talbot (2003: 475, 478) calls the "exaggerated dualism" of the "hegemonic construct of preferred speech patterns." In the United States, this dualism typically locates qualities such as sympathy, support, listening, and pro-social emotion on the feminine side, and reporting or lecturing about facts, confrontational and confident stances, and status-consciousness on the masculine. The physicist, then, in his blurting, evinced emotion and a lack of the control and distance which are central to the "just the facts, ma'am" masculine behavioral linguistic style. That doing so was "awful" should not be surprising; no matter the cultural variation in what is considered linguistically normal for men and for women, it's common for whatever is deemed "men's speech" to be considered more statusful (Hall and Bucholtz 1995), just as being a man carries higher status than being a woman. That he was careful to never say anything like that again should also not be surprising, as there are powerful incentives for men to avoid verbally gendering themselves as female – which, in turn, creates incentives to keep some ways of talking and thinking about nuclear weapons out of the room.

Another way to understand why the physicist "felt like a woman" takes us beyond the level of linguistic behavior, to look into the ways in which gender is encoded within national security discourse itself. What is unusual in this story is only that the physicist used the phrase, "I felt like a woman." But what he is describing – that the professional discourse of nuclear experts excludes conscious attention to human bodies, their vulnerability and their suffering, and precludes space for articulating or even having feelings about the scale of human death and suffering one is planning – is entirely standard. That is, the discourse valorizes, and marks as "expert" and "professional," a series of characteristics and approaches that our culture symbolically codes as "masculine," including dispassion, abstraction, a calculative form of rationality, and scientific and technical knowledge. At the same time, it marks as illegitimate, as inadmissible, other kinds of inputs and other modes of attention and intelligence – and it does so through their association with the "feminine." In other words, the discourse has gender-coded positions within it, and if you dare try to bring in concerns which are coded as being on the feminine side, as the physicist did, you not only violate a code of professional conduct, but you also place yourself in the lower status, subordinate, female position in the discourse (Cohn 1993: 231).

What is the impact of this valorizing of the symbolically coded "masculine" dispassion, abstraction, and technical calculation over the "feminine"-coded attention to human bodies and feelings, which is so fundamental to nuclear strategic discourse? At a bare minimum, it is an understatement to say that the "experts'" discourse allows only an extremely partial set of considerations around the use of nuclear weapons. In the many discussions of nuclear weaponry and warfare I witnessed, I often experienced the feeling that something terribly important was being left out and must be spoken; and yet, it felt almost physically impossible to utter the words, almost as though they could not be pushed out into the smooth, cool, opaque air of the room. There is no room to invoke a seven-year-old boy with his flesh melting away from his bones or a toddler with her skin hanging down in strips. Voicing concerns about the number of casualties in the enemy nation, imagining the suffering of their killed and wounded, is out of bounds. Psychological effects – whether on forces fighting a war or on the citizens who are injured, bereaved, or helplessly watching their babies die from diarrhea due to lack of clean water – none of these are to be talked about, all foreclosed by the way gender is encoded in the discourse (Cohn 1993: 231–32). To borrow a term from defense intellectuals, you might say that the embeddedness of ideas about gender in nuclear strategic discourse, and in national security discourse more broadly, acts as a "preventive deterrent" to holistic, and therefore truly realistic, thinking about nuclear weapons and the holocaust that would result from their use.

12.3   Presidents and the Gendered Discourse of National Security

Unfortunately, defense intellectuals who theorize about nuclear weapons are not the only ones whose thinking about national security is limited and distorted by embedded ideas about gender. The same gendered discourse around weapons of mass destruction has surrounded generations of American presidents. When Assistant Secretary of Defense Paul Nitze reportedly disparaged some of President John F. Kennedy's more cautious decisions during the Cuban Missile Crisis by calling him a "pantywaist" (Powaski 2017: 33), he made it clear that anyone who let himself be governed by fear of triggering a nuclear war was a sissy. In the mid-1980s, during my participant observation among national security elites who move in and out of positions as advisors to presidents, I heard several discussions about whether then-President George H. W. Bush "had the stones for war." At the risk of stating the obvious, the stones referred to were not the type that David used as a weapon to defeat Goliath; this was a discussion about genitals, suggesting that a man is not a truly manly man unless he is willing to go to war (or, more accurately, willing to send others to war). By extension, attempting to solve a conflict through nonmilitary measures would mean you were less than fully manly, a point driven home by the multiple media commentators who described Bush as finally "beating the wimp factor" – his prudence, one might say in a different language – by initiating the first Iraq War in 1990. And Trump has gained popularity among his base in part by framing himself as someone who "has the balls" (an oft-repeated phrase about him; e.g. Hackman 2016, McCarthy 2018, Reeves 2019, etc.) that Obama supposedly lacked when it comes to handling North Korea, Iran, and other potential security threats.

Should we be especially worried about the intersection of gendered national security discourses with the gendered insecurities of this one president? Certainly, Trump seems to live in fear of being feminized. Long before running for president he was known for his leering involvement with beauty pageants, and for bragging on the *Howard Stern Show*, among other venues, about his sexual conquests. A particular point of pride was that he had never changed a diaper, as though this proved he was a real man. Once on the campaign trail, Trump's discourse was laced with "verbal swagger" (Kiesling 2018), including a stream of insults about the physical size of his male competitors – "little Marco Rubio" (Trump on Twitter, February 28, 2016), for instance, and "liddle Bob Corker" (Trump on Twitter, October 24, 2017b). Size seems to loom as an issue for him. When jokesters drew attention to his hand size, invoking the folkloric American notion that hand size corresponds to penis size and, in turn, to virility, Trump defended himself in the eleventh GOP debate by holding his hands up to the cameras and saying, "Look at those hands, are they small hands? . . . I guarantee you there's no problem. I guarantee" (Gass 2016). And in what might be seen as a similar guarantee, when Trump announced (via tweet) that he had decided to call off a military strike on Iran, he prefaced his decision with the assurance that "we were cocked & loaded" (Trump on Twitter, June 21, 2019).[2]

Not surprisingly, in speaking about Kim Jong-un, Trump has done far more to invoke his own masculinity than just alluding to button size. Trump has taunted Jong-un several times with the appellation "Little Rocket Man" (Trump on Twitter, September 23, 2017a), putting him down on the basis of stature while indirectly impugning the size of Jung-un's "rocket," which could be read as yet another phallic stand-in. (Perhaps the indirect reference to the song "Rocket Man" by openly gay pop singer Elton John added an additional layer of emasculation, given the common stereotype of gay men as feminine.) And he has blustered about the nuclear Armageddon he could unleash, with a little too much alliterative pleasure. Trump stated to reporters on August 8, 2017 that Jong-un's continued threats against the US would be "met with fire and fury like the world has never seen" (Shugerman 2017).

Mainstream national security analysts have been reluctant to think seriously – or at all – about the ways that ideas about gender shape national security discourses and practices. So perhaps Trump's disparagements of Kim Jong-un's manhood in one sense did us a favor. Trump has made it glaringly evident that while the literal button or penis size of Trump or Kim Jong-un matters not at all, their need for the world to believe that they are manly men does. Although Trump's attitude toward Jong-un later changed as he apparently came to admire Jong-un's manly authoritarian powerfulness (e.g. "Well he is very talented. Anybody who takes over a situation like he did at twenty-six years of age and is able to run it, and run it tough"),[1] what stays the same is that his perception of Jong-un's masculinity remains central to his approach to foreign policy.

What we now need to remember is that Trump is, in this respect, not the exception we might wish. We need to beware of thinking that once his presidency is over, we can all relax into a world of more conventional politicians who will be guided by some combination of rationality and political self-interest, instead of driven by gendered insecurities. Yes, the fear of being perceived as unmanly may be closer to the surface in Trump. And it may drive his statements and actions in ways less leavened by cognitive capacity and attention span, or by empathy and the ability to imagine the impact of one's actions on others, or by a vision of political leadership as involving responsibility to the citizens of the country or planet as a whole, rather than as a vehicle for self-aggrandizement.

But this is not about individual leaders, individual men or women. Attention to security discourse shows us that independent of the personalities of our political leaders, ideas about masculinity and femininity *already* distort the ways we speak and think about international politics and national security. And they matter. They mattered before Trump, they matter now, and they will matter after Trump. Most national security analysts, from the academy to the mass media to the executive branch, have ignored this reality for too long, to all of our peril.

Notes

1. A much shorter version of this chapter was published as an op-ed in the *New York Times* (Cohn 2018), and longer versions of portions of it were published in Cohn 1987, Cohn 1993, and Cohn and Ruddick 2004. Many of the examples of quotations and observations included throughout this chapter are pulled from these select previously published works.

2. A Reuters article referred to this as a "linguistic misfire involving the phrase 'locked and loaded'" (Trott 2019).

References

Belvedere, Matthew J. 2016. "Trump Asks Why US Can't Use Nukes: MSNBC." *CNBC Digital*, August 3, 2016.

Cohn, Carol. 1987. "Sex and Death in the Rational World of Defense Intellectuals." *Signs* 12, no. 4: 687–718.

1993. "Wars, Wimps, and Women: Talking Gender and Thinking War." In *Gendering War Talk*, edited by Miriam G. Cooke and Angela Woollacott, pp. 227–46. Princeton University Press.

2018. "The Perils of Mixing Masculinity and Missiles." *The New York Times*, January 5, 2018. https://nyti.ms/346DVoO.

Cohn, Carol, and Sara Ruddick. 2004. "A Feminist Ethical Perspective on Weapons of Mass Destruction." In *Ethics and Weapons of Mass Destruction: Religious and Secular Perspectives*, edited by Sohail H. Hashmi and Steven P. Lee, pp. 405–35. Cambridge University Press.

Gass, Nick. 2016. "Trump on Small Hands: 'I Guarantee You There's No Problem.'" *Politico*, March 3, 2016. https://politi.co/32PFiYN.

Hackman, Michelle. 2016. "Donald Trump Called Ted Cruz a 'Pussy' – and the Media Won't Repeat It." *Vox*, February 9, 2016. https://bit.ly/36aghK4.

Hall, Kira, and Mary Bucholtz, eds. 1995. *Gender Articulated: Language and the Socially Constructed Self*. Routledge.

Jong-un, Kim. 2018. "Kim Jong Un's 2018 New Year's Address." *The National Committee on North Korea*, January 1, 2018. www.ncnk.org/node/1427.

Kiesling, Scott F. 2018. "Masculine Stances and the Linguistics of Affect: On Masculine Ease." *NORMA: Nordic Journal for Masculinity Studies* 13, nos. 3–4: 191–212.

Lakoff, George, and Mark Johnson. 1980. *Metaphors We Live By*. University of Chicago Press.

Lakoff, George. 1991. "Metaphor and War: The Metaphor System Used to Justify War in the Gulf." *Peace Research* 23, nos. 2–3: 25–32.

2002. *Moral Politics: How Liberals and Conservatives Think*. University of Chicago Press.

McCarthy, Tom. 2018. "US Steelworkers Say Trump Tariff Plan Has Appeal– 'But About Forty Years Too Late.'" *The Guardian*, March 11, 2018. https://bit.ly/362sBMi.

Powaski, Ronald E. 2017. *American Presidential Statecraft: During the Cold War and After*. Palgrave Macmillan.

Reeves, Megan. 2019. "Amid Outrage and Fanfare, UF Hosts Donald Trump Jr." *Tampa Bay Times*, October 11, 2019. https://bit.ly/31MLq2J.

Shugerman, Emily7. 2017. "Trump Says North Korea Will Be Met With 'Fire and Fury Like the World Has Never Seen' If It Escalates Nuclear Threat." *The Independent*, April 8, 2017. https://bit.ly/32PCdbb.

Talbot, Mary. 2003. "Gender Stereotypes: Reproduction and Challenge." In *The Handbook of Language and Gender*, edited by Janet Holmes and Miriam Meyerhoff, pp. 468–86. Blackwell Publishing.

Thibodeau, Paul H., and Lera Boroditsky. 2011. "Metaphors We Think With: The Role of Metaphor in Reasoning." *PLoS ONE* 6, no. 2: e16782. https://bit.ly/2OGy2bq.

Trott, Bill. 2019. "Trump's Half-Cocked and Loaded Tweet Draws Barrage of Reaction." *Reuters*, June 21, 2019. https://reut.rs/2ol7JyP.

Trump, Donald (@realDonaldTrump). 2016. "Little Marco Rubio is just another Washington D.C. politician that is all talk and no action. #RobotRubio." Twitter, February 28, 2017. https://bit.ly/2WpuVJ2.

2017a. "Just heard Foreign Minister of North Korea speak at U.N. If he echoes thoughts of Little Rocket Man, they won't be around much longer!" Twitter, September 23, 2017. https://bit.ly/32RR5pJ.

2017b. ". . . the entire World WAS laughing and taking advantage of us. People like liddle' Bob Corker have set the U.S. way back. Now we move forward!" Twitter, October 24, 2017. https://bit.ly/2Wi4ftu.

2018. "North Korean Leader Kim Jong Un just stated that the 'Nuclear Button is on his desk at all times.' Will someone from his depleted and food starved regime please inform him that I too have a Nuclear Button, but it is a much bigger & more powerful one than his, and my Button works!" Twitter, January 2, 2018. https://bit.ly/2oi4CHU.

2019. ". . . On Monday they shot down an unmanned drone flying in International Waters. We were cocked & loaded to retaliate last night on 3 different sights when I asked, how many will die. 150 people, sir, was the answer from a General. 10 minutes before the strike I stopped it, not . . ." Twitter, June 21, 2019. https://bit.ly/2pSbWL1.

13   Evaluator in Chief

Brion van Over

Let's set the scene. It's February 2017, and Trump enters a room nearly filled by a long conference table surrounded by comfortable leather rolling chairs. There are some twenty people standing around the table and lining the back wall waiting for the President to enter and be seated; the event has been billed as a "Black History Month Listening Session" (Trump 2017), and most attendees are Black supporters and aides, there to visually and publicly boost the President. It is the talk in this "listening session" that is the focus of the analysis throughout.

While Trump downplays the importance of the event as merely a "little breakfast," the political stakes of the event are undoubtedly high, as a President plagued by accusations of racist and xenophobic remarks is expected to lead a meeting of Black Americans in the public celebration of the lives and accomplishments of some of our greatest Black historical figures.

As he enters, he pulls out a chair for Omarosa Manigault Newman, a former contestant on Trump's reality TV show turned Trump White House official and aide. (A little over a year after this meeting, she was pressured to resign and has since fervently taken up the anti-Trump mantle.) As Trump moves to his seat, flanked by Omarosa on his right and Housing and Urban Development Secretary Ben Carson on his left, the chatter subsides. Trump then takes the floor, beginning a segment of the event I'll call his "opening comments," and is followed by a round of introductions in which each guest seated around the table is invited to introduce themselves. (Note: In the analysis that follows I will indicate participants by their first names, following Trump's practiced use of these for easy reference, as well as to distinguish a married couple who share a surname.)

Hardly a day goes by when those of us consigned to being addressed by the President on Twitter are not made privy to his evaluations of anyone and anything. It therefore may not come as a surprise to hear that both Trump's opening comments and the introductions that follow are littered with evaluations of others, from "you did a fantastic job," to "I think it's a disgrace, the way the press is." The central question I am concerned with here is: What does this barrage of evaluations of others do for Trump? What does he get from the use of this interactional style?

In this chapter, I demonstrate how Trump's repeated assessments, both positive and negative, serve to place him in the role of "evaluator," and thereby position his guests as "evaluatees." With each guest likely noticing that their own turn to be evaluated is soon at hand, each works to provide Trump ample evidence of their fealty in exchange for his positive evaluation. However, this demonstration of commitment and loyalty to Trump and his ideals only works to garner his praise when guests provide evidence that meets Trump's implicit criteria of worthiness, which he repeatedly models in his evaluation of others. As a result, Trump and guests work together to achieve his position as "Evaluator in Chief" and further solidify his public image as the "Boss."

Of course, this is not the first time someone has suggested that men in positions of power may elect themselves to the roles of judge and jury of those they feel entitled to evaluate. In fact, linguistic anthropologists Ochs and Taylor (Ochs and Taylor 1995) identified just such a dynamic, which they deemed "father knows best" (a title derived from the 1950s sitcom of the same name) after observing the dinner table behavior of seven middle-class families in Southern California. The authors found that in a typical interaction the father would become the "family judge," as various problems or topics were raised over the course of a meal. As the judge, the father would problematize the behavior, thoughts, or feelings of his wife or children far more than they would his, thereby taking on the role of "problematizer" and making his wife or children the "problematizee" – the source of the problem that the father identifies. This practice becomes a visible sign of the father's power and authority, and also helps to maintain that authority each time the father takes on the problematizer role and each time the family implicitly or explicitly agrees to participate in being judged.

Ochs and Taylor are thus able to demonstrate one way that normal every-day conversations around the dinner table can become a field where the production and maintenance of social power are played out. The following analysis demonstrates the way a similar dynamic, Trump's persistent evaluations of those around him at a meeting, can become a field on which his own power and authority are made and remade, with the aid and consent of all those who agree to and participate in the production of their own evaluation.

Rather than reproducing Trump's full opening remarks here (about 1,200 words) (Trump 2017), and to give you a sense of the omnipresence of his evaluations of others, I provide an extract of each evaluation deployed by Trump during his opening comments. Far more evaluations follow during the introduction of guests and are reviewed later in this work.[1]

Introducing Paris Dennard, conservative political commentator and consultant

"Paris did such a good job"

"And ((*points*)) Paris has done a- an amazing job in a very hostile *CNN* community"

"I'll take Paris over the seven."

"I ((*points*)) saw you talking about it the other night Paris on something else that was really you did a fantastic job the other night."

Introducing Pastor Darrell Scott, GOP political commentator and consultant

"You have been so helpful Darrell I- You have been really really-"

"I met Darrell when he was defending me on TV and the people on the other side of the argument didn't have a chance right?"

Introducing Ben Carson, Secretary of Housing and Urban Development

"And I want to thank Ben Carson, who's going to be heading up HUD, and it's a big job"

"Nobody's gonna be better than Ben."

Introducing Omarosa Manigault Newman, former *Apprentice* star, and political aide

"I want to thank my television star over here"

"She's been helpful right from the beginning of the campaign"

Evaluating Frederick Douglass, the former slave, abolitionist, writer, and statesman who died in 1895

"Douglass is an example of somebody who's done an amazing job"

"Big impact"

Evaluating Fox News

"But Fox has treated me very nice wherever Fox (news) is, thank you."

Evaluating the group as whole

"This is a great group that's been so special to me, you really helped me a lot"

On the face of it, these evaluations appear to be merely externalizations of how Trump feels about the targets of his evaluations, but in fact they do far more work than that. When we offer an evaluation of something, we are simultaneously "doing" the evaluation, that is, making those thoughts or feelings public, but also sending messages to those listening about the kinds of things I the speaker am likely to evaluate, and whether I'm likely to evaluate those kinds of things positively or negatively. If one were so inclined, one could pay close attention to these evaluations and get a good sense of what counts for Trump as something worthy of evaluation, in which direction he routinely evaluates that thing (positive or negative) and to what degree this is something he just "likes" or really "loves."

Now, let's say you're sitting around a table with a really powerful guy, who really likes to evaluate the people around him. In fact, he's already started doing it and you know it will soon be your turn. While there is typically a range of possible things you might offer when your turn comes around, that range is limited to comments relevant to the occasion and the particular interactional context, in this case, doing "introductions." As is routinely done and expected in introductions, you can use this time to say some things about yourself that don't necessarily highlight your allegiance to Trump, or you can try to figure out what you might be able to say to garner that positive evaluation, since it seems an evaluation of you will be rendered nonetheless.

For the sake of argument, let's say that you wanted to try and get that positive evaluation. The first thing you would need to know is what kind of things he evaluates positively. What seem to be his criteria for deciding whether something gets a positive or negative evaluation? Are there any themes that emerge from listening to him do some of these evaluations over and over? A careful review of his evaluations draws out some patterns.

13.1   Evaluation Themes in the Opening Comments: Establishing the Criteria

The first theme might be summarized as *how much you've helped me further my goals*. An example of this theme can be found in Trump's evaluation of the overall contribution of the group of attendees: "This is a great group that's been so special to me, you really helped me a lot." Here, the group of attendees is positively evaluated on the grounds that "you really helped me a lot" and that doing so can make you "special to me." Presumably, then, those who want to be special to Trump need to "help him a lot," and likely make known exactly how this help has been rendered. This theme can be identified again when Trump evaluates Omarosa, saying "she is a very good person and she's been helpful right from the beginning of the campaign." In this instance, Omarosa is positively evaluated for again "being helpful" and additionally for doing so "right from the beginning," making clear that the length of time one has been "helpful" to Trump is also something that might matter in his personal criteria for positively evaluating others. This theme is found again when Trump evaluates Pastor Darrell Scott's contribution, saying "well these are a lot of my friends, but you have been so helpful Darrell I- you have been really really" before cutting off and shifting to comments on his election win. Here, Trump uses the term "friend" to characterize his relationship with some other attendees but selects Darrell from among members of this category for special attention, apparently for the intensity of his helpfulness – "so helpful."

The next criterion for positive evaluation might be summarized as *publicly defending me against my enemies*. This can be identified in Trump's additional evaluation of Darrell when he says, "I met Darrell when he was defending me on TV and the people on the other side of the argument didn't have a chance right?" Trump's positive evaluation of those who "defend" him in public media contexts is also evident when Trump points at Paris and says, "Paris has done a- an amazing job in a very hostile *CNN* community." For Trump, then, positive evaluations are attached to advocating for Trump's political agenda publicly, in large media contexts, and against those who are "hostile" to him or take up "the other side of the argument." Omarosa is evaluated positively on the same grounds when Trump refers to her as his "television star."

In addition to offering positive evaluations to those who have "been helpful" or "defended" him, Trump sometimes offers positive evaluations of those who are partaking in *major efforts on his behalf*. These evaluations are often distinguished by the presence of intensifiers like "big," as in, "I want to thank Ben Carson, who's going to be heading up HUD, and it's a big job." Here, Ben is evaluated positively, not for what he has done in the service of Trump's campaign or election (after all, Ben was one of Trump's competitors in the Republican primary), but instead with a focus on the size of the contribution Trump believes Ben will make. Positively evaluating the size of a contribution is used again in Trump's evaluation of Frederick Douglass when Trump says, "Douglass is an example of somebody who's done an amazing job," later offering an additional reason for this evaluation when he characterizes Douglass' contribution as having a "big impact."

Finally, Trump offers evaluations on the basis of whether people are perceived as *being nice or saying nice things about me*. Since a disproportionate amount of Trump's talk is often devoted to denouncing those who speak ill of him, it stands to reason that grounds for positive assessment might include doing the opposite. While this theme is clearly related to "defending" him against those who are "hostile" to him, here, the evaluation is also assigned to an entire media organization when Trump evaluates the Fox News agency saying, "but Fox has treated me very nice wherever Fox (news) is, thank you."

Reviewing the above identified themes, we might note that Trump's evaluations seem to be prompted by behaviors that count as displays of loyalty or commitment, whether these be in the form of defending him to his enemies, advocating for his agenda, working hard for him, or complimenting him. In fact, an implicit question that seems to lurk just around the corner of so many of Trump's interactions is the question, "so what have you done for me lately?" Given that this pattern is readily understood and identified, it is likely that these guests have become aware of how important these behaviors are to staying in Trump's favor, and if one wanted to elicit a positive evaluation from Trump, the criteria for doing so would be fairly clear. Let's call this the *tell me what you've done for me lately* dynamic.

We can now turn to see if the guests at this event identify and make use of the above themes that Trump repeatedly models as things likely to receive his

196   *Brion van Over*

praise during his opening comments (spoiler alert: they most certainly do, nearly every time).

13.2   How to Get Love from Trump

Trump begins the round of introductions by inviting Paris Dennard, GOP commentator and consultant, to start. The Paris introduction exchange is interesting, as it is the only one between Trump and a guest that does not follow the recurring pattern that each subsequent introduction follows. This is likely because, as the first exchange, the exchange itself helps to establish the pattern as Paris and Trump work out what needs to be done to get that positive evaluation. Unlike the guests to follow, Paris does not make clear what he has contributed to Trump (what have you done for Trump lately?), but instead remarks on Trump's support for his organization (what Trump has done for him) (Trump 2017; video excerpt starts at 6:20).

PARIS: pleasure to be here Mr. President,
honor to be here
Paris Dennard.
I'm (with) Thurgood Marshall College Fund (that) represents the forty-seven publicly supported historically black colleges and university which I know you are very much in support of.
so it's a pleasure to be here sir.
TRUMP: well I'm glad you're in support of me because uh (.)
I'd be all,
I'd be in the wilderness without you guys
you are so effective I appreciate it

In this instance, Paris doesn't seem to say anything that meets Trump's criteria for positive evaluation. There isn't any talk about how he's defended Trump, or what he's done for Trump. In fact, Paris turns the tables, offering a positive evaluation of Trump for his support of black colleges and universities, temporarily stealing the reins and becoming the evaluator, making Trump the evaluatee. Trump manages to offer Paris a positive evaluation, nonetheless, but only after recharacterizing what Paris said as having purportedly been about supporting Trump, saying "Well I'm glad you're in support of me because …" By taking what Paris said and transforming it into a statement that claims support for Trump, Trump models that what guests should say is something about how they support Trump, not how Trump supports them. This correction may help the guests that follow to offer something that better meets Trump's criteria.

The next introduction proceeds with Bill Cleveland, who introduces himself as "Bill Cleveland, retired Capitol police officer, former vice mayor (of) city of Alexandria, and substitute teacher in Alexandria school system." Bill fails to specify how or what this does for Trump and so is met with merely a "thank you." However, Earl Matthews, who's up next, interjects and provides some additional information that Bill is also a Vietnam veteran, saying "And Bill's ((*touches Bill's shoulder*)) also a Vietnam veteran, sir." This apparently offers Trump something he can evaluate, as he replies, "Oh good for you." While not seen in the themes for positive evaluation established in his opening comments, Bill's status as a Vietnam veteran does speak to his service to the nation, if not to Trump personally. Note, however, that Trump does not thank Bill for his service to the "country," but treats his veteran status as a personal good.

The next guest is Pastor Belinda Scott, who self-identifies as "Darrell's wife" and goes on to have the longest introduction exchange with Trump (video excerpt starts at 7:18).

BELINDA: I'm like you're next ((*laughing*))
           Belinda Scott uh-
           Darrell's wife New Spirit Revival Center
           um
           from Cleveland Ohio,
           Pastor of New Spirit,
           great amount of support in the uh- African American peop- community where we are,
           uhm we love the lord we love our new president,
           and we are praying for our president.
TRUMP: thank you
BELINDA: on a regular basis
OMAROSA: amen
           ((*applause*))
BELINDA: that's what I do what we do
TRUMP: you know the one thing I didn't understand about Belinda I ((*palm point*)) thought they were married maybe five or six years, cause ((*palm point*)) look how they look so young?
           ((*laughter*))
TRUMP: should you say how many years you've been married?
BELINDA: th- thirty? five?
DARRELL: been together thirty-eight
BELINDA: thirty- been together [thirty-eight
TRUMP: [now can you believe that
BELINDA: but- but in the LORD
           ((*laughter*))
BELINDA: thirty-five, yes
DARRELL: thirty-three, [three of the thirty-eight under the blood
TRUMP: [that's great
TRUMP: that's ((*laughter*))
TRUMP: that's actually amazing, I wouldn't have known
BELINDA: but can I say this,
           I am so grateful that our President gives us a ear,
           you know- you- to listen
OMAROSA: that's right

BELINDA:	to the community, to listen,
	and and- and people like-
	like us are just here to constantly put that message out into the community
TRUMP:	thank you Belinda,
	that's so nice

After identifying herself, Belinda goes on to say, "New Spirit Revival Center from Cleveland Ohio, Pastor of New Spirit, great amount of support in the African American community where we are, we love the lord, we love our new president, and we are praying for our president." Like the instance with Bill above, Trump replies here with only a "thank you," which Belinda likely finds insufficient, as she goes on, saying "on a regular basis." With praying for Trump apparently not being something worthy of positive evaluation, Trump looks to produce his own noticing that he can and does go on to positively evaluate. This begins with Trump saying "look how they look so young" and offering for Belinda to say how long they have been married ("thirty-five?"), to which Darrell offers "been together thirty-eight." Trump now finds an opportunity to offer an evaluation, though this is one of his own making, saying "that's great" and "that's actually amazing, I wouldn't have known."

The force of the structure in this event, Trump's need to evaluate each guest, is such that in both the Paris and the Belinda introductions, when Trump finds nothing worthy of evaluating in what his guest has said, he decides to say something himself that he can then go on to evaluate. This allows Trump to invoke and maintain the role of evaluator, even when by his own view there appears to be nothing to evaluate.

The next guest is Darrell Scott, who introduces himself as another pastor at the New Spirit Revival Center (video excerpt starts at 8:28).

DARRELL:	Darrell Scott, pastor New Spirit Revival Center,
	and black (.) Trump (.) supporter.
AUDIENCE:	(Yes)
OMAROSA:	((*laughter*)) ((*applauds*))
AUDIENCE:	((*applauds*))
TRUMP:	thank you
TRUMP:	you have been a great supporter

Darrell opens with a declaration of support for Trump, and makes clear that his being a "Black" Trump supporter matters and is worthy of note in its own right, presumably because common conceptions of Trump's supporters don't include many members of Black communities. Trump again offers his thanks and the now seemingly compulsory evaluation. In this case, Darrell's being Black and being a supporter is all that is necessary to garner Trump's praise – "You have been a great supporter" – presumably because his support is helping Trump to achieve some of his goals, which is one of the themes identified in

Trumps opening comments. Darrell, perhaps unsatisfied, decides to go on (video excerpt starts 8:38).

DARRELL: I was recently contacted,
           by some of the top gang thugs in Chicago,
           for a sit down.
BELINDA: ((*nods*))
           they wanna sit down
DARRELL: they reached out to me because they associated me with you,
           [they respect you
TRUMP: [right
DARRELL: they- they they believe in whatcha doin,
           and they wanna have a sit down
           about lowerin that body count
DARRELL: so in a couple of weeks,
           I'm going into Chicago,
TRUMP: I think that's a great idea because Chicago is totally out of control
           (segment ends 9:00)
           (transcription resumes at 9:25)
DARRELL: but they want to work with this administration
TRUMP: good
DARRELL: they want to,
           they reached out-
           I didn't reach out to them, they [reached out to me,
TRUMP: [I think that's great
DARRELL: they wanna work with this [administration,
TRUMP: [I think it's
DARRELL: they believe in this administration,
           they didn't believe in the prior administration.
           they told me this out of their [mouth
TRUMP: [I think that's great.
DARRELL: but they see hope with you.
TRUMP: I love (it)

Here, Darrell proceeds to tell Trump about his recent contacts with "some of the top gang thugs in Chicago" who want a "sit down" because they "respect" Trump, and that Darrell plans to go to Chicago "in a couple weeks" to advocate for "lowering the body count." This garners an upgraded evaluation from Trump who replies, "I think that's a great idea because Chicago is totally out of control," providing Trump an opportunity to expound on his recurring complaint about the state of inner cities, a popular talking point in his stump speeches. The pattern continues with Darrell emphasizing that it is really Trump who has brought these "street guys" to the table, offering Trump various compliments, or, generally *saying nice things about him*, for which he is paid in ever more enthusiastic positive evaluations from Trump, saying "good," and "I think that's great," and again

"I think that's great," finally stopping only when Trump offers the most upgraded evaluation, "I love it."

This general pattern continues across the remaining participants. The evaluatee offers things for Trump to evaluate that generally conform to the kind of things Trump has positively evaluated earlier in the event, followed by positive evaluations from Trump who is thereby positioned as the evaluator. Below are the remaining evaluatee's bids for positive evaluation as well as the evaluator's (i.e. Trump's) positive evaluations, each of which conforms to this patterning.

Introduction of Gerard Robinson, Executive Director, Center for Advancing Opportunity

GERARD: I was proud to be the leader of the education policy team for Trump–Pence transition.
TRUMP: Thank you, that's great.

Introduction of Ashley Bell, member of Trump transition team, attorney

ASHLEY: Chairman Priebus called me out of my little town to come help run African American outreach for your campaign [. . .] I'll be wanting to help you out at the State Department.
TRUMP: Fantastic. Thank you. Thank you very much.

Introduction of Tucker Davis, West Virginia

TUCKER: I'm Tucker Davis. I ran your campaign in West Virginia, working for you in the-
TRUMP: We did well in West Virginia!

Introduction of Leah LeVell, Republican National Committee

LEAH: I was at the RNC and also at PIC, and I helped launch the video series every week um the midweek message that reached out to millennials and college students and helped launch the college Republican chapter at Howard University.
TRUMP: Good. Good. I heard that.
OMAROSA: That's Bruce LeVell's daughter. We snagged her.
TRUMP: Oh that's good. Oh good. Great job.

Introduction of Monica Alexander, Office of Public Liaison

MONICA: Executive administrative assistant in the Office of Public Liaison, supporting Omarosa.
TRUMP: Good.
MONICA: Spellman graduate.
TRUMP: Okay, well, that's nice.

Introduction of Ja'Ron Smith, congressional staff member

JA'RON: I'm with the Domestic Policy Council, Andrew Bremberg's team, and I'll be focusing on urban affairs and revitalization.

TRUMP: Fantastic!
OMAROSA: And Howard graduate.
TRUMP: Howard graduate. That's good stuff.

13.3   Why Does This Interactive Pattern Matter?

That Trump is a fan of praise, and often heaps it upon himself in the absence of
another to provide this service, is not a new observation. In fact, an editorial in the
New York Times identified a 2017 cabinet meeting wherein member after member
offers their praise during a similar round of introductions (Davis 2017). The results
of the 2016 presidential election also attest to Trump's mastery of bringing (some)
people under his tent, going from the unlikeliest of candidates to growing a legion of
followers. The question becomes, how does Trump manage to continue to trans-
form once stable and routine contexts and practices and bend them to his will,
including taking a meeting purportedly about "listening" to African Americans
during Black History Month and turning it into a fealty forum? And how does he get
others to go along with it?

I suggest the interactional practices outlined here aid Trump in establishing
his "Boss" persona through the public aggregation of supplicants. More specifically, Trump uses evaluative language to (1) establish and normalize standards of behavior, as when he models in his opening comments the kinds of
things that good people worthy of praise ought do, (2) invite others to swear
fealty through their willing participation in the co-construction of their own
evaluations, and (3) encourage them to evaluate themselves on the basis of
Trump's standards. Those who play along win the promise of approval and
avoid the public verbal abuse Trump reserves for those who don't.

This analysis aids our understanding of how the public perception of power
and authority is cultivated through interaction. This knowledge is essential to
our being critical participants in our politics, rather than an unwitting audience
of language games staged for our consumption. Like the "father knows best"
dynamic observed by Ochs and Taylor, the practice identified here makes
visible how Trump's power not only pre-exists events like these, but is made
and remade through the interactions happening in them. Put another way,
power is not only had, but also made, through communication.

Note

1. For this chapter in particular, only segments that include a significant back-and-forth
   between Trump and his constituents have been transcribed in a conversation analytic
   style. Other quotes have been left in conventional orthography. Transcription conventions used for conversation analysis here include the use of CAPITALS to
   indicate talk spoken with special emphasis. Colons after a vowel indicate an elongated vowel sound. A left bracket ([) marks the onset and a right bracket (]) marks the

offset of overlapping talk. Numbers in parentheses – for example, (1.2) – note the length of silences in seconds, while a single period in parentheses (.) indicates a micropause of less than 0.1 seconds. A dash (-) marks the cut-off of the current sound. An equal sign (=) indicates "latching," where talk starts up in especially close temporal proximity to the end of the previous talk. Transcribers' comments and non-verbal action descriptors are italicized in double parentheses ((like this)); single parentheses, (like this), around talk indicate a problematic hearing. Punctuation symbols are used to mark intonation changes rather than as grammatical symbols: a period indicates a falling contour; a question mark, a rising contour; and a comma, a falling-rising contour, as might be found in the midst of a list. Each line of text (without a hard return) indicates talk spoken within a single breath group.

References

Davis, Julie H. 2017. "Trump's Cabinet, with a Prod, Extols the 'Blessing' of Serving Him." *The New York Times*, June 12, 2017. https://nyti.ms/2rjw0pn.
Ochs, Elinor, and Carolyn Taylor. 1995. "The 'Father Knows Best' Dynamic in Family Dinner Narratives." In *Gender Articulated: Language and the Socially Constructed Self*, edited by Kira Hall and Mary Bucholtz, pp. 97–120. Routledge.
Trump, Donald. 2017. "Black History Month Listening Session." C-SPAN video. February 1, 2017. https://cs.pn/2tRKdpX.

14   Fake Alignments

Sylvia Sierra and Natasha Shrikant

> You read all about Dr. Martin Luther King a week ago when somebody said
> I took the statue out of my office, and it turned out that that was fake news.
>
> President Donald Trump, Black History Month Listening
> Session on February 1, 2017

By early 2017, President Donald Trump had been repeatedly and widely accused of being racist and supporting policies that negatively affect minorities. Concerned about his reputation, his team arranged a televised Black History Month Listening Session to be held in the White House on February 1 (Trump 2017). Along with Trump and Vice President Mike Pence, the attendees would include African Americans in Trump's administration – Dr. Ben Carson (Secretary of Housing and Urban Development) and Omarosa Manigault (then-Director of Communications for the Office of Public Liaison) – as well as noteworthy African American leaders in industries such as media, church, military, and private industry (Bobic 2017). Trump knew well that this would be a damage control opportunity: The public would be watching closely to observe how he might connect with the participants and engage with issues important to members of the African American community. But this listening session would be like none other before it. Typically, during such events, a leader listens to participants' concerns, formulates some kind of empathic response, and makes an occasional verbal commitment to an informed administrative response down the line. After this session, though, Trump received harsh criticism from some mainstream media outlets for seeming ill-informed about African American history and for failing to focus on helping the community at stake. Instead, he used much of the time to complain about the seemingly unrelated topic of "fake news" in the media.

Some media outlets, including the *Washington Post* (Wootson 2017) and *CNN* (Merica 2017), pounced in particular on Trump's statement about Frederick Douglass: "Frederick Douglass is an example of somebody who's done an amazing job and is being recognized more and more." They cited Trump's peculiar verb tense and vacuous phrasing as evidence that he was neither familiar with Douglass' achievements nor even aware that Douglass had passed away in 1895. Trump's praise of Douglass, they noted, was also in keeping with his fixation with fame; he may not have known a thing about Douglass, but he understood that Douglass' prominence in public discourse was on the rise. Many headlines further critiqued Trump's failure to listen: "Donald Trump's 'Listening Session' on Black History Month Was Anything But" (Thrasher 2017), "Trump Began His 'Black History Month Listening Session' With a 'Media Complaining Session'" (Bump 2017), and "Trump Blasts Media at African-American 'Listening Session'" (Flores 2017), among others (e.g. Naylor 2017, Nelson 2017). These articles evaluated the event as a failure because Trump seemed self-absorbed, uninterested in engaging with the African American community's needs and struggles. He appeared to be using this meeting as yet another pedestal to preach his anti-media propaganda.

While criticisms of the listening session were numerous, the session participants acted as if they liked Trump. They laughed at his jokes about "fake news" and did not orient to Trump's statements as if they were deviant. Similarly, conservative media (e.g. *Fox News*, *The Drudge Report*, etc.) did not note anything out of the ordinary about Trump's session. How is it that Trump's actions can be evaluated as egotistical, ignorant about African American issues, and obsessed with criticizing media *and* as normal and unremarkable?

One explanation could be the relative positions of power of the parties involved. As president, Trump has long been supported by the African American attendees of this session as well as by conservative news media. What we highlight in this chapter, however, is the role of language use in facilitating alignment between Trump and his African American guests. We show that the conversationalists' identities and relationships are not altogether pre-existing, but rather emerge and are negotiated through the ways they interact with one another (Bucholtz and Hall 2005). Trump did not simply command deference from his participants because of his status. Rather, Trump and his African American interlocutors *collaboratively achieved* congenial relationships through language use, and it is this appearance of friendliness that allowed the conservative media to ignore criticisms about Trump's behavior in the session.

In this chapter, we analyze moments in the listening session where Trump moves seemingly illogically from praising African Americans to complaining about mainstream news media. We show how this move is, in fact, effective in momentarily building relationships. While Trump would go on to make many statements and policy decisions decidedly unfriendly to minority communities, our analysis shows how he can nevertheless use a kind of linguistic sleight of hand to create the impression of being aligned with a community of speakers. In other words, we show how language use in this session functions to sustain enduring racial hierarchies through allowing Trump to ignore issues facing communities of color while still seeming supportive of these communities.

14.1 Talk Activities and Building Relationships

At the listening session, Trump engaged in two distinctive talk activities that we'll analyze here: praising and introducing African Americans, and complaining about the mainstream media. "Talk activity" is actually a formal concept in language studies, used to refer to the collaboratively developed and negotiated meaning of talk itself among speakers (Bateson 1972, Goffman 1974). People constantly shift between different talk activities (Goodwin 1996) or blend multiple activities (Gordon 2008), such as flirting while complimenting. Why should we care about the details of shifting and blending talk activities? Since doing so is a collaborative process, it constructs relationships among those involved. In this chapter, we shed light on the relational work Trump is doing when he seems to shift at random from praising African Americans to commiserating about mainstream media. We also show how one of the African American supporters at the listening session follows Trump's lead by conducting an introduction while simultaneously joking and commiserating about the media. Ultimately, shifting and blending these talk activities contributes to the relational alignment work among Trump and the African Americans present at this event.

Below, we look closely at three excerpts that highlight how Trump and his conversationalists shift and blend talk activities that hinge on repeatedly making jokes about "fake news." First, it's helpful to understand how this short phrase accumulated its meaning in the weeks leading up to this event. Journalists, news pundits, and opposition candidate Hillary Clinton originally used "fake news" to explain how fictitious news stories on websites registered in Macedonia circulated on Facebook, swaying US citizens to vote for Trump in the 2016 election. Trump then co-opted the phrase as an accusation against any media he perceived as being biased towards him and his administration. He initially used the phrase on Twitter, and it subsequently became known as one of his catchphrases.

In the first two excerpts we examine from the listening session, Trump's disparaging jokes about "fake news" indirectly align Trump with the conservative African Americans in this interaction, while praising well-known African American figures functions as Trump's more direct attempt to relate with the broader community. The speakers at the event align with Trump's jokes primarily via laughter. An analysis of a third excerpt demonstrates how conservative commentator Armstrong Williams introduces himself by adopting Trump's humorous anti-media strategy. As he blends his introduction with disparaging the media, he receives additional laughter from the room and approval from Trump. Although shifting talk from praising Black History to disparaging the media might seem random and chaotic, our analysis shows how this process is actually Trump's attempt to align with the conservative African American community.

14.2   "Fake news from these people"

The first example, occurring about two minutes into the listening session, illustrates how Trump initially attempts to align with the broader African American community through praising Reverend Dr. Martin Luther King, Jr. (MLK), but how he then shifts to complaining about the media (Trump, 2017; audio excerpt starts 02:18). We number the following lines for ease of reference in our analysis.[1]

```
 1  TRUMP:  last month we celebrated the life of
 2          Reverend Martin Luther King
 3          Jr. whose incredible example is unique in American history
 4          you read all about (.) ((shifts eye gaze from reading to others))
 5          Dr. Martin Luther King uh: (.)
 6          a week ago when uh somebody said I took the statue out of my office (.)
 7          and it turned out that that was (.)
 8          FA:KE news
 9  ROOM:   ((laughter))
10  TRUMP:  From these people ((gestures towards the reporters in the room))
11          FA:KE news.
```

Through reading his initial remarks, Trump celebrates and praises MLK. He uses "we" in line 1, establishing himself, his conversationalists, and the broader American public as being a singular community that "celebrated the life of Reverend Martin Luther King, Jr." Trump then praises MLK, using "incredible" and "unique" to characterize MLK as an exceptional figure in "American history" (lines 2–3). These empty adjectives echo Trump's earlier characterization of Frederick Douglass as "amazing."

In line 4, Trump goes off-script. He shifts his eye gaze from reading to looking at his conversationalists, and switches pronouns from "we" to "you": "you read all about (.) Dr. Martin Luther King uh: a week ago" (lines 4–6). These verbal and non-verbal cues signal Trump shifting from speaking generally about celebrating MLK to addressing his conversationalists. Trump also shifts from praising MLK as a historical figure to relating a recent news story concerning himself and a statue of MLK, saying, "when uh somebody said I took the statue of out my office" (line 6). Trump then claims that the accusations was false, saying "it turned out that that was (.)," pausing briefly, likely for the effect of comedic timing, before referencing his popular, often-repeated joke, "FA:KE news," in line 8. His emphatic stress and vowel lengthening on "fake" signal to his conversationalists that this is a repeated and already-known reference (Sierra 2016).

Those present in the room demonstrate recognition and appreciation of the joke through laughter.

With this reference to "fake news," Trump foregrounds his political similarities with his current conversationalists, all of whom are conservative Trump supporters. By shifting frames from praising African Americans to complaining about the media, he not only builds shared identity through foregrounding political similarity among participants, but also highlights differences with a common enemy: the media. Through this repeated joke and shifting from praising to complaining, Trump is also denying that he removed the statue of a famous and respected African American figure. This positions Trump as respectful of MLK, and by extension, Trump's African American conversationalists and the larger African American community. The laughter from his conversationalists indicates their alignment with his joke, and subsequently the relational work he is doing. Trump then shifts in lines 8–10 from his general complaint against the media to a specific accusation against the media representatives in the room, pointing at them as he states "fake news . . . from these people." Trump then repeats the phrase "FA:KE news."

Overall, Trump's repeated jokes about "fake news" help him to shift from praising MLK to commiserating about an MLK news story, and ultimately aid in resisting the portrayal of Trump as a disrespectful racist, instead highlighting his similarities with his current African American conversationalists.

14.3 "I don't like watching fake news"

The second example, which occurs about one minute later in the listening session, illustrates how Trump constructs shared identity with his guests through simultaneously praising them and commiserating about the media. Just previous to this excerpt he had said, "I am proud to honor this heritage, and will be honoring it more and more. The folks at the table in almost all cases have been great friends and supporters" (Trump 2017; audio excerpt starts 3:41). Here he begins by praising two of the conservative African American personalities present at the listening session, Pastor Darrell Scott and Paris Dennard (a conservative political speaker), for defending Trump in what he perceives as a hostile media environment. Then he again shifts to commiserating through making another repeated joke about the "fake news."

```
1   TRUMP:     and uh
2              Darrell I met Darrell when he was defending me on television?
3   ROOM:      ((laughter))
4   TRUMP:     and the people ((gazes at Darrell)) that were on the other side of the
               argument didn't have a chance right?=
```

```
 5  DARRELL:    =that's right ((laughing))
 6  ROOM:       ((laughter))
 7  TRUMP:      and ((points)) Paris has done a- an amazing job in a very hostile CNN
                community,
 8  ROOM:       ((laughter))
 9  TRUMP:      he's a- he's all by himself (.)
10              he'll have seven people
11              and Paris
12              and I'll-
13              I'll take Paris over the seven
14  ROOM:       ((laughter))
15  TRUMP:      but I don't watch CNN so I don't get to see you as much as I [used to]
16  ROOM:       ((laughter))
17  TRUMP:      I don't like watching fake news=
18  UNKNOWN:    =no- none of us watch it either [anymore
19  TRUMP:                                      [uhuh ((glances towards speaker))
```

Trump praises Darrell in line 2, foregrounding his shared political identity
with Darrell through stating Darrell was "defending me" in what has already
been established as a hostile context, "on television." Through joking about
being conservatives who have to deal with hostile media, Trump not only
foregrounds shared identity with Darrell but also receives laughter from fellow
conservative audience members in response to this statement. This laughter,
which recurs throughout this excerpt, contributes to affiliation (Glenn 2003)
among those present.

Trump then compliments Darrell by adding, "and the people that were on the
other side of the argument didn't have a chance right?" in line 4, implying that
Darrell is a skilled debater. Darrell aligns with Trump, laughing and affirmatively
answering his question with "That's right ((laughing))" in line 5. Others again align
and bond with Trump and Darrell through their laughter (line 6). Trump then shifts
from introducing to praising when naming another panelist, Paris. Similar to what
he did with Darrell, Trump positions Paris as a skilled debater in a hostile environment (lines 7–13). Here, Trump constructs a shared identity through both praising
and commiserating about the media. This foregrounds his political similarity with
Darrell and Paris through constructing the media as hostile towards not only
Trump, but also the African American media commentators who defend him. In
addition, the fact that Trump is defended by these media commentators might
appeal to Trump's wider base of African American supporters.

Next, Trump begins to shift from praising his invitees to snubbing the
mainstream media by saying, "But I don't watch *CNN* so I don't get to see
you as much as I used to" (line 15). Trump's audience laughs, similar to how
they laughed when he said that he met Darrell when Darrell was defending
Trump on television. Trump then repeats his prior joke, "I don't like watching

fake news" (line 17), shifting fully away from praising to solely complaining about the media. Then someone at the table (who we cannot identify because the camera was focused on Trump) aligns with Trump by declaring on behalf of the group that "none of us watch it either anymore" (line 18). This speaker briefly adopts Trump's strategy of commiserating about the media, a move also highlighted below in the third example.

In this example, Trump's joke about "fake news" facilitates a shift from praising his conversationalists' ability to manage hostile media to simply commiserating explicitly about the media. What we want to underscore is that throughout all of this talk, even though on the surface it seems that Trump is randomly shifting from praising people to complaining about "fake news," he is actually creating and maintaining relationships with his conservative African American conversationalists from start to finish. If anything, his "fake news" jokes serve a crucial role in bringing him together with his African American conversationalists on this occasion.

14.4   "We try to be fair"

Several minutes later in the interaction, conservative commentator Armstrong Williams adopts Trump's strategy of simultaneously praising an individual (in this case, Trump) and commiserating about the media. This allows Williams to align with Trump despite Williams' membership in the media. This strategy receives laughter from the room and approval from Trump (Trump 2017; audio excerpt starts 9:38).

```
 1  WILLIAMS:  um Mr. President,
 2             I'm a-
 3             a member of the
 4             the- uh- what we call the media,
 5             where we try to be fair?
 6  ROOM:      ((laughter))
 7  WILLIAMS:  and objective.
 8  UNKNOWN:   very fair
 9  WILLIAMS:  u:m not ALL media
10             uh seems to be the opposition party.
11             there are those that see the GOOD that you do and we report it (and)
12             I'm just honored to have a seat at the table today.
13  TRUMP:     thank you Armstrong.
```

In light of the tone Trump has set, how can Williams engage in the delicate interactional task of defending the media (and himself) while still maintaining relationships with other participants? Williams begins by displaying respect towards President Trump through the formal address title, "Mr. President." He

then prefaces his claim that the media can be "fair" and "objective" through
using several linguistic moves that both delay and account for the norm
violation (defending the media) that Williams is about to make (Shrikant
2019). First, Williams discloses that he is a member of the media, thus implying
that he is qualified to speak about the media. He hedges and has a false start
("I'm a- a member of the the- uh-", lines 3–4), which indicate that Williams is
aware of the upcoming norm violation and hesitant about making it. Last,
Williams uses "what we call" directly preceding "the media" (line 4). The
formulation "what we call" indicates the shared understanding participants
have about meanings associated with "the media." Through showing that he
is aware of this shared knowledge, Williams is able to maintain alignment with
this group while still acknowledging that he is a member of the media.

    After locating himself as a member of the media, Williams uses "we,"
referencing the media community, and jokes, using question intonation, "we
try to be fair?" (line 5). Through his question intonation on "fair," Williams
tests the water by speaking against the already established position among his
current conversationalists that the media is not fair and does not attempt to be
fair. This joke succeeds in eliciting laughter and alignment from speakers in this
room. Even though Williams is disagreeing with accusations that the media is
not fair, he shows that he is aware that he is disagreeing with the group's
assessment. He is able to elicit laughter and maintain his alignment with his
conversationalists despite his membership of the media.

    Williams then continues describing "not all media" as being "the opposition
party" (lines 9–10). He states that there are "those that see the GOOD that you
do" (line 11), followed by "and we report it" to characterize himself as part of
that group. Thus, Williams defines being "fair" and "objective" as, in part,
reporting about the "good" that Trump does. This further supports our earlier
claim that Williams' joke about the media being "fair" both acknowledges
accusations against the media and serves to distance Williams from this
accusation. These utterances align Williams with Trump while acknowledging
Trump's general distrust of news media. In closing his introduction, Williams
again expresses his deference towards Trump through stating that he is
"honored to have a seat at the table" (line 12), and Trump thanks him (line
13). After thanking Williams, Trump uses this opportunity to again complain
about the media for thirty uninterrupted seconds. While Trump does not accuse
Williams of publishing fake news, he positions Williams as an exception to
mainstream media (saying things like "a lot of the media IS actually the
opposition party ... they're so biased ... it's really a disgrace ..." etc.).
Thus, Williams' self-introduction where he jokes about the media provides
Trump the opportunity to shift completely to complaining about the media yet
again.

How do we know that Trump's prior praising of participants and commiserating about the media is effective in building relationships? In part, because it gets taken up by other conversationalists. They laugh when Trump shifts from praising MLK to joking about "fake news" and when he praises Darrell and Paris while complaining about "fake news." The laughter shows that Trump is bonding and building relationships with these guests. Williams later uses Trump's strategy, aligning himself with Trump, to resist associations of Williams' media outlet with "fake news," and to bond with the conversationalists who laugh at Williams' joke. While Trump's discussion of "fake news" might seem like off-topic complaining, this shifting actually does consistent relational work, where Trump builds alliances – or at the very least, the appearances of them – between himself and African Americans throughout the session.

14.5   Conclusions

In this chapter, we paid close attention to repeated jokes about "fake news"; in turn, we looked at how these jokes facilitated shifts from praising and introducing to complaining and commiserating. Our analysis illustrates how Trump sidesteps racial identity in the Black History Month Listening Session and instead foregrounds political similarities with his conversationalists. We showed how he does this through highlighting shared political identity and perceived shared hostility that Trump and his conversationalists feel they face when engaging with mainstream media. Jokes about "fake news" play a crucial role in the relational work being done by the participants – foregrounding similarities in respect for African American figures, respect for current African Americans who defend Trump on hostile television, and political similarity instead of racial difference. The distinction that is made, in order to construct shared identities among those sitting at the table, is that the media is the opposition because it does not share this group's political ideals and is therefore "fake news."

This close analysis of linguistic data in its context shows us how this interaction is ripe for multiple interpretations because it is much more nuanced than it seems on the surface. On the one hand, when Trump shifts from talking about MLK to "lashing out at the media" as NPR reported, it can seem chaotic and disconnected. However, our analysis shows that these shifts and repeated jokes help speakers bond with one another in this situation. This analysis also helps explain why Trump simultaneously received criticism from the left for sidestepping race, but not from his politically conservative base for the same event. We argue that Trump avoids criticism from his politically conservative base because he constructs himself as a victim who shares experiences of victimization with his African American conversationalists (i.e. dealing with the hostile media). While Trump's experiences as a rich, White, male business tycoon (and now President of the United States) are nowhere near the struggles that African Americans have faced historically and currently, the identity work Trump does here seems to imply that both are oppressed by the media. Thus, through ignoring racial inequality, Trump is able to appeal to his base and attempts to avoid the identity of racist oppressor through adopting the identity of political victim.

While we have revealed that Trump's jokes about "fake news" maintain relationships with his African American conversationalists, and more broadly, his politically conservative base, we want to underscore how his repeated joking about "fake news" has political ramifications. Not only do Trump's comments lend themselves to conflicting interpretations, they also delegitimize the free press in the United States and position Trump as an unquestionable authority as to what counts as "real" news. These political ramifications can be seen in the 2018 mainstream media protest against Trump for violating the First Amendment right to freedom of the press through repeatedly accusing the media of publishing "fake news" and of being the "opposition party" (Bauder 2018). In addition, while we show how listening session attendees co-participate in this process, we also need to acknowledge that Trump is in a position of extreme power (as president), and therefore participants might be more inclined to align with Trump as an authority figure and adopt his framing of the media. In conclusion, we have shown how focusing on close analysis of talk can illuminate how conversational practices that are otherwise puzzling, such as seemingly rambling and disjointed praising, complaining, and introducing, all rely on a vast, hidden store of sociocultural knowledge that is drawn upon to achieve social adhesiveness in a particular group of people at a national televised event.

Note

1. In the transcriptions of the event, we highlight Trump's and his conversationalists' pitch, tone, cadence, and pace, all of which are features we use to infer the meanings that the conversationalists make relevant in interaction. CAPITALS indicate talk spoken with special emphasis. Colons after a vowel indicate an elongated vowel sound. A left bracket ([) marks the onset and a right bracket (]) marks the offset of overlapping talk. Numbers in parentheses – for example, (1.2) – note the length of silences in seconds, while a single period in parentheses (.) indicates a micropause of less than 0.1 seconds. A dash (-) marks the cut-off of the current sound. An equal sign (=) indicates "latching," where talk starts up in especially close temporal proximity to the end of the previous talk. Transcribers' comments and non-verbal actions are italicized in double parentheses ((*like this*)). Punctuation symbols are used to mark intonation changes rather than as grammatical symbols: a period indicates a falling contour; a question mark, a rising

contour; and a comma, a falling-rising contour, as might be found in the midst of a list. Each line of text (without a hard return) indicates talk spoken within a single breath group.

References

Bateson, Gregory. 1972. *Steps to an Ecology of Mind*. Ballantine Books.

Bauder, David. 2018. "US Newspapers to Trump: We're Not Enemies of the People." Associated Press article, August 16, 2018. https://bit.ly/2OEuLbq.

Bobic, Igor. 2017. "Trump Convenes Black History Month 'Listening Session' with People Who Like Him." *The Huffington Post*, February 1, 2017. https://bit.ly/2oK1ep7.

Bucholtz, Mary, and Kira Hall. 2005. "Identity and Interaction: A Sociocultural Linguistic Approach." *Discourse Studies* 7, no. 4–5: 585–614.

Bump, Philip. 2017. "Trump Began His 'Black History Month Listening Session' with a 'Media Complaining Session.'" *The Washington Post*, February 2, 2017. https://wapo.st/2mpW5lk.

Flores, Reena. 2017. "Trump Blasts Media at African-American 'Listening Session.'" CBS News article, February 1, 2017. https://cbsn.ws/2nYntHy.

Glenn, Phillip. 2003. *Laughter in Interaction*. Cambridge University Press.

Goffman, Erving. 1974. *Frame Analysis: An Essay on the Organization of Experience*. Harvard University Press.

Goodwin, Marjorie Harness. 1996. "Shifting Frame." In *Social Interaction, Social Context, and Language: Essays in Honor of Susan Ervin-Tripp*, edited by Dan Isaac Slobin, Julie Gerhardt, Amy Kyratzis, and Jiansheng Guo, pp. 71–82. Lawrence Erlbaum.

Gordon, Cynthia. 2008. "A(p)parent Play: Blending Frames and Reframing in Family Talk." *Language in Society* 37, no. 3: 319–49.

Merica, Dan. 2017. "Trump: Frederick Douglass 'Is Being Recognized More and More.'" *CNN* article, February 2, 2017. https://cnn.it/2vK8Yum.

Naylor, Brian. 2017. "In Black History Month 'Listening Session,' Trump Lashes Out at Media." NPR article, February 1, 2017. https://n.pr/2nWOJ9x.

Nelson, Louis. 2017. "Trump Launches Media Attack during Black History Month Listening Session." *Politico*, February 1, 2017. https://politi.co/2o4Donz.

Shrikant, Natasha. 2019. "'Who's the Face?': Communication and White Identity in a Texas Business Community." *Ethnic and Racial Studies* 42, no. 2: 254–71.

Sierra, Sylvia A. 2016. "Intertextual Media References as Resources for Managing Frames, Epistemics, and Identity in Conversation among Friends." Ph.D. diss., Georgetown University. https://bit.ly/2mtYueU.

Thrasher, Steven W. 2017. "Donald Trump's 'Listening Session' on Black History Month Was Anything But." *The Guardian*, February 2, 2017. https://bit.ly/2o3JyEs.

Trump, Donald. 2017. "Black History Month Listening Session." C-SPAN video, February 1, 2017. www.c-span.org/video/?423342–1/president-trump-holds-african-american-history-month-listening-session.

Wootson, Cleve R. 2017. "Trump Implied Frederick Douglass Was Alive. The Abolitionist's Family Offered a 'History Lesson.'" *The Washington Post*, February 2, 2017. https://wapo.st/2kwLykX.

Part IV

Language, White Nationalism,
and International Responses to Trump

15 Part IV Introduction: Language and Trump's White Nationalist Strongman Politics

Janet McIntosh

In spite of his reality-defying claim that he is "the least racist person that you've ever encountered" (Lopez 2019), Trump's tendency to exclude, caricature, and scapegoat non-Whites has been widely documented. A 2019 *Atlantic* article (Graham et al. 2019) summarizes just a few chapters of his racist past and present, including his anger toward people of color in competition with him (as when he opposed casinos run by Native Americans in the early 1990s–2000s), his anxiety surrounding upwardly mobile African Americans (e.g. on *The Apprentice*), his equivocations about neo-Nazis (see Hodgson, this volume), his administration's flagrant neglect of Puerto Rico compared with Houston when both were slammed by hurricanes, and his generally "very Aryan" view of race. Trump repeatedly lifts from the *Fox News* playbook of racial ideology, presuming that people of color hold themselves back with their own dysfunctions; that Whites are the victims of reverse racism; and that minorities who criticize government policy are "ungrateful" or "unpatriotic" (Waldman 2019). He has pandered time and again to White supremacists, repeatedly denigrated people of color, and reliably attracted voters who score high on measures of racism (Lopez 2019). Though he may deny it, his statements and actions cumulatively point toward the notion that "making America great again" means bringing it back to an era of more overt White supremacy. And whiteness, for Trump, is mapped onto the English language and particular ways of speaking it, while White superiority is encoded in his word choices, his metaphors, and his mockery.

Several chapters in this section address the way language can be weaponized in service of Trump's authoritarian White nationalism. This section introduction furnishes some broader context from linguistic anthropology to address how racism and xenophobia often play out in Trump's linguistic tool kit.

15.1 The Politics of Language Varieties

In human semiotic systems, language varieties – a linguist's phrase for what people usually call "languages" and "dialects" – often stand for something much more than themselves. This is a classic finding in the study of language ideology: opinions about language varieties often mirror peoples' attitudes toward the speakers of those languages. And once the very name of a language can be used to invoke prejudice, all kinds of semiotic creativity follows.

Consider Trump's tweet from October 2012: "Why does Barack Obama's ring have an arabic inscription? Who is this guy?" (Trump on Twitter, October 11, 2012). The tweet links to an article from a conspiratorial right-wing website that spuriously claims Obama's ring is inscribed with the Islamic declaration of faith: "There is no god except Allah" (Mikkelson 2014). But Trump's supporters wouldn't even have to click on the link to know what his tweet was driving at. The way Trump concatenates those two sentences ("Why does . . .?" and "Who is . . .?") sets up the Arabic language on its own to cast doubt on Obama's trustworthiness and identity. The very name of the language also furnishes a quick semiotic trigger for alarmist bigotry about Muslims. Trump's supporters will instantly cast their minds to the birther narrative that Obama is actually "foreign" born and to the long-standing conspiratorial rumor that he's a closet Muslim who hoped to bring sharia law to the United States. Scholars and the media have taken to calling this kind of condensed symbolism "dog-whistling"; it refers to using coded terminology that a target audience will understand, in service of racist fear mongering (Haney López 2015). Trump's paranoid demonization of Muslims reached its peak with his efforts to establish a "complete shutdown of Muslims entering the United States," a stance very likely to stoke the energy of terrorist groups that feed off hostility (Hodges 2019: 86, 90).

But in spite of Trump's Islamophobia, Arabic hasn't been his primary linguistic target. A more prominent bugbear for him has been Spanish, which Trump links to the supposed "animals" and "rapists" migrating from Mexico and elsewhere in Latin America. Latinxs make up approximately 10 percent of the national vote, and although most speak English, Spanish is a powerful symbol of identity and an important medium of communication for millions in the US. But Trump refused to campaign in the language, being the only major-party candidate who never translated his website into Spanish or bought ad time on Spanish-language television or radio (Goldmacher 2016). This eloquent silence was politically calculated: while he might lose some Latinx votes, he counted on his anti-Hispanic stance to garner support from voters who align with Trump's claims – which Santa Ana et al. document in their chapter below – that Spanish-speaking immigrants are "flooding in," "taking over," "bringing crime," and somehow polluting the nation while sucking it dry with their reliance on welfare "handouts." Trump seems oblivious to the fact that crime rates among immigrants are lower than among native-born Americans (Ingraham 2018), or that immigrants have been vital to the American economy. How telling that the Trump campaign's momentary dabbling in Spanish consisted of a single, misused word. At the Republican convention in Cleveland, officials handed out signs that read "Hispanics Para Trump," which didn't even translate the word "Hispanics" and used the incorrect Spanish word for "for" (*para* instead of *por*; Goldmacher 2016). They could hardly be bothered to try.

Trump's neglect of Spanish connects to a nationwide conservative "English-only" (sometimes referred to as "Official English") movement. The US doesn't have a legal policy mandating an official national language, so various organizations have pushed for bills or constitutional amendments that would require English to be used at all levels of government, repealing federal mandates for the translation of government documents and voting ballots into other languages (Crawford 2000). Such organizations usually oppose bilingual education, too, and would withhold citizenship from those who don't pass a certain English language standard – an initiative the Trump administration supported in its proposed immigration legislation in May 2019 (Smith 2019).

But the legal details of such efforts sometimes matter less than the affective hostility that these movements concentrate against Spanish as a language and, by extension, its speakers. At the beginning of his presidential campaign, for instance, Trump admonished his adversary Jeb Bush for his outreach to the Latinx community and his use of Spanish, the language of his Mexican-American wife Columba: "This is a country where we speak English, not Spanish" (Berenson 2015). A tweet produced in 2015 made a similar criticism: "Jeb Bush is crazy, who cares that he speaks Mexican, this is America, English!!" (Gass 2015). Notice how in this tweet, Trump directly maps Spanish onto Mexico, as if it belongs in that territory and should stay there – like the people themselves, presumably. In keeping with this simplistic model of what makes an "American" (a model further documented in Alim and Smitherman's chapter), the Trump administration took down the Spanish-language version of the White House website on January 20, 2017. His Hispanic media outreach team has reportedly been inadequately staffed and compromised by abrupt exits (Bonazzo 2018).

Contrary to Trump and the English-only movement, many multilingual nations have managed to hold together successfully. In Singapore, India, Malaysia, South Africa, Aruba, Luxembourg, and many more, large segments of the population are fluent in three or more languages. But it's been a powerful belief among ethnonationalists in Europe and the United States that nations cohere best when they have only one language (Blommaert and Verschueren 1992). And since Trump speaks only English (in spite of having had two wives with different first languages: Czech and Slovenian) and likes to project himself as an ideal, it makes sense that his monoglot limitations furnish the limits of his model of the nation. How ironic that in Trump's America, millions of English-speakers now feel more profoundly cleaved apart from one other than ever.

15.2 Mock Spanish and Covert Racism

Trump occasionally ventures into Spanish, but not through any embrace of bilingualism. Most notoriously, during the final presidential debate with Hillary Clinton in October 2016, he spoke about his plans to expunge "all of the drug lords" from the country with the following (mispronounced) Spanish word: "We have some bad hombres here and we're gonna get 'em out" (Zezima 2016). Linguistic anthropologist Adam Schwartz (2016) immediately analyzed Trump's usage within Jane Hill's (2008) framework of Mock Spanish. According to Hill, Anglo-Americans often use mispronounced or inaccurate versions of Spanish in an effort to be amusing or "cool," but these uses have a hidden meaning. As Schwartz summarizes it, Mock Spanish is "an often unconsciously strategic effort to silently dominate the folks who are imagined to speak that language" (2016). He goes on: "Trump did not say 'bad men.' He said 'bad HOMBRES.' It was HOMBRES that connected the notion of 'immigrant' not simply to 'men' (the literal translation of that word), but to what the Spanish-ness of his choice could index: MEXICAN men as inherently undesirable, 'illegal,' criminal, violent." As Mendoza-Denton notes in her chapter in this section, Trump's use of Mock Spanish says volumes about his wish to exude (White) American domination, a stance not lost on Latin American strongmen themselves.

Indeed, Trump has repeatedly dipped into select Spanish words or phrases, using them in supposedly jocular ways that in fact have negative connotations. In a speech in Miami in 1999, for instance, Trump said of Fidel Castro: "If I could meet Castro right now, I'd have personally two words for him: 'Adiós, amigo!'" (Trump n.d.). Such "tough talk" in Spanish is nearly identical to the Mock Spanish Hill analyzes from the *Terminator 2: Judgment Day* film, where Arnold Schwarzenegger and others use the phrase "Hasta la vista, baby" to adopt a menacing persona. Such "pejoration" of Spanish words and phrases, to use Hill's word, is one tip-off that Trump is asserting symbolic dominance, rather than engaging in appreciative borrowing or bona fide code switching. Another tip-off is his casual errors. Trump has repeatedly used the word "loco" (crazy), for instance, to denigrate Democrats, the Fed, and the media. (After calling the media "loco" while answering questions on the White House lawn he quipped "I used that word because of the fact that we made a deal with Mexico," as if somehow that made his use of Spanish relevant [Smith 2018].) Using *loco* correctly would require gender and number agreement with preceding nouns: Democrats (*los Demócratas*) would be *locos*, the media (*las redes medias*) would be *locas*, and so forth. Yet every time Trump uses the term, he ends it with the masculine affix, *–o*. After Hurricane Maria devastated Puerto Rico in 2017, an overtly hostile Trump used a deliberately showy mispronunciation of the country's name that sounded something like "pwehto hikow" (On Demand News 2017). Like many of Trump's parodic performances (see Goldstein et al., this volume), this performance seemed at least in part a dig at PC attitudes; he was pretending, in derisive fashion, to pronounce the place name correctly, as if to mock those who care enough to try. More to the point, Trump repeatedly links Spanish to people and conditions he considers undesirable, while his errors reflect a further disregard for – and sometimes deliberate mockery of – the language and, by extension, its speakers.

Trump gets away with this because, as Hill notes, such mock mimicry often passes unnoticed by the broader population. When Anglo-Americans hear Mock Spanish, many simply take it at face value, thinking it funny or cool and nothing more. Others may have a feeling there's something off, but have difficulty putting their finger on what or why. For this reason, Mock Spanish constitutes a form of covert racism that can be hard to throw into relief except with the most egregious juxtapositions. As Hill (2008: 45) notes, "One cannot say, 'I'm not racist, but adios, sucker!'"

15.3   Word Choice and Dehumanization

If some racist language in the Trump era is stealthy, much is overt. Such unguarded verbal practice resonates with Trump's anti-PC stance (see Introduction, this volume). After all, many Trump supporters have reported their resentment of liberal pressure to uplift – or at the very least refrain from denigrating – historically marginalized groups. With the backing of his base, Trump feels emboldened to describe certain non-White social groups as if they are less than human. Mexicans are "rapists" (who, in Trump's vicious imagination, should be shot in the legs or set upon by alligators if they try to cross the border [Shear and Davis 2019]); Muslims are "terrorists" (Boum, below); African immigrants come from "shitholes" (Williams, below). Rumors have swirled that Trump was caught on tape using the n-word during the filming of his pre-presidential reality show, *The Apprentice* (Hutzler 2019). And a short, official article on the WhiteHouse.gov website refers to members of the gang MS-13 as "animals" no fewer than ten times (Trump 2018). While there's no doubt the gang's violence has been heinous, this verbal effort to dehumanize them is so pedantic it would be comical if the implications weren't so serious.

Trump and supporters have also developed a stock vocabulary of dehumanizing terms to discuss migration. The following June 2019 headline from the conspiratorial website Infowars.com uses several: "Hundreds of illegals from Ebola-ridden Congo dumped in Texas, 350 more on the way ... Major threat ignored by mainstream media" (McBreen 2019). Undocumented immigrants are "illegals." They are "dumped" like trash, not dropped off. The central

African nation of Congo is "Ebola-ridden," as if crawling with pestilence – perhaps all 350 of those dropped off are infected? (Far more likely, from a medical and epidemiological standpoint, is that none are.) Meanwhile, the "mainstream media" is in denial of this supposed "threat" to public safety. But Trump's public has learned to adopt his language. Trump's countless references to Latinx migrants as "invaders" has caught on, as seen in November 2019 when a White Milwaukee man allegedly threw battery acid on a Peruvian immigrant walking from his car into a Mexican restaurant, yelling: "Why did you come here and invade my country?" (Moreno 2019). While the suspect is apparently a veteran suffering from PTSD, he, like many Americans in distress, appears to have channeled his malaise into a hostile idiom provided by the president.

Trump and supporters seem to have historical amnesia as to when we have encountered such dehumanizing language before. The Nazis of the Third Reich fomented genocidal impulses by erasing the humanity of Jews and other groups, talking about them as polluted sub-humans. The Hutu political elite in Rwanda in 1994 successfully encouraged mass slaughter of Tutsis with a state campaign that used radio channels to enjoin people to "exterminate the cockroaches" (Ndahiro 2019). Dehumanizing language is also used by right-wing populists across Europe today. Alarmingly, we know from history that it can be a slippery slope from endorsing dehumanizing language to endorsing outright violence. Some linguistic anthropologists have recently amplified their activist efforts to draw attention to the link between language and social justice (Avineri et al. 2019). Jonathan Rosa (2019), for instance, has been among linguistic anthropologists supporting the "Drop the I-Word Campaign," which raises awareness about the stigmatizing political word "illegal" in discussions of (im)migration. What may also be needed is sustained public consciousness-raising about what anthropologists, historians, psychologists, and language theorists alike have noted: As irritating as the PC movement may be to Trump's supporters, cruel word choice can cost lives.

15.4   A Strongman and His Others, and International Responses

The chapters in this section examine Trump's verbal stances toward some of the social groups and polities he frames as "other." There's the "other" within the US, implicated in some of Trump's offhand remarks and carefully teased out in Alim and Smitherman's analysis. Trump uses a common rhetorical strategy, they argue, to draw attention to the supposedly "exceptional" English of one individual of color, in so doing racializing an entire group and setting up an implicit White supremacist model of citizenship and belonging within the United States. Then there's Trump's xenophobia, in which he portrays "others" outside the nation – be they Latinx peoples, or "radical Islamic terrorists" – as if they are vermin trying to infiltrate American borders to sponge resources and take American lives. Trump achieves this portrait through a series of interlocked metaphors that portray the US as a fortress in peril (Santa Ana et al., this section), while his narrative stances conflate supposed infiltrators from the South with so-called terrorists from the Middle East, refusing any diplomatic engagement with or curiosity about Middle Eastern societies (Boum, this section). In referring to migrants from African nations, Trump uses the language of stigma and pollution ("shithole"; see Williams, this section). Meanwhile, his priorities emerge in his language: he prefers people to come from supposedly clean, White-dominant areas of the world (Scandinavia!); he's willing to overlook Islamic identification if the people he knows from a given nation (e.g. Saudi Arabia) are both rich and his personal "friends"; and he favors nationalist leaders who exude tough masculinity like himself (see Mendoza-Denton, this section).

In these chapters, we also locate some of the voices striving to check, neutralize, and respond to Trump's bigotry and tough talk. How Trump's aggressive ethnonationalism lands depends on the audience; that is, it depends on any given country's experience with colonialism and whiteness, and their own historical anxieties about leadership and status. We can infer from Alim and Smitherman's Obama-era interviews with Americans on the linguistic margins that Trump's compliment to a Latinx border agent ("He speaks perfect English!") will likely have been read by its targets as the backhanded remark that it is. We see in Williams' analysis that Trump's language of pollution is profoundly offensive in Southern Africa in part because it is so redolent of the dehumanizing language of apartheid. Williams demonstrates how Southern Africans have responded to Trump through parody, or by adopting a dignified register that claims the high ground while projecting pollution back onto Trump. In the Middle East, Boum shows us, Trump's parsing of the region according to how he can monetize it has led to both cynicism and anxiety. Mendoza-Denton demon-strates how recently-elected Mexican President Andrés Manuel López Obrador tries to deflect Trump's put-downs by tracking an ideal of Mexican rural masculinity, striving to revalorize indigeneity and the com-mon man. By contrast, Brazil's hard-right Bolsonaro seems to have gotten a hit of inspiration as he inhales the vapors from Trump's ethnonationalism. Aligning himself neatly with Trump, Bolsonaro has adopted similar verbal ways of enacting strongman masculinity while targeting vulnerable groups – in his case minorities, women, and LGBTQ+ individuals. This broad inter-national perspective shows us Trump's style is far from unique, and as troubling as it has been to many, it seems to have kindled the fire under other global autocrats.

References

Avineri, Netta, Laura R. Graham, Eric J. Johnson, Robin Conley Riner, and Jonathan Rosa, eds. 2019. *Language and Social Justice in Practice*. Routledge.

Berenson, Tessa. 2015. "Republican Candidates Spar over Spanish on the Campaign Trail." *Time*, September 17, 2015. https://bit.ly/2Y4Bfq2.

Blommaert, Jan, and Jef Verschueren. 1992 "The Role of Language in European Nationalist Ideologies." *Pragmatics* 2, no. 3: 355–75.

Bonazzo, John. 2018. "Trump's Abysmal Hispanic Media Outreach Gets Worse after Top Officials Exit." *Observer*, August 9, 2018. https://bit.ly/33EvikS.

Crawford, James. 2000. *At War with Diversity: US Language Policy in an Age of Anxiety*. Multilingual Matters.

Gass, Nick. 2015. "Trump Goes on Late-Night Twitter Tirade against Megyn Kelly, Jeb Bush." *Politico*, August 25, 2015. https://politi.co/2DBMtZO.

Goldmacher, Shane. 2016. "Trump's English-Only Campaign." *Politico*, September 23, 2016. https://politi.co/35ReTej.

Graham, David A., Adrienne Green, Cullen Murphy, and Parker Richards. 2019. "An Oral History of Trump's Bigotry." *The Atlantic*, June 2019. https://bit.ly /2LflWWu.

Haney López, Ian. 2015 *Dog Whistle Politics: How Coded Racial Appeals Have Reinvented Racism and Wrecked the Middle Class*. Oxford University Press.

Hill, Jane H. 2008. *The Everyday Language of White Racism*. Wiley-Blackwell.

Hodges, Adam. 2019. *When Words Trump Politics: Resisting a Hostile Regime of Language*. Stanford University Press.

Hutzler, Alexandra. 2019. "Donald Trump Used N-Word on 'Apprentice' Set." *Newsweek*, June 25, 2019. https://bit.ly/2P6oBCM.

Ingraham, Christopher. 2018. "Two Charts Demolish the Notion that Immigrants Here Illegally Commit More Crime." *The Washington Post*, June 19, 2018. https://wapo .st/2Y77UeG.

Lopez, German. 2019. "Donald Trump's Long History of Racism, from the 1970s to 2019." *Vox*, July 15, 2019. https://bit.ly/2r2Rt72.

McBreen, Kelen. 2019. "Hundreds of Illegals from Ebola-Ridden Congo Dumped in Texas, 350 More on the Way." *Infowars.com*, June 8, 2019. https://bit.ly /37ZldT8.

Mikkelson, David. 2014. "Barack Obama's Wedding Ring Bears an Arabic Inscription Reading, 'There Is No God but Allah'?" *Snopes*, July 18, 2014. www.snopes.com /fact-check/lord-of-the-ring/.

Moreno, Ivan. 2019. "Family Says Suspect in Acid Attack is Veteran, Suffered PTSD." *AP*, November 4, 2019. https://apnews.com/436fd919ad1e4d0e9d4f221a53d1f12e

Ndahiro, Kennedy. 2019. "In Rwanda, We Know All About Dehumanizing Language." *The Atlantic*, April 13, 2019. https://bit.ly/2rKSmRw.

On Demand News. 2017. "Trump Toys with Puerto Rico Pronunciation." *On Demand News* video, October 6, 2017. twww.youtube.com/watch?v=tM-2xNMQszw.

Rosa, Jonathan. 2019. "Contesting Representations of Migrant 'Illegality' Through the Drop the I-Word Campaign: Rethinking Language Change and Social Change." In *Language and Social Justice in Practice*, edited by Netta Avineri, Laura R. Graham, Eric J. Johnson, Robin Conley Riner, and Jonathan Rosa, pp. 35–43. Routledge.

Schwartz, Adam. 2016. "Trump Relies on Mock Spanish to Talk about Immigration."
    Latin Rebels, October 20, 2016. https://bit.ly/2n4l2Dp.
Shear, Michael D., and Julie Hirschfeld Davis. 2019. "Shoot Migrants' Legs, Build
    Alligator Moat: Behind Trump's Ideas for Border." *The New York Times*,
    October 1, 2019. https://nyti.ms/34508U0.
Smith, David. 2018. "Trump Leaves Rose Garden Listeners Punch-Drunk ... Even
    without Alcohol." *The Guardian*, October 1, 2018. https://bit.ly/2YdkRnm.
    2019. "Trump's 'Merit-Based' Immigration Plan Declared 'Dead on Arrival' by
    Opponents." *The Guardian*, May 16, 2019. https://bit.ly/2Y7B6lW.
Trump, Donald. n.d. "Speech: Donald Trump at the Cuban-American National Foundation –
    Miami, FL – November 15, 1999 (Transcript)." *Factba.se*, n.d. https://bit.ly/2OFUxyZ.
    2018. "What You Need to Know about the Violent Animals of MS-13." *WhiteHouse.
    gov*, May 21, 2018. https://bit.ly/2L9owNp.
Trump, Donald (@realDonaldTrump). 2012. "Why Does Barack Obama's Ring Have
    an Arabic Inscription? http://bit.ly/VMN6Vn Who Is This Guy?" Twitter,
    October 11, 2012. https://bit.ly/35VRxV5.
Waldman, Paul. 2019. "Where Trump's Racist Rants Come From." *The Washington
    Post*, July 30, 2019. https://wapo.st/33W7SYh.
Zezima, Katie. 2016. "Trump on Immigration: There Are 'Bad Hombres' in The United
    States." *The Washington Post*, October 19, 2016. https://wapo.st/2DwGu8u.

16   "Perfect English" and White Supremacy

H. Samy Alim and Geneva Smitherman

In August of 2018, President Trump honored the men and women of US Immigration and Customs Enforcement (ICE) and Customs and Border Protection (CBP) at a White House event called, "Salute to the Heroes" (White House 2018). By late summer of 2018, Donald Trump had not only run an entire presidential campaign with anti-immigrant and anti-Latinx sentiment at its core – referring to Mexican immigrants as "criminals" and "rapists," repeatedly referencing international gang MS-13 to engage in racist fear mongering, and claiming that he would "build a wall" on the US–Mexico border and that "Mexico would pay for it!" (Phillips 2017). He was also working overtime to try to avert what many saw as an inevitable "Blue Wave," whereby Democrats would regain dozens of seats in the House. This was the immediate political context of the "Salute the Heroes" event at the White House.

In a key moment during the event, Trump began telling the story of Latinx Border Patrol agent Adrian Anzaldua, who was being honored for his role in the arrest of two US citizens who were transporting seventy-eight immigrants across the US–Mexico border in April. Dramatically, the immigrants were found locked in the hold of a refrigerated truck in Laredo, Texas, and were all in good health (Dunlap 2018). In what seemed like a spontaneous moment, Trump interrupted his own narration and called Anzaldua up to the podium (Remezcla Estaff 2018; video excerpt starts at the beginning).[1]

TRUMP: The Border Patrol agent who caught the accused and likely really saved many lives, he's here with us. And Adrian – where's Adrian? ((*scanning the audience*)) Adrian's here with us.
AUDIENCE: ((*applause*))
TRUMP: Thank you, Adrian. Great job. Thank you. It's a lot of lives! That's great. Adrian, come here, I wanna ask you a question. So, how did you – come here, come here. You're not nervous, right?
AUDIENCE: ((*laughter and applause*)) ((*camera scans to show Anzaldua making his way to the podium*))

TRUMP: He speaks perfect English. Come here. I wanna ask you about that.
Seventy-eight lives. You saved seventy-eight people. So, how did you feel
that there were people in that trailer? There's a lot of trailers around.
Please. ((*gesturing for Anzaldua to take microphone*))

Anzaldua, clearly surprised by the president's request, recounted the incident, using specific terminology and a style that many in the US would identify
as common to law enforcement officials. After his successful narration, he was
praised and thanked repeatedly by the president: "Fantastic. ((*applause*)) What
a good job he did! What a good job. Now you know tomorrow he's going to be –
he's liked that so much, he didn't know he was gonna do it. ((*smiling at the
audience*)) Tomorrow he will be announcing that he's running for office.
((*audience laughter and cheers*)) Good job! Seventy-eight people saved.
Thank you very much, Adrian." The president then grabbed the podium with
both arms and shifted quickly from a jocular key to a much more serious one:
"Last month under Operation Eagle Shield, right here in the DC area, ICE
officers arrested a hundred and thirty-two illegal aliens, including criminal
aliens charged or convicted of rape, battery, and strangulation. Among those
arrested was a high-ranking MS-13 gang member . . ." (The video clip ends
here, with the entire exchange lasting just under three minutes.)

In the remainder of the chapter, we will show how the above episode is
emblematic of a process we have termed *raciolinguistic exceptionalism*
(defined in the following section). We show how this specific incident highlights the White supremacist, colonial relations through which ideologies of
language and race are formed, embedded, and maintained. Trump's all too
smooth pivot from "complimenting" Anzaldua's "perfect English" to his
repeated xenophobic racializations of Mexicans as criminals, animals, and
monsters functions as a rhetorical strategy to exceptionalize one individual
while racializing and demonizing an entire group. As other chapters in this
volume show, this form of exceptionalism is not the only form of linguistic
racism and discrimination engaged in by Trump – from his repeated mocking of
Indian Prime Minister Narendra Modi's accent in English and his use of "Mock
Asian" to represent Chinese and Japanese businessmen to his reported disgust
with former Attorney General Jeff Sessions' "southern accent" from Alabama
(Benin 2018), his repeated, exaggerated use of "Mock Spanish" phonology
when pronouncing "Puerto Rico" (The Guardian 2017), and his horrid "imitation" of a disabled journalist (Huffington Post 2017; see also Goldstein et al.
this volume), which even some Republicans found reprehensible. While most
progressives readily identify these linguistic performances as racist and discriminatory, in the case of raciolinguistic exceptionalism, it is a bipartisan
process that sometimes easily flies under the radar because the connections
that it relies upon are somewhat more tacit and implicit, at least to hegemonic

228 H. Samy Alim and Geneva Smitherman

White speakers, who constantly have to be reminded not to infantilize People of Color for speaking "such good English."

16.1 Raciolinguistic Exceptionalism

In the following, we show how President Trump's "compliment" – "He speaks perfect English" – functions as a form of raciolinguistic exceptionalism, whereby exceptionalism occurs through White racist evaluations of, and ideologies about, both language and race. In our previous collaboration, *Articulate While Black: Barack Obama, Language, and Race in the US* (2012), we analyzed how then-President Obama was often on the receiving end of such left-handed compliments ("I love Barack Obama. He's soooo articulate!"). In this current case, we examine how President Trump himself participates in these very same forms of raciolinguistic exceptionalism and what that means for Latinx and other groups in the US.

Leading social theorist Imani Perry (2011: 130–31) argues that "racial exceptionalism is the practice of creating meaning out of the existence of people of color who don't fit our stereotypic or racial-narrative-based conceptions." A person of color is placed into a "state of exception," she argues, only when the "normal" state of their group "is assumed deficient." Drawing upon the work of A. Leon Higginbotham, Perry argues that exceptionalizing discourses – intentionally or not, and intuitively or not – accept "the precept of inferiority" as normative. According to Perry, the creation of exceptional states through everyday practices reifies racist interpretive frames. These practices shape how we evaluate inequality and legitimate "the practice of inequality toward those who are not in the exceptionalized group" (ibid.: 131).

While exceptionalizing discourses often escape the attention of members of the hegemonic group in question, those on the social margins often understand the underlying ideological meanings and associations embedded in such "compliments." This is why, in response to President Trump's exceptionalizing comments about Adrian Anzaldua, attorney and *CNN* writer Raul A. Reyes (2018) began his scathing column with these words: "Mr. President, brown people speak English." This simple claim highlights President Trump's assumptions about the relationships between language, race, and nation. Upon addressing a "brown" person (Anzaldua is readily identifiable by his name and brown skin as non-White), Trump assumes both that most Latinxs in the US do not speak English (or if they do, they don't speak it correctly and fluently) and that they are perceived as "foreign" and placed "outside of America."

As White race theorist Tim Wise has written, this is not what most Americans think of as your standard racism, the kind that has plagued the history of this country since its inception. Using the term "enlightened exceptionalism," Wise describes a "form of racism that allows for and even celebrates the achievements of individual persons of color, but only because those individuals generally are seen as different from a less appealing, even pathological black or brown rule." To Wise, Perry, and others, the fact that it is only People of Color who are called upon to "transcend" their race not only proves that America is far from being post-racial, but it also "confirms the salience of race and the machinations of white hegemony" (Wise 2009: 8–11). As an illustrative, theoretical exercise, imagine Trump making the same comment to a White American border patrol agent.

Our discussion of raciolinguistic exceptionalism builds upon this previous work, as well as the language-ideological literature in linguistic anthropology (Schieffelin et al. 1998), particularly Paul Kroskrity's (2011) outlining of linguistic racisms, and the growing area of raciolinguistics (Alim et al. 2016, Rosa 2019). Kroskrity (2020) targets "racist and racializing acts and/or projects that use linguistic resources as a means of discrimination and subordination" in order to "analytically disclose and explicate both overt and covert forms of linguistic racism." In considering racializing "compliments," these processes take on different valences across differently racialized groups because they are shaped within varying sociohistorical and sociopolitical processes of domination, such as settler colonialism, enslavement, and global, racial capitalist exploitation. For example, when Reyes (2016) writes about the racializing "compliment" – "You speak English so well" – directed at Asian Americans, it is both similar to and distinct from the way "You speak good English" is used to target particular Latinx populations (Urciuoli 1996) or the way "You speak so well" (Clemetson 2007) is directed at African Americans.

Numerous studies of language and race by linguistic anthropologists have shown how ideas about People of Color and their speech serve to reinforce racist narratives about Asianness, Blackness, Indigeneity, Latinidad, etc. (Alim et al. 2020). In our earlier work on then-President Barack Obama, we not only described how former US President Barack Obama talked, but also how he was heard by various segments of the American public (Alim and Smitherman 2012). Building upon Alim's (2005) previous research – "Hearing What's Not Said and Missing What Is" – we recognized that White beliefs about Black people and their language depended largely upon Whites' hearing Black speech through the ideological lens of linguistic supremacy, which served to uphold White supremacist logics of both language and race. In this case, White teachers were not only missing various complex aspects of Black linguistic production and variation, but they were also hearing "errors" where there were none, even going so far as to invent syntactic structures not found in any variety of English ("we ain't not," for example). As Flores and Rosa (2015: 151) concluded about this particular example:

This example demonstrates the powerful ways that raciolinguistic ideologies of the white listening subject can stigmatize language use regardless of one's empirical linguistic practices. Thus, even when Standard English learners use forms that seem to correspond to Standard English, they can still be construed as using nonstandard forms from the perspectives of the white listening subject.

As we argued, "More than any other cultural symbol, Barack Obama's multifaceted language use ... served to simultaneously 'Whiten,' 'Blacken,' 'Americanize,' and 'Christianize' [and 'Masculinize'] Barack in the eyes and ears of both Black and White Americans" (Alim and Smitherman 2012: 23). Critically, in presenting a metalinguistic analysis of Barack Obama's language – that is, we talked about the talk about the way Barack Obama talks – we also explored how White racial and linguistic hegemony shaped how his speech was heard and interpreted through ideological processes. These are the same ideological processes – what Flores and Rosa (2015) have termed raciolinguistic ideologies – at work in President Trump's description of Anzaldua's speech, the same processes that underlie narratives and practices of raciolinguistic exceptionalism.

16.2   Raciolinguistic Exceptionalism, Whiteness, and Coloniality

In our previous work (Alim and Smitherman 2012), we not only considered the cultural meanings of "articulate" in relation to Black folks, but we also complicated the conversation by considering phrases like "articulate" and "good English" in relation to other racial and ethnic groups in the US. As we show below, the results demonstrated multiple problematic links between "articulateness" and "whiteness" and "articulateness" and "intelligence" across groups, and showed how language is often loaded with issues of race, class, citizenship, and other forms of social differentiation. Beyond Trump's comments about Anzaldua's "perfect English," we show below how these comments are productively interpreted as parts of larger socio- and raciolinguistic processes impacting Latinxs and other groups in the US.

In terms of reading the social meanings of "articulate" for Latinx, Middle Eastern, Asian, and other Americans, we posed this question in our survey of Americans of the Obama generation (mostly eighteen- to twenty-four-year-olds, with some in their early thirties; see Chapters 1 and 2 of *Articulate While Black*): "If someone referred to you as 'articulate,' how would you feel? Explain your answer." They also submitted information about their age, race, ethnicity, gender, and biographical background. These respondents expressed what we called a "split-view" that depended on their linguistic background as much as, if not more than, their race. In many cases, respondents did not view being complimented as "articulate" as problematic if they were speaking English, but they became more critical when discussing the language of immigrants, their family members, or those with "accents." Because of these Americans' location on the linguistic margins – either they or their parents learned English as a second language – some felt a distinct sense of pride to be referred to as "articulate" since it meant that they had been perceived as mastering English. At the same time, however, these Americans were also able to point out the challenges of belonging to communities where "accents" from languages other than English are linguistically marginalized. These speakers also point out why claims that leftists can't even accept President Trump's compliment to a Person of Color (as heard in conservative outlets) are woefully simplistic readings of language as social action.

In this first example, from a self-identified "biracial (Hispanic and white)" respondent, we see how the "split-view" of those between linguistic worlds gives practices of raciolinguistic exceptionalism meaning. She does not see "articulate" as problematic in English, for example, but makes some complex connections in relation to "color" when speaking of Spanish:

I speak the English that my parents do, so I've never faced the additional challenges of feeling like the only "articulate" person in, for example, an immigrant family that doesn't speak English or a family without parents who are lawyers ... Also, I identify as biracial (Hispanic and white) so I've never felt the need to speak the same way as people who look like me. Interestingly, I have felt pressure to speak Spanish because I ended up with the darkest skin of any of my siblings. I have not felt a similar pressure to speak a certain type of English ...

For this respondent, the link between language and "race" is not as salient as the link between language and "color." She does not experience pressure to speak a particular variety of English, but because of her "darker" skin she has felt social pressure to speak Spanish, as if a higher melanin count leads to a higher degree of Spanish fluency. This respondent's description is similar to existing ideologies of language and race/color expressed by some within Spanish-speaking, Latinx communities, those that assume that darker-skinned Latinxs *should* or *must* speak Spanish while giving lighter-skinned Latinxs a "pass."

This next example comes from someone who describes herself as "Filipino by culture (little blood) and Lebanese by blood (no culture)," but as having been raised "in a predominantly Mexican community" in Texas. She begins, "If someone described me as 'articulate,' I would feel like I had received a great compliment ... I believe that the term articulate can apply across languages and the situations they are used in to mean a clear presentation of complex ideas. Therefore, I view articulate as a compliment." And then, in what she describes as "a complete side-note," she provides further information about her mother's language:

I called my mother at her work today. As she works in an office and several people could have potentially answered the phone, I was not sure if it was her who picked up. To be quite honest, when I heard the woman's voice on the other end of the phone, my immediate thought was, *Nope, that's not mom*. I asked to speak to Soraya, and she said, "Hi!" I said, "Mom! I didn't recognize you . . ." Her response? "I know. Different when I talk right, huh?" . . . I had never considered my mother's way of speaking as "not right." Granted, she has a Filipino accent (so I've been told), but her own assertion that her way of speaking is wrong made me realize even more how powerful language really is.

These next two examples provide heavy insights into the complex nature of raciolinguistic exceptionalism. They also help to show that the underlying cause of Black suspicion and offense when it comes to "articulate" is due to broader, ongoing social processes that relate as much to the deprecation of "Blackness" as they do to linguistic marginalization writ large. The following observation comes from someone who self-identifies as "½ Korean, ½ mixed white" and is an exemplary case of the "split-view." Due to her position on the racial and linguistic margins, she claims that she is not "articulate" and often feels like "she can't gather her thoughts to be expressed in an articulate manner." So, her first response to being referred to as articulate "would be surprise, but also pleased that I'd come across that way." She later complicates her own view by providing an Asian American vantage point to the discussion: "I think, though, that the word contains a bit of surprise in it, as if one is exceeding expectations . . . if someone told me I was 'articulate' after asking where I was from, or if I spoke English, or anything else pointing to my race/ethnicity, then I'd be annoyed." She then explains why this might be particularly frustrating for Asian Americans, who often have to battle the "forever foreigner" stereotype.

Asian-American speech doesn't get stereotyped as inarticulate like black and Latino speech does, but it does sometimes get stereotyped as accented. Maybe the person was trying to give me a compliment, but Asian immigration to the US is not new, the US as a multiracial society is not new, and multiracial people aren't new. I would feel Othered and out of place, even though this is my place.

The various stereotypes that circulate in the US about Asian Americans are discussed at length by Reyes (2007). Drawing on the classic work of Edward Said, Reyes explains that the "forever foreigner" stereotype "draws on discourses of Orientalism, ideologies which shape the image of Asian and Middle Eastern peoples as Other and thus unassimilable due to innate East–West differences that cannot be resolved" (ibid.: 7–8).

The final response in this section is worth quoting in full as it reveals further complexity, and the often-unacknowledged emotional pain of growing up on the linguistic margins of America. This respondent is an indigenous speaker of Hawai'i Creole English, a stigmatized variety of American English:

Answering this question is difficult. I spent the majority of my childhood trying to prove my intelligence. Growing up in an alternative school was difficult. I didn't learn to read or write in English until the 6th grade and even though I was different from my classmates in that most of the community didn't expect us to succeed in a mainstream school I knew from a young age that I had the work ethic and even more important the support to be successful outside of our community. At the same time I struggled with . . . being judged for speaking primarily Pidgin. We were taught that Pidgin would prevent us from being successful, and prevent people from respecting us. So those of us who could, or cared enough, tried to force our tongues to fit into a western system that would only patronize us for our efforts. Because of this, a part of me, the part that so wanted to be successful as a child would feel honored almost at the thought of someone calling me articulate. But the version of me that has learned about the motivations for consolidating communities into a singular language variety makes me feel offended to be placed under that hammer. I know that code switching is a sign of intelligence, even if it's not recognized as one. I know that I have the ability, because of my background, to effectively communicate with people from a broad range of backgrounds in a way that is meaningful to them. I would call this skill articulate if it weren't already tainted with expectations of covering up any language variety that doesn't agree with what some people call 'Educated English.' So for now, I can do without such compliments – I don't need them.

While speaking from a particular vantage point of the linguistically colonized in Hawai'i, this young woman expresses several shared sentiments of those on the linguistic margins in the US. First, we see that Americans on the linguistic margins – whether they speak Arabic, Black Language, Span(gl)ish, Tagalog, or Hawai'i Creole English – learn the dominant ideology that links "articulateness" with "good/perfect English," with "intelligence" and with "whiteness." Second, rather than continue to feel shame, she expresses an alternative ideology that privileges the skills of bilingual and multilingual speakers' abilities to switch in and out of multiple languages. Lastly, she frames "articulate" as a political term. Far from neutral, it is loaded with a cultural-linguistic hegemony that imposes itself upon people and then praises them for "covering up" their own language.

16.3   Conclusion: Anzaldua, Language, and Race at the Border

All of these speakers, when taken together, highlight the associations between race, color, citizenship, coloniality, and language that underlie the seemingly innocent and jocular comments by Trump. Alice Ashton Filmer's "Bilingual Belonging and the Whiteness of (Standard) English(es)" (2007) described these raciolinguistic associations as forming what she referred to as *acoustic identity*. Looking across racial and ethnic groups and across various national contexts, she concluded by noting that:

In every case, the speaker's acoustic identity and sense of bilingual belonging are negotiated and defined within a complex set of historical/sociopolitical/cultural relations and expectations that ultimately conflate the use of (Standard) English(es) with Whiteness and Western imperialism. In light of this evidence, to insist that Standard

Englishes are neutral forms of communication capable of unifying multiracial/ethnic/ cultural societies is to fail to recognize these prevalent, and generally unconscious assumptions and expectations. This brand of linguistic ethnocentrism – a major legacy of Euro-American colonialism – is unethical and must be challenged on the grounds of human and civil rights. (ibid.: 761–62)

In speaking of the major legacy of Euro-American colonialism, it is certainly not lost on us that Adrian Anzaldua shares the same last name as Chicana Feminist theorist Gloria Anzaldúa, who wrote much about questions of language and identity in the borderlands (1987), and who grew up along the Mexico–Texas border, where Adrian Anzaldua serves as a border patrol agent. President Trump's comments constitute a particularly insidious form of what Gloria Anzaldúa described as "linguistic terrorism," the reproduction of White settler colonial violence and colonial relations in and through struggles of language.

Anzaldúa's ideas are particularly relevant to our discussion of raciolinguistic exceptionalism, because these ideas about race, language, citizenship, nation, etc., always index the colonial relations that produce them. In the particular case of President Trump referring to Adrian Anzaldua's speech as "perfect English," we see multiple dimensions of this historical relationship playing out in the short segment that introduced this chapter. Before he started speaking, Anzaldua was already *heard* as linguistically deficient (incapable of speaking English); he was then later praised for his English-speaking ability through raciolinguistic exceptionalism that separated him from the supposedly unwashed, Spanish-speaking Latinx masses ("He speaks perfect English"). Even beyond that, he was infantilized by the president in the same way a teacher might do to a grammar school student after a public speech ("What a good job he did! What a good job. Now you know tomorrow he's going to be . . . he didn't know he was gonna do it. ((*smiling at the audience*)) Tomorrow he will be announcing that he's running for office").

While all of this is troubling, the President's verbal comments were perhaps most deeply unnerving because of the optics at play. Politically, President Trump has been squarely anti-Mexican and anti-immigrant, governing by a clear White supremacist or White nationalist imperative. To many, Adrian Anzaldua, intentionally or not, became the brown face of President Trump's particular brand of "Border Wall" White supremacy, to be used by the President as a shield against accusations of racism and thus allowing him to keep the terms of the debate focused on "legal," not "racial," concerns (e.g. "We are a nation of laws," etc.).

But perhaps the most troubling aspect of this incident of raciolinguistic exceptionalism is how Trump pivots from praise of Anzaldua's language to continue his fear mongering racialization of Mexican immigrants as monsters. Recall that Trump frequently refers to Mexican immigrants as "criminals," "rapists," and "animals." Recall that just seconds after praising Anzaldua, the

President went on to warn Americans that: "Last month under Operation Eagle Shield, right here in the DC area, ICE officers arrested a hundred and thirty-two illegal aliens, including criminal aliens charged or convicted of rape, battery, and strangulation. Among those arrested was a high-ranking MS-13 gang member . . ." (Remezcla Estaff 2018).

Trump's comments on Anzaldua's "perfect English" not only exceptionalize Anzaldua at the expense of Latinxs in the US, whom Trump views as non-English speaking, but the process of racioinguistic exceptionalism at play in this incident positions Latinxs as not having a claim to citizenship and Americanness without use of the English language (and in a manner deemed "perfect," ironically by even those Whites whose language is at best marginally "standard"). In other words, Trump draws a *raciolinguistic* border wall around Adrian Anzaldua, separating him from other less-fluent Latinxs, while using Anzaldua's brownness to help him build a *physical* border wall, excluding "brown" Latinx immigrants from Trump's "white country" across the border. This incident of raciolinguistic exceptionalism throws into stark relief the colonial relations that undergird ideologies of language and race and demonstrates how a so-called simple compliment can be imbricated with questions of citizenship and belonging that ultimately serve to reproduce exclusionary White supremacist notions of Latinx undesirability.

Note

1. Since this transcription is of a monologue, we do not use the detailed style of transcription used for conversations found in other chapters.

References

Alim, H. Samy. 2005. "Hearing What's Not Said and Missing What Is: Black Language in White Public Space." In *Intercultural Discourse and Communication: The Essential Readings*, edited by Scott F. Kiesling and Christina Bratt Paulston, pp. 180–97.Blackwell Publishing.

Alim, H. Samy, A. Reyes, and P. Kroskrity, eds. 2020. *The Oxford Handbook on Language and Race*. Oxford University Press.

Alim, H. Samy, John R. Rickford, and Arnetha F. Ball, eds. 2016. *Raciolinguistics: How Language Shapes Our Ideas about Race*. Oxford University Press.

Alim, H. Samy. and Geneva Smitherman. 2012. *Articulate While Black: Barack Obama, Language, and Race in the US*. Oxford University Press.

Anzaldúa, Gloria. 1987. *Borderlands/La Frontera: The New Mestiza*. Aunt Lute Books.

Benin, Steve. 2018. "There's Something about Trump and Accents He Considers Unfamiliar." *MSNBC*, September 4, 2018. https://on.msnbc.com/2qYACSj.

Clemetson, Lynette. 2007. "The Racial Politics of Speaking Well." *The New York Times*, February 4, 2007. https://nyti.ms/2Pjm2Mb.

Dunlap, Keith. 2018. "Border Patrol Finds Seventy-Eight Illegal Immigrants in Refrigerated Trailer on I-35." *KSAT-TV* article, August 11, 2018. https://bit.ly/2nclJu8.

Filmer, Alice Ashton. 2007. "Bilingual Belonging and the Whiteness of (Standard) English(es)." *Qualitative Inquiry* 13, no. 6: 747–65.

Flores, Nelson, and Jonathan Rosa. 2015. "Undoing Appropriateness: Raciolinguistic Ideologies and Language Diversity in Education." *Harvard Educational Review* 85, no. 2: 149–71.

The Guardian. 2017. "Trump Attempts to Use Spanish Accent to Pronounce Puerto Rico – Video." October 6, 2017. https://bit.ly/2rGnj9y.

Huffington Post. 2017. "Donald Trump Mocks Disabled Reporter." October 24, 2017. https://bit.ly/2OgKUFl.

Kroskrity, Paul V. 2011. "Facing the Rhetoric of Language Endangerment: Voicing the Consequences of Linguistic Racism." *Journal of Linguistic Anthropology* 21, no. 2: 179–92.

    2020. "Theorizing Linguistic Racisms from a Language Ideological Perspective." In *Oxford Handbook on Language and Race*, edited by H. Samy Alim, Angela Reyes, and Paul V. Kroskrity. Oxford University Press.

Perry, Imani. 2011. *More Beautiful and More Terrible: The Embrace and Transcendence of Racial Inequality in the United States*. New York University Press.

Phillips, Amber. 2017. "'They're Rapists': President Trump's Campaign Launch Speech Two Years Later, Annotated." *The Washington Post*, June 16, 2017. https://wapo.st/2rGl85S.

Remezcla Estaff. 2018. "Trump Invites Latino CBP Agent Who Speaks 'Perfect English' to Make Speech at White House Event." *Remezcla*, August 20, 2018. https://bit.ly/2oIRTOl.

Reyes, Angela. 2007. *Language, Identity, and Stereotype among Southeast Asian American Youth: The Other Asian*. Lawrence Erlbaum.

    2016. "The Voicing of Asian American Figures: Korean Linguistic Styles at an Asian American Cram School." In *Raciolinguistics: How Language Shapes Our Ideas about Race*, edited by H. Samy Alim, John R. Rickford, and Arnetha F. Ball, pp. 309–26. Oxford University Press.

Reyes, Raul A. 2018. "Trump's 'Speaks Perfect English' Insult Should Offend All Americans." *CNN* article, August 23, 2018. https://cnn.it/2PtKETs.

Rosa, Jonathan. 2019. *Looking Like a Language, Sounding Like a Race: Raciolinguistic Ideologies and the Learning of Latinidad*. Oxford University Press.

Schieffelin, Bambi B., Kathryn A. Woolard, and Paul V. Kroskrity, eds. 1998. *Language Ideologies: Practice and Theory*. Oxford University Press.

Urciuoli, Bonnie. 1996. *Exposing Prejudice: Puerto Rican Experiences of Language, Race, and Class*. Westview Press.

White House. 2018. "President Donald J. Trump Stands with the Brave Heroes Who Enforce Our Immigration Laws and Secure Our Borders." August 20, 2018. https://bit.ly/2OcVIEv.

Wise, Tim. 2009. *Between Barack and a Hard Place: Racism and White Denial in the Age of Obama*. City Lights Books.

17   Making Our Nation Fear the Powerless

Otto Santa Ana, Marco Antonio Juárez, Magaly Reséndez, John Hernández, Oscar Gaytán, Kimberly Cerón, Celeste Gómez, and Roberto Solís

Immigration has always polarized the nation, and it is currently the signature domestic issue of the United States presidency. It is no exaggeration to state that the words and actions of DT, the sitting president, have triggered great personal loss for hundreds of thousands of immigrant, refugee, and American families. (We use "DT" because we prefer not to invoke his name; it already over-saturates the public sphere. The absence of his name allows readers to focus on his rhetorical excesses, rather than on his celebrity status.) DT is a master of mass media manipulation who grabbed and continues to hold the nation's attention, occupying the White House in part because of a cultural shift that Neil Postman pointed out decades ago: US society no longer lives by the principles set out in the Age of Enlightenment. We now live in the Age of Entertainment where "our presidents . . . and newscasters need worry less about satisfying the demands of their discipline than the demands of good showman-ship" (1986: 98). Martin Kaplan described our plight of a society as one where "entertainment substitutes . . . storytelling for truth telling, sensation for reason, spectacle for seriousness, combat for discourse, play for purpose, sizzle for steak" (2007: 137).

The current president play-acts much of his role as Chief of State, but his very real actions against immigrants are immoral and destructive. In this chapter, we will describe the discourse he has used to villainize immigrants in order to seize and maintain political power.

Our data emerge from the small part we have played in the lawsuits to stop the president from ending Deferred Action for Childhood Arrivals (DACA). The US Supreme Court will ultimately decide the legal fate of young immi-grants who were carried to the US in the arms of their parents.[1] As a team of University of California, Los Angeles (UCLA) undergraduates and their pro-fessor, we analyzed DT's public discourse on immigrants using a replicable empirical method (see Santa Ana et al. 2019a).[2] To offer evidence in these cases, we reviewed over 300 of his speeches and 6,000 tweets, some dating to his campaign and others to his presidency. In them, we identified a pernicious and recurrent narrative that he articulates about immigrants. Below we will describe the metaphors that construct this narrative.

We also suggest it is instructive to compare DT's anti-immigrant discourse to Hitler's discourse demonizing his Jewish compatriots. In the 1930s, the Nazis fabricated a myth that played to the fears of the majority. They scapegoated Jews, blaming them for all the nation's problems and calling them "a dangerous bacillus" (germs, in other words) or "rats" whose very nature is "shrewd" and "criminal" (Roseman [2006]2019). The Nazis claimed that Jews were responsible for Germany's dire circumstances, having supposedly conspired to dominate the world by manipulating international finance. In fact, the Jews were not responsible for the heavy reparation that the World War I victors levied on Germany for its role in the war, nor for the economic collapse following the 1929 stock market crash. Most Aryan Germans had never met a Jew, but the Nazi propaganda machine repeated Hitler's narrative so effectively that Germans soon loathed, feared, and dehumanized Jews, allowing Nazis to send them first to ghettos, and then to ovens. The rapid spread of this deadly mass delusion hinged on a simplifying discourse that Hitler used to frame Jews as sub-human.

17.1   Metaphor Re-imagines Reality: Why the President's Message is Persuasive

How did the Nazis convince a nation to hate? Historians and social psychologists have offered explanations involving the political and economic dynamics of the time. We offer a complementary account grounded in language. To generate support for their genocidal vision, the Nazis exploited the way human beings make sense of their world by promoting a false worldview through metaphorical frameworks that would guide the public's reasoning. The study of metaphor as a crucial reality-building device gained traction with the writings of Lakoff and Johnson (1980) and has since been highly developed in cognitive science and language studies (see Kövecses 2010). A "conceptual metaphor" involves understanding one idea – usually an abstract one – in terms of another that is usually more concrete, seemingly simpler and easier to grasp. Abstractions like "love" or "the nation" are complex and hard to understand, until one can use metaphors (e.g. LOVE AS JOURNEY, for instance, or NATION AS FORTRESS) to make inferences about them, no matter how oversimplifying.

In the material we discuss below, the president is shown to use metaphors to drastically distort the facts about immigration, a worldwide demographic movement spurred by globalization (Santa Ana 2012: 5). The Nazis and the current US president both concocted entire frameworks of thinking that developed false national narratives involving heroes and villains for their respective nations, and each framework pivots on a few key metaphors. The metaphors DT uses are emotionally triggering, invoking such concepts as "flood" (see Santa Ana et al. 2019a: 13–14) and "invader" (ibid.: 17–18) to frame his political narrative. In the discussion that follows, we pull together evidence for the recurrent metaphorical themes that shape his pernicious views. Then, we look at how he has bolstered his grand narrative with distorting overgeneralizations, using a small part of a population to stand in for and supposedly characterize the whole.

17.2   DT's Guiding Metaphors

On the day he announced his run for the presidency in June of 2015, DT made his intent clear when he denounced Mexican immigrants with patently false claims: "The US has become a dumping ground for everybody else's problems," he fulminated. "When Mexico sends its people, they're not sending their best ... They're sending people that have lots of problems, and they're bringing those problems with us. They're bringing drugs. They're bringing crime. They're rapists" (Washington Post Staff 2015). Since then, DT has recurrently stated that the nation is imperiled by the presence of such interlopers. Waves of "criminal immigrants" (Santa Ana et al. 2019a: 28), he repeatedly claims, have poured into America unimpeded, threatening to destroy our nation, while "stupid" politicians (mostly Democrats; see Santa Ana et al. 2019a) are to blame for lax immigration enforcement. Our review revealed DT's fundamental organizing principle regarding the relationship between immigration and the state: US AS BESIEGED FORTRESS. In the paragraphs that follow, we draw on his speeches and tweets to extract the metaphorical elements underlying this grand narrative.

17.2.1   Nation as Border

A wall is easy to understand, but DT's repeated urgent call to "save" the nation with a physical wall erected across a 2,000-mile international boundary that follows a river and crosses deserts, mountains, and metropolitan centers is an extraordinarily over-simplified idea. The fantasy he indulges with this metaphor is that (White) America must be perfectly shielded from the non-Whites coming from the South. For him, anything less than a hermetically sealed wall against such immigrants is both useless and a threat to national survival. He has also falsely claimed that his political opponents want the polar opposite, as when he misattributed the following vision to Hillary Clinton during a campaign rally in Portsmouth, New Hampshire, in 2016: "By 'open borders' she means totally unlimited immigration" (Factba.se 2015). He went on to imply the lack of his imagined shield spelled doom: "Either we win this election, or we lose the country" (Santa Ana et al. 2019b). Crucially, DT continues to repeatedly define the nation itself in terms of its very boundaries, as in this tweet: "A nation WITHOUT BORDERS is not a nation at all. We must have a wall. The rule of law matters" (Trump on Twitter, July 28, 2015e). The theme recurred in his conversation with Howard Kurtz of *Fox News*: "In terms of the border, it's a disgrace. Either we have a border or we don't have a country. You can't have a country without borders" (Fox News Insider 2015).

17.2.2   Immigration as Flood

In keeping with his narrative that our nation is a fortress imperiled because of its breached walls, DT has justified his plans to build a wall by arguing that immigrants are a dangerous flood pouring into the US: "Our border is wide open, and drugs and criminal cartels are pouring into our country on an hourly basis" (Santa Ana et al. 2019a: 17). He has repeated the metaphor often during his candidacy and presidency: "The Mexican border is a sieve. People are pouring into our country" (Fox News Insider 2015). In fact, before his run, the numbers of unauthorized immigrants coming to the US had fallen.[3]

17.2.3   Mexico as Enemy

DT alludes to Mexico as if it is the enemy of the United States; not only the supposed "second deadliest country in the world" (Santa Ana et al. 2019b), but also a threat to American life and security. To bolster the lie that our nation's close ally, major trading partner, and peaceful neighbor is conducting military, economic, or any other kind of warfare against the US, he tweeted: "Mexico is killing the United States economically because their leaders and negotiators are FAR smarter than ours. But nobody beats Trump!" (ibid.). He repeatedly declares Mexico to be a threatening enemy, as in this statement about the "southern border" two years later at an Ohio rally: "Never again will America surrender the security of our people, the safety of our communities, or the sovereignty of our nation" (Abramson 2017). Not only is the supposed enemy, Mexico, "sending" (Trump on Twitter, July 13, 2015d, 6:59 am) its worst people, but with its "tremendous crime problem" (Arter 2017) it is also toxic; the drugs "pouring into this country" are "poisoning our youth" (Santa Ana et al. 2019a: 17). Such imagery further bolsters DT's claim that the wall he proposes is "imperative."

17.2.4   Immigrant as Criminal, Immigrant as Invader

If drugs are supposedly besieging the US from the South, so too are people. DT repeatedly characterizes immigrants from the South as an army of "criminal aliens" and "criminal gangs" that show no remorse toward American citizens; these "bad and dangerous people" coming from Mexico and Central America pour into and threaten the safety of American communities. Consider the following campaign-era tweets: "Druggies, drug dealers, rapists and killers are coming across the southern border. When will the U.S. get smart and stop this travesty?" (Trump on Twitter, June 19, 2015a).[4] And: "El Chapo and the Mexican drug cartels use the border unimpeded like it was a vacuum cleaner sucking drugs and death right into the US ..." (Trump on Twitter, July 13, 2015b, 06:47 am). DT continued shortly thereafter with, "Likewise billions of dollars gets brought into Mexico through the border. We get the killers, drugs & crime, they get the money!" (Trump on Twitter, July 13, 2015c, 06:53 am). He bolstered this "criminal invaders" metaphor in 2018, when several "caravans" of migrants from Central America trekked north to the Mexico–United States border, mostly fleeing violence and seeking asylum. During the run-up to the November 2018 midterm elections, he got mileage out of his "invader" metaphor, as in this sample tweet that, as of October 27, 2019, received 36,600 retweets and 133,000 likes: "Many Gang Members and some very bad people are mixed into the Caravan heading to our Southern Border ... This is an invasion of our Country and our Military is waiting for you!" (Trump on Twitter, October 29, 2018b). The underlying storyline in many presidential speeches and tweets is that the US is under attack, helping to justify the president's overwrought militaristic response.

17.2.5 Immigrant as Animal

According to DT, immigrants are not really human. Addressing law enforcement officials in July 2017, he claimed that immigrant gangs are among the most numerous of immigrants, and their murderous cruelty runs so deep that they "don't like shooting people because it's too quick" (Santa Ana et al. 2019b). He enumerated several vivid and gruesome examples in which a US citizen was murdered by these "animals" (ibid.). Without the construction of a border wall, he argued, the carnage of innocent American civilians will continue:

Think of it. They butcher those little girls. They kidnap, they extort, they rape and they rob. They prey on children. They shouldn't be here. They stomp on their victims. They beat them with clubs. They slash them with machetes, and they stab them with knives. They have transformed peaceful parks and beautiful, quiet neighborhoods into blood-stained killing fields. They're animals. (Trump 2017b)

DT urged his audience to vividly imagine his violent fantasized dystopia to stoke their outrage. When journalists later questioned his exaggeration, he only doubled down, repeating his dehumanizing words. His spokespeople stated that his words were directed only at the MS-13 gang, an international criminal organization whose primary targets in the US are Central American migrants. But DT never apologized for or qualified his hyperbole, instead reiterating it. At a rally in Phoenix in August of 2017, for instance, the president stated that sub-human "illegal immigrants" were being purged from the country: "These are animals. We are getting them out of here. We are throwing them in jail, throwing them out of the country" (Schwartz 2017).

17.2.6 White America as Victim

The supposed invading force DT described wreaks havoc, rape, and all kinds of violence on Americans, by which he implicitly means White Americans. To make his claims more vivid, he has repeatedly named a number of the fourteen individuals who were actually killed by unauthorized immigrants, as can be seen in his campaign rally speech in Naples, FL, in 2016:[5]

All across our nation, innocent Americans have been killed by illegal immigrant criminals who should never have been in our country. Kate Steinle was gunned down in her father's arms in broad daylight on a San Francisco pier. Her killer had been deported five times before. Ninety-year-old Earl Olander was brutally beaten to death in his home by illegal immigrants with criminal records and left on the floor of his home to die. Laura Wilkerson's teenage son, Josh, was tortured and beaten to do by an illegal immigrant he offered to give a ride home. His body was viciously burned. The examples go on and on and on. (Santa Ana et al. 2019a: 15)

DT has invoked these unfortunate individuals and their families as stand-ins for the nation: "Countless innocent Americans have been killed by illegal immigrants" (Santa Ana et al. 2019b). The president repeated a version of this "countless Americans" claim eight times in the eleven speeches we analyzed (Santa Ana et al. 2019a). In fact, "countless Americans" have not been killed and the examples do not "go on and on" (Santa Ana et al. 2019a: 15). We will return to this fallacy (below).

17.2.7 DT as Hero

In the president's fictional war of occupation, Mexican leaders have been sending "the worst of the worst" criminals to terrorize White Americans and destroy the country, while politicians before him have been asleep at the wheel. DT himself, in his rhetoric, is positioned as the great liberator. He has vowed to "find, arrest, jail, and deport" every "criminal alien," and to bring justice to "every mom who has lost her child to illegal immigration" (Santa Ana et al. 2019b). Most absurdly, he has claimed he will "restore" a democracy that we did not know we had lost. Consider these excerpts from his speeches:

To every American who has been waiting for real change, your wait is over – your moment of liberation is at hand. A vote for Trump is a vote to restore Democracy, to heal our economy, and to bring millions of jobs back into every forgotten stretch of this country. (Hains 2016)

The first task for our new Administration will be to liberate our citizens from the crime and terrorism and lawlessness that threatens their communities. (Lopez 2016)

We will bring back our jobs. We will bring back our borders. We will bring back our wealth. And we will bring back our dreams. (Trump 2017a)

DT's claims have been so dramatic that, at a New York law enforcement conference on gangs in 2017, he could not help but remark on his own hyperbole as he referred to himself like some Wild West sheriff, "liberating" towns from immigrants and the MS-13 gang:

One by one, we're liberating our American towns. Can you believe that I'm saying that? I'm talking about liberating our towns. This is like I'd see in a movie: They're liberating the town, like in the old Wild West, right? We're liberating our towns. I never thought I'd be standing up here talking about liberating the towns on Long Island where I grew up, but that's what you're doing. (Haberman and Robbins 2017)

DT has repeated his "liberating" claim often (see, for instance, Hernandez 2018). At a rally in Phoenix on August 21, 2017, he claimed, "We are throwing them out so fast, they never got thrown out of anything like this. We are liberating towns out in Long Island ... We are liberating our towns" (Schwartz 2017). DT's conceptual metaphors add up to a storyline we summarize below, but first, a note on some of the distortions he traffics in.

17.3   Distorted Synecdoche: The President's Shorthand for His Conceptual Metaphors

After so many repetitions of his key metaphors, DT was able to invoke his master narrative in shorthand. Here we mention three expressions in particular that encapsulate his storyline in which he takes a small contingent of people and leverages them as if they somehow characterize the entire phenomenon of immigration. In semiotics, this use of a part of something to stand in for the whole is sometimes called "synecdoche" (see Baumann and Gingrich 2004). In the hands of DT, synecdoche is inevitably distorting, misleading, and politically perilous.

The first synecdoche is "criminal aliens," as in Trump's statement during his October 2016 remarks at the Newtown Athletic Club Sports Training Center in Newtown, Pennsylvania: "We will swiftly remove and deport all criminal aliens from this country, and dismantle the gangs and cartels preying on our citizens. Either we win this election, or we lose the country" (Santa Ana et al. 2019b). Recall that it is not a felony to cross the international border; rather, it is a "civil infraction," a violation of the law that is less serious than a misdemeanor. In contrast, the term *criminal* typically is associated with serious crimes. By repeatedly using this term, the president attributes the acts of two percent of immigrants who actually commit felonious acts to the ninety-eight percent of unauthorized but otherwise law-abiding immigrants. Listening to him, it is not hard to assume that millions of unauthorized immigrants are a dangerous force.

"MS-13" is his second distorting synecdoche. When the president uses this term, he frequently conflates MS-13 with all Latino gangs, and potentially all undocumented immigrants, as in this statement that he delivered during a New York law enforcement conference on MS-13 in 2017: "We are cracking down hard on the foreign criminal gangs that have brought illegal drugs, violence, horrible bloodshed to peaceful neighborhoods all across our country. We are throwing MS-13 the hell out of here so fast" (Lanktree 2017). Yet the Federal Bureau of Investigation (FBI) estimates that the majority (approximately 80 percent) of MS-13 members are not immigrants at all.[6] In many speeches, the president seems to toggle arbitrarily between "illegal immigrants" and "MS-13," muddying the distinction, as is apparent when he spoke at a rally in Arizona: "The people of Arizona know the deadly and heartbreaking consequences of illegal immigration . . . The lost lives, the drugs, the gangs, the cartels, the crisis of smuggling and trafficking, and MS-13" (Schwartz 2017). When the president's audience imagines MS-13 at any mention of immigrants, then he has succeeded at attributing to all undocumented immigrants the incredibly violent behavior of less than one-tenth of one percent (0.08 percent) of them.

Finally, when it comes to White victimhood, DT repeatedly states a handful of roughly a dozen names of Americans actually killed by immigrants as stand-ins for all "beautiful, beautiful, innocent" and largely White Americans (Santa Ana et al. 2019b). He speaks as if each victim had been targeted in a premeditated murder, but his list consists mostly of accidental deaths, such as at the hands of a drunk driver. The fact is that in a nation of 328 million with just over eleven million unauthorized immigrants, immigrants commit fewer crimes of any type than the general US population (Ingraham 2018; see also Bernat 2017). Yet at his first joint session of Congress, the president introduced the relatives of three of the same victims he always mentions, and called on the Department of Homeland Security to create an office focused on the victims of immigrant crime, with instructions to "make public a comprehensive list of criminal actions committed by aliens" (Trump 2017c). Political scientist Peter Beinart compared such actions to those taken by Hitler's government when it took power in 1933. It too began to broadcast "Jewish crime statistics as a way of stoking anti-Semitism . . . . Hitler's Ministry of Justice ordered prosecutors to forward every criminal indictment against a Jew so the ministry's press office could publicize it" (Beinart 2017). DT's smears and exaggerations similarly feed a dangerous beast.

17.4   DT's Supporters: Ardent, Yet Complacent

DT's crude metaphors add up to a storyline that has had mass appeal to his supporters. Our summary of the president's full, hallucinatory narrative about immigrants follows:

The once great castle on the hill, America, is under siege by a foreign force. The fortress walls are broken; our cities and towns have been flooded by ruthless foreign invaders. Criminal aliens, bloodthirsty animals, are victimizing countless American families. The Mexican government has deployed its violent criminals, drug cartels, MS-13, drug pushers, and human traffickers to occupy and destroy our country. Meanwhile America has been governed by weak and stupid politicians. The presence of illegals is a national existential crisis. As the nation's heroic defender, I will liberate our country, rid our nation of this invading force, and build a 'Great Wall' that will allow us to regain control of the border and hence the nation. Only I can make America great again.

As of mid-2020, over 30 percent of the US electorate still accept the president's version of daily events and reject mainstream media reporting of his lies. His rock-solid poll numbers are alarming. History provides multiple examples of national leaders who articulated falsehoods to generate fear about a group, and then exploited that fear to justify actions that undercut their nations' democracies.[7] Our current president's most loyal constituency dismisses any news reports that criticize him, since "journalists are simply trying to bring [him] down" (Rosen 2018). For them, he is the strong leader that the US needs.

It is appropriate to consider how ordinary Germans – not the Nazis – allowed Hitler to bring ruin to their nation. An eyewitness to the horror, author Milton Mayer, interviewed average Germans soon after the war, and found that even after their country had been destroyed, they still applauded Hitler for "clean-[ing] up moral degenerates" (Mayer [1955]2017: 102; see also Sunstein 2018). Many Germans rejected the idea that their government murdered six million Jews. Mayer recorded their shifty hedges about the facts: "Some say it happened and some say it didn't"; "It was wrong, unless they committed treason in wartime. And of course, they did"; or "If it happened, it was wrong. But I don't believe it happened" – and even if it did, "Hitler had nothing to do with it" ([1955]2017: 65, 184). This level of denial and indifference by seemingly upright citizens in response to war crimes was only possible in a nation where most citizens had "quietly" come to accept the Nazi narrative that vilified the Jew. Hitler did not immediately show himself to be a tyrant. His horrors mounted incrementally, "little by little, all around us" (ibid.: 168), as one German citizen put it later, thus allowing him to become one. The regime distracted its citizens through endless dramas, often involving real or imagined enemies, which gradually led to people habituating to being "governed by surprise … Each step was so small, so inconsequential, so well explained" that people could no more see it "developing from day to day than a farmer in his field sees the corn growing. One day it is over his head" (Mayer [1955] 2017: 166–68; see also Sunstein 2018).

The celebrated historian of the Holocaust, Timothy Snyder, recently wrote, "Americans are no wiser than the Europeans who saw democracy yield to fascism, Nazism and communism. Our one advantage is that we might learn from their experience" (2017: 13). Alas, for many the lesson has not sunk in. Millions of Americans have become desensitized to images of imprisoned children who were separated from their parents by DT's administration's policies, and are unmoved by the images of an asylum-seeking Honduran mother and her diapered daughters running from tear gas fired by US Border Patrol agents (see Kyung-Hoon 2018). Church-going American citizens condone policies that turn truly desperate families and genuine refugees away from our borders. Meanwhile DT continues to use the language of the Nazis with his scare mongering: "illegal immigrants, no matter how bad they may be … pour into and infest our country, like MS-13" (Trump on Twitter, June 19, 2018a). When ordinary American citizens come to believe that the most wretched people at our borders are vermin intent on destroying our powerful nation, they will permit DT to treat humans inhumanely.

Notes

1. In 2017 the president attempted to rescind DACA by executive action. DACA allows people who came to the US without documentation before they were 16 to be protected from immediate deportation, if they lived continuously in the US, were under 31 years of age in 2007, and have a high school diploma or GED or an honorable military discharge and no criminal record. DACA grantees obtain limited "consideration of deferred action" for two years, with possible renewal. DACA does not grant "lawful" status, only less likelihood of being deported. Sixteen states took the president to court, claiming he acted to rescind DACA with "racial animus" and "discriminatory intent," a violation of the Equal Protection Clause of the US Constitution.

2. In September 2017 Professor Robert Chang of the Korematsu Center for Law and Equality asked us to produce a report on DT's public discourse toward Latinos and immigrants. The first author had previously served as a plaintiffs' expert in a civil rights case where the public discourse of the Arizona senator who authored SB-1070 expressed "discriminatory intent" and "racial animus" toward Mexican immigrants (Santa Ana 2019). Our report findings, "Final report of the University of California, Los Angeles, DACA Defense Group," were cited in an Amicus Brief submitted to the New York district court. Subsequently our findings became a "declaration" submitted to the 2nd and 9th circuit US Appellate Courts as part of an Amicus Brief, and ultimately, to US Supreme Court. The full pre-publication report presents

our empirical and methodological approach in depth, as well as our findings (Santa Ana et al. 2019a). It can be accessed and downloaded via www.thepresidentsintent.com/iss ue-final-report. The Supreme Court *Amici Curiae* Brief (i.e. *Department of Homeland Security et al., Petitioners, v. Regents of The University of California et al., Respondents*; specifically, see pages 21–4) can be accessed via https://bit.ly/2N2sARj.

3. The nation's unauthorized immigrant population reached a peak of 12.2 million in 2007. Since then, the population has declined to 11.1 million. The number of unauthorized immigrants from Mexico has fallen from a peak of 6.9 million in 2007 to 5.8 million in 2014 (Radford and Noe-Bustamante 2019).

4. We did not edit the grammatical, spelling, or punctuation infelicities of the president's tweets.

5. The frequently named victims are Earl Olander, Casey Chadwick, Marilyn Pharis, Kate Steinle, Grant Ronneback, the son of Jamiel Shaw, Brandon Mendoza, the daughter of Sabine Durden, Sarah Root, Starlette Pitts, the son of Laura Wilkerson, Kris Eggle, and Nick Erfle.

6. In 2018 the US government estimated that MS-13 had 10,000 members (Correa-Cabrera et al. 2018). In 2009, the Federal Bureau of Investigation (FBI) estimated that MS-13 included 30–50,000 members and associate members worldwide, of whom 20 percent (8–10,000) resided in the US (National Gang Intelligence Center 2009: 25).

7. We can point to the demise of contemporary Polish democracy under President Andrzej Duda. He instituted a number of anti-immigrant measures, but with a firewall of support from the anti-immigrant and nationalist core of the electorate, he has instituted other undemocratic moves to limit court and media independence, and even to outlaw unfavorable accounts of the role of Poles during the Holocaust (see Michnik 2011, for example).

References

Abramson, Alana. 2017. "'I Can Be More Presidential than Any President.' Read Trump's Ohio Rally Speech." *Time*, July 26, 2017. https://bit.ly/36a2IdC.

Arter, Melanie. 2017. "Trump: Mexico Will Pay for the Wall – 'It May Be Through Reimbursement.'" *CNSNews.com*, August 28, 2017. https://bit.ly/2JxbQiG.

Baumann, Gerd, and André Gingrich, eds. 2004. *Grammars of Identity/Alterity: A Structural Approach*. Berghahn Books.

Beinart, Peter. 2017. "Trump Scapegoats Unauthorized Immigrants for Crime." *The Atlantic*, March 1, 2017. https://bit.ly/2KWrZB2.

Bernat, Frances. 2017. "Immigration and Crime." In *Oxford Research Encyclopedia of Criminology and Criminal Justice*. Oxford University Press. Oxford Index: A Search and Discovery Gateway, April 2017. https://bit.ly/2WgLmqQ.

Correa-Cabrera, Guadalupe, Mariely Lopez-Santana, and Camilo Pardo. 2018. "Is MS-13 as Dangerous as Trump Suggests?" *The Washington Post*, December 7, 2018. https://wapo.st/2okPZDJ.

Factba.se. 2015. "Remarks: Donald Trump at Toyota of Portsmouth in Portsmouth, NH [Transcript]." *Factba.se*, October 15, 2016. https://bit.ly/2MOHbzz.

Fox News Insider. 2015. "Trump on Immigration Comments: 'I Can Never Apologize for the Truth.'" *Fox News*, July 5, 2015. https://bit.ly/2Pi1o2m.

Haberman, Maggie, and Liz Robbins. 2017. "Trump, on Long Island, Vows an End to Gang Violence." *The New York Times*, July 28, 2017. https://nyti.ms/34aanGP.

Hains, Tim. 2016. "Full Replay/Transcript: Donald Trump Speaks in Greenville, NC." *Real Clear Politics*, September 6, 2016. https://bit.ly/2pZr2y0.

Hernandez, Laura Figueroa. 2018. "Donald Trump's Mantra: We Have 'Liberated Towns' on Long Island." *Newsday*, June 21, 2018. https://nwsdy.li/369sOxc.

Ingraham, Christopher. 2018. "Two Charts Demolish the Notion That Immigrants Here Illegally Commit More Crime." *The Washington Post*, June 19, 2018. https://wapo.st/2ohKyFA.

Kaplan, Martin. 2007. "Welcome to the Infotainment Freak Show." In *What Orwell Didn't Know: Propaganda and the New Face of American Politics*, edited by András Szántó, pp. 137–46. Public Affairs.

Kövecses, Zoltán. 2010. *Metaphor: A Practical Introduction*. 2nd edn. Oxford University Press.

Kyung-Hoon, Kim. 2018. "US Fires Tear Gas into Mexico to Repel Migrants." *Reuters.com*, November 26, 2018. https://reut.rs/2NjGDkf.

Lakoff, George, and Mark Johnson. 1980. *Metaphors We Live By*. University of Chicago Press.

Lanktree, Graham. 2017. "Trump Says Immigrant Gang Members 'Slice and Dice' Young, Beautiful Girls." *Newsweek*, July 26, 2017. https://bit.ly/2Wpb64A.

Lopez, German. 2016. "Eric Holder is Right: Trump's Description of a Dangerous American Hellscape Is Wrong." *Vox*, July 26, 2017. https://bit.ly/32Ssscf.

Mayer, Milton. [1955]2017. *They Thought They Were Free: The Germans, 1933–45*. 2nd edn. University of Chicago Press.

Michnik, Adam. 2011. *In Search of Lost Meaning: The New Eastern Europe*. Edited by Irena Grudzińska Gross. Translated by Roman S. Czarny. University of California Press.

National Gang Intelligence Center. 2009. "National Gang Threat Assessment." Federal Bureau of Investigation Digital. https://bit.ly/2BUcLpf.

Postman, Neil. 1986. *Amusing Ourselves to Death: Public Discourse in the Age of Show Business*. Penguin Books.

Radford, Jynnah, and Luis Noe-Bustamante. 2019. "Facts on U.S. Immigrants, 2017: Statistical Portrait of the Foreign-Born Population in the United States." *Pew Research Center: Hispanic Trends*, June 3, 2019. https://pewrsr.ch/2pSilpo.

Roseman, Mark. [2006]2019. "Holocaust." In *Europe Since 1914: Encyclopedia of the Age of War and Reconstruction*, edited by John M. Merriman and J. M. Winter. *Encyclopedia.com*, October 1, 2019. https://bit.ly/31SBpkt.

Rosen, Jay. 2018. "Why Trump Is Winning and the Press Is Losing." *The New York Review of Books*, April 25, 2018. https://bit.ly/2NjPNNF.

Santa Ana, Otto. 2012. "Arizona's Provincial Responses to Its Global Immigration Challenges: Introduction to *Arizona Firestorm*." In *Arizona Firestorm: Global Immigration Realities, National Media, and Provincial Politics*, edited by Otto Santa Ana and Celeste González de Bustamante, pp. 3–18. Rowman and Littlefield.

    2019. "The Senator's Discriminatory Intent: Presenting Probative Legal Evidence of Unconstitutional Verbal Animus." *Language, Culture and Society* 1, no. 2: 169–95.

Santa Ana, Otto, Marco Antonio Juárez, Magaly Reséndez, John Hernández, Oscar Gaytán, Kimberly Cerón, Celeste Gómez, and Yuina Hirose.

2019a. "Documenting the President's Verbal Animus against Immigrants to Defend DACA Grantees." *The President's Intent*, January 2019. www.thepresidentsintent.com/issue-final-report.

Santa Ana, Otto, Marco Antonio Juárez, Magaly Reséndez, John Hernández, Oscar Gaytán, Kimberly Cerón, Celeste Gómez, and Yuina Hirose. 2019b. "Text Examples." *The President's Intent*, January 2019. www.thepresidentsintent.com/text-examples.

Schwartz, Ian. 2017. "Trump: We Are 'Liberating' Our Towns of Illegal Immigrants, Gangs." *Real Clear Politics*, August 22, 2017. https://bit.ly/2Jn6uGU.

Snyder, Timothy. 2017. *On Tyranny: Twenty Lessons from the Twentieth Century*. Tim Duggan Books.

Sunstein, Cass. 2018. "It Can Happen Here." Review of *They Thought They Were Free: The Germans, 1933–45* by Milton Mayer and *Broken Lives: How Ordinary Germans Experienced the Twentieth Century* by Konrad H. Jarausch. *New York Review of Books*, June 28, 2018. https://bit.ly/31IiGbu.

Trump, Donald. 2017a. "The Inaugural Address." *WhiteHouse.gov*, January 20, 2017. https://bit.ly/31KVole.

2017b. "Remarks by President Trump to Law Enforcement Officials on MS 13." *WhiteHouse.gov*, July 28, 2017. https://bit.ly/2JrCB89.

2017c. "Executive Order: Enhancing Public Safety in the Interior of the United States." *WhiteHouse.gov*, January 25, 2017. https://bit.ly/2Jscr5d.

Trump, Donald (@realDonaldTrump). 2015a. "Druggies, drug dealers, rapists and killers are coming across the southern border. When will the U.S. get smart and stop this travesty?" Twitter, June 19, 2015. https://bit.ly/2BL9CIh.

2015b. "El Chapo and the Mexican drug cartels use the border unimpeded like it was a vacuum cleaner, sucking drugs and death right into the U.S." Twitter, July 13, 2015, 06:47 am. https://bit.ly/2qGEAPp.

2015c. ".... likewise, billions of dollars gets brought into Mexico through the border. We get the killers, drugs & crime, they get the money!" Twitter, July 13, 2015, 06:53 am. https://bit.ly/363qLuN.

2015d. "When will people, and the media, start to apologize to me for my statement, 'Mexico is sending . . .', which turned out to be true? El Chapo." Twitter, July 13, 2015, 06:59 am. https://bit.ly/2WpuC0R.

2015e. "A nation WITHOUT BORDERS is not a nation at all. We must have a wall. The rule of law matters. Jeb just doesn't get it." Twitter, July 28, 2015. https://bit.ly/2JsaUft.

2018a. "Democrats are the problem. They don't care about crime and want illegal immigrants, no matter how bad they may be, to pour into and infest our Country, like MS-13. They can't win on their terrible policies, so they view them as potential voters!" Twitter, June 19, 2018. https://bit.ly/2BL9LeH.

2018b. "Many Gang Members and some very bad people are mixed into the Caravan heading to our Southern Border. Please go back, you will not be admitted into the United States unless you go through the legal process. This is an invasion of our Country and our Military is waiting for you!" Twitter, October 29, 2018. https://bit.ly/32Qon8J.

Washington Post Staff. 2015. "Full Text: Donald Trump Announces a Presidential Bid." *The Washington Post*, June 16, 2015. https://wapo.st/2WfeBKR.

18   We Latin Americans Know a Messianic Autocrat When We See One

Norma Mendoza-Denton

In 2016, during the height of the US presidential election, candidate Trump's rhetoric against Latin Americans, specifically Mexican immigrants, reached a fever pitch, and "bad hombres" became not only a meme but also a much discussed phrase. The tongue-in-cheek debate hinged on what Trump could have possibly meant with his intrasentential (mid-sentence) codeswitch from English to Spanish: Bad men [*hombres*]? Bad hungers [*hambres*]? Bad ombrés? This chapter expands on a previously published article (Mendoza-Denton 2017), which aimed to answer the following two questions: What does Trump's jowl-voweled use of Mock Spanish signal about his attitudes toward Latin Americans? And how are Latin American leaders reacting to the Age of Trump?

I extend that discussion here to narratives of masculinity by and around a handful of Latin American leaders, three from Mexico and one from Brazil (former Mexican presidents Vicente Fox and Enrique Peña Nieto, current president Andrés Manuel López Obrador – AMLO – and current Brazilian president Jair Bolsonaro). Through the examination of storytelling around sex, gender, and their performances, I seek to understand how other countries' messianic strongmen interpret and deal with Donald Trump's threats and tweets, posturing and pronouncements, politics and policies. I argue that these leaders' self-identification and narrative positioning relative to Trump reflect the various discursive ways that American power can be engaged in politics in the region, and that these discourses are in turn inflected through the prism of these leaders' own transnational masculinities and the ways that masculinity is talked about in their respective countries.

18.1   Narrating Masculinity in the Public Sphere

When narrative began as a discipline of study in linguistics forty-five years ago, the focus centered on its recurring "grammar": Labov and Waletzky (1973) hypothesized that narratives could be defined as evaluative recountings of past events that had some stable structural elements. Political/linguistic anthropologists (Duranti

1994), political scientists (Patterson and Monroe 1998), and sociologists (such as Polletta 2006) have further analyzed narratives as sites of cultural contestation that can perform identity-building functions at the collective level. Narrative story-telling additionally provides a biographical window into the individual, since a narrative is necessarily embedded within a point of view. By helping us make sense of our world and our place in history, storytelling produces not only our individual experience but also our collectivity.

Against this backdrop, we may ask how masculinity and its intersection with race, class, and ethnonationalism may be embedded in political narrative. Gender theorists led by R. W. Connell (2016) have posited a hierarchy of masculinities in public spheres; masculinities that "embody, organize, and legitimate the domination of men in the world gender order as a whole" (ibid.: 234). Such public displays of masculinities in the political sphere include what Connell calls "transnational business mascu-linity," which he, along with theorists such as Hooper (1998), contrasts to constructs such as "tough, power-oriented masculinities" enacted and maintained through war and global politics. Both of these types of mas-culinities are at play in the current argument, since the various countries' leaders come from different backgrounds. Jair Bolsonaro, for example, was a figure in the 1980s military dictatorship in Brazil, and his right-wing populism finds its justification in military might and its expression in loudly condemning "bureaucratic" holders of previous presidencies. Trump, on the other hand, is a longtime businessman who avoided the draft as a college student, and who has previously extolled money as the ultimate avenue to power. It is only after ascending to the office of President and Commander-in-Chief that Trump finds himself enamored of signifiers of military might, such as army parades, jet flyovers, and appointing generals to cabinet positions (though he still doesn't listen to them, nor they to him [Graham 2019]).

18.2 Trump and Other World Leaders: Crying, Control, and Masculinity

Donald Trump's speeches as president provide many examples of narratives of masculinity where he elevates himself as the pinnacle of virility, strength, toughness – and whiteness. Wallace Chafe (1998) and other scholars (e.g. Norrick 1988) have written about the ways in which repeated tellings of the same story open a window not only into patterns of language, but also into the workings of the self. In the case of Trump, a revealing narrative of masculinity is found in a series of retellings that Trevor Noah of *The Daily Show* compiled into the satirical Christmas video, "Trump's Mythical Crying Man Yule Log" (The Daily Show 2018). In this video montage, a stone fireplace frames the center of an old-fashioned cathode-ray TV where video clips of Trump are gently licked by flames. Trump, in other words, is the yule log. The clips are taken from Trump's campaign stops, speeches, and conversations with reporters, documenting fifteen distinct instances of Trump retelling the same story with minimal variations. The structure discernible in Trump's narrative series is formulaic, with each instantiation filling in variable details. Here is a summary of the narrative structure, with variable elements in square brackets, optional elements in double square brackets, and gestural elements in double parentheses:

(1) [Tough/Strong] Guy [XY] has had a conversation with Trump.
(2) In that conversation, the toughness dissolves and [XY] starts to cry.
(3) ((*Trump inserts comedic gesture with index and middle fingers sweeping downward across face, to simulate tears.*))
(4) [XY], full of emotion, thanks Trump for saving [America/the farms/steel mills/factories/troops].
(5) Trump can't believe such a tough, strong character was crying [[and thinks [XY] might have been from [insert state that Trump is currently touring]]].
(6) [This person was so tough they probably didn't even cry when they were a baby].
(7) APPLAUSE

The formula above has been recycled on many public occasions, and at each reissuing there is an adjustment. Sometimes, the man is a steelworker, or a miner, or a farmer. Sometimes it's a group of men who are crying. Occasionally there is one holdout in the group who does not cry. This man-crying-before-Trump sequence offers a great example of not only a narrative of masculinity, but also a "comedic gesture," where Trump dramatically drags his hands across his face to show copious crying (Goldstein, Hall, and Ingram, this volume).

While it is well attested that politicians recycle narratives and inflect them to suit their audiences (Fenno 1978), Trump's narratives go one step further, often revolving around self-aggrandizement, situating him as both the pinnacle and arbiter of toughness. Trump has on many occasions expressed his disdain for crying, even going so far as to say "How would China feel if I walked in crying [mock crying voice] 'cause I couldn't make the right deal?" (The Washington Post 2019). During a press conference announcing the death of ISIS leader Abu Bakr al-Baghdadi, Trump triumphantly proclaimed that al-Baghdadi died "like a coward, crying, screaming, and whimpering" (White House 2019b). He mentioned the crying five times in the same news conference, and suggested that the video should be "brought out" so his followers could see it. (No such video seems to exist, and numerous military officials later told the *New York Times* they had "no idea what [Trump] was talking about" in his account of al-Baghdadi's affect [Baker and Schmitt 2019].) Additionally, Trump uses "crying" as an epithet (Cryin' Chuck Schumer), and threatens to beat people up until they cry (e.g. Trump on Twitter, March 22, 2018, where he boasts Joe Biden would "go down fast and hard, crying all the way"; see also McIntosh, "Crybabies and Snowflakes," this volume). As a result of repeated narrative retellings of interchangeable criers, Trump has positioned himself not only as someone who never cries, but also as cause and recipient of others' crying. He constructs himself as so very tough, and having done so much for others, that he moves the less tough to tears of gratitude, or chases villains, dominating them until they're whimpering, crying messes, scared out of their minds (White House 2019b). The recurrence of this leitmotif is precisely what renders it an organizing narrative of Trumpian masculinity.

Another aspect of Trump's self-aggrandizing masculinization hinges on race. Speaker of the House Nancy Pelosi has suggested that building a wall between the US and Mexico "is like a manhood thing" for Trump (DeBonis 2018), connecting his performance of masculinity to his xenophobia. Similarly, Trump calling Mexicans "bad hombres" sounds tough in the sense that he admits they may be tough, but Trump makes himself out as even tougher in his blasé use of Mock Spanish to refer to them (Hill 2008). While inciting panic around gangs like MS-13 by calling them terrorists plays into stereotypes of criminal brown youth, stereotypes about Latinx gangs are already prevalent in the population (Mendoza-Denton 2008), as well as in Congress (ibid). Trump's claim that only he can deal with this problem offers to neuter brown masculinities using the tools of White ethnonationalism. Rather than framing himself as a White civilizer, Trump prefers the trappings of cold-blooded brutality. For example, both Trump and his supporters use the shooting-gun gesture originally introduced by Sarah Palin (see my "Show Must Go On" chapter in this volume).

During his tenure as president, Trump has tended to wax poetic and admiring toward world leaders who display features of nationalist and militaristic masculinity by disregarding human rights; exhibiting swagger, toughness, and hostility toward the opposition and media; displaying violent control; and sometimes exercising outright repression. He's lavished praise on "strongmen" such as Kim Jong-un of North Korea: "Well, he is very talented. Anyone who takes over a situation like he did at 26 years of age and is able to run it and run it tough" (Greenwood 2018); Rodrigo Duterte of the Philippines: "[He did an] unbelievable job on the drug problem" (Nelson 2017); and Turkey's Recep Tayyip Erdoğan on a visit to the White House: "It's a great honor and privilege – because he's become a friend of mine – to introduce President Erdoğan of Turkey. He's running a very difficult part of the world. He's involved very, very strongly and, frankly, he's getting very high marks" (White House 2019a). All of this praise for dictators is sprinkled in with compliments for Trump's perennial favorite Vladimir Putin (Kaczynski et al. 2017). In the self-

Table 18.1 *Summary of Latin American leaders' stances and discursive strategies toward Trump*

Political figure	Country/ political tendency	Time in presidential office	Political figure's alignment with Trump	Discursive strategy
Enrique Peña Nieto (EPN)	Mexico/ ideologically vague neoliberal	2012–2018	Careful alignment while EPN himself in office and Trump running for office	Asking for respect
Vicente Fox	Mexico/center-right populist	2000–2006	Vociferous opposition (no longer in office)	Trolling, ridiculing, caricaturing
Andrés Manuel López Obrador (AMLO)	Mexico/left populist	2019–	Vociferous opposition prior to own election, leading to careful restraint once president	Calling out (initially), transitioning into appeasement and avoidance
Jair Messias Bolsonaro	Brazil/far right, aligned with former dictatorship	2019–	Fawning identification before and after own election	Agreement and imitation

aggrandizement department, Trump has even tweeted a hybrid picture of his head on Rocky Balboa's cinematically muscular body (@realDonaldTrump 2019). Discursively, Trump's glib essentialisms – Mexicans are rapists, Muslims are terrorists, beautiful women need protecting, Americans are dominant heroes – get "read" by his base as decisive, and in this sense, masculine.

Against this background of racism, sexism, a steady drip of praise and admiration for despots, and absurd performances of toughness, Latin American leaders and press have had to contend with Trump. For clarity's sake, I provide a shorthand table (Table 18.1) referring to the leaders I discuss, their stance toward Trump, and the discursive strategy they tend to use to respond to his White supremacist strongman masculinity. I will further explain all of these in text and examples below.

18.3   Trump, Enrique Peña Nieto, and Fox

At the end of August 2016, ten weeks before the United States presidential election, candidate Donald Trump visited the presidential palace in Mexico City at the invitation of then-Mexican president Enrique Peña Nieto (EPN). Despite Trump's racist rhetoric against Mexicans at the start of his presidential campaign, EPN invited him for the purpose of beginning a dialogue, but the invitation backfired, as EPN's submissive behavior resulted in widespread public outcry. In the wake of Trump's visit, a barrage of cartoon images, internet memes, and viral video clips were produced to mock and comment on this dynamic (Mendoza-Denton 2017). Those images presented metonymic relations wherein Trump and EPN stood for their countries in scenarios as dysfunctional lovers. A recurrent anxiety in these widespread images involves the political humiliation of Mexico at the hands of the United States, and the gendered humiliation of its leader at the hands of Trump. Many in Mexico (and abroad) blamed that visit and its photo opportunities for beginning the turnaround in the narrative of Trump's then-flagging campaign (López Segura 2017, Reid 2016). The visit allowed Trump to stand on the world stage, at the presidential palace in Mexico City, and look positively statesmanlike.

During and after the Trump visit, the Mexican public was livid. Political figures protested bitterly, led by then-Mexico City Head of Government and Morena party opposition figure Andrés Manuel López Obrador (AMLO) and former Mexican president Vicente Fox Quesada, whose leadership spanned 2000–2006. Caricaturists and meme-makers feasted on EPN's youth, short stature, and slightly pompadoury quiff to portray him as an imbecilic, incompetent, and impotent man-baby.

Since Trump's election, leadership of Mexico has turned over, and in fact Latin American countries are poised to run twelve elections in just the next few years. Andrés Manuel López Obrador (AMLO) replaced EPN in Mexico. Brazil, the "giant of Latin America" and world's eighth-largest economy, elected a new president, the conservative politician Jair Bolsonaro, a former paratrooper and active military leader from 1977 to 1988 during the bloody Brazilian dictatorship. These Latin American leaders and other public figures by turns vilify and emulate Trump's posturing, alternately attempting to counter, contain, or amplify the unpredictable power of the elephantine neighbor to the North. Certain political commentators (Tharoor 2017, Bowden 2019) have even remarked that Trump has taken a page from banana republic-style politics, and that beyond praising autocrats, he is indeed the first example of a US president acting as a tin horn dictator: "Trump has the typical style of a Latin American caudillo (strongman)," former Colombian President César Gaviria told Andrés Oppenheimer of the *Miami Herald*. "He tells people what they want to hear, scares them, and then says, 'Don't worry, I'll fix it'" (Oppenheimer 2016).

In Mexico, the discursive effects of the cacophony of reactions to Trump's visit resulted in the pummeling of Peña Nieto's masculinity. One of the most prominent actors in this process was former president Vicente Fox, who appointed himself as defender of Mexico's honor and turned up on Twitter as a kind of condescending avuncular troll to EPN and on Trump's feed as an insolent provocateur. Freed from the barely observed protocol constraints of his former role as president, Fox has become famous not only for his salty, populist language, huge cowboy boots, and tough rancher image, but for trolling Trump, calling him a child, swearing at him directly on TV, and popularizing hashtags such as #FuckingWall.

As Ochs (1992: 339–40) explains, "Few features of language directly and exclusively index gender ... [S]ome may presuppose gendered identities for the speaker, the hearer, or overhearers." It was not solely rude words and gestures, then, that would allow Fox to discursively regulate EPN's masculinity, but their deployment in light of the meanings of homophobic slurs in Mexico. As Almaguer (1993), Gutmann (1996), and Núñez Noriega (1999) have noted, in Mexico and Latin America the critical distinction in men's sexual behavior may not be between gay/straight (i.e. Freudian sexual choice) but active/passive (i.e. Freudian sexual aim), with the stakes being about who controls whom. In such an arrangement, "the [sexually receptive] passive, which is understood as feminine, is radically devalued" (Almaguer 1993: 255). Fox has a history of leveraging Mexican homophobic slurs and interpellating (giving an identity to) Mexican voters as overhearers and judges (for examples that played out during Fox's presidential campaign, see Mendoza-Denton 2017).

Anxiety over the possibility of having Trump take advantage of EPN and having the US metonymically penetrate a receptive Mexico is evident in widely circulated images. In Figure 18.1, EPN is pictured in the foreground as a stripper, smiling while offering Trump his backside. At a table in the background sit former Mexican presidents Carlos Salinas de Gortari (presidential term 1988–1994) and Ernesto Zedillo (presidential term 1994–2000). Besides the obvious prostitute-and-john setup, with Trump "making it rain" (i.e. throwing money on performers to show off his wealth), the implication here is that prior Mexican presidents sold out and betrayed today's Mexico by setting up the current geofinancial situation (those two presidents were in charge of implementing NAFTA in the early 1990s).

In the case of Figure 18.1, another possible interpretation would link a deep-rooted underlying racial and gendered anxiety about Trump as a White foreigner whose political presence repeats the history of colonial Mexico. When Hernán Cortés, the Spanish conquistador, landed in Mexico in 1519, he was to be the explorer who "won" Mexico for the Spanish crown. He did not do this alone; he brought soldiers and disease, and secured the cooperation of an indigenous Tabascan woman who was gifted to him as his slave. Her name was Malintzin (aka Marina, or La Malinche). She became Cortés' lover and bore him a son named Martín. In the national psyche and origin story, Martín is the original Mexican; half-European and half-indigenous, the product of betrayal by a White invader and of the rape of an indigenous woman (Palma 1990). Today in Mexico, the word *malinchista* refers to anyone who denounces, denies, or sells

Figure 18.1 Illustration by ElWero Vadelate, 2016. Reproduced with the artist's permission.

Mexico out for personal gain. And malinchista is what EPN was called all over social media in the wake of Trump's visit (Beltrán del Río 2017).

18.4   Andrés Manuel López Obrador and His Dignified Masculine Posture: "Feo, Fuerte, y Formal"

Before being elected to the Mexican presidency at the end of 2018, the leftist, anti-establishment Andrés Manuel López Obrador (AMLO) was the also-ran candidate of almost twenty years, fighting through successive presidential elections with frequent marches and demonstrations against corruption and inequality. AMLO cycled through the various political parties and in 2014, founded his own AMLO-centered leftist party, Morena, *Movimiento Regeneración Nacional* (National Regeneration Movement, the acronym of which strategically plays on the Spanish word for dark-skinned, *moreno/a*). In 2018, AMLO finally was elected President in a landslide, capturing majorities in both the House and the Chamber of Deputies.

Distinguishing himself from the previous Mexican administrations' disastrous economic and foreign policy mistakes, AMLO decried neoliberalism and advocated for brotherhood among nations; the rights of the indigenous and poor; respect for sexual, ethnic, and religious diversity; dignity for migrants; environmentalism; universal education; narrowing the wealth gap; and listening to the lessons of history. After two decades in the wilderness, AMLO's 2018 campaign crystallized into the antithesis of EPN's White urban privilege, fashionable European good looks, neoliberal economics, and corruption-financed luxuries. Bronze-skinned AMLO tracks much closer to an ideal of indigenous Mexican rural masculinity that is captured by the traditional Mexican saying that men should possess the three "F's": *Feo, fuerte, y formal*; that is to say, men should be ugly, strong, and dignified. In this context, ugly refers not to a lack of physical beauty, but to a masculine plainness, a transcendence of both the superfluous and of the necessity for adornment. Constantly bedecked in the formal simplicity of *guayabera* shirts, occasional palm leaf hats, and brown skin, all indexing his rural roots from the state of Tabasco, AMLO as president is practicing populist asceticism and anti-vanity; he has so far given up living in the presidential mansion and flying the presidential jet. The anti-establishment symbolism and political marketing of the appearance of simplicity is evident, especially in contrast to the corruptly luxurious and "malinchista" EPN, to say nothing of Trump.

With more than a dash of self-righteousness and populism, AMLO's campaign platform focused on steering Mexico away from its former corrupt rulers and even more corrupt drug lords, while leveraging Mexico's simmering racial and class resentments to appeal to poor mestizo and indigenous voters. For the first time in the history of the republic, Mexico's presidential inauguration included an indigenous Mexican ceremony, where AMLO received from indigenous leaders a traditional wooden staff representing leadership and power (Diario Crónica 2019). One of his first acts in office was to send a letter demanding that the current King of Spain and the Pope should apologize for colonialism. The Government of Spain rejected the idea, pointed out that one ancestral line in AMLO's own background came from Spain, and accused Mexico of a transhistorical error (judging former acts by today's standards). The Vatican issued a statement saying it had already apologized (ibid.). There appears to be little that is off-limits in AMLO's attempts to recover cultural patrimony and to vindicate Mexican indigenous honor, stretching recuperative claims back to precolonial times. Like Trump, he hews close to a specific and (to his political base) nostalgic version of a national historical narrative and tries to recapture lost glory. In Trump's case, "make America great again" results in tariffs, racism, and xenophobia, while in AMLO's, restoring Mexican national pride results in the revalorization of indigeneity, rurality, and the Mexican common folk.

While campaigning for the presidency, AMLO rebuked EPN for not standing up to Trump, and published a short tome by the title of *Oye, Trump* (López Obrador 2017). Translated as "Listen Up, Trump," the book is a collection of Mexican campaign trail speeches in which AMLO vociferously defended the human rights of migrants, called Trump erratic and arrogant, and compared Trump's talk of migrants to the way Nazis talked about Jews. AMLO's post-election tone toward Trump has calmed down considerably, and now instead of plain-spoken self-righteous opposition, there is an avoidance of conflict-talk and public skirmishes. In an early June 2019 spat over tariffs on products crossing the Mexican border, AMLO explained himself a little bit further by writing Trump a letter, articulating another one of the narratives of masculinity: "Remember that I do not lack bravery, that I am not a coward nor timid, but rather I act on my principles" (López Obrador 2019). What should be remarkable to the reader is that Trump's talk of tariffs and migration elicits AMLO's defensive reaction over masculine qualities such as bravery and cowardice. AMLO's strategy, especially in his *Oye, Trump* book, is to appeal to American history and to the American people directly, reminding them of the closer relationship between the two countries in decades past. As I show in other work (Mendoza-Denton 2017), the historical facts of Mexican oppression are never far from Mexican leaders' or the public's minds. In his book of speeches, AMLO takes the position that one can dialogue directly with the American people, but not with Trump.

18.5   Jair Bolsonaro: The Military Evangelical Homophobe

Jair Messias Bolsonaro, president of Brazil, is the contrasting case to Mexico's AMLO, in that his stance is to plainly admire and vociferously parrot Trump's economic, domestic, and foreign policies, largely mirroring him in his White ethnonationalism. Bolsonaro himself is a military man, cut from a different cloth than either businessman-and-television-star Trump or the Mexican career politicians EPN, Fox, and AMLO. Upon entering Bolsonaro's presidential office, the only presidential portraits on the wall are not those of recent figures Dilma Rousseff or the leftists Lula or Cardoso, but of ARENA party dictators who presided during the murderous military dictatorship (from 1964 to 1985), during which thousands of Brazilians from the political opposition were imprisoned, tortured, or killed. Bolsonaro has long supported torture and has said that the (past) dictatorship's only mistake was that they only tortured but did not kill more of their opponents (Exame 2018, Muñoz Bata 2018).

The policy and stylistic parallels between Bolsonaro and Trump are plentiful, and yet Bolsonaro goes even further in many respects. His campaign was fueled almost entirely by outrageous Twitter statements, since he refused to participate in interviews or debates, claiming that both the media and the judiciary were conspiring against him and vowing that he would not accept any vote that showed him to have lost. Bolsonaro was actually trailing in the polls, and a decisive factor in his electoral win is thought to have been the combination of the support from the evangelical religious lobby and the pretrial imprisonment of his political rivals while they faced corruption charges. Bolsonaro has made many misogynistic, anti-indigenous, anti-black statements in the past, and declared himself to be proudly homophobic, proclaiming that he would rather his son die in a car accident than be gay (Exame 2018), and saying that he had no concern for either of his sons coming home with a black lover because they had been "properly raised," away from a "promiscuous environment" (ibid.). Bolsonaro's support for guns is instrumental in his efforts to wrest land and other capital from Indigenous and Afro-descendant people in Brazil. Before his election, he is quoted as saying, "You can be sure that if I get there [as elected President of Brazil,] there will be no money for NGOs. If it's up to me, every citizen will have a firearm in the house. There will not be a centimeter demarcated for Indigenous reservations or *Quilombolas* [communities of black slave descendants]" (Dolzan 2017). Bolsonaro's right-wing White militarism includes threatening expropriation of indigenous Amazonian land, which would result in its environmentally catastrophic exploitation by logging companies.

In an interview with *Fox News* on the occasion of his United States state visit, Bolsonaro further aligned with Trump, echoing almost word-for-word the text of Trump's campaign speeches: "The vast majority of potential immigrants to the United States do not have good intentions, do not intend to do good to the American people ... we agree with President's Trump's ideas of having the wall" (Shear and Haberman 2019). Later in a joint appearance, Trump stood by, pleasantly surprised, while Bolsonaro declared that he intended to stand with Trump against "fake news" and "gender ideology" (ibid.).

The fixation on countering "gender ideology," another commonality with Trump, has led Bolsonaro into his fair share of outrageous statements about women, some in defense of his two politician sons, one of whom was accused by a former lover of having a small penis (*micropênis*). It seems that as with Trump, genitalia in general and specifically penile size are sources of presidential anxiety (see Cohn, this volume). Bolsonaro defended his son vociferously against the former lover's accusations, and has also referenced penises in other official capacities. He tweeted an X-rated video during carnival and wondered about "golden showers" (Jornal o Globo 2019). He has also worried (on Twitter, during the G20 meetings) about men's public health: specifically, the importance of penile hygiene, lest one's unhealthy member require amputation (Correio da Manhã 2019). This last public service announcement stands in stark contrast to Bolsonaro's formal opposition to the distribution of a welfare ministry pamphlet for adolescent women's health, which shows a medical diagram of the female anatomy (Diário do Centro do Mundo 2019a). While Bolsonaro uses "propriety" and evangelical religion to attack LGBTQ+ Brazilians and women's reproductive health, this does not prevent him from anxiously asking other men for "straight hugs," or from being filmed, shortly after the election and during an interview, with a Japanese tourist in transit at the airport, asking if this tourist was "so little down there," while making a pincer gesture. Video of the gesture itself was used by the *Globo* newspaper against Bolsonaro later when discussing his disastrous economic numbers. His constant references to genitalia have been discussed by psychiatrists in the national press (Diário do Centro do Mundo 2019b).

18.6   Conclusion: Kingdom Come

In 2020, the heads of state of Brazil, Mexico, and the United States together govern more than 650 million people. Although they span the full spectrum from the right (Trump and Bolsonaro) to the left (AMLO), they can all be described as populist messianic autocrats.

In his book *When Words Trump Politics*, Adam Hodges (2019: 20) draws on the notion of a triadic populism that not only advocates for the common people and against the elite, but also accuses the elite of coddling a third group that must be vanquished in order for the state to be successful. In Bolsonaro's case, the targeted groups are minorities, women, and homosexuals. Meanwhile, Trump rails against the left, immigrants, people of color, and women he cannot manipulate. And although it is too early to tell with AMLO, many fear that his target are the *Fifís*, or the bourgeois class of primarily Euro-descent Mexicans against which he continually defines himself (they are nicknamed after the purported name of their fancy dogs).

Every single one of these leaders operates under the diverse narratives of political masculinities in their own societies, each with its own glocal logics and histories of symbolism, repression, and conquest (van Dijk 2005). Each political narrative makes space for a singular messianic autocrat at the top; one who will deliver the people from their current predicament. Each autocrat delusionally deems himself uniquely qualified if not destined for this position, and indeed all claim to be the only option for such deliverance. Finally, each hopes to lead his people to a legendary past, be it a proletarian revolution, a dictatorship, or a time when the country was "great." Mexico's AMLO places himself as the next in line to Benito Juárez, the original president of the

Mexican Revolution (Diario Crónica 2019). Bolsonaro chose to hold up a bible and a book by Churchill in his first televised address (Phillips 2018). And Trump? When asked whether there were people he looked up to from the past, Trump in his infinite self-regard replied that he didn't like the concept of heroes: "Natural ability," he continued, "to me, is much more important than experience" (McGregor 2017).

References

Almaguer, Tomás. 1993. "Chicano Men: A Cartography of Homosexual Identity and Behavior." In *The Lesbian and Gay Studies Reader*, edited by Henry Abelove, Michele Barale, and David M. Halperin, pp. 255–73 Routledge.

Baker, Peter, and Eric Schmitt. 2019. "The 'Whimpering' Terrorist Only Trump Seems to Have Heard." *The New York Times*, November 1, 2019. https://nyti.ms/349Jl2c.

Beltrán del Río, Pascal. 2017. "Milagroso Trump." *Excelsior*, January 24, 2017. https://bit.ly/2kXf8ml.

Bowden, John. 2019. "Conway's Husband: 'Banana Republic' if Trump Got His Wish to Go After Investigators." *Thehill.com*, March 8, 2019. https://tinyurl.com/y6hw2zrb.

Chafe, Wallace. 1998. "Things We Can Learn from Repeated Tellings of the Same Experience." *Narrative Inquiry* 8, no. 2: 269–85.

Connell, R. W. 2016. "Masculinity Politics on a World Scale." In *Women in Culture: An Intersectional Anthology for Gender and Women's Studies*, edited by Bonnie Kime Scott, Susan E. Cayleff, Anne Donadey, and Irene Lara, pp. 234–38. Wiley-Blackwell.

Correio da Manhã. 2019. "Bolsonaro preocupado com o número de amputações de pénis no Brasil." *CMJornal.pt*, April 26, 2019. https://tinyurl.com/s8sm7m3.

The Daily Show. 2018. "Trump's Mythical Crying Man Yule Log." Accessed November 20, 2019. https://tinyurl.com/txro6wx.

DeBonis, Mike. 2018. "'It's a manhood thing for him': Pelosi Comments on the President and His Wall (Nancy Pelosi)." *The Washington Post*, December 11, 2018. https://wapo.st/2mSbH1d.

Diario Crónica. 2019. "Etiqueta: Andrés Manuel López Obrador." Accessed December 1, 2019. https://tinyurl.com/u9zzy64.

Diário do Centro do Mundo. 2019a. "Bolsonaro ataca governo Dilma em live de Facebook por caderneta de saúde da adolescente." *diariodocentrodomundo.com.br*, March 7, 2019. https://tinyurl.com/tne6evy.

2019b. "A obsessão fálica de Bolsonaro: especialistas comentam." *diariodocentrodomundo.com.br*, June 2, 2019. https://tinyurl.com/tq9eece.

Dolzan, Marcio. 2017. "'Não podemos abrir as portas para todo mundo,' diz Bolsonaro em palestra na Hebraica." *Política*, April 3, 2017. https://bit.ly/2SfDt2 C.

Duranti, Alessandro. 1994. *From Grammar to Politics: Linguistic Anthropology in a Western Samoan Village*. University of California Press.

Exame. 2018. "Frases pôlemicas do candidato Jair Bolsonaro." *Exame*, September 24, 2018. https://exame.abril.com.br/brasil/frases-polemicas-do-candidato-jair-bolsonaro/.

Fenno, Richard. 1978. *Home Style: House Members in their Districts*. Little, Brown.
Graham, David A. 2019. "No One Listens to The President." *The Atlantic*, April 19, 2019. https://bit.ly/2ma8mKH.
Greenwood, Max. 2018. "Trump Lavishes Kim with Compliments after Historic Summit." *Thehill.com*, June 16, 2018, https://tinyurl.com/s9dth4z.
Gutmann, Matthew C. 1996. *The Meanings of Macho: Being a Man in Mexico City*. University of California Press.
Hill, Jane H. 2008. *The Everyday Language of White Racism*. Wiley-Blackwell.
Hodges, Adam. 2019. *When Words Trump Politics: Resisting a Hostile Regime of Language*. Stanford University Press.
Hooper, Charlotte. 1998. "Masculinist Practices and Gender Politics: The Operation of Multiple Masculinities in International Relations." In *The "Man" Question in International Relations*, edited by Marysia Zalewski and Jane Parpart, pp. 28–53, Westview Press.
Jornal o Globo. 2019. "Tweet de Bolsonaro com 'golden shower' em carnaval repercute no mundo." *Globo.com*, March 6, 2019. www.youtube.com/watch?v=OJ1hxr7cRJk.
Kaczynski, Andrew, Chris Massie, and Nathan McDermott. 2017. "80 Times Trump Talked about Putin." *CNN* news article, March 2017. https://tinyurl.com/y7dqsacj.
Labov, William and Joshua Waletzky. 1967. "Narrative Analysis." In *Essays on the Verbal and Visual Arts*, edited by June Helm, pp. 12–44, University of Washington Press.
López Obrador, Andrés Manuel. 2017. *Oye, Trump*. Planeta México.
     2019. "Carta al Presidente Trump." Presidential website, May 30, 2019. https://tiny url.com/y3cqjm9e.
López Segura, Jesús. 2017. "Sigue Trump humillando a México sin que Peña reaccione." Accessed January 26, 2017. https://tinyurl.com/rdlxyea.
McGregor, Jena. 2017. "Donald Trump's Revealing Answer to a Simple Question about Heroes." *The Washington Post*, January 17, 2017. https://wapo.st/2mUmDeD.
Mendoza-Denton, Norma. 2008. *Homegirls: Language and Cultural Practice among Latina Youth Gangs*. Wiley/Blackwell.
     2017. "Bad Hombres: Images of Masculinity and Historical Consciousness of U.S./ Mexico Relations in the Age of Trump." *HAU: Journal of Ethnographic Theory* 7, no. 1: 423–32.
Muñoz Bata, Sergio. 2018. "Aterradora decisión en Brasil." *Letras Libres*, October 15, 2018. www.letraslibres.com/mexico/politica/aterradora-decision-en-brasil.
Nelson, Louis. 2017. "Trump Praises Duterte for 'Unbelievable Job' Cracking Down on Drugs in the Philippines." *Politico.com*, May 24, 2017, https://tinyurl.com/w93b9qs.
Norrick, Neal R. 1998. "Retelling Again." *Narrative Inquiry* 8, no. 2: 373–78.
Núñez Noriega, Guillermo. 1999. *Sexo entre varones: poder y resistencia en el campo sexual*. Miguel Ángel Porrúa.
Ochs, Elinor. 1992. "Indexing Gender." In *Rethinking Context: Language as an Interactive Phenomenon*, edited by Alessandro Duranti and Charles Goodwin, pp. 335–38. Cambridge University Press.
Oppenheimer, Andrés. 2016. "Trump, A Latin American Caudillo?" *The Miami Herald* Oppenheimer Report Blog, February 13, 2016. https://tinyurl.com/sj5b4b8.

Palma, Milagros. 1990. "Malinche, el malinchismo o el lado femenino de la sociedad mestiza." *Simbólica de la feminidad*, pp. 13–39. Ediciones Abya-Yala.

Patterson, Molly, and Kristen Monroe. 2003. "Narrative in Political Science." *Annual Review of Political Science* 1: 315–31.

Phillips, Tom. 2018. "Jair Bolsonaro Denies That He Is a Fascist and Paints Himself as a Brazilian Churchill." *Theguardian.com*, October 30, 2018. https://tinyurl.com/yapmvcpu.

Polletta, Francesca. 2006. *It Was Like a Fever: Storytelling in Protest and Politics*. University of Chicago Press.

Reid, Michael. 2016. "The Unspeakable and the Inexplicable: Why Did Enrique Peña Nieto Invite Donald Trump to Visit Mexico?" *The Economist*, September 1, 2016. https://econ.st/2m7BJgy.

Shear, Michael, and Maggie Haberman. 2019. "For Trump, Brazil's President Is Like Looking in the Mirror." *The New York Times*, March 19, 2019. https://tinyurl.com/y2x39u5x.

Tharoor, Ishaan. 2017. "Trump is the U.S.'s first Latin American President." *The Washington Post*, January 25, 2017. https://tinyurl.com/so34j8w.

Trump, Donald (@realDonaldTrump). 2018. "Crazy Joe Biden is Trying to Go Down Hard and Fast." Twitter, March 22, 2018. https://tinyurl.com/rs7xt2p.

2019. Image of Trump's head photoshopped onto Rocky Balboa's body. Twitter, November 27, 2019. https://tinyurl.com/vg7mbxv.

van Dijk, Teun Adrianus. 2005. *Racism and Discourse in Spain and Latin America*. John Benjamins Publishing.

The Washington Post. 2019. "All the People Who Trump Says Cry around Him." Video posted February 13, 2019. www.youtube.com/watch?v=iAv8JPNZ-P8.

White House. 2019a. "Remarks by President Trump and President Erdoğan of Turkey Before Bilateral Meeting." White House Briefing, November 13, 2019. https://tinyurl.com/sycqhp9.

2019b. "Remarks by President Trump on the Death of ISIS leader Abu Bakr Al-Baghdadi." White House Briefing, October 27, 2019. https://tinyurl.com/sl8bbv8.

19 Rejoinders from the Shithole

Quentin Williams

On the campaign trail in 2016, Donald Trump proposed that he "knows words" and has "the best words" (Trump 2017a). In early January 2018, he used these "best words" to denigrate immigrants from Haiti and African countries. Following a bipartisan proposal by Democratic Senator Dick Durbin that would protect thousands of young immigrants from deportation and include 1.6 billion dollars for Trump's border wall, Trump convened a meeting in the Oval Office to discuss immigration policy. Durbin, speaking later to reporters, recounted Trump's lament: the US is accepting immigrants from "shithole" countries in Africa. Trump also railed against immigrants from El Salvador, Guatemala, and Haiti who leave their countries as a result of natural disasters. In particular, Trump fumed that Haitians require temporary protected status, shooting down Durbin's proposal: "We don't need more Haitians. Put me down for wanting more Europeans to come to this country," he added. "Why don't we get more people from Norway?" (Kirby 2018).

In the aftermath of his comments, the outrage from beyond the shores of the US came hard and fast: condemnation from the UN, the Holy See, Uganda, Botswana, the African Union (AU), and the President of El Salvador. US Embassy officials were summoned by far-flung governments to explain Trump's "shithole" remark. Across social media platforms, Trump's comments were condemned as racist.

But Trump himself denied Durbin's account of his words, while aides and supporters soon came to his defense. Unsurprisingly, others present in the Oval Office denied Trump used "vulgar language," but neither could they confirm whether he said the word at all. This is a familiar strategy that we have come to expect from supporters of the US president and the GOP (Grand Old Party). Homeland Security secretary Kirstjen Nielsen, for instance, told a Senate Judiciary Committee: "I did not hear that word [shithole] used," going on to say, "The conversation was very impassioned. I don't dispute that the president was using tough language. Others in the room were also using tough language." Though she could not recall him saying "shithole," she said, he may have used the word "shithouse" (Kim 2018). Baffled by this response? Well, so were others.

The world has long recognized that Trump frequently uses his "best words" to mis-manage his language. He gives incoherent speeches and drifts off mid-tweet, typing non-words such as the now-infamous "covfefe" (Andrews 2017). He coins neologisms such as "bigly" (ignoring the rules of degrees of comparison) and mispronounces basic terms, such as "yuge" (huge). He pointlessly repeats words and phrases ("many, many"), and blunders the names of political groups ("Nazzies" instead of Nazis). But for citizens from Haiti, Africa, the Global South, or indeed anyone not from the Aryan race, Trump's "shithole" utterance was the latest in a long list of racial profanity and insults. It confirmed to us that Donald Trump has lost control of his "best words."

In this chapter, I start by analyzing some of the ideological and linguistic mechanisms by which Trump divulges his racism. I draw on the work of anthropologist Mary Douglas (1966, 1968) to suggest that with his "shithole" language, Trump attempts to frame the Global South as a site of degeneracy, dirt, and matter out of place; essentially, as a form of pollution. In so doing, he encourages paranoid xenophobia of an historically familiar sort. I also analyze some of Trump's attempts to deflect charges of racism, drawing on a theoretical framework by sociologist Edward Bonilla-Silva (2002, 2006), who described several discursive strategies Whites tend to use to defend what he terms "color-blind racism." In the final section, I document how media and institutions in Southern Africa responded to Trump's racist language as they employed discursive strategies of parody, critique, and egalitarianism to encourage non-racialism. By "non-racialism" I do not mean "color-blindness," in the sense that White speakers often proclaim "I don't see color" or "I don't believe in race" as a way to deny the legacy and history of racism. Non-racialism is acutely aware of racial inequities, past and present. As a term taken up by the Civil Rights Movement and in the Brown versus Board of Education decision, it is a specific brand of anti-racism that denotes a utopic society – a not-yet future; a future society without racists. In their rejoinders to Donald Trump, these non-racialist advocates attempt to compensate for his verbal injuries while recognizing the equality and dignity of people throughout the world.

19.1   Trump, Race, and "Pollution"

Trump is surely one of the "whitest" presidents the nation has ever seen, aggressively embodying the qualities of White privilege, nativism, and bigotry (Coates 2017: 341). But his prejudices did not appear suddenly; in fact, they began decades before his political ascendancy, when he was first embroiled in racist discourses with regards to housing practices and an array of public partisan issues. Early in his career in real estate, for instance, he made a concerted effort not to rent apartments to Black and Puerto Rican tenants – a pattern so egregious that in 1973, the Civil Rights Division filed a lawsuit against Trump and his father Fred Trump (Gerstein 2017). He made racist remarks about the Central Park five, a group of young black and brown men unjustly charged with raping and assaulting a white woman in 1989. Trump took out a full-page newspaper ad calling for their execution, telling Larry King, "Maybe hate is what we need" (Segura 2016). Even after the five were exonerated by DNA evidence and compensated by the city of New York, Trump never walked back his comments (Cobb 2019). More recently, he led the Birtherism crusade against President Barack Obama, insisting that Obama was born outside of the United States and thus an illegitimate leader – an unfounded rumor that has given traction to the White supremacist right for years. Since taking office, Trump's list of bigoted policy maneuvers and statements has grown too long to list. But all of this furnishes the clear ideological backdrop for Trump's use of the word "shit-hole." At one level, the word marks a loss of control, constituting a shocking verbal boundary violation for the person in the highest American political office. But at another level it is no accidental slip; rather, it is a coherent expression of Trump's systematic discrimination against minorities and vulnerable people.

The word also draws on a widespread discursive pattern that uses the imagery of pollution to subordinate social groups. Anthropologists have treated pollution as a socially important concept since the 1966 publication of Mary Douglas' book *Purity and Danger*. Douglas opened her argument by exploring those social moments when the profane invades the sacred. Religious institu-tions have historically tried to govern and control these boundaries, protecting the sacred from the profane by drawing discursive and ritualistic lines between purity and its negative twin, impurity. Breaches of the sacred tend to be construed as matter out of place; "dirty" in a deep sense that goes beyond mere physical grime. But in the secular world, too, the things we consider polluted or "dirty" are, Douglas argues, "a by-product of a systematic ordering and classification of matter, in so far as ordering involves rejecting appropriate elements" (Douglas 1966: 34–35). One of Douglas' fundamental insights, then, was that any given notion of pollution or dirtiness emerges from an attempt to establish social order. Imagery of dirt or pollution denotes the "violation" of "a system of values" (Douglas 1968: 338), a challenge to a dominant (or pre-ferred) social scheme.

Across many societies, then, notions of pollution are used to uphold not only religious orders, but also secular bigotry. Discourse about pollution has historically saturated White ideas about racial difference, for instance, fur-nishing a quasi-natural rationalization of brutal hierarchical orders such as slavery, colonialism, and apartheid, in which those with power have a vested interest in keeping others down. Trump's Oval Office allusion to "shithole" nations drew on this historically venerable conceptual structure. When he added he wanted more "people from Norway," it is surely not an accident that his preferred demographic hails from one of the northernmost and whitest societies he could imagine, setting up a racial and geographic foil, as well as an economic one. The Norwegians, in his schema, are pristine and privileged and therefore desirable as immigrants; those from "shithole" nations in the Global South represent a dangerous and almost sub-human population. Never mind that the privilege of Europe and struggles of the Global South are products of colonialism, capitalism, and American foreign policy. For Trump, the differences simply exist as a binary opposition: pure versus impure.

A further insight from Mary Douglas is that imagined pollution is often considered metaphysically contaminating, a stigma that often drives strong, censorious reactions. The prospect of danger or defilement is just what Trump plays on as he hypes his base's anxiety about immigration. His discourse stokes the fear: those entering from Middle Eastern nations are potentially dangerous terrorists; Latinx immigrants from Mexico are "rapists," "criminals," and "animals" (see Santa Ana et al., this volume); and those from sub-Saharan Africa (and other points southern) bring the contamination of the toilets they supposedly come from. Yet in spite of his sweeping, irrational distortions, Trump denies that he is a racist.

19.2   Denial, Equivocation, and Projection: Trump's "Color-Blind" Racism

In this section, I use a micro-linguistic approach to examine some of Trump's other discourse about race, drawing primarily on the framework of Eduardo Bonilla-Silva (2002, 2006). Bonilla-Silva has drawn attention to how White Americans in recent decades have tended to play down the significance of race as a way of distancing themselves from racism, yet still manage to convey racialized opinions. These problematic "color-blind" strategies often attempt to explain racial inequality in terms of other differences. While Bonilla-Silva enumerates several stylistic verbal features associated with color-blind racism, I focus on three in particular: denial, equivocation, and racist projection. I then draw briefly on a theoretical framework developed by linguistic anthropologist Jane Hill (2008) to analyze a complement to these; namely, Trump's apparent indifference to audiences from Africa.

An exceedingly common rhetorical gambit among Whites in the post-civil rights era, says Bonilla-Silva, is pronouncements such as "I'm not a racist," which often appear as "discursive buffers" just before or after statements that might indeed be interpreted as racist (2006: 57). Trump used this stylistic move in the wake of his "shithole" remark. When confronted by a press pool with the reports from the Oval Office, Trump immediately contradicted his critics: "No. No. I am not racist. I am the least racist person you have ever interviewed. That I can tell you" (Brito 2018). He further expounded on Twitter: "Never said anything derogatory about Haitians other than Haiti is, obviously, a very poor and troubled country. Never said 'take them out.' Made up by Dems. I have a wonderful relationship with Haitians. Probably should record future meetings – unfortunately, no trust!" (Donald Trump on Twitter, January 12, 2018). Denial of racism has a long pattern in Trump's discourse. The *Washington Post* compiled a list of six times since 2015 that he explicitly denied being racist or bigoted (Scott 2018). He told Barbara Walters he was "probably the least [bigoted] person you've ever met," and parroted himself to *CNN*'s Don Lemon, saying: "I am the least racist person that you have ever met" (ibid.). When asked in 2016 by a *New York Post* reporter whether his remarks on Mexicans and Muslims reflected racism, Trump replied, "I am not a racist; in fact, I'm the least racist person you've ever encountered" (ibid.). The iterations go on. With his serial denials, Trump is clearly invested in what Bonilla-Silva calls the "anything but race" explanation for his recurrent denigration of people of color.

A second common discursive strategy in color-blind racism is equivocation: "Stating racial views without opening yourself to the charge of racism [by] apparently taking all sides on an issue" (Bonilla-Silva 2002: 50). Some speakers, for instance, use the formulation, "Yes and no, but . . ." to imply they don't wish to take sides, while simultaneously taking an underlying stand on a controversial racial subject. Trump used precisely this style in his infamous remarks after the Charlottesville "Unite the Right" rally in August 2017. The rally had been marked by conflict between White supremacist organizers and protesters, with one protester dying after being brutally rammed by a supremacist's car. Trump's statement afterward was famously equivocal; as journalists pressed him to condemn the actions and ideologies of the rally participants, he said: "I watched [the videos] very closely – much more closely than you people watched it. And you have – you had a group on one side that was bad, and you had a group on the other side that was also very violent" (Trump 2017b). Later in the same press conference, he added, "You had some very bad people in that [Neo-Nazi] group, but you also had people that were very fine people, on both sides" (Holan 2019). The "very fine people, on both sides" remark was widely perceived by his critics as a failure to unequivocally condemn the murderous bigotry of Nazis, and hence as tacit approval of their White nationalism.

A third rhetorical technique of color-blind racism, says Bonilla-Silva, is racial projection, in which a speaker reverses the charge of racism to pin it on a person of color and avoid responsibility themselves. Trump is only too happy to deny that he himself is racist, but quick to lob the charge at others. Consider the following exchange from a November 2018 White House news conference, in which Trump exchanges words with Haitian-American journalist Yamiche Alcindor (PBS NewsHour 2018; video excerpt starts at the beginning).[1]

ALCINDOR: hi Mr. President
            Yamiche Alcindor with PBS NewsHour
            um, on the campaign trail you called yourself a nationalist
            some people saw that as emboldening White nationalists
            now people are [also saying that the Pres-]
TRUMP: [I don't know why you would say that]
            that's such a ra:cist question-
ALCINDOR: there's some people that say [that]=
TRUMP: [no]
ALCINDOR: =now the Republican party is seen as supporting White
            nationalists [because of your rhetoric-]
TRUMP: [oh I don't believe that]
            I don't believe it=
ALCINDOR: =what do you make of that
TRUMP: I don't believe that
            I don't believe –
            I dunno, why do I have my highest poll numbers EVER with African
            Americans
            why do I have among the highest poll numbers
            WITH African Americans
            I mean why do I have my highest poll numbers-
            that's such a RACIST question
            honestly?
            I mean I know you have it written down and you're going to tell me-
            let me you- that's a racist (.) question.
ALCINDOR: um,
            Mr. President I'm gonna ask=
TRUMP: =I love that- you know what the word is?
            I love our country (.)
            I do
            you call – you have nationalists,
            you have globalists.
            I also love the world
            and I don't mind helping the world
            but we have to straighten out our country first
            we have a lot of problems
ALCINDOR: and mis-=
TRUMP: =excuse me
            but to say that
            what you said is so insulting to me.
            it's a very terrible thing that you said-

Trump not only denies that he is a nationalist (which, in this context, is code for "White nationalist"), but also projects racism onto Alcindor herself. Even though Alcindor seeks clarity on Trump's self-ascription and its implications, furthermore, Trump suggests that she look at his rising poll numbers among African Americans, as if such a thing would furnish evidence of his lack of racism. (For the record, Trump garnered 8 percent of the African American vote in the 2016 election; there's been almost nowhere to go but up.) Claiming that "I love the world and I don't mind helping the world" may even be Trump's way of implying he embraces people of all races, including those locales numerically dominated by non-Whites. When he adds, "We have to straighten out our country first," his justification is intended to sound responsible rather than racist – taking us back to the "anything but race" strategy of color-blind racism.

But this putatively world-loving man has some difficulty with his geography, and the difficulty can be traced to his racial attitudes. Take, for example, what some have cheekily referred to as "Nambia-gate." In Southern Africa, we all saw it and we replayed it; Trump twice said "Nambia" and not "Namibia" when he addressed leaders from Africa during a lunch he hosted in New York on September 20, 2017. "I'm greatly honored to host this lunch," Trump opened, "To be joined the Leaders of Cote d'Ivoire, Ethiopia, Ghana, Guinea, Nambia, Nigeria, Senegal, Uganda, and South Africa" (The Washington Post 2017). About three minutes later, he added: "Nambia's health system is increasingly self-sufficient." Jane Hill (2008) has written about a related dynamic in Anglo-American mispronunciations of Spanish. According to Hill, Whites in the USA often engage in a "mock" variety of Spanish, which sometimes involves hyper-anglicization and clumsy spelling or pronunciation. Street and subdivision names in Arizona, for instance, are often distorted from the original Spanish, reflecting a disregard for the language's integrity and, Hill argues, the dignity of the people who speak it as well. Trump's "Nambia" gaffe seems to reflect, at minimum, his ignorance (assuming the gaffe was not conscious) and his disregard for the importance of African nations. For him to have made the error twice before a largely African live audience suggests an insulting level of indifference.

19.3   Non-Racial Linguistic Clap-Backs: Southern African Media and Institutions Respond

Southern African media and institutions have responded with both mockery and objection to Trump's defilement and disrespect, attempting to reclaim a sense of dignity while insinuating that if anyone in these exchanges is a polluter, it's Trump himself. Sometimes, parody is a useful strategy for getting these concepts across. Not long after Trump's "Nambia" blunder, for instance, a Namibian based tourism group, Gondwana Collection, created a video entitled "Trump – 'S**thole Countries' – shithole statement by NAMIBIA" (words that are immediately followed by two poop emojis; EES 2018). The video opens with images of the American flag, Statue of Liberty, and American tourists, before panning across numerous images of Namibia's beautiful landmarks, landscapes, and wildlife. In a parodic version of Trump's voice, the narrator voices over:

Good morning Trump America [sic]. If ever you wanted to leave your so beautiful and perfect country, and come to real shithole country in Africa, we would like to invite you to come to shithole Namibia. One of the best shithole countries out there. No really, we actually have a beautiful underground lake that even looks just like a shithole – Lake Oshikoto. Actually, Namibia is such a shithole country that we converted about forty-two percent of it into various conservation areas where wild shithole animals can roam freely. Not only is our country a shithole place, even our elephants are highly qualified to dump large amounts of shit everywhere ((*here, the image briefly changes over to an animated clay lump of shit with Trumpish hair, eyebrows, and pursed open mouth at a lectern, before returning to beautiful landscapes*)) in our wide-open shithole country. Our desert is such a shithole of a place, believe me, that there hasn't been any proper rain in the last couple of million years, which makes it the oldest shithole desert in the world. But thanks to you not caring about global warming, this could soon end. And we can get lots of rain, while the rest of the shithole countries out there burn or freeze off completely. It is really tough out here, but shithole Nambia has over 300 days of sunshine and our lodges are situated in such a way that one has the perfect view over this beautiful shithole, even while taking a shit. So, you're more than welcome to visit Africa's number one shithole country, known to your president as ((*camera cuts to the actual video of Trump's address, and his own voice*)) "Nambia." (EES 2018)

The parodied voice mocks Trump's racist language as part of an elaborate comedic payback. "Trump" sounds absurd as the pristine scenes from Namibia glaringly contradict Trump's charge that African nations are polluting. The tables are turned, too, as the word "shithole" is ironically used to refer to stunningly beautiful (instead of ugly) places, reasserting that Namibia (and one could even extrapolate this to Africa writ large) is a place that matters rather than being matter out of place. There's just one moment in the video that keys a subterranean message about the meaning of the word "shit"; namely, that moment when a clay Trump-as-lump-of-shit appears. Trump himself, it seems, is the real polluter, by virtue of his offensive words, rather than his race, and his absurd "Nambia" pronunciation furnishes the final punchline of the piece. The video won acclaim from within and outside of Namibia, with dozens of comments applauding its message. Its non-racialized images of Namibia help recuperate a dignified image of the country, hard won over the decades since colonialism.

Political figures and journalists, too, came to the defense of Africa's pride and importance. When news first broke about Trump's "shithole" insult, the media in Southern Africa first under-reported the event, but the relevance of the story intensified, and in the growing outrage, a diplomatic crisis began to brew. South African scholars David Monyane and Bhaso Ndzendze (2018) penned an opinion piece for *The Independent Online* (IOL) news that described Trump's shithole comments as "a new low: one which will leave a number of ambassadors with a lot of cleaning-up to do." They go on: "For President Trump to label

Africa, along with other developing regions, as 'shitholes,' is to betray a glaring ignorance of Africa and its overwhelming importance to America's strategic objectives, global soft power and economic partner[ships]." This piece accomplishes two things. First, it foregrounds the recognition fundamental to non-racial frameworks, reasserting Africa's economic and political importance by way of such words as "strategic," "global power," and "partner." Second, it implies (like the parodic video from Namibia) that Trump himself is the polluting one. After all, his verbal diarrhea has left others holding the mop.

Around the same time, there was a flurry of diplomatic movement against Trump's words coming out of South Africa and beyond. South Africa's African National Congress (ANC) government "demarched" the US embassy representative – in other words, took a formal political step to address diplomatic relations – and demanded an explanation for Trump's "shithole" remark. ANC spokesperson Clayson Monyela affirmed the maneuver, underscoring that relations between the USA and South Africa should "be based on mutual respect and understanding" (News24 Wire 2018). Meanwhile, ANC deputy secretary general Jessie Duarte slammed Trump's comments, saying that although African countries have their problems, "We would not deign to make comments as derogatory about any country facing difficulties" (Gerber 2018). A representative from the official opposition party in South Africa, the Democratic Alliance (DA), tweeted that Trump's comments had been "abhorrent," and that he holds "a patronizing view of Africa and promotes a racist agenda. Africa/US relations will take strain from this, with a leader who has failed to reconcile humanity. The hatred of Obama's roots now extends to an entire continent" (Byran 2018). Meanwhile, the AU released a stern press statement expressing "infuriation, disappointment, and outrage" (ibid.). Taking the moral high ground, the AU suggested Trump's administration had indulged in a "huge misunderstanding of the African continent and its people." His remark, they added, was a "dishonor" to the supposedly defining American values of diversity and human dignity. Though the institution still values the "strategic partnership" of the US, it demanded "an apology to not only to the Africans but to all people of African descent around the globe" (African Union Commission 2018).

In all of these responses, we note several verbal strategies that attempt to reclaim the pride of Africa. Some try to level the playing field by cutting Trump down to size, decrying his racism, and pointing out the ignorance implicit in his "huge misunderstanding." Several boomerang the charge of being polluting right back at him, though again, notice that Trump is framed as polluting not on grounds of race, but on grounds that his dirty, messy insult constitutes matter- (or word-)-out-of-place. This maneuver establishes African politicians, intellectuals, and professionals as qualified to put things to rights and indeed to purify in the wake of a contaminating American president. Other strategies we have just seen emphasize the importance of inclusiveness, underscoring the utopian ideals of mutual respect and equality. And all demand recognition of Africa's strategic, global importance, recovering it from the margins Trump relegated it to. Finally, it's worth noting that all of these rejoinders are coded in a high form of English, reaffirming the authors' globally salient intellectual credentials and status. If Trump attempts to frame sub-Saharan African nations as polluted and contaminating, this language restores their dignity and indeed their importance, enhancing the agency and role of Africa on a global stage.

19.4   Conclusion

Since candidate Trump was first introduced to the media, his "best words" have augmented global discourses of racism, to the point of normalizing them for some. From the Philippines to Brazil, Trumpian racist language has given strongman politicians carte blanche to spread the dirt of social division, nativism, protectionism, White supremacy, and ethnonationalism. Trump's daily archive of racist exhortations on Twitter and television require that we suggest a global language strategy in response. The strategies we see above from Southern Africa furnish one example of how to challenge the spread of Trumpian racist language. First, we need to recognize and call out the ideology and strategy implicit in even seemingly throwaway profanity like Trump's "shithole." Such language is not only messy but also strategic and historically archaic, stoking deep anxieties about pollution and whipping up fear against immigrants. Second, we need to recognize Trump's strategies of denial as part of a wider pattern of White deflection and naïve color-blindness, as Bonilla-Silva reminds us, rather than taking anything at face value. Finally, Southern African institutions have offered us a couple of maneuvers: parodic and/or dignified responses. Parody comes from a place of agency, and it's particularly good for showing up hypocrisy. And the dignified responses shown by so many in South Africa provide reminders the Global South is of strategic importance, deflecting the racist temptation to key people as racially "other," as nothing, as invisible, and as insignificant. Calls to repair through apology assert that such desecrations will not stand unremarked on, while reminders of equality reach toward the utopia of a non-racist world. As unfinished as racial equality is in South Africa, its approach to Trump's racist language at least teaches us this: Non-racial language might be just the right anti-pollutant to Trump's "best words."

Note

1. Transcription conventions most relevant to the analysis in this chapter include the use of CAPITALS to indicate talk spoken with special emphasis. A left bracket ([) marks the onset, and a right bracket (]) marks the offset of overlapping talk. Numbers in parentheses – for example, (1.2) – note the length of silences in seconds, while

a single period in parentheses (.) indicates a micropause of less than 0.1 seconds. A dash (-) marks the cut-off of the current sound. An equal sign (=) indicates "latching," where talk starts up in especially close temporal proximity to the end of the previous talk. Punctuation symbols are used to mark intonation changes rather than as grammatical symbols: a period indicates a falling contour; a question mark, a rising contour; and a comma, a falling-rising contour, as might be found in the midst of a list. Each line of text (without a hard return) indicates talk spoken within a single breath group.

References

African Union Commission. 2018. "African Union Mission – Washington, DC – Reacts to President Trump's 'Shithole Countries' Remarks." *AU.int* [*Union Africaine*], January 12, 2018. https://au.int/fr/node/33622.

Andrews, Travis M. 2017. "Trump Targets Negative Press 'Covfefe' in Garbled Midnight Tweet That Becomes Worldwide Joke." *The Washington Post*, May 31, 2017. https://wapo.st/2scpNbw.

Bonilla-Silva, Eduardo. 2002. "The Linguistics of Color Blind Racism: How to Talk Nasty about Blacks Without Sounding 'Racist.'" *Critical Sociology* 28, nos. 1–2: 41–64.

2006. *Racism Without Racists: Color-Blind Racism and the Persistence of Racial Inequality in America*. Rowman and Littlefield.

Brito, Christopher. 2018. "'I Am Not a Racist': Trump Responds to Reported 'Sh*thole' Comment." CBS News, January 14, 2018. https://cbsn.ws/2KznY3i.

Byran, Bob. 2018. "Union That Represents Entire Continent of Africa Blasts Trump for 'Shithole Countries' Comment." *The Business Insider*, January 12, 2018. https://bit.ly/2r2FiXT.

Coates, Ta-Nehisi. 2017. *We Were Eight Years in Power: An American Tragedy*. One World.

Cobb, Jelani. 2019. "The Central Park Five, Criminal Justice, and Donald Trump." *The New Yorker*, April 19, 2019. http://bit.ly/2pxyK2P.

Douglas, Mary. 1966. *Purity and Danger: An Analysis of Concepts of Pollution and Taboo*. Routledge and Kegan Paul.

1968. "Pollution." In *International Encyclopedia of the Social Sciences*. Vol. 7. Edited by David L. Sills, pp. 336–42. Crowell Collier and Macmillan.

EES. "Trump – 'S**thole Countries' – Shithole Statement by NAMIBIA💩💩." *EES TV* video. January 13, 2018. https://bit.ly/37X7hZy.

Gerber, Jan. 2018. "ANC, DA Take Dim View of Trump's 'Shithole' Comment." *News24*, January 12, 2018. http://bit.ly/2qjcvy5.

Gerstein, Josh. 2018. "FBI Releases Files on Apartments' Race Discrimination Probe in '70s." *Politico*, February 15, 2017. https://politi.co/357MRei.

Hill, Jane H. 2008. *The Everyday Language of White Racism*. Wiley-Blackwell.

Holan, Angie Drobnic. 2019. "In Context: Donald Trump's 'Very Fine People on Both Sides' Remarks (Transcript)." *Politifact*, April 26, 2019. http://bit.ly/2r7nlHg.

Kim, Seung Min. 2018. "Nielsen Testifies: 'I Did Not Hear' Trump Say 'Shithole.'" *Politico*, January 16, 2018. https://politi.co/35hfyFH.

276   *Quentin Williams*

Kirby, Jen. 2018. "Trump Wants Fewer Immigrants from "Shithole Countries" and More from Places like Norway." *Vox*, January 11, 2018. https://bit.ly/2DEMLyY.

Monyane, David, and Ndzendze, Bhaso. 2018. "A Glaring Ignorance Shown of Africa." *The Independent Online*, January 16, 2018. http://bit.ly/2D0gUZn.

News24 Wire. 2018. "US Embassy Must Explain 'Shithole' Comment, Says Dirco." *The Mail and Guardian*, January 14, 2018. http://bit.ly/2QF2J45.

PBS NewsHour. 2018. "Watch: 'That's Such a Racist Question,' Trump Tells News Hour's Yamiche Alcindor." *PBS NewsHour* video. November 7, 2018. https://bit.ly/2svHh7j.

Segura, Liliana. 2016. "Donald Trump's Ugly Attack on the Central Park Five Reflects All-Too-Common Attitude." *The Intercept*, October 11, 2016. http://bit.ly/32YC4Si.

Scott, Eugene. 2018. "Six Times President Trump Said He Is the Least Racist Person." *The Washington Post*, January 17, 2018. https://wapo.st/2XAonrC.

Trump, Donald (@realDonaldTrump). 2018. "Never said anything derogatory about Haitians other than Haiti is, obviously, a very poor and troubled country. Never said "take them out." Made up by Dems. I have a wonderful relationship with Haitians. Probably should record future meetings – unfortunately, no trust!" Twitter, January 12, 2018. https://bit.ly/34GHAdF.

Trump, Donald. 2017a. "Trump: 'I Have the Best Words.'" *The Washington Post* video, 0:22. April 5, 2017. https://wapo.st/33HMJkk.

   2017b. "Remarks by President Trump on Infrastructure." *WhiteHouse.gov*, August 15, 2017. https://bit.ly/33CRllJ.

The Washington Post. 2017. "Watch Trump's Full Speech to African Leaders." *The Washington Post* video. September 21, 2017. https://bit.ly/2rN1oOg.

20   Muslim Enemies, Rich Arab Friends

Aomar Boum

Under the fleeting shade of an acacia tree, Hadji Ali battled a swarm of flies that refused to leave the warmth of his white garment even as he incessantly waved the fly-whisk to keep them away. They seemed to relish the sunny beams that fell on his back. As I got closer to Hadji he ignored, for a moment, the tormenting insects and instead launched a teasing verbal crusade on the Moroccan villager who became American: "Trump will not allow you to return to the United States. We are very happy to have you back in the village after all this time." He grinned as the rest of the assembly of elderly men, youth and children laughed as hard as they could. As a newly naturalized American citizen, I intermittently travel back and forth between Los Angeles and my hometown in southeastern Morocco to visit with my aging parents and extended family. Even in this remote Saharan oasis with its limited and slow internet connection, both soccer and Trump tweets are occasional subjects of the late-afternoon conversations of elderly and young men as they wait for the prayer call. I tried to ignore the teasing and walked away after kissing the old man's hand as our local tradition still dictates. As I paced far from the group, Hadji Ali kept talking about Trump's obsession with money as he shouted, "In Trump's world not all Arabs are the same (*la'rab mashi bhal bhal*)!" A few steps away from the crowd, Jamal, a middle-aged villager, picked his teeth with a piece of wood and shouted loud enough for me to hear him: "Trump is nothing but a *samsar* (real estate broker)! When America wakes up, it might find itself derelict with no house at all because he will sell to the highest bidders: It's the Saudis who are the buyers now!"

This ethnographic vignette reflects a generally held view in the Arab world that Trump's attitude to the Middle East is based on his individual business connections, and no longer has anything to do with America's "soft power," or its traditional public and cultural diplomacy (Nye 2004, Rugh 2006, Schneider 2004, Edwards 2016). Trump's personal relationships with Middle Eastern leaders have disrupted the long-standing bureaucracy and image of American public diplomacy, especially as new policies hinge on Trump's tweets about his personal feelings and relations with Middle Eastern autocrats and leaders, and the bulk of America's foreign policy is now deputized to his son-in-law, Jared

Kushner. These subjective, interpersonal, emotionally mediated alignments and their associated stances are now front and center in US–Saudi diplomacy. By *aligning* with rich Arab Gulf states and *dis-aligning* with the larger majority of Muslims and Arabs, Trump produces a cluster of simplified binary stances evaluating "good/rich" and "bad/poor" Arabs and Muslims. The historical pattern of these stances by Trump and his predecessors has produced a unique signature in the history of American diplomacy toward the Middle East. The pattern began, as I will show, long before Trump; his participation began in earnest only during the early stages of the Obama administration, when Trump emerged as a casual and intermittent *Fox News* critic of Obama's policies during the Arab Spring and after the Iranian Nuclear Deal. By the early stages of the Arab uprisings of 2011, Trump had already aligned himself with the camp of the Saudis who openly disapproved of (1) Obama's support of democratic forces during the Arab Spring, including the Islamists, and (2) American abandonment of authoritarian regimes such as that of Egypt's Hosni Mubarak, who had supported American policies in the region (Gerges 2013).

Since his surprising entry to the White House, Trump has embraced Arab dictators and autocrats in the name of internal political stability and economic benefit, and in return has secured Arab leaders' acquiescent silence vis-à-vis his negative rhetoric on Syrian refugees and Islam (Haynes 2017), as well as his embrace of Israeli Prime Minister Netanyahu. In fact, even after the assassination at the Saudi Consulate in Istanbul of United States resident and *Washington Post* columnist, Jamal Khashoggi, Trump refrained from taking any diplomatic or economic measures against Saudi Arabia and its Crown Prince Mohammed bin Salman (MBS) for fear that he would lose Saudi financial investment in the United States to China or Russia.

20.1   Stance-taking

I read Trump's positionality vis-à-vis Middle Eastern issues and politics through the lens of stance-taking (Du Bois 2007, Jaffe 2009, McIntosh 2009). In much of this research, individual acts of stance-taking that may unfold in single speech events accrue to form an individual's stand, or accrue interactionally to structure relationships, ideologies, and identities (Jaworksi and Thurlow 2009: 221). I will focus for the purposes of this paper on Du Bois' (2007: 163) definition: "Stance is a public act by a social actor, achieved dialogically through overt communicative means, of simultaneously evaluating objects, positioning subjects (self and others), and aligning with other subjects, with respect to any salient dimension of the sociocultural field."

Evaluation, *positioning*, and *alignment* are thus the central components of each act of stance-taking. It bears noting here that the alignment can be to individual social actors, objects, or even to other stances or accrued ideologies. Du Bois (ibid.) also highlights three points in stance research:

(1) Researchers must describe the stance-taker, taking into account not only that person's previous utterances, but also relevant relationships with others; linguistic features; regional, ethnic, and gender categories; social associations and other salient factors.

(2) Researchers should locate the shared object(s) of stance, or what speakers are evaluating.

(3) And finally, we have a responsibility to understand what stances (and counterstances) a stance-taker is responding to; in other words, we should ask ourselves, "why this now?"

One of the striking dimensions of Trump's politically and diplomatically situated stances with respect to the Middle East is the indirect indexicality (Ochs 1993) of Arab and Muslim hierarchies. In linguistic anthropology, we speak of indexes as bits of language or other kinds of "signs" that point to meaning, including social meaning such as stances, activities, or identities (Kiesling 2009). And as Silverstein (2003) and Ochs (1993) have posited, the social meaning indexical signs point to can be quite complex. In direct indexicality, there's a direct or immediate relationship between the sign and its meaning; saying "You!" for instance, directly indexes (points to) to the addressee, while giving a command can directly index a relationship of power between speaker and addressee (Kiesling 2009: 353). But in "indirect indexicality," indexical signs point to larger social constructs, such as masculinity, or shared myths about a social group. For instance, Trump's stance-taking events in tweets and speeches about Middle Eastern Arabs, while directly indexing their purported referents, are simultaneously indirectly indexing deep-rooted orientalist fantasies of Arabs as religious fanatics and rich sheikhs (Little 2008). In the Trumpian Twittersphere, stances toward Middle Eastern people and topics are effectively bipolar: Positive alignment stances are tied to referents' petrodollar status in the global economy, while negative evaluations and disaligning stances indirectly index American fears of violence post-9/11 as well as broader fears of foreigners and contamination (see Williams, this volume). Trump's stances move away from traditional American soft power which has historically recognized the importance of oil but at the same time tried to enforce human rights and respect for individual liberties in the region. For example, a search of Trump's daily tweets using the search engine https://factba.se between January 2015 and early May 2019 reveals a high rate of references to Saudi Arabia (495), Iraq (996), Iran (1,316), Turkey (240), Afghanistan (327), and Israel (772) compared to the rest of Middle Eastern and North African countries: Oman (three), Qatar (fifty-six), Morocco (ten), Algeria (two), Libya (217), Mauritania (zero), Egypt (132), United Arab

Emirates (fourteen), Bahrain (twenty-four), Sudan (seven), and Yemen (seventy-five).

Unsurprisingly, these numbers show that Trump's Middle Eastern priorities are primarily connected to Saudi Arabia, Iran, Iraq, Afghanistan, Israel, and Egypt. Without exception, they are about oil, Islam, Islamic fundamentalism, and refugees. While Trump's tweets mention mostly Saudi Arabia, Iran, Israel, and Egypt, they index a repertoire of meanings which remain consistent through the repertoire of his usage: Saudi royalty are friendly billionaires, al-Sisi of Egypt and Netanyahu of Israel are his partners in fighting Islamic terrorism, and the rest of Arabs and Muslims represent either radical Islamic threats or uncivilized refugees. This narrow focus demonstrates that Arab culture, history, and heritage matter little in Trump's view, and we may even hypothesize, based on an examination of the factba.se corpus, that he uses "Arab" as a geographical locator narrowly designating United Arab Emirates and Saudi Arabia, while aiming to separate it from "Muslim," which he mostly reserves for criticism of his enemies. I contend that Trumpian speeches about "rich Arabs" buying American arms and goods and the total absence of "other Arabs" (by which I mean ordinary people in non-wealthy, but also Arab countries) is consistent with his overall diplomatic and economic view of "America First" which speaks largely to an internal American base and is not only unconcerned with other cultures, but also callous to refugees and immigrants.

20.2   Ambiguous Alignment with Rich Arabs

At the center of Trump's flowing torrent of daily tweets about the Middle East and Saudi Arabia is a geopolitical blackmail strategy. On June 16, 2015, Trump announced his candidacy for the American presidency. He argued that the Middle East and Saudi Arabia are important for the United States only for their financial and energy resources. (I number block quotes for ease of reference in my analysis later in the paper).

(1) Saudi Arabia, they make $1 billion a day. $1 billion a day. I love the Saudis. Many are in this building. They make a billion dollars a day. Whenever they have problems, we send over the ships. We say "we're gonna protect." What are we doing? They've got nothing but money. (Trump 2015a)

The markers of positive evaluation in this stance are overt: "I love the Saudis ... They've got nothing but money." But there is a separate stance as well, embedded in the middle of the first: a negative evaluation of the same referent (i.e. Saudis), where Trump instead aligns with American taxpayers who are ostensibly paying for Saudi security (i.e. the "we" in "What are we doing?" refers to Americans). During the presidential campaign Trump maintained his repeated statement that Saudi Arabia and other Gulf states have nothing to offer but money, and promised that if he gets elected, he will make sure they pay for their security. At the same time, as befitting a salesman with the upper hand, Trump proposed a deal: He argued that *if* the Saudis paid, he would pull out of the deal with Iran and provide military and logistical support for the Saudis and their allies in their fight against the Houthis in Yemen and Iran (Black 2018, Hassan 2017).

Here we must take a detour to explain the historical US actions that Trump the stance-taker is countering; we ask ourselves the question *Why is this stance so overt now?* During the Cold War, President Reagan committed to military and economic support of Saudi Arabia and other Gulf countries for fear that they would fall into the hands of other powers and threaten the oil supply. Despite Israeli attempts to block the sale of AWACS planes and other military equipment to Saudi Arabia, Reagan approved the sale and promised to continue America's support of Israel, arguing that that military deal with Saudi Arabia did not threaten Israel's security. America's military and diplomatic relationship with Saudis throughout the Bush, Clinton, Bush Jr. and Obama administrations continued over the years despite intermittent political challenges. Yet while the bond between the House of Saud (perennial rulers) and Republican and Democratic American presidents remained intact, Trump introduced new diplomatic approaches in tweeting his stances about these relations. It must be stressed that for ordinary Middle Eastern citizens, Trump's political positions about the Middle East are close to those of previous American presidents; for many Middle Eastern tweeters, Saudi Arabia is Trump's "biddable and submissive cow" that has to be "milked." Trump's true deviation from previous administrations is that he pays less attention to upholding America's image of an idealized, free-press, civil-liberties-upholding beacon of democracy in the global political economy. Trump seems to feel from his base a license to adopt more overtly ethnona-tionalist stances, largely doing away with the soft and covert power approaches the US had been nurturing for decades.

Months after his unforeseen win over Democratic candidate Hillary Rodham Clinton, President Trump made a highly publicized trip to Saudi Arabia in May 2017 before he headed to Israel and the West Bank, where he met with Israeli and Palestinian officials. Trump's first international trip to the Middle East held major political significance, especially given his critical discourse and unfavorable talk about Muslim immigrants during the electoral campaign.

On October 2, 2018, during a political rally in Southaven, Mississippi, Trump spoke to a large audience of supporters. A full three years after the first excerpt quoted above, Trump's stance-taking closely parallels his initial assertion on this topic:

(2) We protect Saudi Arabia. Would you say they're rich? And I love the king, King Salman. But I said, "King, we're protecting you. You might not be there for two weeks without us. You have to pay for your military. You have to pay." And Japan is going to also contribute. Japan – we protect Japan. They pay us a small percentage. (Trump 2018)

In this excerpt, Trump aligns with American citizens starting with the first pronoun, "we," and uses direct quotes to introduce a stance where he challenges the rich king and charges him for the country's protection, implying that the House of Saud would immediately collapse if it were not for Trump. Drawing an immediate parallel with Japan serves to imply that Japan might also be vulnerable to deal-making with Trump in exchange for protection.

Trump understands that Americans hold unfavorable views of Saudi Arabia. Yet, he continues to stand up for them despite the global criticism and outcry against their negative human rights record. The recent open alliance between Saudi Arabia and Israel is partly behind Trump's unquestioning support for authoritarian leaders in the Middle East. Ordinary Muslims understand this double standard: America has "never cared about Middle Eastern democracy," noted Abdessamad, a graduate student at Sidi Mohamed Ben Abdellah University in Fez, over a cup of tea, before he added, "Americans have finally dropped the mask of diplomacy and Trump should be thanked for confirming what people already know about the Americans in the Gulf region. Trump openly states today what we have known for decades. America's friends are those with deep pockets." For Trump, King Salman and his son MBS are Arab friends that should be supported despite their dictatorial policies. Like Egypt's President Abdelfettah al-Sisi, MBS has put political opponents in jail and ordered the killings of many. For Trump, the new American diplomacy is less about exporting American human rights values and democracy than supporting dictators who can keep order in the Middle East and cash flowing to America, even at the expense of civilian lives and human rights. The difference in the Trump era is that not only are these stances made explicit, but they're also expressed in highly personal, affective terms in order to play to the priorities and emotions of his base.

20.3   Disaligning with Muslim Enemies

While Trump's diplomatic language about the Gulf region stresses his friendship with a few rich Saudi friends, his discourse about the rest of Middle Eastern and North African Muslims and Arabs takes a different tone. At the center of Trump's negative stance-taking are "Islamic terrorism" and anxiety over "Muslim refugees." It is ironic that Trump and Saudi leaders share common ideas about political Islam. In the aftermath of the Arab uprisings, also known as the Arab Spring, Saudi Arabia and the United Arab Emirates launched a counter-revolutionary campaign against those social and political uprisings for fear that those challenges to dictatorial rule might spill over inside their own borders. The rise of the Muslim Brotherhood in Egypt and its support by Qatar came after the coup d'état led by General Abdelfettah al-Sisi against the democratically elected Mohammed Morsi was opposed by Saudi Arabia and its allies. The Egyptian Muslim Brotherhood has historically taken critical positions against Saudi Arabia, which saw its rise as a threat to the political future of the Saudi royal family.

Aligning with the Saudis, Trump was critical of the Muslim Brotherhood even before he decided to run for the presidency. On September 13, 2012, he called on President Barack Obama to cancel his meeting with then-newly elected Egyptian President Mohammed Morsi in the White House. In early October, he tweeted, "Under Obama Iran has taken over Iraq, al-Qaeda has taken over Libya, the Muslim Brotherhood now controls Egypt. Worst Foreign Policy ever" (Trump on Twitter, October 2, 2012). These stances match the ideological and political positions of Saudi Arabia and the Egyptian military, both of which believed that Obama adopted policies favoring new social and political forces in the Arab world and abandoning traditional allies like former Egyptian President Hosni Mubarak. Trump reacted by indirectly arguing that Obama might be a secret Muslim and calling on the administration to declare a war against "radical Islam." On November 1, 2016, Trump gave a speech in Eau Claire, Wisconsin, where he proclaimed:

(3) We will also keep you safe from terrorism. Hillary Clinton wants a 550 percent increase in Syrian refugees flowing into our country. Who can even believe it? Her plan would mean generations of terrorism and extremism spreading into your schools and throughout your communities. When I am elected president, we will suspend the Syrian refugee program. We have no choice. ((*applause*)) And we will keep radical Islamic terrorists the hell out of our country. ((*applause*)) A Trump administration will also secure and defend the borders of the United States. And as I said, and as you know, we're not playing games, yes, we will build the wall. (Trump 2016a)

Trump engages in many stance-taking strategies here. Using a series of intonational contrasts (e.g. "Hillary Clinton wants") and hypotheticals that are couched as inevitable facts (e.g. "When I am elected president"), along with rhetorical questions (e.g. "Who can even believe it?"), he stokes fear of outsiders, building on prior stances he has taken about Mexican immigrants. First, he establishes a connection between Syrian refugees and Islamic radicalism and then connects both of them to building the wall and securing the southern borders of the United States – despite the fact that there is no proof that Syrian refugees entered the country through the southern border. By connecting the border with refugees and underspecifying or blurring their nationalities, Trump creates a direct relationship between all refugees, crime, and terrorism in the mind of his supporters (Finley and Esposito 2019).

In December 2015, Trump called for a "total ban of Muslims" entering the United States (Trump 2015b). While this statement comes up during the height of his campaign for the Republican nomination, his tweet "Islam hates us" on March 10, 2016 (Trump 2016b), confirms his indexing of Muslims and Islam as "other," and therefore his positioning of the whole Middle Eastern region as a security threat for America. Trump's negative stance-taking and elaboration of his trope of the "threatening Muslim" range from claiming that many Muslims in Jersey City celebrated 9/11 to contemplating the necessity of a Muslim registry in the United States and calling for a temporary ban on Muslims coming to the United States. The Trumpian fear of the Syrian/Muslim refugee crisis (this conflation elides the fact that many refugees might be Christians) is rooted in American fear and anxiety about terrorism and economic as well as political stability in the region especially in the aftermath of 9/11. Consider this statement by Trump on June 16, 2015, at Trump Tower, New York, regarding the Islamic State in Iraq and Syria (ISIS):

(4) Islamic terrorism is eating up large portions of the Middle East. They've become rich. I'm in competition with them. They just built a hotel in Syria. Can you believe this? They built a hotel. When I have to build a hotel, I pay interest. They don't have to pay interest, because they took the oil that, when we left Iraq, I said we should have taken . . . So now ISIS has the oil, and what they don't have, Iran has. (Trump 2015a)

Trump's stance toward Iran and ISIS is articulated in terms of economic benefits and competition. True to his background as a real estate developer, his evaluative statements are framed in terms of financial rewards and gains. Interestingly, the structure of this fragment of his speech is similar to the first three presented earlier in this chapter. One can now discern a strong pattern in Trump's stance-taking. Let's tease this out in Table 20.1.

This table shows the structure of Trump's assessments, from statement through implied alignments, paraphrased for clarity and conciseness by the author. Assessments usually begin with a statement of something that Trump is going to evaluate as incredible or remarkable, and these same statements then interpellate (hail or call) the audience into a state of disbelief with rhetorical questions. Once set up this way, Trump delivers his evaluation. The end alignment appears to always be in favor of "the American people," though he is truly just speaking to his base, as I have noted in the table. However, the various steps to get there also conceal some presuppositions that Trump is bringing in; his evaluations hinge on hidden ideas. For instance, in the second example (i.e. Row 2 of the table), it is implied that Japan and Saudi Arabia are both benefiting from US support and might crumble if that support were withdrawn, leaving them open to geopolitical blackmail. In the third example (i.e. Row 3 of the table), the hidden presuppositions are that Syrian refugees are all Islamic terrorists, that their children would grow up to be terrorists, and that

Table 20.1 *Rhetorical questions and alignments embedded in selected statements made by Trump*

Example	Statement (paraphrased)	Rhetorical question	Evaluation	Alignment
1	Saudi Arabia makes 1B/ day, but we protect them (Trump 2015a).	What are we doing?	Saudi riches = good; taking advantage of us = bad.	Ambiguous alignment with Saudis, strong alignment with base's $ interests.
2	We protect Saudi Arabia (Trump 2018).	Would you say they're rich?	Conditionally good, only if Saudis pay.	Strong alignment with American base.
3	Hillary Clinton wants a 550 percent increase in Syrian refugees (Trump 2016a).	Who can even believe it?	Terrible, it'd mean generations of terrorists in American communities.	Perfect alignment with American base against HRC; coincidental alignment with Saudis against Syria.
4	Islamic terrorism taking over Middle East, terrorists and Iran are now rich (Trump 2012; 2015a).	Can you believe this?	Terrible, DT must pay to build a hotel where in fact America should own all Iraqi oil.	Perfect alignment with American base against terrorism, but also with Saudi Arabia against Iran and Iraq.

they are coming across the southern border, and building a wall is the solution. In the fourth example (i.e. Row 4 of the table), the strong assumption that is quickly glossed over is that Iraqi oil was America's to take. But why should it belong to the United States? The answer to that is likely because the US defeated Saddam Hussein. But why was the United States in Iraq in the first place? What is the background to this position?

After ISIS launched its attacks against the Syrian regime of Bashar al-Assad and the Iraqi government, it established a political base in Raqqa, Syria, which became the capital of its Caliphate. The Islamic State relied largely on the sales of oil from Iraq and Syria to fund its military operations against Iraq, Syria, and the Kurdish civilian population. As far back as the Bush and Obama administrations, Trump had been critical of the way the American government approached the Iraqi oil industry, arguing for an American share of the pie. Oil has become a key denominator between Iran and ISIS; Trump sees this development as a threat to American economy. By arguing that he pays interest when he builds a hotel while ISIS does not, Trump makes the point that America is subsidizing not only the military security of Gulf and Middle Eastern states but also "radical Islamic terrorism" in the whole region. While Saudi Arabia is Trump's key ally and friend in the region, Iran is his principal enemy; Trump believes that the Obama Administration gave the Iranian government major economic dividends when it signed the nuclear deal allowing Iran back into the global oil market. For Trump, America should have maintained the economic sanctions on Iran to force the Iranian's regime breakdown.

20.4   Tweeting Hard Power

On April 27, 2016, candidate Donald Trump delivered a foreign policy speech at the Mayflower Hotel in Washington, DC, where he outlined the foundation of his foreign policy. At the basis of his argument is a call for a non-interventionist approach to the Middle East. He stated:

Unlike other candidates for the presidency, war and aggression will not be my first instinct. You cannot have a foreign policy without diplomacy. A superpower understands that caution and restraint are really truly signs of strength. Although not in government service, I was totally against the war in Iraq, very proudly, saying for many years that it would destabilize the Middle East. Sadly, I was correct, and the biggest beneficiary has been Iran, who is systematically taking over Iraq and gaining access to their very rich oil reserves, something it has wanted to do for decades. (Trump 2016c)

While many Middle Eastern and North African citizens would agree with the negative consequences of the invasion of Iraq on the image of the United States in the Middle East, they would stop short of taking Trump's side about his new vision of America's new Middle East policy.

Trump is neither interested in nor committed to a cultural diplomacy that has historically been at the center of American policy during the Cold War. In the post 9/11 era, President George W. Bush tried to reach out to the Arab World and increase understanding between the United States and the Middle East. Following the fall of the Soviet Union, America was less threatened by Russia in the 1990s, leading to drastic cutbacks in the cultural and public diplomacy programs and the eventual closure of the United States Information Agency (USIA), and by 1999, the integration of public diplomacy activities in the State Department. Cultural diplomacy was tasked to a limited number of individuals.

I do not suggest that a soft-power diplomatic approach toward the Middle and North Africa would lead to an acceptance of American policies in the region. History has, however, shown that cultural and public diplomacy facilitated the celebration of American values throughout the world. In fact, even as Middle Eastern populations have held low opinions about the United States and its policies in the region, they have historically appreciated American democracy and rule of law (Schneider 2004). The open alliance between Trump and certain military and civilian dictators in the Middle East and his reluctance to critique their abuses of human rights have undermined public opinion worldwide regarding the United States. Trump erased the American diplomatic balance between policy and values. Faithful to his "America First" slogan, Trump focused his attention from the beginning on showcasing a "hard" approach to internal and external issues.

20.5   Bots Tweeting Trump

While more than 142 million Middle Easterners use Facebook (Jones and Abrahams 2018), Twitter subscribers continue to represent a small minority, although their numbers have grown over time. Active Twitter users in the Arab world jumped from approximately six million in 2014 to over eight million in 2018. Bahrain, Kuwait, Saudi Arabia, the United Arab Emirates, and Qatar are the leading producers and consumers of tweets in the region (ibid.), with Saudi Arabia topping the list. The popularity of Twitter in the Gulf States is also limited mostly to young and educated users who tend to focus on soft news or celebrities. Therefore, a limited number of Arab speakers respond to or retweet Trump's statements about Middle Eastern issues. Trump's tweets are translated into Arabic and analyzed largely in Satellite television programs on Al Jazeera and other media outlets. However, outside these news outlets, the lack of an Arab Twitter literacy undermines a clear understanding and debate of Trump's tweets (Zagood 2019).

Arab Twitter users have generally remained silent vis-à-vis Trump's tweets. Unable to create a popular online platform that could catch the attention of Trump, Saudi Arabia turned to bots. In November 2017, Trump tweeted his support of the "anti-corruption" crackdown in Saudi Arabia led by MBS against many high-profile members of the royal family as well as military and civilian leaders. Trump wrote: "I have great confidence in King Salman and the Crown Prince of Saudi Arabia, they know exactly what they are doing," adding, "Some of those they are harshly treating have been 'milking' their country for years" (Trump on Twitter, November 6, 2017a). The tweet was later reposted by thousands of fake accounts and bots (Jones and Abrahams 2018). This megaphoning probably helped Saudi Arabia to get public support from President Trump and turn him against the Qatari regime blamed for supporting the Muslim Brotherhood and Hamas. This strategy dates back to the first days of the Saudi blockade against Qatar, when Trump supported Saudi Arabia's move to isolate Qatar despite the concerns of American diplomats and military leaders given the importance of Qatar as home of one of the largest military bases in the Gulf region. In a series of tweets linking Qatar to Islamic fundamentalism, Trump tweeted, "During my recent trip to the Middle East I stated that there can no longer be funding of Radical Ideology. Leaders pointed to Qatar-Look!" (Trump on Twitter, June 6, 2017b). Saudi Arabia weaponized Trump's friendship to put pressure on its tiny competitive neighbor to close Al Jazeera Television and limit its support to the Muslim Brotherhood of Egypt and other leaders of the Arab Spring (Jones and Abrahams 2018).

The use of pro-Trump bots has emerged as an alternative response strategy to Trump's tweets and speeches by different governments in the Arab Gulf. In the absence of an Arab audience for Trump's Twitter feed, Gulf states (especially Saudi Arabia and the United Arab Emirates) resorted to the use of fake accounts to game the tweeting conversations with and about Trump. It is therefore reasonable to argue that the majority of tweets that express an opinion about Trump in the Gulf could be seen as propaganda tweets instead of a reflection of individual opinions in the Arabic Twittersphere. Based on this assumption, we have focused here mostly on the tweets of Trump about the Gulf, Arabs, and Muslims instead of reactions of Arab tweeters to his discourse.

On August 23, 2013, citizen Trump tweeted, "Let the Arab League take care of Syria. Why are these rich Arab countries not paying us for the tremendous cost of such an attack?" Trump argued later that American foreign policy is misguided and that America should focus attention on its internal socio-economic problems. While many experts would agree with his call on focusing on the economic challenges that rural and urban America faces today, they are still in favor of a soft-power approach to the Middle East and other regions (Schneider 2004). After the fall of the Soviet Union, American diplomacy lost its focus on the importance of cultural diplomacy and soft power. Yet histori-cally, American prestige in the world has been based on the exchange of art, culture and values with the intent of fostering understanding. The success of cultural diplomacy is linked to a robust public diplomacy that goes back to the Cold War period. America's ideological and political reach in the world in the aftermath of World War II is linked to successful communication strategies which allowed its soft power to influence what military coercion failed to do, even in times of strife when the United States struggled internally and abroad during the Civil Rights Movement and the Vietnam War. Many experts argue that Trump's hard-power approach to Arab friends and foes has undermined the recent small gains in Arab public opinion after the election of President Barack Obama. Trump has shown less interest in public diplomacy largely because he thinks that it gives the impression of a weak America.

As president, Trump introduced hard-power budgets allocating more resources to defense while cutting financial support to cultural programs in the Middle East and other regions. Yet while cultural programs meant to influence Trumps' enemies in the Middle East are cut or eliminated, Trump tweets emotionally and impulsively, defending his friends throughout the region for buying American military equipment and facilitating the flow of oil to the global market. In his eyes, they are the only Arabs worth talking to and communicating with in the region. And for that reason, as Hadji Ali noted, naturalized Arab-Americans from the region like myself are Trump's enemies because, as Jamal noted, we are not viable buyers in Trump's Middle Eastern market. While Trump takes conditional positive stances vis-à-vis rich Arab friends, villagers like Hadji Ali take negative stances and disalign against me and other Middle Eastern and North African immigrants who live in and tacitly accept Trump's America. Hadji Ali, in his own way, used a similar rhetorical structure to Trump's stances, interpellating his audience through his sarcastic teasing of me, saying that they were happy to have me back. In this complex world of stance-taking where alignments are emotionally mediated, it is very hard to escape the fallout of Trump's stances, even in the most remote oases.

References

Black, Ian. 2018. "Donald Trump and the Middle East." *Political Insight* 9, no. 1: 22–25.

Du Bois, John W. 2007. "The Stance Triangle." In *Stancetaking In Discourse: Subjectivity, Evaluation, Interaction*, edited by Robert Englebretson, pp. 139–82. John Benjamins Publishing Company.

Edwards, Brian T. 2016. *After the American Century: The Ends of US Culture in the Middle East*. Cambridge University Press.

Finley, Laura and Luigi Esposito. 2019. "The Immigrant as Bogeyman: Examining Donald Trump and the Right's Anti-Immigrant, Anti-PC Rhetoric." *Humanity and Society*, April 7: 1–20.

Gerges, Fawaz A. 2013. "The Obama Approach to the Middle East: The End of America's Moment?" *International Affairs* 89, no. 2: 299–323.

Hassan, Oz. 2017. "Trump, Islamophobia, and US–Middle East Relations." *Critical Studies on Security* 5, no. 2: 187–91.

Haynes, Jeffrey. 2017. "Donald Trump, 'Judeo-Christian Values,' and the 'Clash of Civilizations.'" *The Review of Faith and International Affairs* 15, no. 3: 66–75.

Jaffe, Alexandra, ed. 2009. *Stance: Sociolinguistic Perspectives*. Oxford University Press.

Jaworksi, Adam and Crispin Thurlow. 2009. "Taking an Elitist Stance: Ideology and the Discursive Production of Social Distinction." In *Stance: Sociolinguistic Perspectives*, edited by Alexandra Jaffe, pp. 195–226. Oxford University Press.

Jones, Marc and Alexei Abrahams. 2018. "A Plague of Twitter Bots is Roiling the Middle East." *The Washington Post*, June 5, 2018. https://wapo.st/2kzBslW.

Kiesling, Scott F. 2009. "Identity in Sociocultural Anthropology and Language." In *Concise Encyclopedia of Pragmatics*. 2nd edn. Edited by Jacob L. Mey, pp. 352–58. Elsevier.

Little, Douglas. 2008. *American Orientalism: The United States and the Middle East Since 1945*. University of North Carolina Press.

McIntosh, Janet. 2009. "Stance and Distance: Social Boundaries, Self-Lamination, and Metalinguistic Anxiety in White Kenyan Narratives about the African Occult." In

Stance: Sociolinguistic Perspectives, edited by Alexandra Jaffe, pp. 72–91. Oxford University Press.

Nye, Joseph S. 2004. "The Decline of America's Soft Power: Why Washington Should Worry." *Foreign Affairs* 83, no. 3: 16–20.

Ochs, Elinor. 1993. "Indexing Gender." In *Rethinking Context: Language as an Interactive Phenomenon*, edited by Alessandro Duranti and Charles Goodwin, pp. 335–58. Cambridge University Press.

Rugh, William A. 2006. *American Encounters with Arabs: The "Soft Power" of US Public Diplomacy in the Middle East*. Praeger Security International.

Schneider, Cynthia. 2004. "Culture Communicates: US Diplomacy That Works." *Discussion Papers in Diplomacy* 94: 1–22.

Silverstein, Michael. 2003. "Indexical Order and the Dialectics of Sociolinguistic Life." *Language & Communication* 23: 193–229.

Trump, Donald. 2015a. *Trump Candidacy Announcement*, New York, NY. June 16, 2015.

    2015b. *Trump Political Rally*, Mount Pleasant, South Carolina. December 7, 2015.

    2016a. *Trump Political Rally*, Eau Claire, Wisconsin. November 1, 2016.

    2016b. *Trump Interview with CNN*, Washington, DC. March 10, 2016.

    2016c. *Trump's Foreign Policy Speech*, Washington, DC. April 27, 2016.

    2018. *Trump Political Rally*, Southaven, Mississippi. October 2, 2018.

Trump, Donald.(@realDonaldTrump). 2012. @realDonaldTrump. "Under Obama, Iran has taken over Iraq, Al Qaeda has taken over Libya, the Muslim Brotherhood now controls Egypt. Worst foreign policy ever." Twitter, October 2, 2012. https://bit.ly/3c9MaFA.

    2017a. "I have great confidence in King Salman and the Crown Prince of Saudi Arabia . . ." Twitter, November 6, 2017. https://bit.ly/3aejjhH.

    2017b. ". . . there can no longer be funding about Radical Ideology. Leaders pointed to Qatar – Look!" Twitter, June 6, 2017. https://bit.ly/2TlN09v.

Zagood, Mohammed Juma. 2019. "An Analytical Study of the Strategies Used in Translating Trump's Tweets into Arabic." *Arab World English Journal for Translation and Literacy Studies* 3, no. 1: 22–34.

Index

For EU product safety concerns, contact us at Calle de José Abascal, 56–1°,
28003 Madrid, Spain or eugpsr@cambridge.org.

www.ingramcontent.com/pod-product-compliance
Ingram Content Group UK Ltd.
Pitfield, Milton Keynes, MK11 3LW, UK
UKHW020359140625
459647UK00020B/2547